The Making of Fianna Fáil Power in Ireland
1923–1948

The Making of
Fianna Fáil Power in Ireland
1923–1948

RICHARD DUNPHY

CLARENDON PRESS · OXFORD

1995

Oxford University Press, Walton Street, Oxford OX2 6DP
Oxford New York
Athens Auckland Bangkok Bombay
Calcutta Cape Town Dar es Salaam Delhi
Florence Hong Kong Istanbul Karachi
Kuala Lumpur Madras Madrid Melbourne
Mexico City Nairobi Paris Singapore
Taipei Tokyo Toronto
and associated companies in
Berlin Ibadan

Oxford is a trade mark of Oxford University Press

Published in the United States
by Oxford University Press Inc., New York

British Library Cataloguing in Publication Data
Data available

Library of Congress Cataloging in Publication Data
Dunphy, Richard.
The making of Fianna Fáil power in Ireland, 1923–1948 / Richard
Dunphy.
p. cm.
Includes bibliographical references.
1. Ireland—Politics and government—1923–1948. 2. Political
parties—Ireland—History—20th century. 3. Fianna Fáil—History.
I. Title.
DA963.D86 1995
324.2417'083—dc20 94–44524
ISBN 0–19–820474–4

1 3 5 7 9 10 8 6 4 2

Typeset by Graphicraft Typesetters Ltd., Hong Kong
Printed in Great Britain on acid-free paper by
Bookcraft Ltd., Midsomer Norton, Bath, Avon

For Conn O'Neill
(1960–1988)
And for my father
Denis Dunphy
(1909–1994)

PREFACE

A COMMON statement in the literature on Irish politics is that the subject-matter of political competition in Ireland, and the explanation for political alignments, is essentially incomprehensible without reference to the peculiarities of Ireland's colonial history and the divisions which marked the final stages of the national independence struggle.

Irish political alignments, it has frequently been argued, cannot be accommodated within any of the categories developed in the Western European context—left–right, rural–urban, clerical–anticlerical, etc. If comparisons are to be useful, we should look at other post-colonial, recently independent countries. It is as if Ireland is to be considered a Western European country by geographical accident. Yet the fact is that in terms of per capita income, economic development, literacy, and communications, and in terms of its democratic political system and political traditions, Ireland has much more in common with Western Europe than with most post-colonial, recently independent states.

The tendency to regard Irish politics as essentially divorced from the major political cleavages of most European countries has been reinforced by two factors: the marked hostility to the study of social class and material forces which Irish nationalism has for long inculcated in many Irish intellectuals and analysts, and which, as O'Dowd has pointed out, is in fact shared by many of the present generation of post-nationalist intellectuals;[1] and the fact that many non-Irish— in particular many North American and British—commentators have tended to fall prey to the mystical sway of Irish political language. It is as if, by definition, parties with names such as *Fianna Fáil, Fine Gael, Sinn Féin,* or *Clann na Poblachta* must be expressing some inaccessible, spiritual essence rooted in the national consciousness of the Celtic race. This is, of course, to put the point rather crudely, not to say polemically. But there can be no escaping

[1] L. O'Dowd, 'Neglecting the Material Dimension: Irish Intellectuals and the Problem of Identity', *Irish Review*, 3 (1987), 8–17.

the fact that the inevitable conclusion to so many studies of Irish political alignments is that Irish politics is, in a phrase, *sui generis*.

More recently, there has been a 'gradual if nevertheless pronounced shift in conventional political science treatments of the Irish case. A shift which has seen an emphasis on the peculiarities of Irish political life being slowly replaced by a new emphasis on essential comparability.'[2] In such a vein, the present work sets out, not to deny the obvious peculiarities of modern Irish politics, or that interesting comparisons may be drawn between Ireland and certain other recently independent states; rather, it attempts to explain the evolution of the political system in Ireland during the first two and a half decades of independence in terms which make the nature of political alignments more readily understood by analysts of other European countries. It attempts this by focusing on one of the central puzzles of Irish politics—the predominance of Fianna Fáil, despite the reversal of many of that party's original policies and the obvious changes in its social support base which occurred during those decades.[3]

The predominance of Fianna Fáil from the early 1930s until at least the early to mid-1940s, at any rate, can with justification be described as hegemonic: that is to say, the party did not simply enjoy an electoral superiority, but succeeded in establishing its intellectual, moral, and cultural leadership. This point should not be obscured by the fact that a substantial number of Irish people remained so alienated from de Valera and his comrades as never to consider voting for the party. Fianna Fáil's rivals and opponents never really succeeded in challenging the leadership role of Fianna Fáil during the first decade of the party's rule—be it in the sphere of economic development (e.g. the general acquiescence, on the part of Fine Gael and Labour, from the mid-1930s, in the policy of protection), national identity (e.g. the rapid acceptance of de Valera's Constitution of 1937—by 1949, Fine Gael were even attempting to go one further than the 'dictionary republic'), national security (e.g. all-party support for the policy of neutrality during the war), or

[2] P. Mair, 'Explaining the Absence of Class Politics in Ireland', *Proceedings of the British Academy*, 79 (1992), 383–410.

[3] Of course, Fianna Fáil is not entirely unique. Its position in Irish life can perhaps be compared to that attained in the post-war period by the Swedish Social Democrats, the Japanese Liberal Democrats, and the Italian Christian Democrats. See M. Gallagher, *Political Parties in the Republic of Ireland* (Manchester, 1985), 10.

religious and moral identity. By the mid-1940s the party's hegemonic position was under threat—as a result of general policy stagnation combined with rising post-war socio-economic expectations. Again, the failure clearly to articulate any alternative line of development enabled Fianna Fáil, after a period of political uncertainty and economic crisis, to reconstitute its centrality.

Implicit in the attempt to render Fianna Fáil's centrality within Irish political life more comprehensible within the European context is the belief that Irish politics is not so *sui generis* as is usually asserted. After all, just because Irish political parties do not bear names such as *social democrat, Christian democrat, conservative, liberal,* and so on does not mean that their behaviour in opposition and in office, and the articulation of their political, cultural, social, and economic concerns, may not bear comparison with such parties.[4] One commentator has even suggested that the party's appeal in the 1930s bore a superficial resemblance to that of the German Nazi Party. Although he is quick to point out that Fianna Fáil's commitment to parliamentary democracy was never seriously in doubt in the 1930s, and that it resembled the Nazi Party 'only in respect of certain secondary characteristics', he makes the valuable point that

even such an apparently unique party as Fianna Fáil cannot be fully understood if examined only in a purely Irish context, and . . . certain aspects of its image and policies which contributed greatly to its appeal in Ireland in the 1930s were also striking a chord with people in other European countries at that time.[5]

My focus will be on three aspects of the Fianna Fáil phenomenon: the evolution and articulation of its strategy for economic development, in opposition and in government; the nature of its political strategy—more precisely, the ideological assertion of its claim to moral and intellectual leadership of the Irish nation; and the objective forces which influenced, shaped, limited, and conditioned the party's plans for the economic, cultural, and political direction of the southern Irish state.

I will look, therefore, first at the party's relationship to the forces of production and its mediation of conflicting social and economic

---

[4] For an important discussion of this question, see M. Laver, 'Are Irish Parties Peculiar?', *Proceedings of the British Academy*, 79 (1992), 359–81.
[5] Gallagher, *Political Parties in the Republic of Ireland*, 37–40.

interests; second, at its articulation of its conception of Irish national identity, its role in setting the political agenda in the Ireland
of the 1930s and 1940s, and its use of broadly accepted concep-
tions of religion, morality, and nationalism to outmanœuvre its opponents; and, third, at the limitations inherent in its economic
programme in particular—in part given by the size of the Irish
home market and the closeness of Irish economic ties with the
United Kingdom; in part due to the nature of the party programme,
which found itself relying upon the economic potential of the Irish
manufacturing bourgeoisie, and consequently came up against the
historical reluctance of this class to invest in Irish industry.

In Chapter 1 I examine previous approaches to the study of
Fianna Fáil and explain how the present work relates to the ongo-
ing debates within Irish political science. Chapters 2 and 3 trace the
development of the party's strategy from the end of the civil war to
the election of the first Fianna Fáil government in 1932, focusing on
the background to the foundation of the party, 1923–6, and the
party's early years in opposition, 1926–32, during which it formulated its economic, social, and political programme. Chapter 4 traces
the implementation of its economic development strategy during
the period 1932–8, focusing on its political aspects. Chapter 5 examines the importance of the war years for the consolidation of
Fianna Fáil dominance; traces the progress of economic policy
debates within the Government and the party; looks at the loss of
momentum and of direction after the war; and examines the emergence of new threats and challenges to Fianna Fáil and its descent
into opposition in 1948. The Conclusion explores some of the lessons which the study of Fianna Fáil's past might hold for those
pondering the future of the party in the 1990s.

R. D.

Dundee
June 1994

ACKNOWLEDGEMENTS

THIS book has its origins in a Ph.D. thesis which I completed at the European University Institute in Florence under the joint supervision of professors Ian Budge and Joe Lee. I am indebted to them both for their constant help and encouragement.

Amongst fellow academics working in the field of Irish politics and history, I would like in particular to thank Paul Bew, Michael Gallagher, Ellen Hazelkorn, Stephen Hopkins, Dermot McCann, and Henry Patterson.

The staff at the various libraries and archive departments where I have worked have been unfailingly helpful and considerate: Trinity College Dublin library, University College Dublin archives department, National Archives of Ireland, National Library of Ireland, European University Institute library, National Library of Scotland, University of Dundee library.

A number of friends have contributed to the making of this book by enriching my view of Ireland, of politics, and of things in general. I am especially indebted to the late Beatrice Behan, Steve Derrick, Kim Duke, Nardo and Deirdre Dunphy, Stephanie and Ken Gardner, Paddy Gillan, Moira Leydon, Steve Mathewson, Peter McDermott, Grahame Miller, Pete Millward, Theresa Moriarty, Alison Muir, James Newell, the late Gerald O'Connor, Joan O'Mahoney, Gerard O'Neill, Maura O'Neill, Seamas O'Tuathail, Dorinda Outram, Chris and Sandra Skillen, the late Eamon Smullen, Serena Sordi, Liz Steiner-Scott, and Tam Wilkinson.

My greatest debt by far is to Conn O'Neill, whose death on 10 December 1988 at the age of 28 years robbed me of my best friend and closest comrade. Conn was my main interlocutor on all matters Irish. He understood why I wanted to write a book such as this, and hopefully he would have approved of the outcome.

CONTENTS

ABBREVIATIONS

ACA	Army Comrades Association
CIU	Congress of Irish Unions
DTUC	Dublin Trades Union Council
EPO	Emergency Powers Order
FII	Federation of Irish Industry
FIM	Federation of Irish Manufacturers
Finance	Department of Finance
FUE	Federated Union of Employers
GAA	Gaelic Athletic Association
GATT	General Agreement on Tariffs and Trade
IDA	Industrial Development Association
ILP	Irish Labour Party
Industry and Commerce	Department of Industry and Commerce
INTO	Irish National Teachers' Organization
IRA	Irish Republican Army
ITGWU	Irish Transport and General Workers' Union
ITUC	Irish Trades Union Congress
IWL	Irish Worker League
IWWU	Irish Women Workers' Union
JLC	Joint Labour Committee
Labour	Department of Labour
NAI	National Archives of Ireland
NAIDA	National Agricultural and Industrial Development Association
NLI	National Library of Ireland
NLP	National Labour Party
RWG	Revolutionary Workers' Groups
Supplies	Department of Supplies
Taoiseach	Department of the Taoiseach
TD	parliamentary deputy
TUC	Trade Union Conference
UCDA	University College Dublin Archives
WUI	Workers' Union of Ireland

NOTE ON SOURCES

IRELAND finally gained a national archives in 1991. Documents previously held in the State Paper Office are currently stored there. Since the passage of the National Archives Act, 1986, the position for researchers seeking access to Irish government departmental archives (up to 31 December 1960) has improved. At the time of writing, the archives of a number of government departments were still being processed, although some relevant material had just become available. Problems, however, included the unavailability of Department of Finance files for the period 1941–8, and the unavailability of much Department of Industry and Commerce material. I had been repeatedly assured that the release of both was imminent. Cabinet minutes and minutes of the various committees established during the war years have been available for some time; but de Valera's innate suspicion of the written record means that supposition must play an unacceptably large role in attempting to deduce from cabinet records the main contours of intra-party debate during the period of Fianna Fáil rule under examination.

Valuable collections of private papers are spread between the National Library of Ireland and the archives department of University College Dublin. Some important collections of private papers were inaccessible. The de Valera Papers have only just become available, for example. This would be more serious, perhaps, if this book was a general history of Fianna Fáil. The Lemass Papers are also as yet unavailable to researchers. The Frank Aiken Papers, in University College Dublin archives department, are unlikely to be processed and released before late 1995 at the earliest, I am informed. However, the recently released Seán MacEntee Papers contain much interesting material on internal party matters and have proven invaluable.

The question of personal relationships between party leaders and ministers can only be partially answered by a reconstruction based upon newspaper articles and recollections long after the events under consideration. Caution is obviously advised. The memoirs of the late Todd Andrews, whilst extremely interesting and useful in this respect, are very much an exception in the Irish case. No Fianna Fáil cabinet minister of the period has ever penned his personal memoirs. The culture of the early Fianna Fáil, with its emphasis upon party unity, iron loyalty to the party and its 'Chief', and its own form of democratic centralism, militated against such openness. Here, as elsewhere, secrecy and suspicion confront the historical researcher or political analyst attempting to understand the historical evolution of party policy.

Fianna Fáil and Irish Political Studies

The process by which a demoralized, dispirited, and defeated minority which emerged from the Irish civil war in 1923 succeeded in becoming the government of the country less than a decade later, and in giving birth to a political party which has exercised clear political dominance ever since, has fascinated and, to an extent, mesmerized political commentators.

Arguably, however, this very mesmerization has deflected serious and detailed investigation of the nature and role of the party, and of how it has contributed to the reproduction of its own central role in Irish political life. Despite the fact that Fianna Fáil has held governmental office for almost two-thirds of the life of the independent Irish state, that its share of the popular vote never fell below 40 per cent in a general election between 1932 and 1992, and averaged above 45 per cent in that period, and that it has been able to draw support with remarkable consistency from all social strata, conveying the impression that it is politically immune to the negative effects of social conflict, no major study of the party's evolution exists. Instead, much of the discussion concerning the growth and maintenance of Fianna Fáil's political dominance has tended to take place within the framework of a general discussion of the peculiarities of the Irish party system, or Irish political culture. Whilst it would obviously be foolish to ignore the insights produced by such debates, the framing of the question in this context may have the effect of diverting attention from important ideological and political factors.

The present work aims at a partial redress of the balance by focusing on the specific role of Fianna Fáil and its involvement with Irish society. While such historical monographs are sometimes charged with a tendency towards over-induction, their very paucity in the Irish context—I refer, of course, to the writing on Irish political parties—increases their attractiveness. Moreover, it is often by more rigorous examination of the particular and the peculiar that one comes better to appreciate the common characteristics present and common tendencies at work in different social and political formations.

Garvin, for example, commenting on the centrality of Fianna Fáil in Irish political life, has hinted at the existence of similarities with Italian Christian Democracy. Comparing the two, he suggests that 'in a sense, much of the real politics of the Republic takes place, usually in camera, within the Fianna Fáil party or between Fianna Fáil and the major social institutions and interest groups of the Republic, rather than among the three main parties in the political system'.[1] The same could obviously be said of Italian Christian Democracy from the early 1950s onwards. Indeed, the similarities between the two parties are more striking than Garvin suggests: both tend to project themselves as movements rather than as political parties; neither can be adequately described as a conservative party—rather as a political formation which has sought the maintenance of its popular base at the expense of considerable policy compromises and often internal dissension (although the latter is certainly more evident in the Italian case); both have relied upon powerful ideologies—in Fianna Fáil's case Irish nationalism, in Italian Christian Democracy's case anti-Communism—reinforced by the social and cultural presence of the Catholic Church; and both enjoy a useful relationship with sections of the trade-union movement. Finally, both have held office for so long as to assume the appearance, not so much of a series of administrations, as of a regime—although, in Fianna Fáil's case, there have, of course, been interruptions in its exercise of governmental power.

The detailed study of the Fianna Fáil case may, then, facilitate a more informed comparison between the Irish political experience and that of other European countries.

The present analysis of Fianna Fáil's political dominance focuses on the party's relationship to social class and to the distribution, reproduction, and exercise of power in Irish society. A question which has often been raised is whether it is possible to analyse Irish politics in terms of social class, given the apparent lack of social bases in Irish political alignments. In an influential article

---

[1] T. Garvin, 'Theory, Culture and Fianna Fáil: A Review', in M. Kelly, L. O'Dowd, and J. Wickham (eds.), *Power, Conflict and Inequality* (Dublin, 1982), 173.

published in 1974, Whyte, whilst acknowledging the existence of class tensions in Ireland, and indeed Fianna Fáil's superior appeal to the 'less well-off sections of the community', nevertheless concludes—on the basis of opinion-poll survey data collected during the late 1960s—with an assertion of the continuing centrality of the Irish independence struggle to any understanding of the absence of open class politics.[2]

Other writers have pointed out that Irish politics, even at surface level, is not so unmarked by the influence of class as is often assumed. Thus Garvin writes:

If we look at the Fine Gael, Labour Party and Sinn Féin the Workers' Party support profiles, there is a clear 'class' effect, Fine Gael being a party with an obvious middle-class centre of gravity, the Labour Party being based on skilled and unskilled workers and Sinn Féin the Workers' Party being even more pronouncedly proletarian . . . the most important feature of Fianna Fáil's support profile . . . is the massive cross-class endorsement that it gets persistently, both in opinion polls and in elections, from the population.[3]

Mair, commenting on similar findings in a 1969 Gallup poll, writes:

In one way this shows how Irish politics are much more strongly linked to social cleavages than is normally taken to be the case, and, while this is only half the story, insofar as it excludes Fianna Fáil, it does provide an apt demonstration of how the exigencies of party competition smother this distinct social opposition.[4]

What needs to be explained is not the lack of social bases in Irish politics, but the remarkable success of Fianna Fáil in constructing an inter-class bloc (at least in electoral terms) under its political leadership—an achievement which has had the effect of forcing other political parties with a 'clear "class" effect', such as Fine Gael and Labour, into marriages of convenience, thereby obscuring the class content of political competition in the Republic of Ireland.

My focus, as stated, is on the political strategy employed by Fianna Fáil to construct, consolidate, and maintain, through changing economic and social conditions, the alliance of social forces which has guaranteed its predominance; in other words, its consensus-building strategy. Fianna Fáil's relationship with different

[2] J. Whyte, 'Ireland: Politics without Social Bases', in R. Rose (ed.), *Political Behaviour: A Comparative Handbook* (London, 1974), 647–8.

[3] Garvin, 'Theory, Culture and Fianna Fáil', 173–4.

[4] P. Mair, 'The Autonomy of the Political', *Comparative Politics*, 11 (1979), 459.

classes, social groups, and political forces, and its use of the state apparatus to alter, maintain, or reinforce (as the case may be) the distribution of power, will be studied.

In what way, exactly, does a political party affect the distribution of power or the balance of forces in a society? Following Therborn's analytical schema for the study of state power,[5] I will bear in mind the party's role in relation to three factors: the relations and forces of production, the character of the state apparatus, and the particular ideological superstructure with its specific forms of subject formation.

First, it will prove beneficial to review some of the characteristic explanations offered for Fianna Fáil dominance and some of the assumptions implicit in previous writing on the party, bearing in mind that most treatment of Fianna Fáil has taken place within the context of general academic debates about the nature of the Irish party system, political cleavages, electoral behaviour, political culture, the role of clientelism, and so on.

Previous writing on Fianna Fáil has tended to ascribe the party's dominance to such factors as the predominance of nationalist ideology in Irish society, or the *peasant culture* of Ireland with its propensity for clientelism and its hostility to class politics. Alternatively, electoral studies have frequently tended to emphasize the internal dynamics of the party system. A lively contribution to the debate about the nature of Fianna Fáil has been made by Garvin, whose argument that Ireland presents a case of the 'periphery-dominated centre' raises questions about the social bases of the early Fianna Fáil, and of its rivals, which require investigation. Finally, Marxist writing on Irish politics is notoriously thin on the ground and until the recent work of writers such as Bew, Gibbon, Patterson, and Hazelkorn has been dominated by the shadow of the 'unfinished national revolution'. Thus we may add a fifth approach to the study of Fianna Fáil politics which treats the evolution of the party as a process by which it abandoned its 'radical' origins, grew fat with the spoils of office, and became accommodated to the established order. Clearly this, too, raises important questions about the social origins of the party and the nature of its early radicalism. I wish to question some of the arguments advanced in support of all these approaches before outlining the areas in which the present study concentrates.

[5] G. Therborn, *What does the Ruling Class do when it Rules?* (London, 1980), 145.

'THE REPUBLICAN PARTY'

The most common explanation for Fianna Fáil's political strength is that which attributes it to a monopoly of nationalist feeling, expressed in the form of a quest for sovereignty and identity within post-independence Ireland—a quest which superseded all attempts to appeal to class or sectional interest. This is certainly the explanation most favoured by Fianna Fáil ideologues; the party's subtitle, 'the Republican Party', and its insistence that it is a 'national movement' and not a mere political party, together with its astute use of nationalist rhetoric, bear witness to this.

The thesis that Fianna Fáil supremacy can be traced to its monopolistic hold on the nationalist susceptibilities of the Irish people has become a commonplace, indeed almost sacrosanct, part of the conventional wisdom regarding Irish politics. Even when the role of economic and social factors is acknowledged, it is generally held to be of subsidiary importance to the party's republicanism. Perhaps one of the most extreme statements of this position (in so far as he rejects the influence of socio-economic factors altogether) has been offered by Carty.[6]

Carty has argued emphatically that Irish political alignments have nothing whatsoever to do with social or economic cleavages, but rather revolve around constitutional or nationalist-inspired issues. Moreover, the cleavages which are rooted in such issues have been fostered by political élites, acting as free and independent agents. (Here, at least, the reproduction of nationalist ideology is treated as a question of political strategy; however, the refusal to countenance the existence of objective constraints prevents a rigorous investigation of the political choices facing Carty's political élites.) Thus Carty claims that his analysis

demonstrates that the stable blocs that underlie the political parties are not rooted in more basic socio-economic divisions of the society, nor, it seems, have they ever been. To account for the pronounced stability of these voter alignments it is necessary to turn to an investigation of Irish partisan identifications.[7]

Irish political culture permitted the post-independence political élites to construct partisan cleavages completely unrelated to

---

[6] R. K. Carty, *Party and Parish Pump: Electoral Politics in Ireland* (Brandon, 1983).   [7] Ibid. 76.

socio-economic cleavages. 'Élites do not simply respond and react to demands, they actively create and define them, choosing issues which will evoke electoral response.'[8]

The highly voluntaristic nature of such an argument has been noted by Sinnott; yet he does not really dispute the predominant role of nationalist ideology in securing the hegemony of Fianna Fáil. 'The basis of this achievement', he writes, 'was that the party could make the best claim to represent the nationalist consensus established in 1918,' a nationalist consensus apparently facilitated by the fact that the secession from the United Kingdom removed the agrarian–industrial conflict by severing the 'agrarian sector'.[9] No mention is made here of the bitter and persistent conflicts over industrial policy, and over social and economic policy in general; an agrarian consensus seems to be simply assumed; all other conflicts appear to be relatively unimportant.

Electoral studies have also tended to repeat this line of argument in one form or another. Gallagher has commented on the first four decades of political competition after independence that

The only detectable difference between the major parties themselves was that Fianna Fáil, being descended from those who had opposed the 1921 Treaty settlement establishing the Irish Free State, appeared more nationalist than Fine Gael, claiming a greater commitment to the 'recovery' of Northern Ireland and to the revival of the Irish language.[10]

Although he later admits the decline in 'nationalist and constitutionalist subjects' from the late 1950s onwards and devotes considerable attention to the cultural and social changes taking place in Irish society since then, the success of Fianna Fáil is attributed to its vagueness, its 'flexibility', its 'winning strategy'. This 'winning strategy'—never fully specified—seems ultimately to be reducible to the party's nationalism. In fact, I will argue that specific policies and policy compromises played a central role in Fianna Fáil's political strategy, that the differences between the major parties have been more wide-ranging than suggested by Gallagher, and that Fianna Fáil's 'winning strategy' has consisted precisely in its quick

---

[8] Carty, *Party and Parish Pump*, 97.

[9] R. Sinnott, 'Interpretations of the Irish Party System', *European Journal of Political Research*, 12/4 (1984), 300–4.

[10] M. Gallagher, 'Societal Change and Party Adaptation in the Republic of Ireland, 1960–1981', *European Journal of Political Research*, 9 (1981), 271–5, 282.

adaptation to changes in the balance of social forces (Gallagher argues that Fianna Fáil has adapted least of all the Irish political parties 'because it saw least reason to change').

Mair has introduced an interesting and original investigation of the political weakness of the Irish Labour Party with the standard observation that Labour suffered from 'an inability to compete with the dominant politics of nationalism' and thus with 'the larger parties . . . which have effectively rendered irrelevant the Labour demand that the electorate mobilise around strictly social and economic issues'.[11] This last comment is not entirely accurate; the Labour Party has, throughout most of its history, been as given to nationalist rhetoric as either of the two main parties, and even in the 1920s it possessed economic and social policies which were neither as coherent nor as attractive as those of Fianna Fáil—a point he later acknowledges without modifying his initial judgement.

The importance of the strategic choices made by the Labour Party—and by Fianna Fáil—are, however, highlighted in Mair's later work on Irish political parties. He writes:

Labour's marginal role in the Irish party system cannot simply be explained by historical inertia and by reference to the legacy of 1918, of the late 1920s, or even of the 1940s. Rather, it is in large part due to the logic of party strategy, and to the choices and decisions of the Labour leadership . . .[12]

This is a significant observation, which invites us to explore further the role of party strategy in both the marginalization of Labour and the rise of Fianna Fáil, rather than just assuming an *a priori* and self-reproducing nationalist consensus.

In fact, the argument that support for Fianna Fáil has historically been rooted, above all, in nationalist sentiment suffers from a number of obvious flaws. Apart from the dubious assumption, often present, of a political culture immune, at least in the short term, to change, there are a number of historical observations which must be made.

First, both before and after the civil war the great majority of the electorate delivered a decisive rejection of the republican forces, opting for peace, stability, and moderation, much as they had in

[11] P. Mair, 'Labour and the Irish Party System Revisited: Party Competition in the 1920s', *Economic and Social Review*, 9/1 (1978), 59–65.

[12] P. Mair, *The Changing Irish Party System: Organisation, Ideology and Electoral Competition* (London, 1987), 58.

1916. Support for Fianna Fáil only began to grow *after* the party had taken the oath of allegiance to the king and had entered parliament, which scarcely suggests an irredentist public opinion even in the bitter climate of the 1920s. Moreover, in 1927 the electorate decimated the rump of Sinn Féin, unseating, in a most unsentimental manner, such republican notables as Count Plunkett (father of one of the 1916 martyrs), Mary MacSwiney (sister of the martyred Lord Mayor of Cork), and Brian O'Higgins. Never again would abstentionist Sinn Féin offer a significant electoral challenge, a fact usually, and probably correctly, attributed to the political impotence of aspirant politicians who refuse in advance to take their seats if elected.

Second, from its inception Fianna Fáil fought on the basis of an economic and social programme with specific appeal to broad sections of the electorate. Nationalist rhetoric helped to subdue nascent class themes; but the appeal to nationalism was tied up with concrete policy proposals which enjoyed widespread popularity—for example, economic protectionism with its promise of prosperity for Irish business men and employment expansion for workers; or wartime neutrality—perhaps the most universally popular policy of all. Thus, in the party's 1932 election manifesto, emphasis was placed on economic, social, and health policies and the question of partition was relegated discreetly to the sidelines.

Third, the fact is that Fianna Fáil's performance in office on the so-called national issues has been in striking contrast to the rhetoric. No move whatsoever was made during de Valera's period as Taoiseach towards ending partition; indeed, as has often been commented, the society created in the southern Irish state was one singularly unlikely to appeal to the Protestants of Northern Ireland. The former Fianna Fáil ideologue and cabinet minister, Kevin Boland, has drawn the conclusion that perhaps de Valera's party was more interested in *maintaining* the status quo produced by partition, and hence its own political dominance in the southern state.[13] John Bowman has noted the failure of Fianna Fáil to make any effective move towards ending partition.[14] Furthermore, Fianna Fáil has presided over the virtual disappearance of the Irish language, the preservation, and indeed restoration, of which was, and remains, one

---

[13] K. Boland, *The Rise and Decline of Fianna Fáil* (Dublin, 1982).
[14] J. Bowman, *De Valera and the Ulster Question* (Oxford, 1982).

of the party's fundamental constitutional aims. This failure to match rhetoric with achievement has not produced any noticeable fluctuation in the party's popular support; parties which have challenged Fianna Fáil solely from the republican angle have been notoriously unsuccessful—for example, Córas na Poblachta (1941), Aontacht Éireann (1970s), and, of course, Sinn Féin. (I deliberately omit Clann na Poblachta from this list, as that party's brief success owed as much, if not more, to dissatisfaction with Fianna Fáil's socio-economic policies as to the 'national question'.)

The party has, however, been significantly less insulated from electoral set-backs in times of economic difficulty—1937, 1943, 1948, and 1954—and has itself been able to benefit from the negative effects of its opponents' economic policies. Of course, this may signify that the electorate's faith in Fianna Fáil's nationalist credentials has been so unshakeable that the party is not vulnerable on this front; or it may signify that the real importance of the nationalist dimension has been exaggerated. The question is more open than is often assumed.

Fourth, the decline in nationalist rhetoric since the end of the Second World War and the emergence of new discourses concerned with the problems of economic growth and stability of government[15] did not produce any noticeable decline in Fianna Fáil support either; indeed, the party experienced one of its best ever results in the 1977 general election, which it fought on the basis of an extravagantly populist economic programme. Nor did the problematical re-emergence of the 'green card' under the leadership of Charles Haughey prove the panacea which had been hoped. As Tom Gallagher has pointed out, Haughey's election as party leader in 1979 'was due largely to internal dissatisfaction with Mr Lynch's handling of the economy and of industrial relations'.[16]

Finally, assertions that Fianna Fáil's mass popular support is rooted in the almost innate nationalism of the Irish people raise enormous

---

[15] See P. Mair, 'Ireland, 1948–81', in I. Budge, D. Robertson, and D. Hearl (eds.), *Ideology, Strategy and Party Change* (Cambridge, 1987), 137–42. Mair argues that 'appeals to nationalism have played an insignificant role in electoral mobilisation in post-war Ireland' and that Fianna Fáil sought to articulate a rather different discourse: 'an appeal to national unity which is expressed in social rather than territorial terms, and which stems from the party's self-image as the builder of a modern Ireland standing securely in the face of a hostile international environment.'

[16] T. Gallagher, 'The Dimensions of Fianna Fáil Rule in Ireland', *West European Politics*, 4/1 (1981), 63.

problems of verification. Methodological problems obviously exist with attempts to utilize concepts such as class interest, or even self-interest. But how does one go about measuring national consciousness, republican feeling, anti-Britishness? Opinion surveys, attempting to measure public attitudes on nationalist issues, exist only since the late 1960s. No survey data exist for the 1920s, 1930s, or 1940s. Even if it could be established, on the basis of empirical data, that nationalist myths have played an important part in cementing Fianna Fáil electoral support since the 1960s—which is by no means an agreed conclusion—it would be ahistorical to attempt to explain the party's development and consolidation in an earlier period on the basis of such findings.

These observations should make us hesitant to subscribe too quickly or uncritically to the notion that the determinant of Fianna Fáil dominance is its inheritance of a nationalist tradition deeply rooted in the political culture of the country—a myth which 'the Republican Party', always anxious to project itself as riding high above class or sectional interests and disputes, has assiduously reproduced.

The most which can be said is that the party's perceived commitment to nationalism plays an important role in bonding together its members and faithful supporters; but the argument that nationalism or republicanism is the real or fundamental source of Fianna Fáil dominance is far from proven.

THE 'PERSONALIST' POLITICAL CULTURE ARGUMENT

On occasion the claim has been made that the political culture of Ireland is a 'peasant culture', characterized by strong personalist traditions, attachment to politicians rather than to political ideology, distrust of the state apparatus, religious conservatism, and entrenched individualism which encourages hostility to the politics of class. Even the urbanization of Irish society which has taken place inexorably throughout the twentieth century is not considered to have changed much fundamentally; Ireland, even urban Ireland, is a nation of 'up-rooted peasants'.

The clearest statement of this position has perhaps been made by Chubb. In an article published in 1963,[17] which had a seminal

---

[17] B. Chubb, 'Going about Persecuting Civil Servants: The Role of the Irish Parliamentary Representatives', *Political Studies*, 11/3 (1963).

influence on further research of the period, he outlined an argument which he subsequently developed[18] in his highly popular textbook on Irish politics:

with the exception of Dublin, and perhaps Cork, all towns are country towns, i.e. centres of rural regions. Prominent in them are the shopkeepers and tradesmen, who are closely connected with the farmers, and very like them in their parochialism and in the value they put upon personal contact. Even in Dublin most people are country-born or the children of country-born people, with rural connections . . .[19]

Adherents of this approach have identified the importance of clientelism, patronage, and brokerage as a significant feature of Irish politics. Clientelism, it is argued, by emphasizing the personal relationship between politician and 'client', discourages horizontal organization and collective expression of social grievances, and contributes to the de-ideologization of Irish politics. Not only does this enforce the conservative nature of political life, but it clearly favours the most highly developed and best organized electoral and brokerage machine, i.e. Fianna Fáil. Thus several major studies have been devoted to case analyses of the Fianna Fáil electoral machine and its effectiveness in fulfilling the role allocated to politicians by the political culture.[20]

A number of criticisms may be made of the degree of emphasis which has been placed upon the role of clientelism. First, at its crudest level, it would seem unable adequately to account for the enormous degree of party stability in Irish politics. Carty, despite the criticisms expressed earlier of his analysis, is undoubtedly right to point to the high level of consistency in support for Irish political parties, the intensity of party identification, and the singularly unimpressive electoral performance of 'charismatic' politicians who have broken with their party to stand as independents. (Exceptions exist, but they are in no measure as common as emphasis upon the role of clientelism, or the effects of the single-transferable-vote electoral system, would lead us to expect.) Thus, factors other than

---

[18] B. Chubb, *The Government and Politics of Ireland* (Oxford, 1974).

[19] Chubb, 'Going about Persecuting Civil Servants', 273.

[20] See e.g. P. Sacks, *The Donegal Mafia: An Irish Political Machine* (New Haven, Conn., 1966); P. Sacks, 'Bailiwicks, Locality and Religion: Three Elements in an Irish Dáil Constituency Election', *Economic and Social Review*, 1/4 (1970); M. Bax, 'Patronage Irish Style: Irish Politicians as Brokers', *Sociologische Gids*, 18/3 (1970); and M. Manning, *Irish Political Parties* (Dublin, 1971).

clientelist relationships must significantly influence voting behaviour. Furthermore, it has been pointed out that

The quantitative multiplication of brokerage ties has not led to brokerage becoming . . . qualitatively stronger . . . there has been a distinct marginalisation in each particular consequent relation of this type. No longer is it possible to use brokerage to achieve large-scale frauds, as it was in the days of the Congested Districts Boards. The majority of broker–client deals are quite trivial in content, and often constitute no more than personalised forms of obtaining normal legal entitlements.[21]

On the basis of research conducted in greater Dublin in the early 1980s, Komito has challenged the tendency to emphasize the role of clientelist relations in Irish politics.[22] He argues that 'brokerage alone does not create clientelist politics', that 'clientelist links do not necessarily imply clientelist politics, unless such links dominate the entire political system'. Komito has pointed out that few voters in Dublin (no more than 20 per cent) have ever contacted a politician; moreover, a politician's role is essentially the diffusion of information made inaccessible by the structure of the Irish bureaucracy. Unlike the case of politicians in southern European countries such as Italy and Greece, Irish politicians are seldom in a position to offer real patronage prizes to their clients. Nor can Irish politicians control clients' voting behaviour: the most which can usually be hoped for is an enhanced local reputation which will increase an individual's competitiveness *vis-à-vis* other politicians of his or her own party. As Komito makes clear, not only is it the case that 'the significance of brokerage in Irish politics may be exaggerated'; but, moreover, there is little firm evidence to support the theory that either brokerage or clientelism influences significantly party loyalties, as opposed to intra-party competition:

Once committed to a particular party, personalistic preference is as good a way as any to decide amongst rival party candidates, and so survey results may underplay party loyalty. Personalism or brokerage does not explain party loyalties. After all, brokerage is not unique to Irish politics and politicians. Politicians in other countries commonly articulate, and are expected to articulate, constituents' demands . . .

---

[21] P. Gibbon and M. D. Higgins, 'Patronage, Tradition and Modernisation: The case of the Irish Gombeenman', *Economic and Social Review*, 6/1 (1974), 40–1.

[22] L. Komito, 'Irish Clientelism: A Reappraisal', *Economic and Social Review*, 15 (1984), 176, 180–90.

Nor can clientelism, brokerage, and localism be ascribed to 'peasant culture'. The problem with such an analysis is twofold: 'both its cultural determinism and its assumption of a homogeneous rural community are open to question.'[23] This latter assumption is underlined by Komito's remark that 'in Irish studies, social and economic distinctions among clients are often ignored and a rural/traditional versus urban/modern dichotomy is presumed. Such studies may mask political and economic inequalities while presuming a functionalist consensus.'[24]

Despite the importance of clientelism and localism as an aspect of Fianna Fáil's organizational effect, Ireland has not suffered, like many Third World countries, from personalism and cultural malintegration destroying the legitimacy of the state. 'In the comparative context, the striking feature of Irish "localism" was less its proneness to faction than the effectiveness with which it could transcend, without abandoning, its roots.'[25] Moreover, 'the ethic of personalism did not transcend partisan division or stand opposed to democracy, but instead was expressed within it'.[26] Not the least reason why this was so is that, whilst the use of clientelism mediated against the emergence of class or interest-group politics, Fianna Fáil was also acutely conscious of the potentially fissile effect of clientelism. Strong party discipline, emphasis upon the primacy of political parties, and a strategy which prioritized the unity of Fianna Fáil's constituency helped party democracy flourish. To quote Lee again, 'one reason why Fianna Fáil would overtake Cumann na nGaedheal was precisely because it realised the limited ability of local "notables" to deliver the vote, and put its faith instead in far more elaborate national organization'.[27]

We may conclude, then, that the 'peasant-culture' model and the focus on clientelism often inspired by it have contributed to the study of Fianna Fáil political dominance by correctly highlighting the role of patronage, clientelism, and brokerage as *an aspect* of the party's reproduction of its centrality; but that two fundamental weaknesses remain. First, the emphasis placed on this factor may

[23] I. McAllister and D. O'Connell, 'The Political Sociology of Party Support in Ireland: A Reassessment', *Comparative Politics*, 16/2 (1984), 191.

[24] Komito, 'Irish Clientelism', 174.

[25] J. J. Lee, *Ireland, 1912–1985: Politics and Society* (Cambridge, 1989), 81.

[26] J. Prager, *Building Democracy in Ireland: Political Order and Cultural Integration in a Newly Independent Nation* (Cambridge, 1986), 223.

[27] Lee, *Ireland, 1912–1985*, 82.

exaggerate its importance with regard to the formation and maintenance of party loyalty and the determination of voting behaviour.
Second, the simple attribution of this to 'peasant culture' may lead
to a one-sided focus on the supposed rural–traditional versus urban–modern dichotomy in Irish society at the expense of adequate
treatment of other divisions and tensions, and a dangerous simpli-
fication, without adequate empirical justification, of much of the
urban reality of Irish life, thereby possibly diverting attention from
new forms of social control and political domination.

In other words, both the structure of power in Irish society and
the ideological and political role of parties in securing their support
bases have been dealt with inadequately.

FIANNA FÁIL AND THE 'PARTY-SYSTEM APPROACH'

Although it can scarcely be regarded as a distinctive approach to
the study of Fianna Fáil, there has been a tendency to attribute the
changes in the balance of political forces which took place in Ireland in the late 1920s and early 1930s to the logistics of the Irish
party system as it developed in the post-civil-war period. A clear
statement of this position was made by Mair in 1978, although
subsequently modified considerably:

The decline in the Labour Party's electoral fortunes from September 1927
onwards can be directly attributed to the logistics of the sharply polarised
party system which developed in this period, which, though potentially
operational throughout the first decade of independence, did not actually
emerge until the entry of Fianna Fáil into Dáil Éireann in August 1927, and
which was accentuated by the 'anti-system' character of Fianna Fáil's
opposition.[28]

Of course, Fianna Fáil's entry into Dáil Éireann marked an important turning-point in the party's credibility as a party of government; and, conversely, adversely affected the fortunes of the Labour
Party, which had hitherto played the role of opposition to Cumann
na nGaedheal. However, Mair seems here to be attributing *causal*
significance to this event, and to the 'sharply polarised party system' which it helped to bring into operation.

Both here, and in a later article,[29] Mair acknowledges the

---

[28] Mair, 'Labour and the Irish Party System Revisited', 62.
[29] Mair, 'The Autonomy of the Political'.

importance of Fianna Fáil's economic and social policies in setting the political agenda in Ireland from the late 1920s onwards, and its astuteness in creating and sustaining 'an electoral culture which maintains an over-riding concern with a party's talent for government'.[30] Yet, while the role of Fianna Fáil (and Cumann na nGaedheal) in *creating* the increasing polarization of the party system is implicitly acknowledged, an initial sharp, albeit partly dormant, polarization of the electorate (prior, even, to the birth of Fianna Fáil in 1926) is explicitly assumed.

The political issues which are held to have so sharply polarized the electorate in the early years of independence are held to be, first, the question of the Anglo-Irish Treaty (or, more broadly, the 'national question'), and, second, the direction of economic development and of social policy. Fianna Fáil's absence from the centre of the political stage until August 1927—due to its boycott of Dáil Éireann—is said to have artificially submerged the importance of the civil-war divisions and granted an equally artificial boost to the Labour Party. With Fianna Fáil's Dáil entry, all this changed; the 'real' lines of division in Irish society could now find political expression; Labour could not even hope to hold its own on the socio-economic plane, as its essentially welfarist policies possessed only minority appeal.

But was the electorate really so sharply polarized around the Treaty question? Even in 1922—i.e. before the civil war—when the Treaty issue was clearly to the centre of the stage, and with an electoral pact operating, albeit with violations, between the pro-Treaty and anti-Treaty wings of Sinn Féin, no less than thirty of the ninety contested seats went to candidates who belonged to neither wing of Sinn Féin. Moreover, this was in a situation marked by intimidation of non-Sinn Féin candidates.[31] Within this group Labour was predominant. The post-civil-war period saw not merely the 'centre' (as Mair refers to those groups not directly involved in the Treaty split) holding, but also, after a brief respite, the inexorable decline of the Sinn Féin (anti-Treaty) party.

It is not sufficient to trace the dramatic reversal of this position after September 1927 simply to the entrance of Fianna Fáil into the

[30] Ibid. 462.
[31] For a discussion of the circumstances in which the election took place, see M. Gallagher, 'The Pact General Election of 1922', *Irish Historical Studies*, 21/84 (1981), 408–11.

Dáil, assuming that a public opinion which had really been galvanized around the Treaty issue all along was thereby prompted into
action. Fianna Fáil's break with the Sinn Féin rump consisted of
much more than simply a break with abstentionism; as will be
argued in Chapters 3 and 4, Fianna Fáil, from the outset, sought to
articulate its nationalism in concrete economic and social terms
which combined a development strategy appealing to the interests
of important strata such as the small farmers and petty bourgeoisie
with welfarist policies and overtures to the trade-union movement
designed to secure working-class support; Fianna Fáil's appeal to
the working class was in some respects just as 'welfarist' as Labour's,
but the latter possessed neither a political nor an economic strategy.

Moreover, Labour was hopelessly divided, as was the trade-
union movement. The lack of policy coherence was accompanied
by a severe lack of funds and a failure to nominate sufficient candidates to present a credible governmental alternative in any case.
The Labour Party was fatally fissile: 'Of its seventeen TDs [parlia-
mentary deputies] elected in 1922, three were independent by August
1923. Of the fourteen elected then, one was independent by June
1927. Of the thirteen elected in September 1927, four fought the
election of 1932 as independents.'[32]

Labour's failure to think in strategic terms was shown by the
refusal of its leader, T. J. O'Connell, to support the anti-land annuities campaign, thereby forfeiting the possibility of winning small
farmer support. Not only did Fianna Fáil poach the issue from
radical Irish Republican Army (IRA) leaders such as Peadar
O'Donnell, but its programme of land division offered a powerful
attraction to those landless agricultural labourers who formed one
of Labour's main sources of support.

That the party system became more obviously polarized in the
late 1920s is clearly not in dispute. The interesting question is why
it became polarized in the way that it did. If primary significance is
to be attached to Fianna Fáil's Dáil entrance, assuming an existent,
but dormant, polarization since the end of the civil war which was
then activated, the following question needs to be asked: would
Fianna Fáil have been able to oust Cumann na nGaedheal from
power by 1932 if it had, upon entering the Dáil, continued upon
the old Sinn Féin path of showing indifference to social and

---

[32] D. R. O'Connor Lysaght, *The Republic of Ireland* (Dublin, 1970), 89.

economic problems, offering merely vague generalizations about
'less taxation' and 'more prosperity'? If not, then to what extent
might the party's success in maintaining and consolidating the spurt
which Dáil entry undoubtedly gave it be attributed to its role in
creating a new political agenda? The question is of importance in
assessing the significance of Fianna Fáil's break with the old Sinn
Féin strategy, and not merely in terms of abstentionist politics.

In summary, the changes which occurred during the late 1920s
and early 1930s cannot be attributed to the dynamics of the party
system, on the assumption of the determinant effect of the civil war
upon the political alignment of the electorate. Mair is on much
stronger ground when, in a later work, he argues that:

> while parties and party systems persist, it is also necessary to emphasise
> that they do not persist *per se*, but persist under certain conditions and
> within certain circumstances. These conditions and circumstances may be
> environmental—that is, they may relate to the social structure, the prevail-
> ing value system, the institutional context, and so on—but they may also
> belong in the party arena itself, and have much to do with the strategy
> of the parties, their ideological appeals and the manner in which they
> compete.
>
> In other words, the capacity of parties to persist is not predetermined
> and the rules of the political game are not necessarily set irrevocably from
> the beginning of mass politics . . .
>
> In short, there is nothing inevitable about the persistent dominance of
> Fianna Fáil in contemporary Irish politics. Nor is it inevitable that Fine Gael
> remained the main challenger to Fianna Fáil, nor that Labour remains on
> the margins.[33]

Undoubtedly the perceptible rise in anti-Treaty propaganda and
agitation, and the reaction which this provoked, characterized Fianna
Fáil's rise to power; but this must be studied within the context of
the party's overall strategy, embracing the joint articulation of social, economic, and political grievances. In short, the situation was
a lot more fluid than a concentration upon the causal significance
of Fianna Fáil's Dáil entrance would suggest.

THE PERIPHERY 'INVADES' THE CENTRE

We have already mentioned the predominant role allocated by Carty
to political élites, and the problems which this highly voluntaristic

---

[33] Mair, *The Changing Irish Party System*, 59–60.

approach entails. Carty has developed his theory in debate with Garvin, who has sought to portray the social cleavages underlying Irish politics in terms of a centre–periphery dichotomy. According to Garvin, the fundamental conflict in Irish politics has been between a modernized, urbanized, Anglicized, and economically advanced 'centre' and a less well-off, rural, Gaelic 'periphery'. This conflict finds expression in the political competition between Cumann na nGaedheal–Fine Gael and Fianna Fáil. The latter is essentially a rural phenomenon, which began its life in the western periphery—where it has always maintained a high level of support—and gradually made inroads amongst the more urban areas, giving birth to the phenomenon of the 'periphery-dominated centre'.

Fianna Fáil, the argument goes, not only held the old Sinn Féin vote in the west, but managed to mobilize 'young and recently mobilised voters, particularly in the west' between 1923 and 1932.[34] It fought on the basis of a 'populist, autarkic and anti-urban programme [which] reflected well the mass support for the party at this time, as it reflected well the thinking of de Valera, himself a westerner in social background'.[35]

The fact that Fianna Fáil managed to maintain its dominance for so long, despite the economic and social changes which occurred, is attributed to the 'invasion' of the 'centre' taking place 'during the last phase of political mobilisation in Irish society between 1923 and 1932, and at a time when the national question dominated domestic politics'.[36]

However, as Sinnott has noted, there is little evidence for such a conclusion.

Fianna Fáil's vote increase was not uniformly correlated with increase in turn-out . . . the newly mobilised voters were not dominantly peripheral . . . the periphery's contribution to the total Fianna Fáil vote remained remarkably stable over the period in question . . . From the outset Fianna Fáil advanced on all fronts and behaved much more as a national party than as a party representing one side of a centre–periphery conflict.[37]

[34] T. Garvin, 'Political Cleavages, Party Politics and Urbanisation in Ireland—The Case of the Periphery-Dominated Centre', *European Journal of Political Research*, 11/4 (1974), 309.

[35] T. Garvin, 'Political Action and Ideology in Dublin', *Social Studies*, 6/1 (1977), 176; 'The Destiny of the Soldiers: Tradition and Modernity in the Politics of de Valera's Ireland', *Political Studies*, 26/3 (1978), 333.

[36] Garvin, 'Political Cleavages, Party Politics and Urbanisation', 309–10.

[37] Sinnott, 'Interpretations of the Irish Party System', 298–9.

It can also be argued that Garvin ignores much of the social reality behind the electoral statistics. Sinnott is undoubtedly correct to point out that Fianna Fáil's advance in the 'centre' was already well under way before the party came to power, and that it polled 43 per cent here in 1933. However, it should also be pointed out that the very presentation of the problem in this context obscures the fact that there was a considerable population imbalance between the regions. Throughout the century the population of western Ireland has been declining—and the decline has been manifest first and foremost among the young and the impoverished—the people from whom Fianna Fáil might be expected to have drawn most of its support in the 1920s and 1930s. Thus, between 1911 and 1936 the population of Connaught and the three Ulster counties which were to form part of the Irish Free State fell from 942,000 to 805,000. In the same period the population of Leinster (Dublin included) rose from 1,162,000 to 1,220,000. (These areas do not exactly correspond to the 'centre' and 'periphery' as defined by Garvin, but the discrepancy is, if anything, likely to be more pronounced.) So, even if the Fianna Fáil vote was proportionately higher in the west and the border counties, this does not prove that anything like a majority of Fianna Fáil voters came from these areas.

Nor does Garvin really address the question of who, exactly, voted for Fianna Fáil in the 'peripheral' areas. Farmers? Petty bourgeoisie? Landless labourers or small-scale service workers? The unemployed? While he certainly acknowledges the long tradition of agrarian strife, not only between landlords and tenants but between the farmers and the landless and disinherited, his attempt to fit Irish socio-political conflicts within the framework of the centre–periphery cleavage underplays the significance of rural (and urban) social conflicts. The result is a less than fully satisfactory picture of the social nature of the early Fianna Fáil and a less than rigorous treatment of the political strategy employed by the party to supersede the tensions within a class bloc composed of potentially fissile elements, which ensured its passage to power.

In some respects, the presentation of the Fianna Fáil programme and political appeal as anti-urban is misleading; that of its rival, Cumann na nGaedheal, was, if anything, more so, placing unfettered faith in the development of the cattle trade as the motor for economic expansion and rejecting any substantial policy of industrialization. Fianna Fáil not only formulated concrete economic and social policies aimed at the urban working class, basing its economic development strategy upon the envisaged industrialization of Irish society, at least in part; it also articulated those policies in terms which it knew would appear favourably to its audience, whether rural or urban, petty bourgeois, bourgeois, or working class.

Thus, Seán Lemass, a central figure in the presentation of Fianna Fáil policy to the Dublin working class (and one of a Dublin-based group of republicans who set about the original organization of the party), was, as early as November 1924, fighting a by-election in a working-class Dublin constituency with the full support of the Dublin-based Council for the Unemployed, and on the basis that

when the Republicans came into control of the machinery of government they would see that it moved in the interests of the whole Irish people and not in the interests of a small privileged class. They cared nothing for the old catch-cries about the rights of property and the sacredness of interests.[38]

After the formal launch of Fianna Fáil in 1926, the appeal to Dublin workers and consumers grew more specific. Emigration, Lemass told the Dáil in 1929, 'represented the fruits of the policy of allowing the farmers to do whatever they liked with the land, regardless of its effects upon the community'. And the man who boasted that 'I am not, never have been, and probably never will be a farmer' told the Dáil: 'I represent Dublin, and I feel justified in speaking especially about the position in Dublin because of the fact that unemployment is worse in Dublin than in any other part of the State.'[39] We shall have more to say later about the fate of such sentiments during Fianna Fáil's long tenure in office; and it might well be argued that Lemass's expressed views were not necessarily shared by a majority of his front-bench colleagues, and that the importance of his opening to the working class was as yet far from universally accepted within the party. But it should suffice for now to note that these remarks reflect a fundamental facet of Fianna Fáil's political appeal and mass support in the late 1920s which cannot be described as 'western', 'peripheral', or 'anti-urban'.

Nor does the description of Cumann na nGaedheal–Fine Gael as a party of the 'centre' enlighten us much. It was Fianna Fáil policy which advocated the industrialization of Ireland, while that of

---

[38] Quoted in B. Farrell, *Seán Lemass* (Dublin, 1983), 11.　　　[39] Ibid. 31.

Cumann na nGaedheal–Fine Gael remained staunchly committed to the interests of the larger farmers, maintaining Ireland as an agricultural appendage of the UK economy. Moreover, the Cumann na nGaedheal commitment to the Irish language was highly pronounced throughout the 1920s—indeed, emphasized, as proof of the party's nationalist credentials (Garvin deduces that support for the language is a characteristic of 'periphery' and is strongly correlated with support for Fianna Fáil); and the party's outlook was deeply influenced by the social teachings of the Catholic Church, tinged with clericalism and with subsequent hostility to 'foreign influence'—scarcely an indicator of 'modernism' or of cultural anglocentricity. What evidence, then, is there to regard it in such terms?

If it is Garvin's contention that Cumann na nGaedheal was supported by those strata which were more modern in the sense that they were more viable economically according to capitalist economic criteria, then undoubtedly he has a point. But one suspects that more is intended. Arguably, the centre–periphery debate tends to obscure economic and political conflicts between, and within, social classes and to simplify shifting correlations of political and social forces. The outcome, as far as the analysis of the politics of Fianna Fáil is concerned, is once again to underplay the significance of the party's political and economic strategy.

THE REVOLUTION BETRAYED? THE DILEMMA OF THE NATIONALIST LEFT

The final approach I will examine is concerned not so much with the rise of Fianna Fáil as with its 'decline'—a decline which—to be sure—is not yet fully manifest in electoral terms, but which is traced to its degeneration from a 'popular', 'national-democratic', or 'radical' movement (all the terms have been used) into a conservative, bourgeois party. This approach has tended to dominate much Marxist writing on Irish politics.

This theory of the decline of Fianna Fáil has long found favour on the left wing of Irish republicanism. The late Peadar O'Donnell, an influential socialist republican theorist and activist, has argued explicitly that the big mistake of the socialist republicans of the 1920s and 1930s was that they did not join up with Fianna Fáil, thereby helping to rescue the party, and de Valera, from the clutches of the bourgeoisie and from de Valera's own innate conservatism. According to O'Donnell, the Fianna Fáil members of that time 'were basically the same kind of people as ourselves . . . except sometimes more realistic . . . Oscar Traynor [later a Fianna Fáil TD] was one of the best socialist republicans I knew.'[40] Following O'Donnell, others have developed this line of argument, which rests not so much upon the contention that there were radicals or socialists within the early Fianna Fáil (for which there is undoubtedly some evidence), but upon the belief that such elements determined the character, or potentially could have determined the character, of the party in its early days.

According to this school, the basic form which class struggle is said to have taken in twentieth-century Ireland is the struggle against British imperialism. From this, two conclusions are drawn: that completion of the 'national revolution' is the primary struggle facing the Irish left; and that, in some sense, republicanism, or radical nationalism, is thereby the natural ideology of the Irish working class. Thus, the civil war is seen in terms of a straightforward conflict between left and right, with the small-farmer and essentially petty-bourgeois forces which formed the backbone of the republican movement regarded as revolutionary, in a socialist sense. These, of course, were the principal forces which were to give birth to Fianna Fáil; indeed, one of the principal icons of the nationalist left, Countess Markievicz, ended her life as a member of Fianna Fáil.

The greater part of the history of that party is seen in terms of a betrayal of its revolutionary origins and a surrender to the established order. This betrayal is manifest not least in the party's failure to realize the end of partition and its role in government in upholding the status quo of a partitioned Ireland. According to the analysis, Fianna Fáil dominance has been maintained through the fostering of false consciousness amongst the working class and other strata; this has been achieved, first and foremost, by the shrewd manipulation of the allegedly natural republican sentiments of these social groups by a party which has long since abandoned the completion of the 'national liberation struggle'. This is the line of argument followed explicitly by O'Donnell's comrade and fellow Republican Congress leader, George Gilmore, in a pamphlet which had a considerable influence amongst the nationalist left.[41]

[40] Interview with Peadar O'Donnell.
[41] G. Gilmore, *The Irish Republican Congress* (Cork, 1974).

Such analyses find common ground with more orthodox approaches in that they both see Fianna Fáil's monopoly of nationalist sentiment as the key to the party's success. Indeed, the socialist republicans also find common ground with (decidedly non-socialist) ultra-nationalist ideologues such as Kevin Boland, who has attributed the 'decline' of Fianna Fáil to its evolution from a national party to a sectional party, dominated by the rich and privileged.[42] The socialist republicans generally conclude with the claim that the wrestling of the leadership of the 'national revolution' from Fianna Fáil is the prerequisite for the success of the Irish left. This conclusion has underpinned the political strategies of the Republican Congress in the 1930s, Clann na Poblachta in the 1940s and 1950s, and elements of the republican movement since the 1960s. Their singular lack of success should give pause for thought.

In fact, such an analysis is flawed: it obscures the limits of Fianna Fáil radicalism, and of Irish republicanism as a revolutionary ideology, which were inherent from the start. The republican economic programme left no doubt as to the central role of private enterprise in developing the economy. Fianna Fáil economic policy aimed at the creation of an indigenous manufacturing bourgeoisie; social-welfare proposals and the expansion of employment and housing schemes, combined with approaches to the trade-union movement, would help secure working-class support, but there was never any question of violating the rights of private property despite Lemass's rhetoric.[43] Indeed, Lemass's refusal to nationalize the railways, which was one of the factors leading to the general election of 1933—an election deemed necessary to relieve Fianna Fáil of dependence upon Labour Party support—was an early warning which should have given the republican left grave cause for concern.

Moreover, no action whatsoever was taken to interfere with the workings of the banks and the financial institutions. Again, despite campaign rhetoric, Fianna Fáil showed itself unwilling, or unable, to violate capitalist economic rationale by stemming the outflow of capital to more profitable destinations. The Fianna Fáil agricultural policy, which has often been hailed as a radical assault upon the

---

[42] Boland, *The Rise and Decline of Fianna Fáil*, esp. 96–104.

[43] Whether Lemass ever believed his rhetoric, whether he was simply politically astute, or whether he was a sheer pragmatist who, in the early years, was prepared to rough-handle the bourgeoisie if necessary to get results, is an interesting question—but probably an unanswerable one.

big estates, actually reinforced the private ownership of land more than ever—before the party, inevitably, and without too much fuss, bowed to the laws of capitalist economic development and gave up the struggle to multiply the ranks of the small farmers, accepting land clearance.

Far from being revolutionary, this 'Catholic version of Jacobinism—the creed of small property owners'[44] was inherently conservative in both cultural and economic terms. Moreover, republicanism has always served to reorientate social discontent away from the arena of class conflict. As O'Connor Lysaght puts it, Fianna Fáil 'showed itself assiduous in making minor changes'. Such changes, including long-overdue development of housing and social welfare, were extremely important to an impoverished people, and should not be too lightly dismissed; but they were in no way fundamental structural changes which offered any prospect of a disruption of the balance of economic power in Irish society. Important, but decidedly non-revolutionary, economic and social changes, articulated in terms of 'nation' rather than 'class', helped to secure the allegiance of sections of the working class and other less-well-off groups to a party committed without ambiguity to the preservation and development of Irish capitalism.

It is difficult to see how a successful challenge to Fianna Fáil could have been mounted from a republican position; the real basis of its success lay, not in its manipulation of false consciousness on the national issue, but in its ability to make compromises within the framework of its commitment to capitalism—to grant much needed economic and social concessions, within the limits dictated by its prior commitment to the development of private enterprise. It was the absence of an alternative which could highlight and analyse these limits which gave Fianna Fáil a relatively easy passage. From the point of view of the political and intellectual left, the emphasis placed upon the dubious concept of false consciousness, with its tendency to underestimate the importance of reformist material concessions, has played a negative role.

CONCLUSION

A recurring criticism of the analyses of the Fianna Fáil phenomenon examined so far is that they fail to pay sufficient attention to the

---

[44] O'Connor Lysaght, *The Republic of Ireland*, 102.

strategic importance of the political choices of parties—to the field of tactical and strategic possibilities present in any historical situation. How did this group of republicans, emerging from the ramshackle ruins of Sinn Féin, manage to construct a party which achieved political dominance in such a short period of time? How did it maintain that dominance despite near economic collapse, despite the clear failure to realize either of the party's two principal aims—reunification and restoration of the language—despite the failure of many of the earlier radical hopes to materialize, and despite a complete economic volte-face in the late 1950s, when Fianna Fáil effectively abandoned the policies which, it had always claimed, could alone lay the economic foundations of national independence? How did the party manage persistently to succeed in keeping the politics of class conflict at bay, in a society in which poverty and affluence have always coexisted? What is the common thread which runs throughout the history of this remarkably successful political machine? It is the apparent elusiveness of convincing answers to questions such as these which has so confounded political commentators, encouraging the tendency to take refuge in deterministic theories.

This study will focus on the period from 1923 to 1948, although the interpretation offered may also have relevance for understanding the reconstruction of Fianna Fáil dominance in later years. The year 1948 can reasonably be taken as marking the culmination of the successes obtained as a result of the economic and political strategy pursued during the first phase in the party's history. From 1948 to 1957 Irish politics were in a state of flux; cracks were beginning to appear in Fianna Fáil's hegemony, but the very paucity of responses of other political forces to the severe economic crisis eventually permitted the recreation of Fianna Fáil dominance on a new basis. In any case, the period from 1948 to 1957 can be regarded as a transition phase between two distinct eras in Irish politics, marked by little that was new or interesting and by a singular lack of new initiatives on the part of Fianna Fáil itself.

First, I will examine the origins and nature of those social and political forces which gave rise to Fianna Fáil, arguing that the party programme aimed at realizing the economic project of the class of relatively small producers and native industrial manufacturers, numerically strong and fairly homogeneous in terms of ideology, *but without restricting itself to that project*. The Fianna Fáil policy of protection satisfied the desire of the native manufacturing class (existent and aspirant) to create an autonomous centre of capitalist development. It also held out hopes of employment expansion for workers. This ran counter, however, to the interests of large farmers and export-orientated capital; it also involved low standards of living, compared to the industrialized countries, for most citizens, and increased emigration.

The negative effects of this policy were mitigated at the political level by a programme of economic and social concessions—which stopped short of threatening the logic of capitalist accumulation. The failure of the republican left and the Labour Party fully to realize the importance of such concessions was matched by the failure of Cumann na nGaedheal–Fine Gael to transcend the politics of narrow economic corporatism. Even when Fianna Fáil's rivals have realized the necessity to forge social alliances, the result has often been reluctant, piecemeal, and ineffective. Thus the process by which Fianna Fáil secured the support of electorally and politically decisive sections of the working class and other marginalized groups cannot merely be attributed to objective factors, such as the weakness of working-class consciousness in Ireland or the drainage effects of emigration upon the potentially most dissatisfied sections of the community. The party's strategy, which combined an element of politically inspired economic populism with a successful moral and ideological offensive, requires careful analysis.

The failure of the attempt to create an autonomous centre of capitalist development, due to the laws of international economics and the extremely restricted size and potential of the home market, can already be detected from the late 1930s onwards. After a brief respite during the Second World War, the degenerative processes at work in the Irish economy resumed in the late 1940s. The unprecedented emigration crisis of the 1950s led, after much hesitation and ineptitude, to the abandonment of the goal of self-sufficiency and to a new industrialization drive led by foreign capital. Powerful material forces existed to support such a change in direction—not least some of those industrial concerns which had been fostered by the original policies of Fianna Fáil but which now saw their expansion possibilities exhausted by the saturation of the home market.

Although it is beyond the time scope of the present work, I will comment very briefly upon some of the changes which have taken place since the 1950s.

With the advent of the new economic policy, Fianna Fáil's political strategy was once again decisive for the successful reorientation of Irish capitalism. Bew and Patterson have commented on those aspects of that strategy (many of which are already present in the 1920s and 1930s), such as: the defusing of potential rifts within the bourgeoisie by the gradualist approach adopted towards the rationalization of industry—essentially, an insistence upon the supremacy of political over purely economic criteria which was often to the chagrin of the most efficient sectors of the bourgeoisie, and not without conflicts within Fianna Fáil itself; the incorporation of the labour movement through the new institutionalized role allotted to the trade unions within the economic planning (or programming) apparatus; and the maintenance of the support given to the party by increasingly uneconomic petty bourgeois, small farmers included, at least in part by direct subsidy.[45]

The period since the 1950s has also seen a retreat from cultural isolation and the gradual integration of Ireland into the cultural mainstream of the advanced capitalist countries. Cautious secularization and the breakdown of cultural nationalism have been accompanied by the lessening attractiveness of nationalist ideology. As the economic basis of partition has been eroded, with the desire for increased economic co-operation between north and south, the attraction of anti-partition rhetoric for the economically dominant groups has arguably diminished. Membership of the European Community since 1973 (the European Union since 1993) has further contributed to what has been quite a decisive shift in Irish political culture.

The failure, however, to sustain economic vitality, and the exposure of this small open economy to the worst excesses of the international economic crises of the 1970s and 1980s, have seen Fianna Fáil struggling to maintain its dominance in conditions favourable neither to economic populism nor to political and cultural nationalism. Increasingly the party finds itself in the throes of an identity crisis—torn between the twin attractions of capitalist entrenchment tempered by political populism and the limited

---

[45] P. Bew and H. Patterson, *Seán Lemass and the Making of Modern Ireland, 1945–66* (Dublin, 1982), ch. 2 *passim*.

possibilities for a Lemass-type neo-Keynesianism coupled with new overtures to the trade unions. Leading personalities, such as Charles Haughey, have shown themselves perfectly capable of giving expression to both 'ways forward' at one and the same time.[46] Fianna Fáil's failure to resolve this identity crisis is manifest in its unprecedented failure to secure a majority in six successive general elections. Its disappointment in the 1984 European Parliament elections, when, despite increasing its representation, it secured one of its lowest shares of the vote for many years, was followed in the autumn of 1985 by the formation, largely by Fianna Fáil dissidents, of a new and more 'orthodox' conservative party—the Progressive Democrats. Indeed, the factionalism and scandal which preceded the birth of the Progressive Democrats have robbed Fianna Fáil of much of its proud record of iron self-discipline and moral self-confidence.

Although the lacklustre politics of Ireland's most recent Fine Gael–Labour coalition government (1982–7), which, like its predecessors, proved unable to temper economic harshness with any appeal to the popular imagination, allowed Fianna Fáil to return to power as a minority government in 1987, further losses in the general election of 1989 forced the previously unthinkable upon Charles Haughey and his party: the formation of a coalition government with the Progressive Democrats as junior partners. It is difficult to exaggerate the shock with which the decision to cling on to power by entering a coalition—always regarded as anathema—was greeted by party activists; or the disorientating effect upon the party's political sub-culture and self-identity. Writing in 1987, O'Carroll could reasonably assert:

Coalition was seen to be anathema, reflecting the dilemma of all who would claim the absolute. In the world of true believers, whether of Fianna Fáil or of traditional Catholicism, the untrue and the bad cannot be joined with the true and the good. Accordingly, the only alignment, for the foreseeable future, can be Fianna Fáil versus the rest. The only coalition possibilities are among 'the rest'.[47]

---

[46] For example, see Haughey's 1983 statement (quoted in Gallagher, *Political Parties in the Republic of Ireland*, 26) that 'the Fianna Fáil that I lead is not, and will not be, a party of the right or of the left. It is the party of the nation'.

[47] J. P. O'Carroll, 'Strokes, Cute Hoors and Sneaking Regarders: The Influence of Local Culture on Irish Political Style', *Irish Political Studies*, 2 (1987), 84.

Yet by the summer of 1989 anathema had become reality. Moreover, although the controversial Haughey had finally been replaced with the ambitious but uninspiring Albert Reynolds, further humiliating losses were suffered by Fianna Fáil in the general election of November 1992. In the aftermath of that election—which both confirmed that Fianna Fáil's problems were not reducible to the 'Haughey factor' and called into question whether the party can win an overall parliamentary majority in the foreseeable future—Fianna Fáil swallowed the bitter pill of coalition for a second time and formed an unprecedented alliance with the Labour Party. The new administration collapsed in November 1994, amid a series of scandals concerning Fianna Fáil's role in office. Reynolds was replaced as party leader by Bertie Ahern, and a three-party coalition of Fine Gael, Labour and Democratic Left took office without recourse to fresh elections.

Fianna Fáil has entered the 1990s in the grip of a profound identity crisis, with both the unity of the party and its ability to reproduce its old historical bloc of social forces under threat. Never have the party's long-term prospects seemed so uncertain. It is against this background that we turn to a historical analysis of Ireland's premier party, in the hope that an analysis of its past may offer some guide as to its present and future prospects.

2

The Birth of Fianna Fáil
1923–1926

POLITICAL FORCES BEFORE 1923

The Irish civil war (June 1922–April 1923) marked the disintegration of Sinn Féin, which had led the struggle for independence. Sinn Féin had been a socially conservative movement, led by the urban middle classes, but containing within it representatives of most social strata. Amongst the movement's leaders there was a preponderance of 'traders, small manufacturers and the professions; in the country . . . civil servants, primary teachers, and priests'.[1]

This movement had demanded the subordination of all social concerns to nationalism. In a society numerically dominated by small manufacturers, farmers, traders, agricultural labourers, and domestic servants, it felt little necessity to seek a compromise with the numerically weak forces of organized labour which had been effectively deprived of political leadership by the Labour Party's decision to stand aside at the general election of 1918. Labour had in effect accepted the demand for national unity for the duration of the independence struggle. Sinn Féin displayed a hostility towards the organized working-class movement from the outset: 'when the working-class took part in social struggles it came up against the hostility of Sinn Féin, which was at least as violent as that of the police or the British army.'[2]

Arthur Griffith, the Sinn Féin president, had been particularly virulent in condemning the strike of Dublin workers for higher wages in 1913 and in siding with the employers: 'whenever Griffith saw socialist influence he sensed British influence. "The man", he wrote, "who injures Ireland, whether he does it in the name of imperialism or socialism, is Ireland's enemy." '[3] In Griffith's mind

---

[1] M. Goldring, *Faith of our Fathers: The Formation of Irish Nationalist Ideology* (Dublin, 1982), 20–1.   [2] Ibid. 79.
[3] Patrick Lynch, quoted in S. O'Faolain, *The Irish* (London, 1980), 150.

there was no doubt that the workers' strike in 1913 constituted 'injuring Ireland'.

Of course, Sinn Féin underwent a rapid expansion after 1916, and this involved more than just numerical change: it saw a transformation of the party's approach to the question of the use of political violence to achieve national independence. But there is precious little to suggest that the antagonism towards organized labour of the pre-1916 Sinn Féin underwent much of a change; many of the post-1916 Sinn Féin leaders, de Valera included, shared fully Griffith's hostility to working-class politics, even if they enjoyed a greater degree of 'psychological autonomy' from the employers.

Yet, the working class aside, Sinn Féin's ranks were far from free of social conflict, particularly during the post-1916 rapid expansion of the party. At least two potential sources of class tension existed within the movement. First, the small farmers, landless labourers, and other less-well-off strata were not content to postpone indefinitely their demands for social reform and land redistribution until emigration had taken its toll; acts of land seizure by the rural poor were not uncommon during the War of Independence, and frequently the IRA, under orders from the republican leadership, intervened to restore the seized land to its former owners. These, moreover, were the people who came to form the backbone of the movement, especially after the 1918 general election, when Sinn Féin became a truly mass national movement.

Second, the rather vague Sinn Féin programme 'was designed to create the conditions whereby an independent Irish manufacturing class could come into existence. The keystone of the policy was protection from foreign competition.'[4] Whilst the policy of protection appealed to the economic interests of small and increasingly bankrupt manufacturers and farmers, it was bound to meet with opposition from larger farmers, dependent upon the cattle trade with Britain, and the small number of relatively successful larger manufacturers, as well as from a conservative state bureaucracy. It was essentially an economic policy which aimed, as yet in an idealistic sense and without too many specifics, at the transformation of the urban and rural petty bourgeoisie through the development of the home market. It offered the small man the possibility of

---

[4] B. Probert, *Beyond Orange and Green* (London, 1978), 37.

becoming a slightly bigger man if only he would bide his time, and fall in behind the national independence struggle.

That Sinn Féin would succeed in keeping class politics off the agenda was by no means certain, even at the height of its unity in 1918. As Rumpf and Hepburn have observed: 'It is therefore evident that while Sinn Féin support was often socially radical, its social programme, national leadership and (in many areas) local leadership was very moderate. A split along class lines did not seem impossible in the early months of 1918.'[5]

When the split eventually came, it was around the Anglo-Irish Treaty settlement of 1921. At first sight, the issues involved seem to have been entirely constitutional; the opponents of the Treaty objected to four principal restrictions on Irish sovereignty: Ireland was to have dominion status and to become known as the Irish Free State instead of becoming a fully independent republic; the king was to be recognized as the head of state in Ireland; all members of the Irish parliament would have to swear an oath of allegiance to the king; and the British were to retain control of certain Irish ports and other facilities in time of war. (The issue of the partition of Ireland, which the Treaty also ratified, was not really such a cause of concern to the republicans as they remained convinced that the Northern Ireland state could not possibly survive more than a few years anyway.)

But as first Sinn Féin, and then the IRA, split over the terms of the Treaty and drifted towards civil war, it became obvious that socio-economic factors played some part in determining the constellation of opposing forces. Certainly, to portray the civil war in terms of a pure class struggle is to posit an unsustainable hypothesis; and Garvin is surely right to draw attention to the relatively small part played by both proletariat and bourgeoisie.[6] However, to ignore the influence of social class upon civil-war allegiances is to posit an equally unsustainable hypothesis: that of the 'sacra insula'— an Ireland oblivious to all but the 'things of the spirit'—a hypothesis for which there is little supporting historical evidence.

During the War of Independence the economic grievances of the landless poor (and, indeed, the petty bourgeoisie) had frequently

    [5] E. Rumpf and A. C. Hepburn, *Nationalism and Socialism in Twentieth Century Ireland* (Liverpool, 1977), 21.
    [6] T. Garvin, *Nationalist Revolutionaries in Ireland, 1858–1928* (Oxford, 1987), 174.

been expressed in terms of loyalty to the Republic and hostility to the ruling circles whose interests led them to pursue a policy of close co-operation and integration with the British economy, and hence cast them in the role of 'pro-British elements'. This had been an ideological theme of the left-wing republicans who justified the land seizures perpetrated by the poor, and it was to remain a theme in Fianna Fáil propaganda for many years to come. With the civil war, those who opted for a settlement with Britain placed themselves precariously in the shoes of the 'pro-British elements'—all the more so as they were supported by the economically dominant groups—with the result that those who felt they had least to lose, socially and economically, tended to express their discontent in militant republicanism.

It had long been a cardinal principle of Irish republicanism that the British connection was the source of all the country's ills—economic and social as well as political; and that the completion of the national revolution would result in material, as well as spiritual, well-being. Given this well-entrenched aspect of nationalist ideology, it was perhaps to be expected that the economic ills of the 1920s should be attributed so easily to the abandonment of the nationalist policy of protection for Irish industry by the civil-war victors, and their acceptance of Ireland's role as an agricultural exporter to the British market. Given the close integration, within Irish nationalism, of economic, cultural, and political ends, it is necessary to deconstruct expressions of nationalist sentiments which initially appear of a purely political or constitutional nature.

Of course, while the articulation of economic interests remained bound up with nationalist and religious ideology, then arguably the threat to the rule of the economically dominant classes was weakened, and the possibility of the emergence of independent organizations of the working class and the rural poor was correspondingly reduced—a state of affairs which Fianna Fáil did much to reproduce.

Various writers have commented on the class dimension to the civil war. Rumpf and Hepburn have commented on the fact that the anti-Treaty forces tended to be supported by small western farmers and the sons of landless men, while the pro-Treaty forces counted on the support of the big bourgeoisie, larger farmers, and substantial sections of the professional strata. The high level of support which the anti-Treaty forces received from the relatively prosperous counties of Munster, where a high percentage of the population was engaged in agriculture, suggests, moreover, the adherence of both labourers and small-town petty bourgeoisie.[7]

Pyne, whilst noting the importance of factors such as personal antipathies and regional variations in anti-government traditional patterns of behaviour, and the unsatisfactory nature of a purely socio-economic analysis of the civil-war split, has pointed to similar 'legitimate if tentative generalisations'. He has concluded that 'while the Treaty was opposed by people from every social level, the bulk of its opponents could broadly be described as lower middle-class', and has pointed out that the evidence of the 1923 general-election returns leads to the general conclusions that the anti-Treaty forces

tended to be supported by the less well-off sections of the agricultural community, whose housing conditions were far from ideal and who were considerably affected by emigration. The classes furthest down the social pyramid believed that the establishment of a Gaelic nation State, completely cut off from the English sphere of influence, would help them to increased rights and improved conditions.[8]

Put very simply, those with least to lose, and everything to gain, tended to oppose the Treaty in the hope that an alternative settlement might give them enough land to support their families or some security of livelihood.

The civil war had witnessed an upsurge of social radicalism, involving, as in the immediately preceding period, the seizure of land in some areas by small farmers and landless men. Liam Mellows, one of the more intellectual of the republican leaders, gave concrete expression to this radicalism, declaring that 'under the Republic all industry will be controlled by the State for the workers' and farmers' benefit'. But the majority of the anti-Treaty leaders

kept apart from such aims because they did not want the republican ideal to be confused by social issues. The anti-Treatyites, both physical-force men and politicians, neglected to develop a coherent social programme, and thus failed to secure the widespread public support which they needed to win the civil war.[9]

Indeed, years later, at a Fianna Fáil conference, a delegate was to answer attacks upon Fianna Fáil's allegedly revolutionary designs

[7] Rumpf and Hepburn, *Nationalism and Socialism in Twentieth Century Ireland*, 36, 61.

[8] P. Pyne, 'The Third Sinn Féin Party, 1923–26', *Economic and Social Review*, 1 (1969–70), 242–3.   [9] Ibid. 242.

by boasting that 'an out-break of communism in Galway in 1920' was 'put down' by the IRA within twelve hours. They 'told the ring-leader to surrender at once the land he had seized'.[10] Of course, the incident reported here occurred before the start of the civil war; the point is that the quotation sums up the attitude of many anti-Treaty leaders in such matters.

Evidently, the urban middle classes and embryonic national bour-geoisie who had led the Sinn Féin movement during the struggle for independence had yet to readjust to the changed circumstances of 1922–3 and to develop a strategy for maintaining their hegemony over the small farmers, landless labourers, and others who formed the main source of 'left republican' discontent. Thus Mellows might write: 'The commercial interests and the merchants were on the side of the Treaty. We are back to Wolfe Tone, and it is just as well, relying on the men of no property.'[11] But the deep suspicion within the republican movement of any attempt to raise questions of so-cial reform, which might bring class tension within the ranks to the surface, and which had earlier led the underground Sinn Féin to establish land courts to punish the seizure of land by landless ele-ments,[12] continued to persist amongst many of the leaders of the *anti-Treaty* forces during the civil-war period and after.

As regards the urban working class, the claims of several writers that workers tended to be pro-Treaty[13] seem to rest on the fact that Labour Party electoral transfers in 1922 went to pro-Treaty rather than anti-Treaty parties.[14] In any case, there seems to be no doubt that urban workers played little part in the struggle against the Treaty; indeed, Pyne suggests that non-agricultural workers in general showed little support for 'the cause of the Republic'.[15] Mellows re-cognized this; writing from his prison cell, he lamented the failure of the republican forces with the words 'the workers were not with us'.

The reasons why the working class should have regarded the struggle for the Republic with less than overwhelming enthusiasm at this time are not difficult to discern. First, as we have seen, the ideology of Sinn Féin and the republican movement had simply

---

[10] *Irish Press*, 29 Oct. 1931.   [11] Quoted in O'Faolain, *The Irish*, 152.
[12] Rumpf and Hepburn, *Nationalism and Socialism in Twentieth Century Ire-land*, 53.
[13] Ibid. 67; J. Meenan, *The Irish Economy since 1922* (Liverpool, 1970), 31.
[14] Gallagher, 'The Pact General Election of 1922', 420.
[15] Pyne, 'The Third Sinn Féin Party', 243.

no place for the *organized* working class. (And it should not be forgotten that Dublin workers, in particular, though numerically a minority group, had a strong tradition of recent struggle—the memories of 1913 were still fresh and raw.) The 'men of no property' of whom Mellows spoke were really, for the majority of his fellow republicans at any rate, 'men of little property' or 'men of no land'.

Second, the Sinn Féin leadership's failure to articulate a sufficiently coherent or radical economic strategy to maintain the unity of an electoral bloc which included urban middle classes, small farmers, and landless labourers was exceeded by its downright hostility to the needs and interests of urban workers. Some, like Countess Markievicz, had taken the workers' side in 1913, but to the majority the very notion of an urban working class, with its spectre of the industrial revolution, was simply un-Irish and strangely out of place in the Gaelic Ireland of small businesses and strident individualism[16] which they envisaged. Lyons has commented on this aspect of the Sinn Féin ideological patrimony that 'the obverse of the cult of the peasant was a recoil from corrupt and stinking towns and cities, and from that it was but a step to condemn "modern civilisation" in general, more particularly as exemplified by England'.[17] Besides, given a conflict of interest between the working class and the small capitalists whose interests the republican policy of protection appealed to most intimately, the republicans tended naturally to side with the latter.

Third, Labour's decision not to contest the 1918 general election, which saw the emergence of Sinn Féin as the hegemonic force in the land, contributed to Labour's marginalization throughout the Treaty debates and the sequence of events leading up to the civil war. The Labour Party stood apart from the civil-war conflict and this was reflected in the disappointing results it obtained in 1923; disappointing, not because potential Labour voters necessarily rallied behind one or other of the warring Sinn Féin factions; but because, as several sources agree, the urban working class (who might be considered a 'natural' constituency of the Labour Party) viewed an election dominated by the civil-war issue with large-scale apathy and abstained in greater numbers than other sections of the community.[18]

---

[16] Goldring, *Faith of our Fathers*, 21–4.
[17] F. S. L. Lyons, *Culture and Anarchy in Ireland* (Oxford, 1982), 81.
[18] J. A. Gaughan, *Thomas Johnson* (Dublin, 1980), 222; A. Mitchell, *Labour in Irish Politics, 1890–1930* (Dublin, 1974), 190.

So urban workers appear to have looked on largely in apathy as Irish society was torn apart by a bitter civil war in which the immediate issues at stake were clearly of a constitutional nature, but in which the alignment of political forces was also clearly influenced by socio-economic factors. In short, the pro-Treaty forces, supported by the social weight of the big bourgeoisie, larger farmers, and—although arguably of less importance—the Anglo-Irish ascendancy, inflicted a devastating defeat on the republican forces, whose bedrock of support was the small farmers, petty bourgeoisie, and lower professional classes. This is the background to the emergence of the political and economic strategy which, not without much internal debate, conflict, and tension, was eventually to guarantee the rise of Fianna Fáil to dominance in the new Irish state.

FROM THE ASHES OF THE CIVIL WAR: THE EMERGENCE
OF THE NEW IDENTITY

The civil war formally ended, in total military defeat for the anti-Treaty, republican forces, on 30 April 1923. A disastrous military strategy, compounded by the lack of a political one, and the loss of popular sympathy, left the republicans impotent, although sporadic acts of terrorism were to continue for some years, culminating in the assassination of the Minister for Home Affairs, Kevin O'Higgins, in July 1927.

Political power in the new state rested in the hands of the pro-Treaty wing of the old Sinn Féin, reconstituted in April 1923 as Cumann na nGaedheal. The new government could count on the support of the greater part of the commercial classes, the big farmers, the intelligentsia, the media, and the churches. During the civil war the Catholic Church had excommunicated the republicans, insisting that

in all this there is no question of mere politics, but of what is morally right or wrong . . . [and impressing] on the people the duty of supporting the national government, whatever it is . . . Unless they learn to do so they can have no government, and if they can have no government they can have no nation.[19]

Moreover, the great majority of the people were war-weary and had an earnest desire for peace. Although the particularly bitter

---

[19] Quoted in R. Fanning, *Independent Ireland* (Dublin, 1983), 19.

nature of the conflict, augmented by atrocities on both sides, left burning scars on the social body, the Government could reap the benefits of a widely felt longing for a return to law and order and social stability. Besides, most Irish people were prepared to bestow upon a Dublin parliament and government, even one which they may not initially have favoured, a legitimacy which they withheld from a parliament and government in London. The new police force (the *Gardaí*—recruited and trained in 1922–3 and formally established in 1924) was undeniably Irish, composed largely of old (pro-Treaty) IRA men, piously Catholic and accepted by the community. Moreover, the trumpeting of the Irish language—recognized in the Free State constitution of 1922 as the 'national language'—helped to consolidate legitimacy.[20] In short, despite the bitterness, devastation, and damage caused by the civil war, the new Government could draw upon a considerable reservoir of support, reinforced by the disarray of its opponents, and was backed by a formidable array of forces.

There is no doubting the popularity of the pro-Treaty forces at this time. In elections held in August 1923 Cumann na nGaedheal won 39.0 per cent of the vote (sixty-three seats); the even more conservative Farmers' Party won 12.1 per cent (fifteen seats); independents (often old Unionists, and generally pro-Treaty) won 10.9 per cent (fourteen seats); Labour won 10.6 per cent (fourteen seats). The anti-Treaty forces, who by now had a monopoly of the name Sinn Féin, succeeded in winning 27.4 per cent and forty-four seats in the new Dáil.[21] The performance of the anti-Treaty forces was far from disappointing, taking into consideration the circumstances under which they were operating: many of their leaders and candidates were in prison; their political activities were subject to repression and harassment by the police; they were badly short of funds and demoralized by military defeat. Indeed, their success in obtaining 27.4 per cent surpassed their expectations and surprised many of their leaders. One such leader, Seán MacEntee, expressed the hope that perhaps it would be possible after all to make real headway through political action. Within the republican movement, the election further strengthened the hand of the 'politicians', such as Eamon de Valera, at the expense of the 'gunmen'. It has been

[20] T. Garvin, *The Evolution of Irish Nationalist Politics* (Dublin, 1981), 152.
[21] C. O'Leary, *Irish Elections, 1918–1977* (Dublin, 1979), 101.

argued[22] that the manner in which the civil war ended had already given a considerable boost to de Valera, who had been marginalized to a good extent while the war was in progress, and it is indeed open to question whether de Valera's ascendancy within the post-civil-war movement would have been so undisputed had most of the senior leaders not lost their lives in the course of the conflict.

The pattern of Sinn Féin support in 1923 leads to the conclusion that it remained heavily dependent upon the small farmers and lower middle classes and devoid of the national appeal which had characterized the old, united Sinn Féin movement in 1918.[23] Sinn Féin, in other words, remained dependent for its support upon the very social strata, largely rural, upon whom emigration was once more beginning to take its heaviest toll.

Before examining the party's response to this situation, let us consider the ideological complexion of the defeated republicans, thousands of whom began to be released from prison from 1923 onwards. It has sometimes been argued that Fianna Fáil began life as a radical, almost socialist, party which might well have been 'won' to a revolutionary position had the left wing of the IRA and the labour movement thrown in their lot with de Valera. This, as we have seen, is the familiar line of argument advocated by sections of the nationalist left. My purpose, here, is to examine the distinct limits to Fianna Fáil's radicalism; these limits, inherent from the start, are reflected in the essentially petty-bourgeois ideology of the republican movement.

Poulantzas has defined the petty bourgeoisie as those engaged in small-scale ownership;[24] this definition includes small farmers, artisan producers, small businesses where the owner of the means of production is also the direct producer, as well as retail traders.[25] According to Poulantzas, the economic experience of the petty bourgeoisie has specific and detectable ideological effects as a result of its ambiguous position *vis-à-vis* the working class, on the one hand, and the bourgeoisie, on the other. Attached to his or her property, like the bourgeois, the petty bourgeois exhibits respect for property, social conservatism, hostility towards taxation and high

[22] T. Ryle Dwyer, *Eamon de Valera* (Dublin, 1980), 71.
[23] Pyne, 'The Third Sinn Féin Party', 243–4.
[24] N. Poulantzas, *Classes in Contemporary Capitalism* (London, 1975), 285–90.
[25] For an outline of this argument, see D. O'Connell, 'Class, Nation and State: The Real Fianna Fáil Story, 1927–1957', unpub. paper (Dublin, 1982), 18.

public expenditure, and so on; however, being a direct producer, like the worker, he or she often displays an antagonism towards the 'rich and idle' and towards extravagance or waste (or, in Poulantzas's words, a 'status quo anti-capitalism'), and a concern with hard work and meritocracy.

The Ireland of the 1920s was one dominated by the small producer. Brown has written:

In 1926, 53 per cent of the state's recorded gainfully employed population was engaged in one way or another in agriculture . . . Only one fifth of the farmers were employers of labour. A majority were farmers farming their land . . . on their own account or with the help of relatives. Roughly one quarter of the persons engaged in agriculture depended for their livelihood on farms of 1–15 acres, a further quarter on farms of 15–30 acres with the rest occupied on farms of over 30 acres. Some 301,084 people were employed in various ways on farms of less than 30 acres, 121,820 on farms of 30–50 acres, 117,255 on farms of 50–100 acres, 61,155 on farms of 100–200 acres, and only 34,298 on farms of 200 acres and over. As can readily be seen from these figures, small and medium-sized farms were the predominant feature of Irish agriculture.[26]

Other writers have noted the relatively tiny size of the working class, which, in 1926, accounted for only 13 per cent of those gainully employed (the figure relates to those in industrial employment). Indeed, in that year 'there were as many domestic servants— 85,000—as factory workers'.[27]

It was from the Ireland of the small producer that the rank and file of the republican movement seems to have been derived, together, in all likelihood, with the bulk of its electoral support; and it was its economic interests which the Sinn Féin policies of industrial protection and land redistribution aimed primarily at promoting. To the landless was held out the possibility of becoming a small farmer; to the employee in a small manufacturing firm or family business, the possibility of setting up in business. That republican ideology might reflect the economic experiences and expectations of such strata is scarcely surprising.

The ideological outlook of the republicans is marked by a number of recurrent themes—individualism, moralism bordering on puritanism, egalitarianism, and exclusivism—which will reappear time

---

[26] T. Brown, *Ireland: A Social and Cultural History* (London, 1981), 19.
[27] J. A. Murphy, *Ireland in the Twentieth Century* (Dublin, 1975), 111–12.

and time again in our analysis of the political discourse of Fianna Fáil, not only in its early years, but long after it had ceased to be the vehicle for the economic and social advancement of the 'small man'.

This ideology was, of course, one which the republicans shared in many respects with the pro-Treaty wing of Sinn Féin. However, as we have already hinted and as we will see more clearly later, Cumann na nGaedheal underwent a process of transformation almost from its inception; its clear emergence as the favoured party of the old (anti-Sinn Féin) establishment permitted the founders of Fianna Fáil to claim as their own the full force of republican ideological orthodoxy.

Commenting on a pamphlet, *The Ethics of Sinn Féin*, published by the party's National Council in September 1917, Goldring has this to say about the spirit of individualism which permeated the republican movement:

What dominates this text is the emphasis placed on the individual rather than on his adhesion to a social group or class. Independence is first and foremost a personal matter. The Sinn Féiner's moral obligations are many and restrictive. His conduct must be above reproach. His personality stainless. He must learn the Irish language, write on Irish paper, abstain from alcohol and tobacco. This alone, however, was not enough. He must integrate all these moral decisions into the personal decision to break with England. Sinn Féin (Ourselves Alone) became Me Féin (Myself Alone).[28]

This overwhelming concern with individual initiative went hand in hand with a contemptuous and fundamentally hostile attitude to the concept of class and of class politics and lies behind what has become a familiar theme throughout the history of Fianna Fáil—a concern with the 'rights' of the worker, the small farmer, the 'common man', combined with antagonism towards the forces of organized labour and the advocacy of class interests, invariably seen as 'sectional' and 'anti-national'. Not for nothing do Rumpf and Hepburn remark that de Valera's supporters saw him as a champion of their rights more than they ever saw him as a champion of their interests.[29]

The hostility towards the notion of class is well expressed in the

---

[28] Goldring, *Faith of our Fathers*, 21–2.
[29] Rumpf and Hepburn, *Nationalism and Socialism in Twentieth Century Ireland*, 99.

memoirs of Fianna Fáil founder member and former senior civil servant, Todd Andrews. Writing of the attitudes of the republicans in the aftermath of the civil war, Andrews first attacks the Free State for its involvement with the old ruling class—the 'landed gentry or wealthy unionists'—and then states quite categorically:

We assumed that except for the usual tendency for tuppence-halfpenny to look down on tuppence the Irish nation in the mass was a classless society. There was no social immobility based on birth or inherited wealth. To us the make-up of the Senate was just one example of the extent the Free Staters were prepared to go to keep in step with the manners, customs and values of the British.[30]

Class, for Andrews, as probably for the majority of the republicans, was simply 'un-Irish'. Regardless of the chronic unemployment and poverty, bordering in some areas on starvation; regardless of the slum housing conditions in Dublin, among the worst in Europe; regardless of the existence of wealthy Catholic farmers and manufacturers; regardless, even, of the severe economic plight of the republicans themselves, tens of thousands of whom were forced to emigrate in the 1920s—'class' was a thing to be associated exclusively with the British and the Protestants whom the Free State government had appointed in considerable numbers to membership of the new senate.

Extreme individualism often bordered on moral puritanism. According to Andrews:

We held strongly to the social ethos of republicanism in that, with one exception, we were puritanical in outlook and behaviour. We didn't drink. We respected women and . . . knew nothing about them. We disapproved of any kind of ostentation. We disapproved of the wearing of formal clothes—tuxedos, evening or morning dress, and above all silk hats. We disapproved of horse racing and everything and everyone associated with it. We disapproved of any form of gambling. We disapproved of golf and tennis and the plus-fours and white flannels that went with them. We disapproved of anyone who took an interest in food.[31]

This disapproval is not unconnected with what Poulantzas calls 'status quo anti-capitalism'. Whilst the ruling class is identified as the Anglo-Irish Protestant ascendancy (and behind it, the British), the republican petty-bourgeois leaders could lay all the vices of the

---

[30] C. S. Andrews, *Man of No Property* (Dublin, 1982), 13.   [31] Ibid. 29.

country, from poverty to unemployment, from sexual promiscuity to alcoholism, and, not least, intellectual non-conformity, at the feet of 'foreign capitalism', 'foreign imperialism', or, simply, 'foreign influence'. Another aspect of this moral puritanism concerns the authoritarian and at times contemptuous disposition of the republicans towards the mass of the Irish people when the latter are seen as hopelessly under the sway of this 'foreign influence' and failing to live up to the 'National Ideal'. Garvin has commented that 'the perception of the Irish people as corrupt and enslaved, and the cult of militarised youth, aggravated tendencies toward political and moral elitism among many separatists and the IRA'.[32]

As noted, the Catholic Church excommunicated the republicans during the civil war, and, as a consequence, the persistence of certain anti-clerical, or, to be more exact, anti-church hierarchy, tendencies within the republican movement and Fianna Fáil is to be observed during the 1920s and 1930s. One of the leading participants in the republican army during the civil war later commented, albeit somewhat optimistically, that 'the Church drove one half of the people against them with the result that they never regained the power they once had'.[33]

However, it must also be added that the republicans retained the sympathy of some priests; and, as Keogh makes clear,[34] the bishops, though strongly supportive of the Treaty, were generally opposed to the policy of executions by way of reprisal, pursued by the Government. The republicans could hope for sufficient countervailing tendencies within the Church to render an outright break avoidable.

Peadar O'Donnell has recounted how he and other IRA leaders were invited, during the civil war, by a group of pro-republican priests to attend a secret meeting to discuss the short-lived idea of the formation of an 'Irish Catholic Church'—as a breakaway from the Roman Catholic Church. According to O'Donnell, the priests' proposal met with a cool response from the IRA leaders, who sensed that without clear doctrinal coherence the project would be a damaging farce.[35]

Keogh adds that

---

[32] Garvin, *Nationalist Revolutionaries in Ireland*, 120–1.

[33] Dan Breen, quoted in Lyons, *Culture and Anarchy in Ireland*, 150.

[34] D. Keogh, *The Vatican, the Bishops and Irish Politics, 1919–1939* (Cork, 1986), 77–100.   [35] Interview with Peadar O'Donnell.

among the clergy, particularly the newly ordained men coming out of the Irish colleges in Rome, Paris and Salamanca, there was great sympathy for de Valera . . . it is probable that by 1924 de Valera had good cause to feel optimistic about the 'return of the younger priests as a preliminary step on the road to victory'.

Indeed, it was a priest, Fr John Hagan, Rector of the Irish College in Rome, who exercised an important influence on de Valera—both in helping to stimulate discussion on the need to found a new party, and in reassuring de Valera about the morality of entering the Dáil.[36]

The clear entrenchment of the Catholic Church's authority under the Free State regime—its control over education, the ban on divorce (1925), the stringent censorship laws in accordance with Catholic moral teaching (1923 and 1929)—not only went unchallenged by the overwhelming majority of republicans, but was intensified when Fianna Fáil was in office. Clearly, Breen's words are something of an exaggeration, to say the least. One reason for the receptiveness of the republicans to the Church's authority has been suggested by Lyons:

it is probably fair to say that most republicans in the 1920s, like most Fenians in the 1860s, distinguished in their own minds and to their own satisfaction between spiritual matters, in which they willingly acknowledged ecclesiastical authority, and public life, where laymen had to exercise their private judgement. This delicate balance could only be maintained so long as the boundary between the spiritual and the political was not defined too precisely, but the Church itself was unlikely to demand that it should be.[37]

Undoubtedly, there is something in this. But there are a number of other reasons for the remarkable ease with which those vanquished in the civil war accepted the authority of the Church in the new state they inherited. The first has been noted by Fanning:

Though the Treaty remained 'the dream that went bust', though the island remained partitioned and the republic a mirage, there remained Catholic ideals to bind together a riven nation. Catholicism, always central to so much of Irish nationalist ideology, thus took on an additional significance in the search for national identity.[38]

---

[36] Keogh, *The Vatican, the Bishops and Irish Politics*, 130, 159.
[37] Lyons, *Culture and Anarchy in Ireland*, 151.
[38] Fanning, *Independent Ireland*, 59.

The binding force of Catholic teaching in the new state is not to be underestimated. For those political and social forces aspiring to power, playing the 'Catholic card' allowed them to cast potential rivals outside the realm of social acceptability. The Protestant, the Anglo-Irish, the intellectual, the socialist ideology of some sections of the working class—all were simply materialist, pagan, Anglo-Saxon, and un-Irish values. The attempt to create an autonomous centre of capitalist development, which was the essence of the economic policies of the early Fianna Fáil governments, would necessitate measures directed against potential working-class and large-farmer protests, 'for Irish capital was fighting for its survival and could not withstand militant attacks from labour'.[39] Catholicism, with its hostility to class, its emphasis upon the moral obligation to submit to authority, and its effective isolation of nonconformist elements, would provide not merely an electoral asset, but would act in times of social tension as an invaluable social cement.

A further factor is that, although 'a current of mild anti-clericalism ran through much of the separatist movement', this 'was not the systematic, secularist anti-clericalism of continental ideologues but rather a belief that the priests were failing in their duty by not supporting purist republicanism wholeheartedly'.[40] Indeed, in the Irish case, there has been an extreme confusion and ambiguity in the ideological positions of self-professed radical nationalists, and Catholic, nationalist, socialist, corporatist, Marxist, and fascist ideas would continue for many years to run together in the minds of republicans.[41]

Finally, the moral puritanism of the republicans can be seen as a secular reflection of the strongly authoritarian and puritanical teachings of the Church. The former Fianna Fáil cabinet minister, Kevin Boland, writing as late as 1982, has this to say on the subject of public morality:

From the very outset there was a fully promulgated, though unwritten, rule that any departure from a high standard of personal integrity would entail expulsion from the party . . . the accepted principle now seems to be that 'a person's private life is his own business'. It sounds reasonable enough until it is examined, and it seems to be accepted by the Irish public . . . It is a principle that is not appropriate for anyone who opts for public life

---

[39] Probert, *Beyond Orange and Green*, 41.
[40] Garvin, *Nationalist Revolutionaries in Ireland*, 127–8.   [41] Ibid. 124.

and it is one that is dangerous from the point of view of public morality and the proper conduct of the State's affairs.[42]

The egalitarian aspect of republican ideology has sometimes been held out as evidence of socially radical, or even revolutionary, origins, later betrayed as Fianna Fáil became fat with the spoils of office. But, on closer examination, it becomes evident that this egalitarianism also had its limitations and was not nearly as revolutionary as some commentators, including many of the republicans themselves, would in good faith have us believe.

What was under attack was the notion of aristocracy, not the existence of socio-economic inequalities. The Anglo-Irish ruling class, together with the 'ranchers', distinguished by inheritance, by blood, and by titles, would make way for those who had worked their way to the top. Hard work, forbearance, meritocracy—these were the cornerstones of the republican egalitarianism. Those who worked their way to success would not be 'bourgeois' but patriots who, in bringing wealth to themselves, would bring credit to the nation. Such individuals could be described as having 'become modestly wealthy through their own enterprise and industry and through government policy'.[43] As Andrews puts it:

There were three words which were always virtually taboo in republican circles—peasant, bourgeois and intellectual. Theoretically, we have no peasants in Ireland. No republican would admit to being a bourgeois. Intellectual was a particularly pejorative term because it suggested falsity and pretentiousness.

Indeed, further on he provides us with the key to understanding the ethos of the republican movement. The republicans, he argues, were

egalitarian in that they accept the proposition that all men are created equal. This means that Jack is as good as his master but it also means that his master is as good as Jack. In the nature of things there are rich and powerful men who by any standards are good men; there is no merit in poverty.[44]

---

[42] Boland, *The Rise and Decline of Fianna Fáil*, 92–3. Mr Boland's views, in turn, sound reasonable enough until one remembers that the principle that 'a person's *private* life is everyone's business' was not merely applied to people who opted for public life, but became part of the ethos of Irish society. In this, the moral creed of the republicans and that of the Church were at one.

[43] Ibid. 96.   [44] Andrews, *Man of No Property*, 34, 98.

This is a profoundly conservative outlook which reflects an acceptance of social inequality and a fundamental commitment to private property which was challenged only by a tiny minority of republicans who were quickly marginalized. It is not difficult to see why such egalitarianism as existed within the republican movement was apparently unruffled by the social conservatism and complete lack of structural reforms which characterized Fianna Fáil rule in the 1930s and 1940s. The 'social republic' would be one which created conditions to allow the emergent national bourgeoisie to come into its own; not one which set about the socialization of the means of production or the radical redistribution of wealth. In a telling comment in a newspaper interview in the 1970s, Fianna Fáil leader and cabinet minister, Frank Aiken, answered a question about the party's 'loss of radicalism' in the 1940s by saying that 'our radicalism had been implemented'.[45]

In spite of such evidence, the image of the third Sinn Féin and its successor, Fianna Fáil, as a revolutionary force in the early days 'remains one of Irish political folklore's central myths'.[46] One of the most potent concepts sustaining this myth has been that of 'the men of no property'.

The phrase originated with Wolfe Tone, the founding father of Irish republicanism. Without going into the debate over the true content of Tone's remarks,[47] the phrase had, by the 1920s, become part of the ideological arsenal of the petty bourgeoisie. The 'men of no property' were in fact the 'men of little property', hoping for more land, a bigger home market for their products, or, in the case of the landless labourers or lower-middle-class professionals, an opportunity to set themselves up as farmers or to reap the advantages of social advancement which they hoped the newly independent state would offer. To quote Andrews once again:

We were the children of unimportant people—the men of no property of whom Wolfe Tone spoke—who had no ambition beyond rearing their families to be educated and decent citizens. McCarthy, Dermot Lawlor and I graduated in commerce; McHenry in engineering. With the exception of

---

[45] *Sunday Independent*, 15 Feb. 1976.

[46] O'Connell, 'Class, Nation and State', 23.

[47] For critical comments, see A. Morgan and B. Purdie (eds.), *Ireland: Divided Nation, Divided Class* (London, 1980), 76–7. For a wider discussion of Tone's philosophy, see Marianne Elliott's path-breaking biography, *Wolfe Tone: Prophet of Irish Independence* (New Haven, Conn., and London, 1989).

McCarthy, who set up as a public accountant, and Kerlin, whose people had a small wallpaper business, we all entered the public service.[48]

While the author is coy about the social ambitions of his generation of republicans, it is nevertheless obvious that those he cites— by all accounts not untypical, though better educated than many of their comrades—hardly constitute a cross-section of the poorest strata of society. The 'men of no property' who feature so prominently in Fianna Fáil propaganda from the outset are not the unemployed or the urban workers; the phrase bears witness to the flattering self-image of the lower middle classes. The failure of many commentators to grasp this has led to the perpetuation of myths about the class nature and revolutionary potential of the early republican party.

One final aspect of the ideology of the republicans requires comment: what can best be described as their exclusivism. Having rejected the Treaty and fought a civil war, despite the approval of the Treaty by the Dáil and by a majority of the Irish people, having battled for the salvation of the soul of the nation in the belief that the people had no right to sell their birthright, the republicans came to regard those who were not with them, not merely as against them, but as scarcely of the same species. This identification of *truth*, of the Republic, and ultimately of the Irish nation itself, with the republican movement, and later with Fianna Fáil, was undoubtedly augmented by the persecution and social isolation which the republicans endured in the aftermath of the civil war.

Fianna Fáil was launched in 1926 as a 'national movement'. To many of its followers Fianna Fáil *was* Ireland, and the people had no more right to turn their backs on it than they had to turn their backs on their country in the bitter days of the civil war.

It was not a normal political party because it had this noble and historic ideal. It was the national movement. No member had any doubt about that. They had set out from La Scala on the line of national advance and the winning of elections was essential to that advance. That was why they won them and why the occasional defeat—regarded as a temporary aberration by the people—had a revivifying effect.[49]

The ambiguity towards the democratic process which is implicit in such an outlook has often attracted comment; at least as

[48] Andrews, *Man of No Property*, 28.
[49] Boland, *The Rise and Decline of Fianna Fáil*, 33.

significant is the strength which this exclusivism afforded the republicans when they faced the task of extending their ideological and political hegemony over the nation, and in particular over organized labour. O'Carroll has argued, in this respect, that de Valera enhanced his authority and that of his party 'by a process of cultural management which owed its success to its ability to confirm to his followers his view of the "superiority and integrity" of his values over those of his opponents', and that this messianic aura 'made him a very formidable opponent'.[50]

We will see later how Fianna Fáil always sought to articulate the interests of the social forces which it represented in such a way as to identify them with the interests of the nation; let it suffice for now to note that this identification of the party with the nation, which has a long history in Irish politics, was a predominant feature of the ideological complexion of the republicans in the post-civil-war period, powerfully strengthened by the events of those years.

This brief analysis of republican ideology prior to the formal launch of Fianna Fáil in 1926 sets the stage for many themes which will occur and reoccur as we trace the party's ascent to power in 1932 and its consolidation of its position over the years. Let us now return to the state of Ireland in the post-civil-war period. First, I will examine the economic situation and the response of the Free State government; then I will look at the reaction of Sinn Féin to the country's increasingly desperate economic plight. It was precisely the failure of the existing republican organization which was to provide the impetus for the founding of Fianna Fáil by Eamon de Valera and other prominent Sinn Féin leaders.

ECONOMIC AND SOCIAL CONDITIONS IN THE 1920S

The economy of the new state suffered from many objective constraints. An almost complete lack of an industrial base, a large number of unproductive people—due to the peculiar demographic patterns which had developed especially after the Great Famine of the 1840s—and the country's close proximity to the advanced industrial economy of the United Kingdom, which tended to reproduce the underdevelopment of the Irish economy, were all factors

[50] J. P. O'Carroll, 'Eamon de Valera, Charisma and Political Development', in J. A. Murphy and J. P. O'Carroll (eds.), *De Valera and his Times* (Cork, 1983), 17, 23.

posing considerable problems for any government. The situation was further complicated by the post-war depression in agricultural prices, which led to lower living standards for the agricultural community in the early 1920s, and by particularly bad weather conditions.[51]

It must also be said, however, that the new state enjoyed certain advantages which could certainly have facilitated greater policy flexibility.

The last years of the Union had been prosperous ones and capital was available for investment. This was reflected by the successful floatation of the various National Loans; of the twenty-three million pounds subscribed, twenty millions were raised internally. The new state started life unhampered by the burden of a National Debt ... with overseas assets of 200 million pounds, a very substantial sum for a small country. This figure probably understates the total, for some Irish residents continued to use London rather than Irish banks and stockbrokers for their financial transactions, and these were not necessarily disclosed to the Free State authorities.[52]

Even allowing for the objective economic and political constraints facing the new government, one is struck by two overwhelming features of its response to the economic crisis: its effective abandonment of the economic goals of the national revolution and its total failure to effect even the minimum of social reform necessary to sustain a sufficient level of popular support. In short, Cumann na nGaedheal's economic strategy effectively abandoned the hopes and aspirations of those petty-bourgeois strata which had looked to Sinn Féin and national independence in the hope of greater prosperity; and the party lacked a political strategy which might have utilized social policy in a drive to establish political hegemony.

From the outset, the Government made clear its complete commitment to the cattle trade, and its distaste for any governmental initiatives to encourage industrial investment. Government policy was defined by the Minister for Agriculture, Patrick Hogan, as 'helping the farmer who helped himself and letting the rest go to the devil'. In effect, this meant the abandonment of any serious attempt

---

[51] Brown, *Ireland: A Social and Cultural History*, 14–15; Pyne, 'The Third Sinn Féin Party', 244.

[52] K. Daniel, 'Griffith on his Noble Head: The Determinants of Cumann na nGaedheal Economic Policy, 1922–1932', *Irish Economic and Social History*, 3 (1976), 57.

to build up an indigenous manufacturing industry by fostering industrialization through protection, coupled with a policy of keeping both taxation and public expenditure to a minimum.

In June 1923 the Government appointed the Fiscal Inquiry Committee to investigate and report on the subject of protection. This was the first of three commissions of experts—the others being the Commission on Agriculture of 1924 and the Banking Commission of 1927—which, as Daly points out,[53] effectively determined economic policy during the 1920s. Hopes that the Committee's Report would lead to the enforcement of a policy of protection for Irish industry were soon dashed: caution, conservatism, and attention to the possible detrimental effects of tariffs on agricultural exports informed the Report's findings.

The Report identified many small manufacturing concerns which looked to the home market and which anxiously awaited state assistance to ensure their survival and growth.

On the other hand, the industries that were then regarded as the major industries showed no desire for protection . . . This reflected, no doubt, the clash between industries that looked to export markets and industries which, in the circumstances of the time, were thankful to hold what they could of the home market.[54]

Indeed, the Report painted so gloomy a picture of the state of Irish industry as almost to convey the impression that an industrial development strategy was a waste of time.[55] It is clear, from the Report's findings, that, in their battle against protectionism, the large farmers could count on the support of the small but influential stratum of export-orientated industrialists. Fanning adds that the Tariff Commission 'in its first two years . . . managed to report on a mere three of a dozen or so applications before it'.[56]

The renunciation of the economic policy of the nationalist movement was undisguised. Kevin O'Higgins dismissed Griffith's protectionist policies with the words: 'The propagandist writings of one man cannot be accepted simply as revealed truth, requiring no

[53] M. Daly, *Industrial Development and Irish National Identity, 1922–1939* (Dublin, 1992), 16. Daly sums up the views of the three commissions rather succinctly: 'The experts favoured the status quo. Ireland would maintain parity and financial links with sterling, produce food for Britain, and retain a free-trade industrial sector.'
[54] Meenan, *The Irish Economy since 1922*, 139.
[55] R. Geary, 'Irish Economic Development since the Treaty', *Studies*, 11 (1951), 404–5.   [56] Fanning, *Independent Ireland*, 77.

further investigation.'[57] Griffith's death, in August 1922, cleared the way for this repudiation of his economic programme by his colleagues, although, as we will see, opposition to the shift remained within the ranks of Cumann na nGaedheal.

The principle that 'national development in Ireland . . . is practically synonymous with agricultural development',[58] and the corresponding government refusal to aid developing industries, spelt doom for many of the urban petty bourgeoisie—and for the thousands of workers who found themselves thrown out of work. As later Fianna Fáil propaganda was to stress, almost 200 factories were forced to close down during this period,[59] a fact which stands in sharp contrast to the claim made by W. T. Cosgrave, President of the Executive Council (or Prime Minister), in 1925 that eight to ten factories had been opened since his Government had taken office.[60]

Active state intervention to help the development of agriculture did not, however, apparently conflict with the *laissez-faire* principles of the new administration and its influential supporters. Here, too, however, the policy was a conservative one:

More efficient production could only have been obtained by discouraging dry cattle production (by such means as an export tax) thus inducing farmers to shift to more intensive lines of production such as tillage and dairying which, although resulting in a lower profit per acre, would have produced a higher gross output. This would, however, have run contrary to the policy of maximising farmers' incomes . . . it would also have meant favouring the smaller producers against the large grass farmers who formed the main political base of Cumann na nGaedheal. Effort was therefore concentrated on cutting the costs of existing methods of production, which meant not only the farmer's inputs but also his rates and taxes, and the costs of all the goods he needed to purchase for himself and his family.[61]

The Government sought to improve the quality of agricultural produce, and thus increase the competitiveness of exports to the UK market, by regulating livestock breeding and standardizing dairy products. An Agricultural Credit Corporation was established in 1927 to provide farmers who were in debt with state aid in the form of low-cost credit. The 1923 Land Act sped up the process by which

[57] Quoted in F. S. L. Lyons, *Ireland since the Famine* (London, 1973), 600.
[58] Patrick Hogan, quoted in Fanning, *Independent Ireland*, 74.
[59] Fianna Fáil, *The Fianna Fáil Story* (Dublin, 1951), 12.
[60] *Irish Times*, 9 Mar. 1925.   [61] Daniel, 'Griffith on his Noble Head', 62.

all remaining leasehold land was purchased from the Anglo-Irish gentry by the Land Commission and passed into the hands of the farmers.

This one-sided concentration upon the development of agriculture, based upon the prosperity of the large grass farmers—tillage declined throughout the 1920s and flour and animal feeding stuffs had to be imported—implicitly accepted the existence of widespread emigration. Throughout the 1920s emigration mounted, with the counties affected worst being those in the west and south of the country.

Nor did the allegedly sacred principle of the free working of the labour market inhibit the Government from giving strong backing to the cuts in farm labourers' wages effected by the farmers within a year of the ending of the civil war; indeed, it necessitated such backing.

Increased agricultural incomes, it was argued, would lead to increased demand for goods and services, and thus not only stimulate the non-agricultural sectors but also create an expanding market which Irish industry, when it became established, could exploit. From this point of view, policy needed to aim at the maximization of farmers' incomes; in other words, the emphasis should be on net profits, not on gross output.[62]

A policy which aimed at the maximization of farmers' incomes was to prove compatible neither with income security for agricultural labourers nor maximization of agricultural production.

Cuts in the wages of urban workers soon followed. In July 1923 the wages of Dublin dockers were cut by two shillings and before long building workers, coalmen, carters, tradesmen, transport, and manufacturing workers all had their wages cut or frozen. Kevin O'Higgins reacted to the subsequent inability of many families to pay their debts by telling the Dáil that 'the ceasing of the bailiff to function is the first sign of a crumbling civilisation'.[63]

The summer of 1923 saw seamen and firemen, as well as the dockers, out on strike, and rising rural discontent as agricultural labourers fought to resist wage cuts. Attacks on farmers were frequently reported, especially in the Waterford area. Retaliations took the form of the burning of the cottages of labourers and of trade-union officials, and in September a labourer was shot.[64] For their

---

[62] Ibid. 61.   [63] Quoted in Lyons, *Ireland since the Famine*, 487–8.
[64] *Irish Independent*, 11 Sept. 1923.

part, the labourers attacked farmers' property, spiked meadows, and burnt machinery. For some time Waterford farmers had been on the defensive, but that situation began to change.

For hard-line Government supporters like Sir John Keane, the Labour movement in his own county was an obstacle to a national economic policy of which he was a staunch advocate. Accordingly, it had to be crushed at all costs. Very obviously, the Government had to have a vested interest in this ... 1923 was the year to do it.[65]

With the end of the civil war the Government was soon 'firmly in control of most of the country, and determined to quash any challenge to its authority'. The subsequent intervention of the military sealed the fate of the strike.

In late July the Employers' Federation of Dublin met with employers from Cork and Waterford to agree on a campaign for all-round reductions in wages.[66] Before long building workers, bacon curers, and others were on strike, not only in Dublin but in many provincial centres. The drapers came out on strike in September. For many workers, urban and rural, the period was one of bitter struggle—and ultimately of harsh defeat.

Certainly divisions within the labour movement contributed to the difficulties facing those engaged in industrial struggle. A bitter split in the Irish Transport and General Workers' Union (ITGWU) between supporters of the militant leader, James Larkin, and conservative union leaders seriously weakened the trade-union movement. The difficulties were compounded by the refusal of the leadership of the Labour Party to give full support to the strikers' struggle.

The plight of the labourers was an acid test of the political strategy of the Irish Labour Party [ILP] and Trade Union Conference [TUC]. The failure of the Labour leaders to appreciate the crucial importance of maintaining trade union organization among rural workers is evidence of the essentially conservative nature of its policy.[67]

Labour was certainly under heavy pressure. A press campaign urged Labour to give a 'clear statement' that it had 'constructive rather than revolutionary ideas'.[68] The leadership did not hesitate to do so.

---

[65] E. O'Connor, 'Agrarian Unrest and the Labour Movement in County Waterford, 1917–1923', *Saothar* (1980), 46–7.   [66] *Irish Independent*, 28 July 1923.
[67] O'Connor, 'Agrarian Unrest and the Labour Movement', 40.
[68] *Irish Independent*, 13 July 1923.

In an address to a Labour Club gathering in September, the party leader, Thomas Johnson, made it clear that there would be no 'new departure' for the party. He continued:

It was quite possible for the Labour group [of Dáil deputies] to wear itself out raising controversial issues at every step, and they had been advised to [so] proceed by certain interests. If that was the hope of their supporters, he was afraid that it would be disappointed.[69]

In short, the Labour Party refused to give political leadership to outbursts of defensive agitation by sections of the working class (indeed, the Labour Deputy for Waterford, scene of much of the unrest, subsequently became a Cumann na nGaedheal Senator), and, devoid of such leadership, the struggles petered out. We have already noted the large-scale apathy with which urban workers seem to have greeted the general elections of 1923; evidence, perhaps, of the gap which existed between the Labour Party and urban workers was that some party leaders could think of no better explanation for the setbacks which the party suffered in that contest than to blame the 'ingratitude' of the workers: the Vice-President of the Cork Workers' Council, for example, proposed disbanding it because of the 'base ingratitude of the workers' in voting for their 'enemies'.[70]

There was no doubt where the sympathies of the Government, and, more broadly, of the state apparatus, lay throughout this period of social unrest. Official attitudes were summed up in a very clear manner by the Assistant Commissioner of the newly formed *Gardaí*, Walsh, in a confidential report he submitted to the Government on 13 October 1923. The report, concerned with labour unrest in Cork, identified as the root cause of the trouble the fact that the employers had been paying too high wages. According to Walsh, the workers were 'very highly organized' and had become 'masters of the situation': 'the union will not be deposed from its position of supremacy without a struggle, and this the employers seem incapable of making.' The conclusion was that the state might have to stiffen the backbone of the employers, and should prepare to deal the workers a blow through tough police action: 'strong action would be necessary to deal with the situation which would arise [when the strike was broken]. The advanced sections of the

[69] Ibid., 21 Sept. 1923.   [70] Ibid., 1 Sept. 1923.

workers would soon get out of hand.'[71] Liberal theories of the state apart, this public servant had no doubt where he stood—and clearly assumed that his political masters were of a similar frame of mind.

Of course, they were. The Government, in 1923, circulated advice to the *Gardaí* to get tough with unions, especially the ITGWU. Union legislation, inherited from British rule, was investigated to see what could be done, and the opinion was circulated that 'a great many of the practices which have grown up in recent times in the conduct of trade disputes and which have been acquiesced in by the authorities [and] have come to be regarded as a proper exercise of legal rights by the trade unions, are beyond the actual rights given by the Trade Disputes Act of 1906'.[72]

As the Government gave full effect to its policy of keeping wages down, and extending assistance to agriculture only, poverty escalated, both unemployment and emigration rose, and the trade-union movement was greatly weakened. In February 1925 58,000 people were registered as being out of work, the largest number for the period of the 1920s. During the years 1924–7 more than 100,000 people, mostly young farm labourers and unemployed workers, emigrated to North America or Australia.[73] The trade unions found their membership cut to 95,000 by 1926—less even than at the height of the 1913 defeat.

The outlook for the unemployed was bleak. The Government, it is fair to say, did not consider itself as having any duty to create employment for those who found themselves without a livelihood, and even toyed with schemes to abolish unemployment assistance altogether.[74] The 'bottom line' *vis-à-vis* any state role in employment creation was spelt out in unambiguous terms in a memorandum, submitted to the Government in October 1927 by Commissioner Monahan of Cork:

If it is necessary to provide work artificially, those for whom it is provided have no right of any kind to a wage higher than the community who provide it choose to fix . . . it should be fixed so low that those who are taken on will not be satisfied to remain in the job a day longer than is necessary.[75]

[71] UCDA MacNeill Papers LA1/H/71.   [72] NAI Labour W705.

[73] Pyne, 'The Third Sinn Féin Party', 245.

[74] See e.g. the reports from a Government inspector, Commissioner Monahan of Cork, in July 1927, which dismissed talk of poverty or hardship and recommended that responsibility for the unemployed be left to the St Vincent de Paul Society—a Catholic charity (UCDA McGilligan Papers P35a/30).

[75] UCDA McGilligan Papers P35a/30.

The dire economic situation for the bulk of the urban and rural poor was compounded by the social policies of the Government in other fields. 'Almost Gladstonian in its approach, it exerted itself to keep taxation down to a minimum and to regulate expenditure accordingly.'[76] In short, the Department of Finance, whose first secretary, J. J. McElligott, has been described as 'an unashamed, unreconstructed laissez-faire ideologue',[77] was given a free hand to implement its policy of strict balancing of the budget through keeping public expenditure, and especially social expenditure, to an absolute minimum.

Fanning, writing of the Department's attitude, has this to say:

Defenders of the established socio-economic order, theirs was no brave new world envisaging independence as an opportunity for change. If change, indeed, there was, it was often for the worse. The levels of social expenditure inherited from a powerful and wealthy empire were deemed inappropriate for a poor, small country . . . Hence the notorious cut in the old age pension in 1924 from ten shillings to nine shillings a week . . . Hence also the willingness of Blythe (Minister for Finance from 1923 to 1932), having decided to cut pensions, to inquire into 'the possibility of doing away with the national health insurance and labour exchanges, neither of which seemed necessary in the Free State'.[78]

Appeals by the Dublin unemployed met with curt statements to the effect that the Government was doing all it could, and an extremely restrictive unemployment insurance scheme meant that in 1928 only 11,000 workers and their families were actually eligible for unemployment benefit.[79] In fact, such was the political atmosphere aroused by Government policy that a defensive Labour leader, Thomas Johnson, warned of 'a desire to curtail the activities of trade unions to make strikes illegal' and went on to accuse the Government of wanting 'to deprive the Irish people of the benefits of social legislation passed by the UK parliament, such as old age pensions, unemployment and health insurance, maternity and workmen's compensation, because they placed a slight burden on the employing class'.[80]

In the field of housing, the Government's policy could be summed

---

[76] Lyons, *Ireland since the Famine*, 607.

[77] J. J. Lee, 'Ireland and the Marshall Plan', unpub. lecture delivered at the European University Institute, Florence (Feb. 1985).

[78] Fanning, *Independent Ireland*, 64–5.   [79] Ibid. 72.

[80] *Irish Times*, 2 Feb. 1925.

up as follows: 'They [the cabinet] are convinced that if any real success is to be attained it must be by private enterprise.'[81] The same report quotes Cosgrave as having said:

we have discovered that neither the state nor the municipality, nor any of the state or semi-state organizations, are in a position to deal with the subject in a satisfactory manner. Accordingly, the Government propose to elicit private enterprise by grants that may encourage the enterprising builder to undertake the work with reasonable hopes of making a fair profit.

And again: 'the Government had come definitely to the conclusion that there was only one real method of making this service a success, and that was by giving private enterprise full and complete freedom.' Grants to private builders were made available to the tune of £100 for a house valued at £500. Unfortunately for the poorest sections of the community, most in need of improved housing, the manner in which the grants were made available ensured that only the building of houses by those with money was facilitated.

Throughout the 1920s rent arrears, particularly on the part of labourers, mounted. A report submitted to the Minister for Local Government gives the average yearly figure for rent arrears for the period 1925–30 at £37,000—more than 20 per cent of the total rent due.[82] The areas worst affected were Kerry, Leitrim, Mayo, and Clare. A similar situation was to be found among urban workers. Despite this background, the Minister, General Richard Mulcahy, could later declare:

The general circumstances at the time, and these building costs, were such that the Government could not, without serious prejudice to its credit and to its financial reputation, have risked putting any considerable amount of borrowed money into housing, and particularly housing for the working-classes, and more particularly housing for the poorly-paid working-classes.[83]

This refusal to contemplate state intervention to bring about even the mildest of social reform as a means of alleviating the economic plight of the poor was accompanied by a self-justificatory rhetoric which can only be described as callous—and which was to provide Fianna Fáil with plentiful ammunition. With more than 800,000 people living in overcrowded conditions (overcrowding being

[81] *Irish Independent*, 26 Feb. 1924.   [82] UCDA Mulcahy Papers P7/C/53.
[83] Ibid.

defined as more than two people per room), many of them concentrated in north Dublin where the slum conditions were among the worst in Europe; with high infant mortality rates—in north Dublin, again, the death-rate per 1,000 children aged between 1 and 5 was 25.6; and with cases of death from starvation being reported to the authorities, the Minister for Finance, Patrick McGilligan, could tell the Dáil: 'there are certain limited funds at our disposal. People may have to die in this country and die through starvation.'[84]

Reporting on just such an instance of death through starvation, a Government committee could tell Mulcahy that relief 'should be distributed as sparingly as possible. The principle of the state helping those who helped themselves should be rigidly adhered to.' Another Government inspector, reporting on the poor of Achill island in County Mayo, could recommend their wholesale 'removal', adding that 'I would not consider very much whether my suggestion is "congenial" or otherwise to the people no more than I would consider the whims of a drowning man.'[85] The Victorian attitudes embodied in such statements scarcely need commenting upon.

Indeed, as social unrest appeared to mount throughout the mid-1920s, bourgeois forces were pushing the Government to go even further. A campaign for the complete abolition of income tax was mounted in 1925. The Dublin and Cork Chambers of Commerce expressed support,[86] as did the Cork United Cattle Traders Association.[87] On 6 March the Dublin Mercantile Association, representing 1,500 firms and businesses, sent a memorandum to Cosgrave and the Ministers for Finance and Industry and Commerce seeking, in addition to action on the question of income tax, the abolition of Corporation profit tax (or exemption of the first £10,000) and the reduction of taxation on such items as tea and sugar. A week later, a meeting of business men was held in the Hibernian Hotel in Dublin to form a 'No Income Tax Committee'.[88]

This pressure from sections of the bourgeoisie for the radical reduction of both state revenue and expenditure found a sympathetic hearing in Government circles: the danger of a flight of capital out of the country led the Cosgrave Government to adopt an extremely conservative monetary policy, tying the currency to

[84] Brown, *Ireland: A Social and Cultural History*, 16; Fanning, *Independent Ireland*, 100.   [85] Quoted in Fanning, *Independent Ireland*, 71–2.
[86] *Irish Times*, 25 Feb. 1925.   [87] Ibid., 28 Feb. 1925.
[88] Ibid., 13 Mar. 1925.

sterling and keeping taxation and public expenditure to a minimum. One of the economic arguments attracting bourgeois support for Sinn Féin in the pre-independence period had been that 'Ireland had been over-taxed under British rule and that the country could be administered much more cheaply under native rule'.[89] With this promise at least, the Free State administration kept faith: 'the standard rate of income tax which had been twenty-five per cent in 1924, had been reduced to fifteen per cent in 1928.'[90] Indeed, it is clear that the tax burden upon the wealthy was not as excessive as their protests suggest: a report from the revenue commissioners, dealing with this period, states that 'the farming community in reality pays very little income tax';[91] and the total income tax paid for the year 1925/6 by 1,500 so-called 'super-income tax payers' came to only £1.6 million. This must be contrasted with the figure of £11 million, which was the income earned in the form of interest on capital invested outside the state in the year 1927 (total accumulated capital invested abroad—£195.09 million).[92] Despite the fact that the standard rate of income tax remained below the UK level from the mid-1920s onwards, capital continued to be invested abroad. Moreover, the Government's determination to reduce the tax burden on its supporters led it 'to rely heavily on regressive taxes . . . the Free State's taxation system was considerably more regressive than that of the United Kingdom . . . thus the system . . . tended to penalise the mass of the people, who had supported independence as against the middle and upper classes, the latter being composed largely of ex-Unionists.'[93]

The mobilization of the propertied around the question of income tax might scarcely seem necessary given the clear commitment of the Government to follow policies in line with their chief demands in any case. However, such mobilization did have the important political effect of putting the labour movement on the defensive, especially as the demand for a reduction in tax and public expenditure was, ironically, articulated together with an assault on the high cost of living. Faced with the prospect of outright abolition of income tax—and the further cuts in social

[89] Meenan, *The Irish Economy since 1922*, 240.
[90] J. O'Hagan, 'Analysis of the Size of the Government Sector, 1926–1952', *Economic and Social Review*, 12 (1980), 25.
[91] UCDA McGilligan Papers P35a/21.   [92] Ibid. P35a/18, P35a/19.
[93] Daniel, 'Griffith on his Noble Head', 60.

expenditure which that would necessitate—the Labour leadership chose to do battle around precisely this question—*abolition*—effectively conceding the struggle against any *reduction* in income tax.[94]

Finally, it may be noted that certain of Cumann na nGaedheal's political allies, such as the Farmers' Party, adopted an even more aggressive stance on the economic issues of the day. The Farmers' Party offered strong opposition to the Shannon hydroelectric scheme which was begun in 1925 and which was the sole exception to the prevailing antagonism towards both state enterprise and industrial development during the life of the Cumann na nGaedheal administration. As Oliver St John Gogarty put it, the Farmers' Party existed 'in order to oppose everything'.

The civil-war victors, then, not only committed themselves to economic policies which were bound to frustrate the hopes and expectations of large sections of the petty bourgeoisie and which did nothing to stem the tide of escalating poverty, unemployment, and emigration, particularly affecting urban workers and farm labourers; they also failed to make even the minimum of compromise necessary to maintain their political dominance. It has been argued that the achievement of political hegemony by forces representing the vital economic interests of a social group requires an ability to project the particular as representative or typical of the universal; that it necessitates a process of 'equilibria in which the interests of the dominant group prevail, but only up to a certain point, i.e. stopping short of narrow corporate and economic interest'.[95] In this respect, the civil-war victors failed spectacularly. Neither the political forces grouped around Cumann na nGaedheal, nor the classes most intimately associated with them, were prepared to 'stop short of narrow corporate and economic interest'.

Nor were they able to substitute for economic compromise an appeal to nationalist or anti-imperialist rhetoric which is often a feature of post-colonial government. Having signed the treaty with the United Kingdom, accepted dominion status and the oath of allegiance, and fought a bitter civil war, with UK aid, against those who refused to settle for less than full formal political independence, their nationalist credentials would scarcely support such rhetoric.

---

[94] *Irish Times*, 9 Mar. 1925.
[95] A. Gramsci, *Selections from Prison Notebooks* (London, 1982), 182.

Moreover, an economic policy which envisaged continuing dependence on the UK market for agricultural exports represented a further break with the nationalist platform. Not only that, the Free State Government found itself supported by many who had always opposed national independence: both old 'home rulers' of the Irish parliamentary party and ex-Unionists. Finally, having fought a civil war for the Treaty, the actual terms of the settlement came to acquire a sanctity in the eyes of many Cumann na nGaedheal members. What had for Collins been merely a 'stepping-stone to freedom' now became for many of the Government's supporters an end in itself.

How did the Government hope to maintain itself as the dominant force in Irish politics? In short, by an appeal to the desire of the middle classes for law and order and to war-weariness. As we have noted, this was a powerful factor leading to the political victory of the pro-Treaty forces in the first place. But, given the political and social effects of the Government's economic policies and its isolation on the matter of nationalism, there were strict limits to the amount of political capital it could hope to accumulate by increasingly harsh security policies. In by-election after by-election Cumann na nGaedheal politicians accused their opponents of being 'destructionists', terrorists, and even communists, justifying the application of severe emergency legislation to 'draw their teeth'. Kevin O'Higgins even boasted at an election meeting in Sligo of the execution of republican prisoners during the civil war: 'I stand over those seventy-seven executions and over seven hundred and seventy-seven more if they become necessary.'[96] This elevation of security policy into what amounted to the chief plank in the Government's strategy for marshalling popular support reached its pinnacle in the wave of anti-communist hysteria and repression of left-wing political organizations which was unleashed prior to the 1932 general election. Such might serve the purpose of helping to heal the divisions within Cumann na nGaedheal ranks and of rallying the hard core of the Government's supporters; but it was no recipe for winning broad sections of the population.

Given this basic failure in politics, it is hard to escape the conclusion that, by the mid-1920s, the country was already ripe for an alternative. But whence would the alternative—the force for

[96] *Irish Times*, 19 Jan. 1925.

change—come? Who would provide the leadership in the process of reconstruction, both political and economic?

THE SEARCH FOR A POLITICAL ALTERNATIVE

It was from the ranks of the rural poor in particular that the flood of emigrants was drawn. These were precisely the people who had tended to support the republicans during the civil war. Indeed, poverty, unemployment, and emigration hit hardest at the ranks of the republican activists, who, in any case, found themselves subject to discrimination in the hunt for what work was available. In short, their plight mirrored, in a concentrated and condensed form, the disillusioning economic experiences of large sections of the lower social strata, from which they were largely drawn, during the years of the Cumann na nGaedheal Government.

Such work as the Government did help to stimulate, on roads and drainage schemes, went to demobilized Free State soldiers and supporters of the Government.[97] The newly created police force was almost entirely made up of men carefully screened for their pro-Treaty loyalties.[98] Moreover, the economic plight of the republicans was further aggravated by harassment; the bitterness of the civil war died slowly and the newly constituted forces of the state were all too eager, on occasion, to engage in gratuitous outbursts of 'republican-baiting'—a situation which was worsened by the acts of IRA terrorism which continued well into the late 1920s.

The republicans had good reason to reorganize in opposition to the Free State regime, but the effectiveness of the opposition offered by the reconstituted Sinn Féin was reduced significantly by two factors: the party's neglect of specific social and economic policies, and its policy of non-recognition of the institutions of the state.

In the summer of 1923, the Sinn Féin president, Eamon de Valera, was arrested while he was addressing an election rally in Ennis and spent the next year in jail. It has been argued that it was during this period that the more hardline republicans, such as Mary MacSwiney, managed to persuade the party to elevate non-recognition of the institutions of the state and abstention from parliament into a fundamental principle; de Valera, it is argued, had previously regarded abstention as a tactical matter and, upon his release from prison,

---

[97] Andrews, *Man of No Property*, 14.   [98] Fanning, *Independent Ireland*, 66.

had to begin the fight to 'bring the policy back to the point it should never have changed from'.[99] While this is true, there is also no doubt that de Valera himself, mediating between the various Sinn Féin factions, did much to sustain the myth of the 'existing republic'. The effect of this myth was that Sinn Féin was forced to stand on the sidelines as it became increasingly cut off from the mainstream of political life; for, short of starting another civil war, which the defeated republicans were in no position to do, there was no way to overturn the rapidly entrenched governmental machinery of the new state. This marginalization is evident in the tone of Sinn Féin addresses throughout the period 1923–6.

Two themes dominate these addresses: an increasingly desperate refusal to accept the existence of the institutions of the state (which became more pronounced, if anything, as the policy came under attack from within Sinn Féin); and frustration with the failure of the people to rally behind the republican flag. Thus, at a by-election meeting in Cavan on 25 January 1925, de Valera was reported as saying:

The Free State Constitution made them a state subject to England. He had never been a willing subject of England. Did they want an English king as their king? If they did not want that they should not vote for a man who would take an oath of allegiance to him. No matter what the newspapers said, no decent republican would ever enter the present Dáil. No man who stood for the independence of the country, or who had any sense of personal or national self-respect, would take an oath to a foreign king.[100]

And just over a week later Lemass, speaking in north Dublin, declared in a similar vein:

Ireland today is ruled by a British garrison, organized by the Masonic lodges, speaking through the Free State parliament, and playing the cards of England all the time. If this nation is to get a chance to live we must sweep the Free State and all that it stands for out of existence . . . Partial independence has given us poverty, unemployment and a burden of taxation. The Free State cannot be secure while there are half-a-dozen people who profess the republican creed.[101]

When the people failed to respond with the anticipated fervour, disillusionment with the masses and anger preceded self-criticism.

---

[99] Ryle Dwyer, *Eamon de Valera*, 73–4; T. O'Neill, 'In Search of a Political Path: Irish Republicanism, 1922–1977', *Historical Studies*, 10 (1976), 158–61.
[100] *Irish Times*, 26 Jan. 1925.   [101] Ibid., 2 Feb. 1925.

De Valera, speaking at the graves of IRA volunteers in Tipperary, chided the nation:

Recently an opportunity was given to the people to declare their will. They did not declare that will *as we know it to be their will,* and, perhaps, there are people listening today who, if you had an election here tomorrow, would be a party to misrepresenting the national position. It is a shame that Irishmen who know what the majority of the people want—this country free and independent—should go to the polls and register their votes in such a way that it will be held that these are votes for the Free State. I do not know what it is. It is the result, so far as I can see, of the teaching that you have been listening to for the past three years . . . there is no use in looking to a small body of men to free the nation. It is for the people to right the wrong they did a couple of years ago and which apparently they have been doing since.[102]

There is much that could be said of such speech, rich as it is in self-righteous exclusivism and paternalism. But what is interesting in the present context is the evident frustration which had begun to take hold; and, indeed, there was much to be frustrated about. Apart from an initial burst of enthusiasm, Sinn Féin had gone into a state of steady decline by 1924. A rapidly worsening financial situation went hand in hand with a fall-off in membership—the number of registered branches fell from 1,025 in June 1924 to just over half that number in July 1925—and extremely disappointing election results. Initial by-election successes were followed by defeat in March 1925 and a disastrous performance at the first local-government elections in June 1925, when, despite the fact that Cumann na nGaedheal did not contest on a party ticket, Sinn Féin captured only 11 per cent of the poll.[103]

The futility of parliamentary abstentionism and non-recognition of the state was matched by the lack of tangible economic and social policies. Sinn Féin's economic programme was a set of vague generalizations which combined the main thrust of Griffith's old policy with principles drawn from the Democratic Programme of the first Dáil. While sounding radical, it lacked substance; and the increasingly hopeless plight of the people whose votes the republicans needed to survive as a political force demanded something more concrete than rhetoric. De Valera, challenged at an election

---

[102] Ibid., 18 Mar. 1925 (emphasis added).
[103] Pyne, 'The Third Sinn Féin Party', 41–2.

meeting in January 1925 as to Sinn Féin's economic policy, replied that:

The answer to that could be given not in his words but in the words of the representative assembly, the National Parliament, and contained in the democratic programme adopted on 1 May 1919 . . . they not only proclaimed their political independence but their economic independence, so that they might make their people happy and prosperous.

And he continued:

England's economic grip was more dangerous than her political grip of the country. They had a wonderful country, rich in natural resources, and if there had been a definite movement, a definite attempt, made by a national authority to use these resources for the nation's benefit, it would be one of the most self-contained nations in the world.[104]

Small wonder that many of de Valera's listeners came away with little idea of what the Sinn Féin policy amounted to. As one commentator has put it: 'a preliminary policy draft was attacked in the columns of the *Irish Statesman* on the grounds that it was so vague and obscure that "it could be adopted by the most reactionary Tory . . ." '.[105] In effect, the republican attempt to blame all the country's ills upon 'England' failed to rally popular support, despite the much-heralded nationalist bias in Irish public opinion, precisely because it failed to offer concrete policy alternatives to Cumann na nGaedheal.

The realization that this was so was one of the main factors behind the launch of Fianna Fáil. From the outset, Fianna Fáil sought to accommodate, in a concrete fashion, certain demands of all the strata from which the republicans drew their support, plus the urban working class. This ability to project the vital interests, and reproduce the ideological self-image, of the petty bourgeoisie (part of which was to emerge under Fianna Fáil rule as an indigenous, national bourgeoisie), whilst at the same time offering concrete advantages to other social groups, was to be developed into a fundamental plank in the party's strategy for building and maintaining its political hegemony—a fact too often overlooked by commentators who focus on the nationalist aspect of the party's rhetoric. In this fundamental respect, Fianna Fáil was to mark a break with the Sinn Féin tradition as decisive as the party's abandonment of

---

[104] *Irish Times*, 5 Jan. 1925.　　　[105] Pyne, 'The Third Sinn Féin Party', 246.

abstentionism and its entrance into the parliamentary arena, which have usually been highlighted as critical.

De Valera and Sinn Féin had gone into the elections of 1925 with little more than bitterness over the provisions of the Treaty and visions of a united Irish republic; their economic programme was virtually non-existent, and combed from the programme of the first Dáil of 1919. The result was rejection by an electorate which demanded more than rhetoric. The result was also a considerable boost to the process of revisionism within the republican movement.

In May 1925 the Standing Committee of Sinn Féin secretly adopted the resolution that: 'the president may act on the assumption that the question of republicans entering the Free State "parliament" if the oath were removed is an open question, to be decided on its merits when the question arises as a practical issue.' Speculation began in the press that the movement was on the verge of abandoning abstentionism. In July the IRA, disillusioned by the electoral failure of Sinn Féin and suspicious of politicians, began to move towards the separation of the military and political wings of the republican movement—a process which was formally completed when the IRA Army Convention voted, in November, to vest control of the army in the Army Council, as opposed to the republican 'government'. The IRA chief of staff, Frank Aiken, a close supporter of de Valera, began to take his distance from those of his colleagues who were moving away from politics altogether.

Sinn Féin was now visibly crumbling, unable to offer its own supporters, never mind the country at large, a credible alternative to the continuing emigration which seemed to be the result of Government policies. The revisionist criticism now heard within the ranks concerned the two main obstacles to the construction of an alternative political hegemony to that of the Cumann na nGaedheal bloc, itself tottering on increasingly shaky foundations. These were, as we have seen, the now hopeless policy of non-recognition of the state, and the welding of concrete economic and social demands of various classes and social groups into a coherent political strategy.

Sinn Féin had pledged in 1925 that republicans 'will be as able and as efficient administrators as any of the alleged "business" groups'.[106] Such an attitude reflected many of the ideological

[106] *An Phoblacht*, 20 June 1925.

self-perceptions of the petty bourgeoisie. Although divorced from any concrete programme, the emphasis on hard work and efficiency and concern to keep taxation to a minimum might have been expected to appeal to petty-bourgeois groups.[107] The problem, however, was to incorporate sufficient demands of the landless men and urban working class, as well as to articulate more clearly the economic concerns of the petty bourgeoisie itself, so as to attract the many potential supporters who had voted for the Government and its allies or, in many cases, simply abstained.

As a letter to the party publication, *Sinn Féin*, put it:

The country is hungry for a construction programme. The people are sick of such platitudes as the Sinn Féin economic programme. They want a real, live full-blooded constructive policy, with facts and figures, over which the Republican government will stand when it comes in to function.[108]

In the absence of such a programme, there was little the republicans could hope to do except to watch the emigrants leave. No one seems to have realized the necessary preconditions for the achievement of political supremacy better than Seán Lemass, who was to become a key figure in the representation of Fianna Fáil policy to both the urban working class and the new national bourgeoisie. In a series of highly critical articles in the republican newspaper, *An Phoblacht*, written in late 1925 and early 1926, he emphasized the need to rebuild the party from the bottom up, with an essentially new brand of politics—new not only to Sinn Féin, but also, we might add, to Cumann na nGaedheal. The idealist insistence upon the 'existing republic' was dealt with thus:

We must free ourselves of all the tags and tatters, the remnants of a brighter past that now serve only to bind our arms and deny us freedom of action. We must forget all the petty conceits and formulae which bedeck us, like rouge on the face of a corpse, and face the facts, the hard facts which we must overcome . . . There are some who would have us sit by the roadside and debate abstruse points about a 'de jure' this and a 'de facto' that, but

---

[107] See e.g. de Valera's message to P. J. Ruttledge the previous year, that 'we must stand for fair play and justice between all classes, and push co-operation and such enterprises as will be of advantage to all. The more we lean to the economic side the better it will be for the political objective but it must be a national programme for the common good, not a class programme' (quoted in O'Neill, 'In Search of a Political Path', 156–7).

[108] Quoted in Pyne, 'The Third Sinn Féin Party', 250.

the reality we want is away in the distance—and we cannot get there unless we move.[109]

Lemass realized the need for 'immediate objectives', 'capable of realization within a reasonable period of time'.[110] His message to the republican faithful was straightforward: 'teach them [the Irish people] that National Independence means real concrete advantages for the common people and not merely an idealists' paradise, and they will be with us.'[111] As early as February 1925 Lemass, who had been urging his more hesitant revisionist colleagues to adopt more distinct and radical social and economic policies, had used his position as a key member of the party's economics subcommittee to propose circulating the economic programme of the Australian Labour Party. Faced with opposition, he had resigned from the economics subcommittee to concentrate on organizational work— thereby consolidating his influence on the future direction of Fianna Fáil.[112]

The programme which was to emerge with the birth of Fianna Fáil would promise salvation for the petty bourgeoisie whilst offering sufficient concrete gains to enlist the support of large sections of the rural and urban poor. This explains why it gained such rapid popularity, not only with the Sinn Féin faithful, but also with many republicans who had dropped out of active politics, disillusioned in the aftermath of the civil war; and why the 'ideologically pure', essentially right-wing, rump within Sinn Féin, represented by such figures as Mary MacSwiney, who had no longer any real policy to offer to any class or social group, was almost completely marginalized within a few years.

The immediate factor which gave the decisive push to the process of revisionism within Sinn Féin was the leaking of the findings of the Boundary Commission in November 1925. Established to ratify the boundary between Northern Ireland and the Irish Free State, it had been widely hoped by republicans and 'Free Staters' alike that the Commission would recommend the transfer of large parts of the territory of Northern Ireland, where Catholics were in the majority, to the Free State, thereby undermining the northern state. However, it now became clear that the Free State was to gain

[109] *An Phoblacht*, 22 Jan. 1926.   [110] Ibid., 29 Jan. 1926.
[111] Ibid., 5 Feb. 1926.   [112] Farrell, *Seán Lemass*, 12–13.

much less than expected—small parts of south Fermanagh and south Armagh—and was actually to lose parts of Donegal where Protestants were in a majority, something which had never been envisaged. The inability of the Government to make any substantial alterations to this arrangement—attacked by de Valera as an 'ignominious bargain'—led it, in desperation, to propose that the Commission report be 'burned or buried'.[113] The actual Boundary Agreement, signed in December 1925, left the border between north and south unaltered.

This blow to the Government's prestige, and to the hopes of Irish nationalists in general, caused serious dissension within the Government's ranks which the republican opposition was unable to take advantage of. 'No longer could Cosgrave and his colleagues even try to claim that the treaty by which they had set such store would serve as an instrument for the reunification of Ireland.'[114] Three Cumann na nGaedheal TDs broke away, in protest, to form a new party, Clann Éireann. Coming on top of an attempted mutiny in the army in 1924, which had led to the temporary appearance of another party, the National Party, this event showed the fragility of the unity of the Government forces.

An appeal from Labour for Sinn Féin deputies to enter the Dáil for the purpose of defeating the boundary agreement met with a sympathetic response from some Sinn Féin leaders, but de Valera was adamant that the organization had fought on the basis of abstention and would require a new mandate from the people if it was to abandon that policy. Perhaps the launching of a new party had already taken root, and de Valera felt that a split in 1925 would be premature; at any rate, revisionism had taken a firm hold in Dublin, where the Reorganization Committee, under Lemass, was engaged in a steady overhaul of the party, as can be seen from the 'Organization Notes' published each week in *An Phoblacht*.

The formal split came in March 1926, by which time Lemass was already heading his letters to the pro-de Valera faction with his preferred title for the new party—'The Republican Party'. A special conference, convened to consider de Valera's motion that once the oath of allegiance was removed 'it becomes a question not of principle but of policy whether or not republican representatives enter the Dáil', narrowly rejected the motion—by 223 votes to 218. The

---

[113] Cosgrave, quoted in Fanning, *Independent Ireland*, 91. [114] Ibid.

next day de Valera resigned as Sinn Féin president. On 29 March ten leading revisionists, including Lemass, Gerry Boland, MacEntee, and P. J. Brennan, tendered their resignations from the Sinn Féin Standing Committee. On 2 April a meeting was held to decide the name of the new republican organization: de Valera, sensitive to the mystic pull of the Gaelic and the political value of a certain ambiguity, insisted upon *Fianna Fáil* as against Lemass's preferred title. Eventually a compromise was agreed—*Fianna Fáil the Republican Party*. Then, on 16 April, *An Phoblacht* announced the formation of a provisional Organization Committee, charged with the task of laying the foundations for the new republican party, and urged all Sinn Féin branches and officers to contact it.

There seems to be no doubt that the founding fathers of Fianna Fáil were only too happy to leave the old Sinn Féin behind them. They had long come to recognize its inability to function as a vehicle for the construction of their political supremacy. Bowman has noted that 'senior Fianna Fáil politicians were pleased to have left some of their former colleagues in the trenches; they saw them as cranks who were determined to remain strangers to political reality'.[115] This is borne out by the comment of one of the early Fianna Fáil organizers, Gerry Boland, who stated many years later: 'we could have won, but it would not have been advantageous. We wanted a new organization.' Indeed, de Valera himself is quoted as saying that 'it mattered very little to me whether we had a majority or a minority at the *Ard-Fheis*'.[116]

An interesting insight into the possible motivation of the revisionists in launching the new organization is contained in a letter from de Valera to the Irish-American republican organizer, Joe McGarrity. De Valera wrote:

It is vital that the Free State be shaken at the next general election, for if an opportunity is given it to consolidate itself further as an institution—if the present Free State members are replaced by Farmers and Labourers and other class interests, the national interest as a whole will be submerged in the clashing of the rival economic groups. It seems to be a case of now or never—at least in our time.[117]

This abhorrence of the alien environment of class politics—the spectre of 'Farmers' and 'Labourers' fighting for economic resources

---

[115] Bowman, *De Valera and the Ulster Question*, 95.
[116] Quoted in Fanning, *Independent Ireland*, 96.   [117] Ibid.

—is not untypical of the small producers who felt their interests betrayed, unrepresented, and squeezed out of existence in the hostile climate of the 1920s. Without wishing to portray de Valera as a conscious front man for any particular class—which he almost certainly was not—his words can be read as an authentic expression of the desperate urge for survival felt by many of this social group at this juncture. If they were not given a new organizational means of expression which might allow them to advance their political dominance under the banner of the 'national interest', then the spectre of class politics between the forces represented by the apparently disintegrating Cumann na nGaedheal bloc, on the one hand, and organized labour, on the other, might become a reality. In fact, de Valera and his potential supporters probably had less to fear than they may have anticipated. Success in political struggle is rarely guaranteed, certainly in democratic conditions, by the narrow advocacy of the economic interests of a social group, devoid of understanding of cultural and ideological realities and of the ability to make the compromises necessary to win support beyond the ranks of the immediate social group concerned. The 'Farmers', of whom de Valera wrote, had failed totally to realize this; the Labour Party, and the left republican groups, seldom managed to advance beyond a purely defensive position either.

It has often been argued that the factors leading to the birth of Fianna Fáil were purely of a constitutional and tactical political nature: that the issue at stake was that of the 'pursuit of the Republic' in the face of Cumann na nGaedheal 'neo-colonialism'. This is certainly the self-perception of Fianna Fáil ideologues; but it is also forwarded, in one form or another, by many commentators who insist that

the differences that divided the two groups—the oath of allegiance and the Crown—were largely symbolic and constitutional . . . there were no basic differences between the two groups' aspirations for a free Ireland . . . national and constitutional questions came to distinguish the major parties, and national party competition largely revolved around the symbolic rather than substantive issues.[118]

Kevin Boland has written:

The really decisive factor, which swung so many in favour of the decision to form a new party, was the ratification of the Boundary Agreement by the

[118] *Carty, Party and Parish Pump*, 42.

'elected native government under contract with the enemy to maintain his overlordship' . . . The party arose out of, and was founded on, the shock of the acceptance of partition and on the determination of the republicans to undo it.[119]

Growing disillusionment within Sinn Féin with the policy of abstention was certainly increased by the Boundary Commission affair. Moreover, neither the importance of nationalist sentiment in motivating the founders of Fianna Fáil, nor the significance of personal temperament in determining who left and who remained in Sinn Féin, can be denied.

Nevertheless, the catalyst leading to the birth of Fianna Fáil was Sinn Féin's complete failure to defend the vital economic and social interests of those groups from which it drew its support. Sinn Féin's inability to advance concrete policy alternatives and its lack of credibility due to non-recognition of the state were rapidly undermining its electoral prospects. A political vacuum existed by the mid-1920s which a new party could hope to fill. This vacuum reflected also the failure of both the Free State Government parties and the Labour Party leadership to produce a political strategy capable of building a sufficiently wide alliance of social forces. The basic difference between Fianna Fáil and its rivals, whilst articulated in terms of the 'national issue', was really a question of political strategy. The founders of Fianna Fáil, unlike their Cumann na nGaedheal or Labour counterparts, understood perfectly well the necessity of actively constructing their supremacy by tapping the grievances of different social classes and groups. They understood the importance of 'concrete objectives' and 'concrete advantages' in enlisting the support of the 'common people' behind their banner.

Fianna Fáil sought to unite under its leadership those whose hopes had been dashed by the abandonment of Griffith's policies by Cumann na nGaedheal, and who had seen their children forced into emigration. In the name of the 'national interest', it did so by appealing to all those who felt that the Free State policy of serving as 'England's larder' had brushed them aside.

We must now turn our attention to the organization of the new republican party, the precise nature of the political strategy which emerged, the ideological articulation of its economic programme, and the political forces and material conditions with which it had to grapple on its way to governmental office in 1932.

[119] Boland, *The Rise and Decline of Fianna Fáil*, 16–17.

3

The Road to Power 1926–1932

The inaugural meeting of Fianna Fáil took place on 16 May 1926 in La Scala theatre in Dublin. Before we turn our attention to that meeting, and the first formal party conference in November, a number of pertinent features of the new organization should be noted.

It has sometimes been implied that, organizationally at least, Fianna Fáil took up where the old Sinn Féin left off, albeit with a greater degree of effectiveness. Boland, for example, states quite explicitly that the Sinn Féin model of organization was adopted.[1] There is certainly some evidence to suggest that, on the surface, this is true. One of the main sources of recruitment for Fianna Fáil had indeed been Sinn Féin; the number of affiliated Sinn Féin *cumainn* (branches) fell from 275 to 173 between March and April 1926 and, at the level of national leadership, there was a considerable overlap between the old and the new (seventeen of the thirty-seven Sinn Féin Standing Committee members and twenty-one of the party's forty-seven TDs joined Fianna Fáil; moreover, they were later joined by some highly regarded Sinn Féin leaders, such as Oscar Traynor and Seán Moylan, who had at first greeted the new departure with caution). But this should not blind us to significant organizational differences between Fianna Fáil and Sinn Féin. These differences are not simply related to the fact that Fianna Fáil *cumainn* were a good deal more extensive than Sinn Féin *cumainn* had been;[2] they consist in the membership composition, political ideology, and structural orientation of the new party.

First, it seems clear that the existing Sinn Féin network was by no means the most important source of recruitment. Arguably of greater importance was the large pool of disillusioned republicans who had not been politically active at all since the end of the civil war;

[1] Boland, *The Rise and Decline of Fianna Fáil*, 17.
[2] O'Leary, *Irish Elections, 1918–1977*, 25.

many of them may not even have voted in 1923. Indeed, it was not so much the old Sinn Féin model of organization, as the IRA model, which was adopted. Party organizers toured the country, contacting local IRA commanders, many of whom, because of their (real or legendary) exploits during the war of independence and civil war, had established themselves as heroic or charismatic figureheads in their localities. In this way, numerous old IRA companies were transformed into Fianna Fáil *cumainn*. Also of importance was the network established among republicans imprisoned during the civil-war period. Indeed, it is reasonable to assume that it was some time before all those who followed de Valera into Fianna Fáil actually severed their connections with the IRA, and certainly many of them regarded their republican oath of allegiance as still binding with the force of military discipline.

This fact is significant from a number of angles. The highly disciplined nature of Fianna Fáil has frequently attracted comment, both positive and negative. Boland has recalled with obvious pride that party activists

voted and canvassed exactly as the strategists at national and local level planned. In the early days candidates were not allowed to canvass at all. In many rural constituencies in particular, the constituencies were divided among the candidates with mathematical accuracy and there were no breaches of the plan.[3]

Carty, too, has emphasized the desire of party leaders to build a strong, efficient, and enduring party machine, firmly anchored to the grass roots (the basic party unit was the parish *cumann*, which soon existed in every parish throughout the Free State) rather than the fleeting power of local influential figures.[4] This development— facilitated by the fact that IRA commanders in general owed their charisma to their military office, rather than personal appeal alone— permitted Fianna Fáil to transcend the fissile tendencies encouraged by the Irish electoral system, to which practically all other political formations in Ireland at this time fell victim. Just to ram the point home, Fianna Fáil candidates were required to pledge that, in the event of their being elected to any public office, 'if called upon by a two-thirds majority of the National Executive of Fianna Fáil to resign that office, I shall immediately do so'.

[3] Boland, *The Rise and Decline of Fianna Fáil*, 21.
[4] Carty, *Party and Parish Pump*, 103 and *passim*.

Obviously, efficiency was not the only product of such an approach to organization. Fianna Fáil's brand of democratic centralism greatly obstructed the operation of internal party debate. Differences of opinion, of policy, and of ideological outlook certainly existed, especially in the early days. But only indirectly could the party rank and file hope to influence policy or strategy, and dissident or critical elements were quickly neutralized without any real possibility of mustering significant support for their positions. Only at ministerial level were real political differences able to emerge and here, too, they were more often smothered than resolved under the veil of unanimity. Prager has commented upon the authoritarianism inherent in Fianna Fáil's politics from the outset; the individual's relation to political authority was mediated by a hierarchical authority structure and popular acquiescence by the rank and file to the vision of party leaders was such that 'political accountability extended no further than the élite's articulation of that vision'.[5]

Comment has frequently been forthcoming upon the lack of intermediate policy-making structures, the lack of accountability of party leaders to the general membership, the concentration of real power within the upper echelons of the parliamentary party, the failure of the annual *Ard-Fheis* to develop as a real policy-making body, and the elevation of total obedience to the party leadership into a fundamental and inviolable principle of party membership. This last point obviously raises the question of the charismatic leadership, said to have been exercised by de Valera and to have been of such importance in securing his party's predominance. Therborn has argued that the social stratum most vulnerable to the appeal of the charismatic leader is the petty bourgeoisie:

the [petty-bourgeois] need for protection then becomes a craving for an individual *protector*, who will constitute and control an anti-bureaucratic part of the state machine; the petty bourgeoisie hopes to entrust its interests to such a populist leader, to whom it will have direct access, and to whom it will be able to appeal over the heads of capitalist officials.[6]

A similar method of leadership was predominant at all levels of Fianna Fáil. What the organization developed was not simply a cult of de Valera, but a structurally anchored cult of leadership, which has been one of its most consistent features, and which concentration

[5] Prager, *Building Democracy in Ireland*, 216–17.
[6] Therborn, *What does the Ruling Class do when it Rules?*, 122.

upon the relative qualities of de Valera, Lemass, Lynch, Haughey, or Reynolds might well serve to obscure. We have already seen that the party was initially organized largely on the basis of local IRA commanders—often local charismatic figures who bequeathed to the party a method of exercising power which has been the object of numerous clientelist and brokerage studies. This structural orientation towards a particular method of the exercise of power is another facet of the legendary Fianna Fáil party discipline. Clearly, the party's inheritance of IRA power structures is of pivotal importance, and neither undue concentration upon the Sinn Féin model of organization, nor careless assimilation of the IRA to Sinn Féin, really enlightens us much. Dogma, not discipline, was the predominant feature of the old Sinn Féin.

It is precisely the rejection of a dogmatic approach to politics which was the second major consequence for the new organization of its anchorage in the mass of republicans who had not been active in Sinn Féin, or had tired of it. They were weary of the failed policy of no compromise and disgusted at the complete incapacity of Sinn Féin to defend their interests at a time of severe economic hardship. They had seen Sinn Féin flounder for want of any policy— political, economic, or social. It is scarcely surprising that the new party's lack of dogmatism should attract them; or that de Valera's abandonment of parliamentary abstentionism should provoke so little opposition, when the oath of loyalty to the British crown was transformed into an 'empty formula'.

This political pragmatism was personified by de Valera, whose ability tactically to manipulate his supporters by issuing 'firm statements followed by intricate qualifications'[7] was considerable; it went hand in hand with a conscious electoral orientation. This, too, marked a break with the Sinn Féin method of organization, concerned as it had been as much with the administration of the affairs of 'the Republic' as with the winning of electoral contests.

Fianna Fáil was, from the beginning, totally electorally orientated. The party's ideals would be realized by winning a parliamentary majority; desired changes would be effected by the actions of a Fianna Fáil government. Repeated comments about the ambivalence of some party members towards the question of whether or

---

[7] T. Desmond Williams, 'De Valera in Power', in F. McManus (ed.), *The Years of the Great Test*, 1926–39 (Cork, 1967), 33.

not armed force still had a place in Irish politics, and whether the
Free State should receive *de jure* or *de facto* recognition, has dis-
tracted attention from another fact worthy of mention: Fianna Fáil
lacked any theory of society or of the state which might have re-
motely justified the hopes vested in its early radicalism by some
socialist republicans. Its approach to the exercise of power was
both parliamentary and paternalistic; it adhered to no concept of
the progressive or gradual democratization of the state apparatus—
characteristic of social democratic parties of the time—and its understanding of the role of a political party never included the idea
that a party ought to seek to democratize society in such a way as
to reduce its own centrality. Accordingly, no attention was paid to
questions of which internal organizational structures might facilitate
fundamental alterations in the exercise of power in society; organizational questions inevitably centred on the question of greater
electoral efficiency. No attempts were made to supplement, reinforce, or check the electoral machine by the sort of auxiliary organizations which are again characteristic of working-class parties,
both social democratic and communist. The cultural politics of the
party involved the mobilization of pre-existing convictions and
beliefs and their imposition on new institutions. Admittedly, social
bodies for members existed, most notably *Craobh na Féinne* (Irish
language body), and music festivals were sponsored; Lemass and
Boland told the 1929 *Ard-Fheis* that 'everything should be done to
counteract the tendency in recent years to concentrate exclusively
on purely political matters, and members should realise that work
done to foster the Irish language, games and customs was useful
work for the Fianna Fáil movement'.[8] But the party lacked any
concept of political power fundamentally different from that of its
opponents. This might seem rather obvious; but it is necessary to
ponder the implications. In the absence of any such theory of state
power, thoughts of altering the structure of power floundered and
were quickly abandoned. Much of the, often naïve, disillusionment
with the failure of Fianna Fáil's republican radicalism stems largely
from this fact.

The mobilization of the electorate was the first task which
the party set itself. Garvin has shown that the period up to 1933

---

[8] Quoted in B. Reynolds, 'The Formation and Development of Fianna Fáil, 1926–
1932', Ph.D. thesis (Dublin, 1976), 173–4.

witnessed a 'rapid and permanent rise in turn-out levels'.[9] This mobilization of the electorate affected all areas of the country, but especially the east; not only were the small farmers and rural proletariat electorally mobilized during the 1920s; so, too, was the Dublin working class, which had recorded low turn-outs at elections in the early 1920s. Moreover, working-class electoral politics in the city was at this stage dominated by independent candidates such as the renowned Alfie Byrne. This section of society, then, was prone to the appeal of any party which could accommodate sufficient of its needs within its political programme to offer some hope of social and economic amelioration.

By the end of August 1926, Fianna Fáil had already circulated a pamphlet on voter registration, and a full check of the electoral register was under way by mid-September. Fianna Fáil recognized the importance of local government elections long before its opponents did;[10] although the restricted nature of the property franchise might be expected to have adversely affected the party's fortunes, the experience gained in this field was used to build the organization and to lay the ground for future parliamentary successes; for Fianna Fáil, the two inevitably went hand in hand.

In contrast with the severe financial difficulties of its predecessor, the new party seems to have been on a sound financial footing from the beginning. Although information on party finance is notoriously hard to come by, a number of observations may be made, even if some of the conclusions must of necessity be tentative.

First, the party did not hesitate to seek financial support from business men who might hope to benefit from its policies. Tommy Mullins, one of those most involved in the early organization, has admitted that the party wrote to 200 or so 'wealthy friends' asking them for money; and Robert Briscoe cheerfully recalls that collecting funds was easier than he had anticipated because of what he coyly terms 'the reckless generosity' of many such supporters.[11] Reynolds claims that business men in Wexford and Cork, attracted by the policy of protection, began supporting the party once it entered the Dáil.[12] Indeed, Gerry Boland is quoted by his son as

[9] T. Garvin, 'Nationalist Élites, Irish Voters, and Irish Political Development: A Comparative Perspective', *Economic and Social Review*, 8/3 (1977), 172–9.

[10] Carty, *Party and Parish Pump*, 107.

[11] R. Briscoe, *For the Life of Me* (Boston, 1958), 227.

[12] Reynolds, 'The Formation and Development of Fianna Fáil', 139.

bemoaning the influx of 'big subscriptions' from the early 1930s onwards.[13] What constitutes 'big' is, of course, open to endless dispute; and it seems likely, in view of the preceding comments, that this method of party financing was in operation from the outset. But it is certainly of interest that when a subscription of £500 was received from prominent business man and former Cumann na nGaedheal minister, Joe McGrath, in 1931, Boland's initial efforts to return the money were overturned by the Fianna Fáil National Executive on the insistence of Lemass. Thereafter the financial ties between the party and the business community were not in dispute.[14]

Boland's contention that this relationship must have gained a privileged position for the party's business backers where the formulation of party policy was concerned is supported by another veteran, Todd Andrews, who claims that 'heavy subscriptions to party funds have redounded to the benefit of the subscribers'.[15] Seán MacEntee has left proof of at least one such incident, albeit a fairly minor one. In 1938 he received a cheque for £20 from Smith and Pearson Ltd. (structural engineers) for the party's election fund, together with a letter demanding retention of protection of fabricated steel. MacEntee wrote to Lemass on the company's behalf, requesting action.[16]

Also important initially was the financial backing received from wealthy Irish-Americans whose taste for radicalism in any shape or form is questionable. De Valera had collected some £20,000 in the United States by 1927 and he visited that country in December 1927, and again, for six months, in November 1929, to raise funds and establish Fianna Fáil support committees.[17] A steady flow of money was available from the United States from 1926 onwards from, *inter alia*, the American Association for the Recognition of the Irish Republic. The party's balance sheet, published in 1927, showed that, of its income of £30,402 2s. 5d. in that year, no less than £29,782 15s. 10d. came from abroad. Remarkably, a profit was actually shown in this year despite two elections.[18]

[13] Boland, *The Rise and Decline of Fianna Fáil*, 62.

[14] The private papers of Seán MacEntee contain copies of correspondence with numerous wealthy business backers throughout the 1930s, in particular, and receipts for some of the donations received. Amongst those donating were Johnston, Mooney, and O'Brien (bakers), Cahill and Co. (printers), and John Hughes and Co. (tea importers) (UCDA MacEntee Papers P67/360).

[15] Andrews, *Man of No Property*, 251.   [16] UCDA MacEntee Papers P67/360.

[17] Lord Longford and T. P. O'Neill, *Eamon de Valera* (London, 1970), 247, 269.

[18] Reynolds, 'The Formation and Development of Fianna Fáil', 163.

Further funds were made available as a result of the outcome of the so-called Sinn Féin Funds Case. When the New York Supreme Court decided, in 1927, that money donated to Dáil Éireann in the early days of the national independence struggle should be returned to the original subscribers rather than to the Free State government, many of these American sympathizers with Irish republicanism gave the money to de Valera to be used for 'other national purposes'.[19] The money was used to buy new party headquarters and to launch a daily newspaper, *the Irish Press*, in 1931.[20] Significantly, business backing was sought for the launch of the paper, and all of its directors, except de Valera, were wealthy business men.

Obviously, dependence upon the goodwill of successful Irish-Americans also had implications for the development of the party. Cronin has recorded how the IRA, following its move to the left during the late 1920s, found itself under severe pressure from its US financial backers. In fact, the IRA's financial support from the United States dried up and was not forthcoming again until after 1934, by which time the movement had effectively abandoned its flirtation with socialism.[21] It is unlikely that there was much significant difference between those sections of Irish-American opinion which financially backed the IRA and those which, in the late 1920s, backed Fianna Fáil.

The third main source of party finance would appear to have been the annual national collection. It is probable, however, that the real significance of the collection lay in its function as a form of party activity and a measurement of organizational strength. In 1927 the collection yielded the party about £2,000 at some 160–200 church gates in areas where the party was strongest. By the early 1930s this amount had risen to about £5,000.[22] Even so, this seems a relatively small amount compared with the sums—admittedly impossible to estimate properly—which the party was receiving from the United States and from business circles. The 1928 *Ard-Fheis* was told that £30,000 had been raised through 'collections'.[23] There is no way of knowing how much came from business men, or who donated. Given the estimates for church-gate collections, the lion's

[19] S. Cronin, *The McGarrity Papers* (Dublin, 1972), 160–1.
[20] Briscoe, *For the Life of Me*, 231.
[21] Cronin, *The McGarrity Papers*, 160–1.
[22] W. Moss, *Political Parties in the Irish Free State* (Columbia, NY, 1933), 92.
[23] Reynolds, 'The Formation and Development of Fianna Fáil', 163.

share of the donations would seem to have come from other than the 'plain people of Ireland'.

The national collection did serve, however, as a catalyst of organizational expansion and consolidation. Returns were used by the leadership to assess the vitality of each region and weak areas were targeted; scarcely an *Ard-Fheis* went by without detailed discussion of organizational problems.[24] It is interesting to note that Dublin was well organized from the start and that the impetus for organizing the rest of the country came from the capital.

Organizational success was immediate and impressive. By November 1926 the party had 460 *cumainn*; this had risen to 800 by the spring of 1927; more than 1,000 party units were operative by that summer. A team of up to twenty-five speakers was available on a more or less full-time basis to tour the country.[25] By November 1926 more than 400 public meetings had been held, with party speakers present. These meetings were used to mobilize supporters, present party policy, and serve as education classes.[26] After Dáil entry involved many of these party leaders in parliamentary life, a headquarters team which included two full-time organizers was appointed to continue the necessary work. At a local level it was inevitably the TD or prospective candidate who became the organizer; or perhaps it would be more accurate to say that it was the local organizer who tended to gain parliamentary selection, as many of the early Dáil deputies had been local or national IRA leaders, involved in party organization from the outset. In any event, the predominance of the parliamentary party and its close personalistic ties to the mass membership ensured that 'Fianna Fáil, like many of its predecessor parties, understood itself to be more of a support organization than a legislative or policy-making assembly'.[27]

Fianna Fáil's concentration upon party organization was in sharp contrast to its opponents' behaviour. Cumann na nGaedheal 'never grasped the possibilities inherent in mass organization'[28] and many of its leaders maintained a haughty contempt for the whole business of mass mobilization. Indeed, General Mulcahy, in later life, spoke of a deliberate attempt after 1924 to wind down the organization in

[24] Carty, *Party and Parish Pump*, 107.   [25] Briscoe, *For the Life of Me*, 230.
[26] Reynolds, 'The Formation and Development of Fianna Fáil', 52.
[27] Garvin, *The Evolution of Irish Nationalist Politics*, 157.
[28] Manning, *Irish Political Parties*, 6.

the country on the understanding that party branches were merely a hindrance to the Government's work.[29] Cumann na nGaedheal, it seems, would succeed merely on the basis of its moral superiority. The Labour Party never proved capable of imposing upon its local cadres and politicians the discipline necessary to build an effective organization, and was fatally hampered by the splintering of the trade-union movement.

Fianna Fáil organization was boosted by the launch of a weekly newspaper, the *Nation*, in 1927 under the editorship of one of the party's most consistent and shrewd populists, Seán T. O'Kelly. The *Nation* provided a valuable means of communication between members and between the party and the public, and an indispensable way in which to combat the propaganda of the overwhelmingly hostile established press (although it is interesting to note that, in contrast to the national press, many provincial papers were won over to Fianna Fáil between 1927 and 1932). It also relieved the party of the potential embarrassment of sharing with the IRA the existent republican press such as *An Phoblacht*.

For Fianna Fáil, organization was about the business of winning elections, and the business of winning elections was crucially linked to questions of policy and strategy. The experience of Sinn Féin had taught the proponents of the new departure precisely this lesson. Already in April 1926—a month before the formal launch—a statement of the fundamental aims of the party was issued. The initial draft of this statement listed the party's aims as being:

1. To secure the unity and independence of Ireland as a Republic.
2. To restore the Irish language as the spoken language of the people and to develop a distinctive national life in accordance with Irish traditions and ideals.
3. To make the resources and wealth of Ireland subservient to the needs and welfare of all the people of Ireland.
4. To make Ireland, as far as possible, economically self-contained and self-sufficing.
5. To establish as many families as practicable on the land.
6. By suitable distribution of power to promote the ruralization of essential industries as opposed to their concentration in cities.[30]

---

[29] Fanning, *Independent Ireland*, 102.

[30] Boland (*The Rise and Decline of Fianna Fáil*, 36) adds a seventh aim—to carry out the Democratic Programme of the first Dáil—but this does not appear in de Valera's original policy statement.

Even at this early stage there was manifest a tendency, which was to become more marked later, to place more emphasis on policy and less on nationalist rhetoric. The latter retained an important place in the party's arsenal—but no longer the sole, essential place; it was, rather, a back-up weapon with which to put rivals on the defensive and to consolidate a bloc of social forces attracted by various aspects of the party's programme. Soon, constitutional issues had been largely reduced to the single issue of the oath of allegiance, and so it was to remain until the party's advent to office.

The detailed evolution of Fianna Fáil's economic and social policies will be examined in the next section. Here, we may observe that the need to relate to socio-economic cleavages, and to come up with policies which could appeal to economically dissatisfied groups, was spelt out in an editorial in *An Phoblacht* on 11 June 1926. Under the title 'A new alignment needed? Organization born of activity', this editorial castigated those who thought that the party's success could be guaranteed without relating to the everyday lives of 'the people'. In language reminiscent of Lemass's articles the previous year, the editorial urged the party to 'sectionalize'—i.e. to come up with policies and a mode of political discourse which would appeal to 'the peasant farmer and the wage earner' who stood to benefit from and would therefore support a programme based on complete separation from Britain.

At the party's inaugural meeting de Valera, having delivered himself of a sharp attack upon the oath of allegiance and pledged the party to 'peaceful reunification', concentrated upon economic and social issues, identifying himself and his party with James Connolly—founder of the Labour Party and 1916 martyr—thereby stealing Labour's clothes. He launched an attack upon unemployment, poverty, and bad housing. Familiar themes of subsequent Fianna Fáil propaganda were aired—the promise of protection for Irish industry and the pledge that the 'ranches' would be broken up into small farms. And the finance for such sweeping reforms?

A loan would have been given, I believe, from the vast deposits which were held in our banks . . . Even if it were not possible to get all the initial capital we required at home, I believe we could have gone to our race abroad and placed with them an additional loan of from twenty-five to fifty millions [of pounds].

In other words, no action to reform the banking or financial institutions was proposed, and no real attention paid to the necessity of altering their patterns of investment (noises made in this direction on occasion by Lemass and a few others never came to anything). In the last analysis, the Fianna Fáil programme was to be financed by investment in Irish industry by wealthy Irish-Americans. In retrospect, the limitations of such a programme are obvious. But in the circumstances of the time, it was the promise of a new economic deal, and not its limitations, which excited the imagination and appealed to the social categories most in need.

De Valera took up another theme which I will deal with more substantially later: a populist attack on the cost of state bureaucracy. Not surprisingly given the personal experiences of most republicans, his attack was focused on the cost of the army, police, and civil service ('secretaries to secretaries to secretaries'). This was coupled with a pledge to reduce the number of Dáil deputies from 153 to 100 and to abolish the Senate. It is significant that the pro-Cumann na nGaedheal *Irish Independent* had run a series of articles attacking government 'waste', department by department, and that the cry had been taken up by the provincial press.[31] Soon Fianna Fáil was linking the question of cuts in old age pensions to the allegedly high level of salaries paid to senior civil servants and TDs, and promising to restore old age pensions until the top salaries were cut.[32]

An Information Bureau was established with the purpose of advising *cumainn* on policy; of equal importance at least was to be its role in collecting facts and statistics on economic matters in particular, providing back-up service for Fianna Fáil TDs, and 'issuing as speedily as possible for circulation among Fianna Fáil Deputies . . . a précis giving all material helpful to the aims of the party or injurious to Cumann na nGaedheal (e.g. analysis of the Poor Law Commission Report showing distress in the country)'. Interestingly, in view of Fianna Fáil's subsequent failure to challenge the impartiality of the civil service, the Bureau was conceived of by its instigator, Frank Gallagher, as having another function:

both to those working on its staff and to those in receipt of its information the Bureau would be the nucleus of a training ground for a Civil Service with a National outlook on all branches of Irish affairs. Those anxious to train in such a Department might be given the opportunity of an unpaid

---

[31] Reynolds, 'The Formation and Development of Fianna Fáil', 57.
[32] See e.g. the resolutions passed by Fianna Fáil county councils in Cork, Galway, and Clare in August 1926 (NAI Finance S088/0004/26).

apprenticeship which would thus provide the Bureau with helpers at no cost and the country with young men and women trained to look at public affairs with Irish eyes.[33]

'Notes for Speakers', issued by the party's Publicity Department, declared: 'Speakers should give wide publicity to those points in the programme of action set out in our printed leaflet, *especially to the social and economic policy.*'[34] Militant attacks on emigration went hand in hand with advocacy of protection. The process by which rural and urban working-class support was ascertained for an economic developmental strategy which would prove to be costly, inefficient, and uncompetitive was under way.

So, too, were preparations for the party's first formal *Ard-Fheis*, which opened in Dublin on 24 November 1926. This was, in many ways, simply a ratification of the policy statements which had been made at the May meeting and since. Attended by some 500 delegates, the *Ard-Fheis* ratified an elaboration of the party's original policy statement which had been issued by the General Policy Committee earlier in the month and which pledged the party 'with a view to the realization of [its] ultimate aims', *inter alia*, to:

Develop the natural resources of the country, including its mineral wealth and sources of power, encourage native industries that minister to the needs of the people, and protect them by adequate tariffs;

Establish a Tariff Commission independent of political and sectional interests to act as an Advisory Board to the Government, with power to publish its findings and recommendations for the guidance of the people, and to suggest safeguards so that the advantages of protection may be shared by the community as a whole;

Encourage the creation of an Irish Mercantile Marine;

Set about the reafforestation of the country on a national scale;

Make a survey of the transport requirements of the country, with a view to facilitating internal communication and the equable distribution of commodities whilst utilising to the fullest extent native sources of motor power;

Complete land purchase, break up the large grazing ranches, and distribute them as economic farms amongst young farmers and agricultural labourers, such as those at present compelled to emigrate.

In addition to this impressive list of commitments there was a pledge to help the ailing *Gaeltacht* (Irish language) communities

---

[33] Quotations from 'Memo re information Bureau', submitted by Frank Gallagher (NLI Gallagher Papers MS 18357).

[34] NLI Gallagher Papers MS 18357 (emphasis added).

by developing 'the fishing and other industries suitable to the Gaeltacht so as to enable the young native speakers to live at home'. Furthermore, there were pledges on protection of the rights of town tenants, and discussion of a state bank and a tax on native capital invested abroad. In other words, there was a continuous elaboration of the party's programme in a manner which was not at all vague and ambiguous, but calculated to facilitate the party's electoral penetration of Irish society.

The *Ard-Fheis* reiterated opposition to the oath of allegiance, but irredentist rhetoric was at a minimum. Instead, a further attempt was made to woo working-class support with attention paid to questions of social welfare and health insurance. A commitment to full employment was given with the promise to provide 'employment in lieu of pensions for all pensioners under sixty years of age, who are not otherwise unfitted for work'.[35]

Having examined the first steps taken by Fianna Fáil to establish itself, forge its new identity, outline its policies, and give concrete form to its embryonic political strategy, I will consider the evolution of its social and economic policies in the years up to electoral victory in 1932. Then I will raise the question of the party's mode of ideological discourse, the projection of its self-image, its manipulation of popular sentiments, and its success in ideologically disarming its opponents and rivals. Finally, I will trace the acceleration of the power struggle in Irish society during this period at the political level.

'IRELAND FOR THE IRISH': FIANNA FÁIL AND SOCIO-ECONOMIC DEVELOPMENT

There is no doubt that the economic and political situation in the late 1920s and early 1930s was favourable to the economic strategy being forged by Fianna Fáil. Central to this strategy was full-scale industrial protection. Protection would enable the growth of an Irish industrial base by freeing Irish manufacturers from competition with foreign firms; the expansion of the economy would lead to a substantial increase in employment, and the general increase in spending power would also have a beneficial effect on agriculture.

[35] Quotations from Policy Committee statement (UCDA Brennan Papers P50/1); for further comments, see M. McInerney, *Eamon de Valera, 1882–1975: The Controversial Giant of Modern Ireland* (Dublin, 1976), 56.

Industry, then, not agriculture, would be the driving force behind economic development. Protection was never advocated with an eye to one class alone. The profit-making opportunities which protected home markets would offer to Irish capitalists and the prospects of increased employment which industrial expansion held out to Irish workers were always emphasized together. Clearly, this dual approach entails inherent potential contradictions, unless a sustained increase in income per capita can be achieved. Economic development may rely as much upon increased labour productivity as upon expansion of the labour force,[36] in which case the sort of employment expansion promised by Fianna Fáil would require an adequate level of economic growth. It might also be noted that protected industries often tended to pay low wages, by British standards—the obvious comparison for most Irish people—and that downward pressure on labour costs became a key priority for the domestic bourgeoisie struggling to consolidate itself. Moreover, protection can often lead to overpricing and inefficiency which affects the consumer. It is precisely this last aspect which was taken up by opponents of Fianna Fáil policy in the 1930s. Cumann na nGaedheal, in particular, focused almost exclusively upon the inflationary effects of protection. This may well have been a serious political mistake: the limitations of Fianna Fáil economic policy, as far as its working-class support base was concerned, were not effectively stated by addressing the worker as a consumer—if his or her first priority was security of employment.

In November 1927 Lemass called for the replacement of the existing tariff commission with members 'who have a knowledge of agricultural and industrial conditions'.[37] He proposed that the new commission should have the right to enforce attendance of witnesses, to examine them under oath, and to make recommendations to the government which would publish reports within three months if the commission requested this. It should have the power to investigate in any industry, regardless of whether a request had been made or not. At the same time Lemass reassured manufacturers that 'unless we can insure that the benefits derived from the imposition of protection are reserved for the Irish manufacturers as well as the consumers it is a dangerous policy to embark upon

---

[36] M. Peillon, *Contemporary Irish Society: An Introduction* (Dublin, 1982), 160.
[37] NAI Finance F21/21/27.

protection'.[38] As Daly points out, he was reacting to a growing realization on the part of Irish capitalists that protection, unless accompanied by measures designed to ensure native control over industries supplying the home market, could lead to worse consequences than ever. Foreign companies, taking advantage of the few tariffs introduced during the 1920s, established a dominant position in many sectors of the Irish market, including soap and tobacco manufacture and confectionery.

Lemass, in 1928, estimated that there were 459 foreign companies accounting for capital investment of £73 million and profits of £4 million, and argued that there were 'many foreign companies operating in Ireland which we would be better without'. Such a statement, in itself, would hardly have been encouraging news for those employed by such companies; but it must have been music to the ears of Irish capitalists in competition with foreign rivals—and at a time when Cumann na nGaedheal was attempting to use the fear of foreign take-over bids as an argument against the introduction of industrial tariffs at all. Pressure for the introduction of a full-blooded '"Irish-Ireland" for Business' policy had been forthcoming from the Dublin Industrial Development Association (IDA), which recommended in 1928 that Irish-owned investments should receive preferential tax treatment and that there should be free tax dividends for certain industries.[39] The 1929 Fianna Fáil *Ard-Fheis* endorsed the central demands of the Dublin IDA and passed a resolution requiring that the Companies Act be amended so that all companies registered abroad be licensed and that all other companies should have a majority of their directors resident in the state, and that shareholders' meetings be held in the state.

Lemass's emphasis that protection would lead to profit for investors was repeated throughout the late 1920s and must be set alongside his insistence that 'even if manufacturers were "slack or inefficient" in applying for tariffs, the government should be prepared to intervene on behalf of the workers whose "interests are of much greater importance to the nation than the interests of a small group of owners"'.[40] Of course, state intervention to apply protective measures on behalf of workers also dovetailed with the desire of manufacturers to see those of their competitors who had no

[38] Quoted in M. Daly, 'An "Irish Ireland" for Business? The Control of Manufactures Acts, 1932 and 1934', *Irish Historical Studies*, 24/94 (1984), 252.
[39] Ibid. 246–8, 250–2.　　　　　　　　　[40] Farrell, *Seán Lemass*, 27.

need of protection ruined. The latter, needless to say, also employed workers, whose interests seem to have been considered only indirectly.

From 1927 to 1932 Fianna Fáil intervened constantly to advocate protection for sector after sector of the Irish economy—flour, wool, coach-building, boots and shoes, paper and cardboard, butter, bacon, dairy products, fish barrels, sugar beet, malt. Time and time again the case for protection was aired and always with forthright insistence upon the golden prospects for Irish industry which such a strategy would entail.

Lemass, advocating 'the building up of industries here which are being controlled by natives of the country', claimed that the profit-making opportunities afforded by protection would be 'one way in which to induce' Irish investors to reinvest in Ireland some £200 million which was invested abroad.[41] This modest appeal to the pockets of investors must be set against his occasional more radical-sounding pronouncements on the subject of financial control. It was these latter statements which never came to anything.

In January 1932 de Valera told a party rally that 'Fianna Fáil was founded with the idea of giving an opportunity to all those who had the right national [outlook] of getting together again; to secure Ireland for Irish people—so that the wealth of the country will be available for Irish people'.[42] Significant, here, is the omission of the definite article—the wealth of Ireland was to be secured, not for *the* Irish people, but for 'Irish people'. Which Irish people? The answer came not long after: 'if you put capital into Irish industry and back up Irish industry—we'll see to it that it's not broken by unfair competition.' A few days later he told a meeting in Offaly that 'one couldn't expect an Irish manufacturer to show enterprise if he is driven out of the home market by a foreign combine selling goods here'.[43] Having recognized the need to see that protection would not be abused by manufacturers seeking easy excess profits, de Valera assured his audience that 'personally he believed that such protection would not be used for profiteering purposes'. De Valera's naïve, but touching, faith in the piety of the Irish bourgeoisie stands in sharp contrast to the hard-headed approach of wealthy business man and Fianna Fáil TD, T. P. Dowdall, who told the Cork Chamber

---

[41] Dáil Debates, 17 July 1931.   [42] *Irish Press*, 2 Jan. 1932.
[43] Ibid., 8 Jan. 1932.

of Commerce a few years later that: 'trading should be left in the hands of the business community. With regard to the statement that people were taking advantage of the tariffs, it was only human nature to do so, and personally he would avail of them to make as much profit as he could.'[44]

By 1932 Fianna Fáil had secured the confidence of substantial sectors of Irish industry. By 1930 its programme was in line with that of the National Agricultural and Industrial Development Association (NAIDA) (an employers' organization), and from 1931 it had the support of the Farmers' Protection Association. Although these organizations did not openly campaign on a partisan ticket, it is significant that, during the 1932 election, the NAIDA launched a campaign in favour of Irish industrial development and the manufacture of goods in Ireland which, until then, had been imported. Running full-page advertisements in newspapers, the NAIDA quoted the number of jobs which could be made available through the further development of Irish industry geared to the home market.

This had been the principal theme in Fianna Fáil's concerted drive to rally working-class and rural labourer support. The message that unemployment was due to the Government's failure to protect Irish industry, and that Irish manufacturers, if given a fair chance, would prove capable of ensuring full employment, was constantly repeated—sometimes with the proviso that, if the private sector failed initially to fulfil expectations, the state would step in and instigate temporary and emergency employment-creating schemes. This linking of the solution to unemployment with the question of protection for Irish industry certainly wrong-footed the Labour Party, while the Government party was (correctly) accused of failing to publish accurate unemployment figures; as many unemployed people failed to register, because of the inadequate benefit system, the problem was considerably understated.

In a debate on the cost of salaries and expenses of the Department of the President (i.e. prime minister) and the Executive Council,[45] Lemass skilfully proposed that the Government estimate be referred back for reconsideration 'for the purpose of giving the Dáil an opportunity of expressing its view on the policies of the Government in relation to unemployment'. Having accused the Government of failing to publish the census figures of 1926 in order to

[44] *Evening Herald*, 30 Jan. 1935.   [45] Dáil Debates, 4 June 1930.

obscure the real extent of unemployment and emigration, he went on to estimate the former at between 50,000 and 75,000. Unemployment in Ireland, he argued, was not due to the same causes as unemployment in the United Kingdom or the United States. Irish unemployment was a different species altogether—it was, in a word, unnatural:

The outstanding fact of unemployment in this country is that it need not exist at all. The solution of unemployment depends in the long run upon the development of industry . . . it cannot be done any other way except we reconcile ourselves to a permanent reduction in the number of people living in the country and unless we ensure development of industry here.

Lemass then explained that Fianna Fáil

have urged in the past and still urge that during any period of depression which now exists here [*sic*] in which a large number of people are without work the state should embark upon schemes of work providing public utility services which are needed so as to relieve the depression and continue its work on these lines until the depression has passed.

The highly conditional and temporary role allocated to the state should not pass unnoticed. Farrell's assessment that behind Lemass's seemingly radical rhetoric was no socialist but a 'moderate Keynesian', profoundly influenced by Griffith and attached to private enterprise (but with some recognition of its 'dangers and inadequacies'), is perfectly correct.[46]

Lemass also linked the problem of housing to the lack of a policy of protection. There were 50,000 houses needed in the Free State, he declared. 'Why are the producers of building materials not encouraged and why not employ people to build these houses.' It was a disgrace that the Killaloe Slate Factory sold its slates to Glasgow Corporation while Dublin Corporation did not buy them. He concluded by demanding the rejection of the Government amendment on its own expenses to express dissatisfaction with the Government.

Faced with this offensive, Labour's T. J. O'Connell could do no more than congratulate Lemass on his speech whilst timidly suggesting that 'wholesale protection' might not 'entirely meet the problem'. From the Government benches the response was just as inadequate. One Government supporter complained that the

---

[46] Farrell, *Seán Lemass*, 26–30.

Government was being put unfairly on trial for its eight years' work and added: 'I have been a member of St Vincent de Paul for fifty years . . . The slums have improved immensely since I first visited them and they will gradually disappear.' The Minister for Industry and Commerce, Patrick McGilligan, replied rather huffily to Lemass that it was not his fault if people did not register as unemployed.

The Fianna Fáil offensive to win working-class support continued. De Valera told a party meeting in Offaly in January 1932 that

If the people noted the large quantity of goods they imported unnecessarily they would understand why they had so much unemployment. If every Irish person was clothed in clothes made in Ireland, this would provide employment for 25,000 people; if all the things they used were manufactured in Ireland, then they could provide employment for 80,000 people— no other country could point to such a certain solution for its economic problems as the Irish Free State.[47]

Days later, he told supporters in Kanturk:

As regards the biggest problem of all, the problem of unemployment—we are a comparatively rich country in natural resources, rich in everything to provide all the necessities of life, but we are still faced with unemployment. *This is due solely to the large imports of goods into this country.* A complete analysis of all these imports would show that a total of 85,000 people would be given employment in the manufacture of goods at home.[48]

Lemass, with an eye to the votes of workers in his own constituency, where the railways were an important employer, sought to underline his party's self-projection as an agent of economic growth and employment expansion by declaring that 'Fianna Fáil was the pro-railway party; the development of industry couldn't be brought about unless railways were preserved—this could only be done if the cream of traffic taken from them by the road transport was returned'.[49]

Fianna Fáil agricultural policy involved an appeal to the small farmers and agricultural labourers, ostensibly against the interests of the large graziers, who depended on the export of live cattle to the UK market—the 'ranchers'. The evidence suggests that large farmers at least did well during the 1920s. Until 1929 those farmers who were efficient enough to be able to avail of the favourable

---

[47] *Irish Press*, 8 Jan. 1932.   [48] *Irish Times*, 17 Jan. 1932 (emphasis added).
[49] *Irish Press*, 2 Feb. 1932.

conditions fostered by the Government, and who possessed the necessary collateral to benefit from the establishment of the Agricultural Credit Corporation in 1927, certainly profited as a result. In 1929 Irish butter and eggs enjoyed top prices in the UK market. In the same year agricultural exports stood at £47 million—a figure not reached again until 1948; and the volume of exports was not exceeded until 1960. The value of exports was 77 per cent of that of imports—a figure only improved upon during the war years, when imports were scarce.[50] However, from 1929 prices fell. Farmers found it increasingly difficult to compete in the UK market and were thwarted by the United Kingdom's tendency to resort to protection in the face of international economic depression. To the satisfaction of the Irish Government, cattle exporters continued to do well, but there were no jobs to be created in that sector. Indeed, Daly bemoans the 'unimpressive' performance of agriculture in general and suggests that 'the economic development model of the 1920s was not only bedeviled by poor economic conditions but based upon false assumptions'. The farmers, contrary to Government belief, could not 'raise all boats', and both unemployment and emigration remained high.[51] (Moreover, it was stated Government policy not to spend money on 'unproductive' schemes to relieve seasonal unemployment.[52]) Orridge adds that 'the export statistics . . . indicate that Ireland tended to specialize in the low value end of the productive processes in which it was involved. It shipped live cattle, many of them unfattened, to be fattened, slaughtered, and processed in Great Britain, thus allowing much of the value added before the meat reached the consumer to be realised elsewhere.'[53]

In other words, not only was the relationship between Irish agriculture and the rest of the economy profoundly unhealthy, but only a minority of the agricultural population really benefited from the Government's policies.

Small farmers and agricultural labourers faced many (and by no means similar) problems which the Government did little or nothing to alleviate, and sometimes even aggravated. Small farmers had

[50] J. Meenan, 'From Free Trade to Self-Sufficiency', in McManus (ed.), *The Years of the Great Test*, 72–3.

[51] M. Daly, *Social and Economic History of Ireland* (Dublin, 1981), 141–2.

[52] NAI Finance S009/0011/27.

[53] A. Orridge, 'The Blueshirts and the "Economic War": A Study of Ireland in the Context of Dependency Theory', *Political Studies*, 31 (1983), 353.

not had their demands for more land met—a frustration which they shared with many labourers. While those schemes which the Government did embark upon, such as the Shannon Electricity Scheme, helped reduce farmers' production costs, it was the larger farmers who benefited most. No subsidy was available for pig farming—an important mainstay of the small farm economy—until 1931; and small farmers lacked the capital resources to join improvement schemes—credit loans depended on land security. Indeed, Cumann na nGaedheal's neglect of the small farmers was to prove a source of friction within that party.

Agricultural labourers faced an even bleaker situation. Their organizations had been crushed as a result of the failure of the movement for wage improvement in 1924; labourers' wages were declining throughout the period under examination; they were not entitled to unemployment benefit and had no vote at local-government level. Not surprisingly, their numbers were in a state of decline. Daly tells us that 'it was felt that industrial protection would raise farm labourers' wages, and this was undesirable. So, too, was any legislation controlling their wages or hours of work.'[54] The reason given was that this would prove a burden on the farmers. Government policy was aimed at keeping the labourers in a state of insecurity and near poverty.

It is against this background that Fianna Fáil's drive to enlist small-farmer and labourer support should be seen. It has been argued that 'the problems of agriculture were seen [by Fianna Fáil] as peripheral to industrial expansion: it was stressed that the expansion and dispersal of industrial units would be instrumental in solving the problems of agriculture'.[55] This is certainly true, and is borne out by de Valera's remark in 1934 that 'the best way to help the farmers in the long run is to increase the home market by building up the industrial population, because the people employed in the factories would require the farmers to produce more food for them'.[56] However, the party's agricultural programme was emphasized by Fianna Fáil, not merely because of considerations to do with electoral arithmetic, but also because of the ideological function of the small homestead which became an important part of the party's evocation of petty-bourgeois sentiments in general. Unlike

[54] Daly, *Social and Economic History of Ireland*, 140.
[55] J. Smyth, 'The Changing Nature of Imperialism in Ireland', *Bulletin of the Conference of Socialist Economists*, 3 (1974), 69.   [56] *Irish Press*, 28 May 1934.

the argument for industrial protection, much of the party's agricultural policy never really made much economic sense—and of all the party's policies it was the one which failed most dramatically; its rationale was largely political and ideological.

In addition to tariffs for bacon, butter, eggs, and other agricultural products, Fianna Fáil advocated fixed prices for butter and wheat. Strong emphasis was placed upon tillage, as opposed to grazing, and production of food for the home market rather than production for export was urged. The party

was committed to a policy of reorientating agriculture towards domestic subsistence rather than international trade. The ultimate aim was to greatly increase labour-intensive arable farming to support a larger population and the main initial scheme to this end was a programme to encourage wheat growing.[57]

All of this naturally appealed to the small farmers, who saw themselves elevated at the expense of the graziers, and to the unemployed farm labourers, to whom it offered new employment prospects. The demand that subsidies be introduced to encourage wheat production was further welcome news. (The granting of subsidies—including hidden subsidies in the form of social-security benefits—to unproductive agricultural elements was to be a consistent feature of Fianna Fáil strategy for retaining the loyalty of these strata down the years and helps to explain the paradox noted by Peillon: Fianna Fáil's ability to command the support of small farmers while 'doing nothing' to defend their interests.[58]

On top of this, the party advocated the speeding up of the Land Commission's task of dividing the large estates up among small farmers and the landless, and the withholding of the land annuities payable to the UK exchequer.

The annuities, which came to about £5 million each year, were the debt paid by Irish farmers to the UK Government arising from the transfer of much of the farming land of Ireland from Anglo-Irish landlords to Irish farmers. The annuities were paid to the Land Commission, which, in turn, transferred them to the British. Apart from being a financial burden, the payment of the annuities was heavy with political implications. There was a widespread feeling that the payment of money to the UK Government for land which

---

[57] Orridge, 'The Blueshirts and the "Economic War"', 358.
[58] Peillon, *Contemporary Irish Society*, 110.

was Irish in the first place was both profoundly unjust and an insult to national pride. Indeed, the real significance of the annuities issue is probably political rather than economic; the mythology surrounding the question touched upon the farmer's ideological perception of himself as the descendant of the cruelly expropriated, restored to his rightful inheritance.

Agitation for the abolition of the land annuities had been started by left-wing republicans, such as Peadar O'Donnell, during the mid-1920s, and a number of local campaigns to withhold payment got under way. From the start, the agitators sought to involve Fianna Fáil, and O'Donnell was informed by Lemass that the party was anxious to take up the issue provided it could do so in such a way that it would not appear to be jeopardizing the ownership of property.[59] Fianna Fáil adopted the issue as its own in 1928, although the party advocated merely withholding payment by the Irish Government to the UK Government and not outright abolition of the annuities.

The money saved on the annuity payments, Fianna Fáil argued, would be used to improve the lot of Irish agriculture in the form of subsidies to the small-farm sector. On occasion, Fianna Fáil speakers such as Lemass could also link the promise of improved social services and housing to the projected saving on the annuity payments; for example, he declared in the Dáil in May 1930 that 'there is no hope of improving the social services until expenditure of land annuities is stopped'.[60] Indeed, Fianna Fáil's opponents could accuse it, with some justification, of having pledged the savings on the annuities many times over. The pledge to withhold land annuities was a policy which commanded widespread support far and beyond the small-farmer community, linked as it was to matters of national pride.

Workers and agricultural labourers were enticed by, *inter alia*, the promise of employment expansion and greater job security; a minimum wage for agricultural labourers was promised; and a 1932 Fianna Fáil election poster exhorted workers to 'End Unemployment! Vote Fianna Fáil!'[61] The poster showed imports being unloaded at the docks whilst the unemployed hung their heads in despair. The commercial petty bourgeoisie (and, to some extent

[59] Interview with Peadar O'Donnell.   [60] Dáil Debates, 28 May 1930.
[61] Reproduced in J. J. Lee and G. O'Tuathaigh, *The Age of de Valera* (Dublin, 1983), 65.

also, the professional strata) were enticed by the prospects of greater employment opportunities for their children and greater prosperity as a result of a general increase in spending power within the community: a remark by Fianna Fáil TD, James Geoghegan, is enlightening in this respect: 'deplorable as it might be', he told supporters, 'to waste money in the country, it was much worse to send it out of it, because even unwisely circulated in the country itself, it came eventually to the shopkeeper and the farmer.'[62] Professional groups were further reassured by promises that there would be no reductions in the salaries of the 'small men'; during the 1932 election campaign Fianna Fáil produced leaflets specifically aimed at the lower ranks of the civil service.

The general recourse internationally to protection from 1931 made it seem that it was the opponents of protection, and not Fianna Fáil, who were out of line with reality. The occasion was not lost on Lemass, who gleefully described the limited tariffs imposed in 1931 as a forced reaction to developments in UK economic policy as 'a further indication of the conversion of the Cumann na nGaedheal party to the policy of Fianna Fáil'.[63]

By the general election of 1932 Fianna Fáil's skilful articulation of the case for protection[64] had placed its opponents completely on the defensive. Of course, protection, although the central plank in Fianna Fáil's economic programme, was not the whole story. Considerable attention was given to pressing social problems, and policies were elaborated whose content was often quite modest but whose presentation made the Labour Party appear timid and inadequate by comparison. This is not to deny Labour's role in introducing and initiating discussion on the subject of social-welfare legislation. Indeed, at least one Fianna Fáil *cumann* was moved, during the late 1920s, to complain that

within the past eight months, legislation dealing with such important social questions as unemployment and the Old Age Pensions has been introduced. It was not due to the initiative of Fianna Fáil that legislation of this kind was discussed. That the Fianna Fáil *Teachtaí* [deputies] figured

---

[62] *Irish Independent*, 7 Aug. 1931.

[63] Quoted in R. Fanning, *The Irish Department of Finance, 1922–1958* (Dublin, 1978), 206.

[64] See e.g. the advertisement which appeared in the *Irish Press* on 13 February 1932 which linked protection to economic security for workers, farmers, shopkeepers, and manufacturers.

prominently in the lengthy discussion on these it is true, but why had they to leave the introduction of these motions to the Irish Labour Party?[65]

The point is, however, that Fianna Fáil quickly realized the political value of a programme of social reforms; pensions and social-welfare assistance were a relatively small price to pay to ensure the adherence of the most desperate social strata (numerically, and therefore electorally, important) to its strategy for economic development. When social policy initiatives were articulated in terms of Fianna Fáil's economic programme and its perceived political radicalism, the Labour Party—which lacked both an economic programme and radical credentials—was quickly outflanked.

Appalling housing conditions were widespread during the 1920s. Daly has estimated that the Dublin tenement problem was probably worse in 1939 than it had been in 1914, when there had been some 6,317 slum tenements housing 111,350 people; and that the worst deterioration occurred between 1914 and 1926.[66] This state of affairs did not change much during the last years of the Cosgrave administration. A report of a meeting of Dun Laoghaire council on 4 May 1931 records concern that the poor were being put out of their homes by landlords who wanted to build 'better class houses', capable of yielding greater rents.[67] Many tenants, it seems, were having to 'beg from door to door the means of their sustenance' because of rents which could be as high as eight shillings per week for a single room (before the war, the same accommodation averaged around two shillings). 'Working-class' families were officially defined, since 1908, as those earning less than thirty shillings per week, while as late as 1931–5 the average weekly wage for agricultural labourers, over the age of 21 with no rent allowance, was merely twenty-one shillings and three pence.[68] This destitution was by no means confined to Dun Laoghaire.

The Government made grants available to private individuals and public-utility societies, rather than to local authorities; naturally, this adversely affected working-class families and those unable to pay high rents, as these were most dependent upon local-authority action. During the period 1924–9 a total of 11,627 houses

---

[65] Resolution passed by the Erskine Childers Fianna Fáil *cumann* (UCDA McGilligan Papers P35c/165).
[66] Daly, *Social and Economic History of Ireland*, 191.
[67] UCDA Mulcahy Papers P7/C/53.   [68] UCDA McGilligan Papers P35c/176.

was built by private individuals and public-utility societies with the aid of £839,738 in government grants. This contrasts with a mere 3,939 houses built by local authorities in the same period with the aid of £320,296. Moreover, amazing as it may seem in view of the gravity of the housing crisis, more than 10 per cent of the £1,350,000 allocated under the various housing acts since 1924 remained unused, allowing the Department of Local Government and Public Health proudly to record a saving of £157,756. Following something of a struggle between the Minister concerned, Mulcahy, and the Department of Finance, the situation was somewhat eased in 1931 when, against Finance's wishes, the Local Loans Fund was opened up 'for the making of advances to Local Authorities for the erection of working-class houses'. As a result, 'loans amounting to 200,000 pounds were sanctioned during the year'.[69] This led to the construction of 1,825 houses by local authorities during the year ending 31 March 1931 (compared with 2,610 by private individuals and public-utility societies). The corresponding figures for local-authority construction during the two previous years were 789 (1930) and 1,058 (1929).

Clearly, then, policy tended to facilitate housing construction by the better-off sections of the community; and, while Mulcahy might hope to earn some credit for the slight improvement registered in time for the 1932 general election, his Fianna Fáil opponents could easily accuse the Government of doing too little, too late.

Lemass had linked the questions of housing construction, employment creation, and protection for the building industry in the context of the party's overall economic strategy. Fianna Fáil followed this up with a pledge that 'the first concern of a Fianna Fáil government will be to provide suitable dwellings for working-class families at rents which they can afford to pay'. In a burst of radical rhetoric, Robert Briscoe told a meeting in Dublin in January 1932 that 'Fianna Fáil would tackle the housing problem and would take responsibility for the housing problem, and would tackle it no matter what the opposition from the building merchants'.[70] (Since the building merchants were subsequently to make considerable fortunes from Fianna Fáil's construction programme, and were to become one of the legendary mainstays of the party's business backing, Mr Briscoe's words of fire assume a certain retrospective irony.)

---

[69] From a civil-service memo (UCDA Mulcahy Papers P7/C/53).
[70] *Irish Press*, 29 Jan. 1932.

The party fought the 1932 election with policies which included: a pledge to establish a National Housing Council to embark upon a programme of slum clearance and construction of houses in both rural and urban areas—a target of 40,000 new houses within five years was spoken of; the fixing of rents within the means of working-class families; and control over ground rents, which were a source of controversy and annoyance principally to the lower middle strata. Allied to this was a promise to increase the grants and loans available to private individuals and public-utility societies, and to encourage the use of Irish building materials. There was, it seemed, something in it for almost everyone: the workers, the middle strata—and the contractors.

In addition to the housing situation, poverty was rampant throughout the Free State during the 1920s. As we have seen, estimates of the number of unemployed ranged from 50,000 to 80,000. A further indication of the extent of the problem is probably the numbers receiving home assistance under the Poor Law. These numbers increased steadily during the last years of Cumann na nGaedheal rule, from 47,963 (1925–6) to 77,474 (1930–1).[71] In Dublin, 38,000 men passed through the Dublin Shelter for Men in 1929, 300 receiving breakfast there on Christmas morning. On 4 January 1930 the Dublin Poor Relief Act was brought into being. Administered by Dublin Commissioners, it received 5,000 applicants by 15 January, with only 50 per cent or so approved.

Like health care and help for the unemployed, the cost fell upon the ratepayers, and the propertied classes at once sprang into action to ward off this encroachment upon their wealth. Already in 1927, the Government had taken action against local councils which were deemed to have overspent on welfare payments.[72] Now, the Dublin Chamber of Commerce protested to the Government before the Bill was passed and organized a protest meeting under the auspices of the Businessmen's Association once the Act became law. The *Irish Times* reported that 'businessmen are angry at having to pay increased rates to support immigrant paupers and say savings in electricity as a result of the Shannon Scheme will be offset by increased rates'.

On 17 January 1930 the same paper reported the objectives of the Association as being to voice a protest over ministerial refusal

[71] Lyons, *Ireland since the Famine*, 609.
[72] O'Connor Lysaght, *The Republic of Ireland*, 97.

to consult them prior to the passing of the Bill and 'to call attention to the necessity for an organization such as the Businessmen's Association, if the interests of the business community were to be adequately safeguarded and if it was desired to prevent a recurrence of what had happened in connection with the Poor Relief Bill'. Mr George Jacob, speaking at the annual general meeting of the Dublin Chamber of Commerce later that month, said that in relation to the Poor Relief Scheme they had made deputations and had given directions about the administration and distribution of the relief, so that the increase in the rates would be far less than it might otherwise have been. In this way the business class succeeded in getting poor relief reduced. Indeed, in 1929 and 1930 a series of meetings had been held between the Government and business organizations at which pressure to balance the budget and decrease expenditure had been applied. For example, in April 1929 the Association of Chambers of Commerce of the Irish Free State had met the Minister for Finance to press him to reduce income tax and stamp duties, abolish corporation profits tax, and impose taxes on co-operative societies,[73] and in January 1929 the West Limerick Farmers' Association had urged a reduction in taxation, linking this to what was now a common theme in Fianna Fáil propaganda: reductions in ministers' and civil servants' salaries, in the number of TDs, and in the size of the army.[74]

The business organizations were pushing at an open door. Cumann na nGaedheal showed itself willing to face defeat in March 1930 rather than back down on a Bill to reduce old age pensions. A one shilling per week cut in old age pensions in 1924 (Finance had wanted a two shillings cut) was not restored until 1928, and soon further cuts were on the way. The 1931 budget reduced old age pensions and health and unemployment insurance payments. These cutbacks were to create profound unrest with the Government in such seemingly unlikely quarters as the police and the army, as well as amongst the teachers. Indeed, the Government had chosen to ignore warnings from within its own ranks; in November 1927, for example, the Cumann na nGaedheal Dublin city north constituency chairman had complained that the cut in old age pensions was 'a sad mistake' according to 80 per cent of the people.[75]

[73] NAI Finance F043/0004/29.   [74] Ibid. F049/0002/29.
[75] Ibid. S088/0004/26.

This situation obviously left Fianna Fáil with the opportunity to make political capital, particularly as there was little chance of being outflanked by the leaders of the Labour Party, whose virtual paranoia had led them to campaign in 1927 on the basis of a commitment to ensure 'rigorous control of all public expenditure'.[76] That is not to say, however, that organized labour was entirely passive or dormant. An Irish National Unemployed Movement was launched in 1926, partly under communist influence, and organized big marches in the late 1920s and early 1930s. A major rally of unemployed was held in central Dublin in November 1932 and a national conference of local groups followed in December. Fianna Fáil was pushed forward, at least in part, by forces within the labour movement as well as within its own ranks.

Its social proposals, despite being described rather fancifully by one commentator as 'more advanced than any non-socialist party offered before Roosevelt's New Deal',[77] did not constitute anything like a revolution. Modest (but highly significant for the recipients) increases in old age pensions and unemployment payments, new pensions for widows and orphans, and extension of health insurance were the main features of the social programme which helped to clinch victory in 1932 and to secure it thereafter, without seriously alienating those business groups whose increased profit margins as a result of protection more than compensated for any loss incurred.

Fianna Fáil's political success was not in any sense inevitable, given its strategy; the limitations and internal contradictions of its position cannot be overlooked. If its rivals and opponents had reacted differently, or if the party itself had failed to break so completely with the old Sinn Féin *political strategy*, and to realize the importance of economic and social policies in building an interclass electoral bloc, then the outcome might have been very different.

The limitations and contradictions which are evident with respect to Fianna Fáil's socio-economic programme can be discussed in the context of four interrelated issues: the role of the state and of the private sector in economic life; the party's attitude to private property; taxation policy; and the party's inaction on banking and finance.

[76] UCDA Mulcahy Papers P7/C/44.
[77] O'Leary, *Irish Elections, 1918–1977*, 22.

We have already seen the highly conditional nature of Fianna Fáil's advocacy of a role for the state in employment creation; this position, and the party's corresponding acceptance of the primacy of capitalist leadership in the economy, never altered—a point which has sometimes been obscured by concentration upon the expansion of semi-state bodies during the party's years in power. De Valera had pledged, in October 1931, that 'if Fianna Fáil got into power factories would be established, and if they were not established by private enterprise the State would establish them'.[78] And again, weeks later, he told supporters that 'a time might come when the State might have to enter into an enterprise like the production of boots, and if private enterprise did not give the youth of the country, who could now emigrate, an opportunity of using their brains at home, then the State would have to step in and do so'.

Here we have the Fianna Fáil position in a nutshell: the state would embark upon employment creation only as a last and somewhat reluctant remedy to private capital's failure to generate employment. In actuality, expansion of the state sector during Fianna Fáil's years in power was undertaken largely in 'highly capital intensive sectors . . . taken over by the state due to the reluctance of private capital to invest in these sectors'.[79] 'The lack of private capital, the timidity of private capitalists, the necessity to supply some public services and rescue others—these were the fundamental reasons for the formation of the state-sponsored bodies.'[80] The employment-creation schemes to be undertaken by the state in times of depression were almost exclusively concerned with the provision of necessary infrastructural requirements which private capital could not adequately undertake, but had need of. Thus, the role allocated to the state in the Fianna Fáil developmental strategy can be seen as functional to the expansion and consolidation of the leading role of the national bourgeoisie. Almost all of the economic developments urged by de Valera in the late 1920s—the training of fishermen and the provision of easy loans for the purchase of their boats and equipment, the development of peat for electricity generation and fuel, the co-ordination of road, rail, and canal transport under a single management—can be related to the infrastructural requirements of the private sector.

[78] *Irish Independent*, 5 Oct. 1931.
[79] Smyth, 'The Changing Nature of Imperialism in Ireland', 68.
[80] Lyons, *Ireland since the Famine*, 619.

The role of the state did not even include competing with the private sector, never mind replacing it. The only firm to be nationalized by Fianna Fáil when in power during the 1930s was a foreign-owned sugar company. Significantly, when the Minister for Finance urged, in June 1930, that the interests of private gas suppliers should be safeguarded by subjecting the state-sponsored Electricity Supply Board to taxation, Fianna Fáil's Seán Lemass supported the idea.[81] Lemass, who has sometimes been portrayed almost as a quasi-socialist and has certainly been seen as a champion of state enterprise, argued against monopolies on the grounds that 'the operation of the ordinary economic laws' of competition ensured efficiency.[82] Fianna Fáil leader Frank Aiken is quoted by party co-founder Todd Andrews as conceiving that 'production [of turf] was to be left in the hands of private enterprise and the role of the state was merely that of creating conditions calculated to stimulate maximum turf production'. In the event, it became clear that the stimulation of maximum production required a much wider role for the state than Aiken, or perhaps many other of his colleagues, would have liked. Andrews, who was a member of the Fianna Fáil National Executive from 1927, also tells us that during the 1920s, 'from time to time, prompted by my socialist beliefs, I put forward proposals for setting up nationalised clothing and shoe industries but in the political circumstances of the time these ideas must have seemed naïve and unrealistic'.[83] The 'political circumstances of the time' were the unthinkable nature of questioning the primacy of private ownership of the means of production—an attitude which Fianna Fáil shared with its Cumann na nGaedheal opponents. The picture is completed by the remark of de Valera's biographers that, as private industry developed behind the barrier of protection, it would absorb labour which would be released by state undertakings.[84]

The limited nature of the state role envisaged by Fianna Fáil should be clear enough. Fianna Fáil had committed itself to a policy of full employment, a promise to end emigration and to facilitate an expansion of the population supported by the Irish economy, and increased social services. Yet it refused to commit the state to a policy of wealth creation. The ownership of capital and the creation

[81] Dáil Debates, 4 June 1930.   [82] Farrell, *Seán Lemass*, 28.
[83] Andrews, *Man of No Property*, 123, 230.
[84] Longford and O'Neill, *Eamon de Valera*, 328.

of wealth was to remain firmly in private hands. A so-called 'Economic Plan for the Free State', drafted in early 1932, made it clear that 'It must be emphasised that under the plan there is no suggestion of interference with private property and there will be no confiscation', and that 'no government Department shall administer directly or indirectly any business whether agricultural, industrial, distributive or productive other than the administration of the financial credit scheme except as hereinafter set out'.[85] Whence would the money come to finance improved conditions for the mass of the population? From the taxation of wealth or control over the means of exchange? From control over the direction of private investment? As we will see, the party's deference to private property was to block off these options. As Lee and O'Tuathaigh put it, 'the first flush of success had begun to fade by 1937. There simply wasn't the money to finance the social and economic policy any longer . . . de Valera himself conceded privately that he was at his wits' end in economic and social matters, and didn't know where to turn next.'[86]

Fianna Fáil's promise of full employment depended largely upon the goodwill and patriotism of Irish capitalists. It was *hoped* that they could be persuaded or enticed into investing in Ireland, thereby creating new jobs; and it was further *hoped* that their profits, gained behind protection barriers, would, in one way or another, filter down to the rest of the community. There was little historical basis to justify such expectations. The same people who organized themselves to resist paying a meagre pittance to the poor through increased rates were relied upon by de Valera and Lemass to bring increased prosperity to the Irish people. Speaking in December 1928, Lemass had said that 'those who controlled industry had always exercised a large influence over national policy'—and had gone on to attack ownership of Irish industry by foreign capitalists as threatening national sovereignty. But what of ownership of Irish industry by Irish capitalists? What real likelihood was there that Irish business men would facilitate the provision of employment 'at an adequate wage to all suitable able-bodied workers'?[87]

Ironically, one of the most acute statements of the class limitations

[85] NLI Gallagher Papers MS 17256.
[86] Lee and O'Tuathaigh, *The Age of de Valera*, 139.
[87] From a 1932 Fianna Fáil election leaflet (UCDA Mulcahy Papers P7/C/140).

of Fianna Fáil's economic programme came from within the party (we have already examined the reasons why such dissent was easily contained). Dublin's Erskine Childers *cumann*—how representative it was we will never know—pleaded with party leaders as follows:

The protection of Irish industries from the dumping of foreign made products is a good and proper demand. But the protectionist policy of Fianna Fáil, if achieved, will benefit the manufacturing class in Ireland. With their industries protected, their profits will considerably increase. To the question of protection there are two sides. Will an Ireland of protected industries mean that the manufacturers whose industries are protected be allowed to avail of their privileged positions to force workers to toil for low wages and long hours? Will they be allowed to pursue the policy obtaining in many Irish-owned industries at present, of employing children at the age of fourteen and dismissing them when they reach the insurable age of sixteen? To questions of such practical and vital importance must Fianna Fáil veer its attention. If Fianna Fáil refuse to consider the other side of the question of protection, then it can rightly be said that between the economics of Seán Lemass and Arthur Griffith there is no difference. Arthur Griffith stood for an Ireland controlled by the greedy mercenary manufacturing class. Does Fianna Fáil stand for the same?[88]

Lemass had declared in 1924 that the republicans 'cared nothing for the old catch-cries about the rights of private property and the sacredness of interests'. Nothing could be more misleading. Fianna Fáil was careful, in the 1932 election campaign, to emphasize its acceptance of property rights. On 1 February 1932 the party journal declared:

Dealing with the Fianna Fáil policy, Mr de Valera declared that there was nothing communistic, nothing socialistic, and nothing that interfered with the rights of private property contained in it. It was the assumption by the State of the paramount right, to try and organize the efforts of the community for the benefit of the community as a whole.[89]

If this was not sufficiently reassuring, it was quickly pointed out that Pope Pius himself had said something similar; Seán T. O'Kelly reminded voters that Cosgrave's claim that it was no duty of the government to encourage provision of employment was 'in direct negation of the Papal Encyclicals'.

---

[88] Undated, but clearly from the late 1920s (UCDA McGilligan Papers P35c/165).
[89] *Irish Press*, 1 Feb. 1932.

Earlier in the campaign, a Fianna Fáil advertisement in the *Irish Independent*—a newspaper sympathetic to Cumann na nGaedheal and unfailingly reflective of the business community's point of view —had hit back at claims that Fianna Fáil would deprive farmers of their land, declaring that 'the exact reverse is the truth', and pledging the party against the introduction of a land tax.[90] On the same day the *Irish Press* continued: 'We believe in the diffusion of property and ownership, and are convinced that this would lead to much more satisfactory social conditions and to a much higher life for the individual.'[91]

It was this conception of the function of property, and not Lemass's earlier rhetoric, which was enshrined in de Valera's new Constitution in 1937—a Constitution which made public ownership 'much more difficult than under the Free State Constitution'.[92]

Now there is a clear contradiction inherent in all of this. Fianna Fáil had promised to redistribute land to the small farmers and landless labourers. But did those already in possession of the land not possess property rights as 'natural' and 'inalienable' as the rights of those aspiring to ownership? If Fianna Fáil was unwilling to take land away from the large farmers, whence would the land come which was to be redistributed? It did not. The work of the Land Commission was run down during the mid-1930s.

A further weakness in the party's position was its confused and badly handled attempt to exploit the issue of taxation. We have seen that Cumann na nGaedheal, responding to pressure from sections of the bourgeoisie, had cut the standard rate of income tax during the 1920s. Demands for the reduction of taxation were a constant theme in business circles. Fianna Fáil spokesman, Seán MacEntee, sought to make political capital out of the issue, linking it to attacks on 'waste' and calls for reduction in public expenditure. As far as appeals to the petty bourgeoisie and self-employed were concerned, MacEntee's attacks upon taxation may well have been of an ideological more than a practical nature, since it seems likely that small farmers, small-scale producers, and the self-employed paid little direct tax.

There is obviously some contradiction between a commitment to increase social services and involve the state in the provision of,

---

[90] *Irish Independent*, 9 Jan. 1932.   [91] *Irish Press*, 9 Jan. 1932.
[92] McInerney, *Eamon de Valera, 1882–1975*, 77.

at least some, additional employment through the creation of industrial and social infrastructure, and a pledge to reduce public expenditure. Various commentators have noted that the end results of government action during the 1930s were not as MacEntee had suggested. O'Hagan tells us that there was a rise in the public sector's share of expenditure after Fianna Fáil's election to power, although he estimates that additional taxation only accounted for a small percentage of the additional expenditure.[93] Daly reports that civil-service numbers rose by about one-third during the period 1932–43, and that both taxation and public expenditure rose.[94] Clearly, then, the Fianna Fáil socio-economic programme would necessitate increased public expenditure and, at the very least, no reduction in the level of overall taxation. Why, therefore, did party leaders such as MacEntee choose to take up an issue which the party seems to have been singularly ill-equipped to exploit convincingly? The answer takes us to the heart of an important contradiction within Fianna Fáil, which was to persist down through the years and which has at times been reduced, rather simplistically, to the personal rivalry between MacEntee and Lemass. The issue at stake was, in essence, as follows: how far should the party defer to the immediate and unmediated interests of the bourgeoisie, whose consolidation Fianna Fáil aimed at and upon whom it depended for the successful implementation of its developmental strategy; and how far should it impose sacrifices upon that class, and make concessions to other social forces, in order to secure political and social stability and ensure its own dominance.

The former approach was characteristic of Cumann na nGaedheal and led to its political defeat; the latter strategy emerged as characteristic of Fianna Fáil. This is not to suggest that this choice was undertaken in unison and without problems. It is the persistent tension between MacEntee's conservatism and the greater political astuteness and opportunism of Lemass which was to condition both the achievement and the limitations of Fianna Fáil: success in keeping the party's opponents in a subaltern state and the majority of the population tied to a bourgeois project of economic development; failure to embark upon any real innovation which might have fundamentally altered Irish society, and consequent economic stagnation

---

[93] O'Hagan, 'Analysis of the Size of the Government Sector', 22–6.
[94] Daly, *Social and Economic History of Ireland*, 151.

and recurring emigration and poverty. Of course, this is to state the case too baldly and without full attention to objective factors. This contradiction within Fianna Fáil first came to light during the debate over the Government's Finance Bill in 1930. MacEntee, speaking in a vein which must have stolen the breath of the Farmers' Party veterans, attacked the Government's 'reckless borrowing'. Lemass was careful to emphasize that the borrowing was 'reckless' only because it was 'haphazard'.[95]

In the course of the 1932 election campaign differences surfaced again. In November 1931 MacEntee took up his favourite theme:

The proper way to meet the deficit was by cutting down expenditure, not by the imposition of further taxation. If they had the 1,250,000 pounds paid to ex-R.I.C. pensioners, the 1,500,000 pounds spent on an army which General Seán MacEoin had said was useless for any national defence, and the land annuities, there would have been no need to throw fresh burdens on any section of the community.[96]

Earlier in the month he had told the Dáil that Cumann na nGaedheal stood for 'taxation before economy', whereas Fianna Fáil stood for 'economy before taxation'.

Lemass had his say a month later. He did not disagree, of course, with his party colleague's attack upon Free State pensions or the land annuities—there was truly no disagreement here. But he was careful to correct any wrong impression which might have been given and to keep his options open: 'having saved every possible penny and if there was still a deficiency, then, only, should be considered the imposition of additional taxation.'[97]

A further weakness in the Fianna Fáil position relates to the all-important questions of banking and finance. We have already noted de Valera's cautious remarks in May 1926. Lemass, in a conscious effort to capture Labour votes from June 1927, sounded much more radical when, speaking on a Labour Party motion on unemployment in the Dáil, he declared unemployment to be due to 'the financial system in operation in this country'. He had two proposals to make to attract capital investment to Irish industry. The first sounded more radical than it actually was: a tax on exportable capital. The second was decidedly less threatening: income tax concessions on capital invested in Ireland and in Irish industries.[98]

[95] Quotations from Lemass in Farrell, *Seán Lemass*, 29.
[96] *Leinster Leader*, 28 Nov. 1931.   [97] *Meath Chronicle*, 19 Dec. 1931.
[98] Farrell, *Seán Lemass*, 26.

During the 1920s and early 1930s no effort was made by the Government to alter the situation whereby the Irish currency remained tied to the British; the value of the Irish pound was fixed by the Bank of England (*de facto*, of course, not *de jure*) and the volume of the issue of Irish banknotes by the amount of British securities and banknotes held by Irish banks. The Currency Commission, established in 1927, had little more than a supervisory role over the activities of the shareholding banks. No control was exercised over the export of capital, and considerable amounts were, in fact, invested abroad. 'Both Commercial and Post Office savings banks held most of their assets (fifty-six per cent in 1927) in the UK.' Indeed, money was rarely invested in Ireland; the Irish financial institutions preferred more profitable destinations for the capital entrusted to them to the risks of investment in Irish industrial development. By the late 1920s the total accumulated amounts invested abroad had come to £200 million, representing 'estimated fractions of the national capital resources varying from one-fifth to five-sevenths'.[99]

Cumann na nGaedheal's *laissez-faire* economic doctrines forbade any attempt to alter this situation. Finance Minister Ernest Blythe declared that it had been decided not to establish a central bank because it would have been 'in opposition to the wishes of the existing institutions'. Labour leader, T. J. O'Connell, was warned by business man TD William Hewat that 'any interference with the stability of the currency or with the exchange rate would quickly be followed by a flight of capital'.[100] The Currency Commission, all were reassured, would have a 'psychological effect on the banks' in the direction of greater patriotism.

Cumann na nGaedheal was at pains to assure the banks that it intended defending their interests against accusations that the interest rates they charged were too high. In a revealing memorandum, written by Finance Secretary McElligott to the Irish Banks' Standing Committee in October 1929, the Government position was spelt out quite clearly. Requesting information which would enable the Government to defend the banks' policy in parliament, McElligott added: 'I am to add that the Minister trusts that the Committee will not regard his request for a statement as putting the Irish Banks on

[99] O'Connor Lysaght, *The Republic of Ireland*, 94–5.
[100] Quoted in M. Moynihan, *Currency and Central Banking in Ireland, 1922–60* (Dublin, 1975), 73–5.

their defence on this matter or as requiring them to justify the action they have taken.'[101]

Fianna Fáil economic strategy depended crucially upon the reorientation of Irish capital investment patterns. How did the party plan to achieve this? In reality, it seems that it did not have much idea. The 1932 election campaign had featured pledges to establish a state bank and Lemass sometimes made noises in this direction. But the issue, upon which so much depended, was never fully thought out, or fought out; in the end, it was the commitment to the interests of private capital and the rights of private property which was to prove decisive. Here, again, was another weakness which Labour in the 1920s failed to exploit—largely because Labour was no clearer in its intentions.

We have seen the limited nature of the reforms urged by Lemass in 1927. On 24 October 1931 the *Irish Independent* reported him as advocating:

A national currency backed up by the national credit with an exchange value determined by its purchasing power here. If they had such a currency, those who imported foreign produce could only take out their profits in the form of Irish produce, and an adverse balance of trade would not be possible.

The limited nature of the reform advocated, the implication that profits would continue to leave the country, and the apparent primacy given to the balance of payments question, are as significant as the talk about a 'national currency'. During Fianna Fáil's tenure of office, other party figures, such as Frank Aiken, would express a keen interest in questions of monetary reform, but no substantial action was ever taken forcibly to redirect the pattern of capital investment. De Valera, in even vaguer form than Lemass, is quoted as advocating 'native control' of Irish currency and credit during the late 1920s.[102] Later, his biographers quote his 1932 remarks about 'going outside the system' should he try but fail to do his 'full work' from within. As they quickly add, 'he never did go outside the system'.[103] What, exactly, de Valera understood by 'the system' is an interesting but forever unanswerable question.

Fianna Fáil in power relied upon incentives, and principally upon the promise of greater profits as a result of protection, to attract

[101] NAI Finance F009/0009/29.
[102] Longford and O'Neill, *Eamon de Valera*, 329.   [103] Ibid. 334.

capital investment back to Ireland. But if the promise of greater profits is the sole, or even principal, means envisaged to alter long-established investment patterns by a bourgeoisie historically reluctant to invest at home, how does this square with the promise given in February 1932 to end the downward pressure on workers' wages? With a profit-motivated bourgeoisie doing its best to resist 'inflationary' wage demands, a party which had made the promise of greater profits almost its sole policy instrument was faced with an impossible contradiction.

Before moving that far ahead, let us turn to the reaction of Fianna Fáil's main rivals to social and economic developments in the late 1920s and early 1930s. We have dealt with the main outlines of Cumann na nGaedheal policy and there is no need to cover old ground again. A number of additional points may be made, however.

First, it must be remembered that the abandonment of the economic goals of the national revolution struck hard at an important source of Cumann na nGaedheal's legitimacy. As the leaders most opposed to protection—O'Higgins, Hogan, MacNeill, Fitzgerald, McGilligan—gained total predominance, the party faced internal turmoil related to the debate over economic development. In the summer of 1927 the Minister for Posts and Telegraphs and party chairman, J. J. Walsh, resigned, declaring: 'the party itself has gone bodily over to the most reactionary elements of the State ... A government cannot depend on the votes of ranchers and importers and at the same time develop industry and agriculture.'[104]

Walsh had earlier given O'Higgins a list of business men who would finance Cumann na nGaedheal's 1927 election campaign in return for the protection of their industries. (An interesting question, which unfortunately we cannot answer, would be how many of these same business men subsequently financed Fianna Fáil.) O'Higgins is reported to have torn the list up and burnt it.[105] Walsh may have been alone inside the cabinet by this stage;[106] but his dissent was not an isolated incidence. On 13 April 1927 Father Malachy MacBrennan, member of the Standing Committee of

---

[104] Quoted in Fanning, *Independent Ireland*, 101.
[105] T. De Vere White, 'Social Life in Ireland, 1927–37', in McManus (ed.), *The Years of the Great Test*, 28.
[106] Daly, *Industrial Development and Irish National Identity*, 35. Daly's claim that 'Walsh was an isolated figure' is certainly true of the cabinet by the time of his resignation, but not of the party as a whole.

Cumann na nGaedheal, tendered his resignation from the party on the grounds that the Government was neglecting the plight of small farmers: 'If employment be not provided for them on productive work of some kind, the emigration must continue and semi-starvation for very large numbers as well.'[107] Father MacBrennan's resignation was important because the welfare of small-farmer communities was a subject dear to the hearts of politically minded Catholic clergy, to whom Cumann na nGaedheal turned for legitimization of its rule. Fianna Fáil's success in breaking down clerical suspicion and hostility was not simply due to its growing respectability; the failure of Cumann na nGaedheal to realize the social ideals of the clergy also played a part. In January 1927 a forlorn and depressed General Mulcahy had lamented to a friend of 'personal differences of which there are plenty already'. Cosgrave, he feared, intended putting him out of the cabinet after the next election and this might mean 'further disintegration'.[108] While Mulcahy's problems did not relate directly to economic strategy, there can be no doubt that many of the 'personal differences' referred to did.

Cumann na nGaedheal was, in fact, undergoing fundamental and disorientating changes. It was shedding the original Michael Collins-type 'republican pro-Treaty' support which it had enjoyed and was becoming 'the centre of a coalition of not particularly popular sectional groups, many of them with pre-1916 roots, and united only in their fear of the "wild men" of de Valera's party and the reactionary character of their political and social outlook'.[109]

The party was becoming indistinguishable from the Farmers' Party and the ex-Unionist and business-orientated TDs whom it was shortly to absorb. Its image as a bastion of privilege, complacency, and élitism was an obvious target for Fianna Fáil propaganda. Putting itself forward as the party of 'the plain people of Ireland', Fianna Fáil attacked Cumann na nGaedheal as the puppet of Freemasons and Unionists—a message which was to prove more effective than dire warnings about communism. Moreover, the Government's capitulation to the intellectual hegemony of free-trade ideology, which has been traced by Daly,[110] was such that Lemass was not exaggerating too heavily when he declared in 1930: 'judging by the recent speeches of Mr Fitzgerald and Dr O'Higgins, if Griffith

[107] UCDA Mulcahy Papers P7b/65.   [108] Ibid.
[109] Garvin, *The Evolution of Irish Nationalist Politics*, 147–8.
[110] Daly, *Industrial Development and Irish National Identity*, ch. 2.

lived and spoke today he would be liable to be sent to jail for sedition.'[111]

Cumann na nGaedheal had no convincing answer to such charges. The party's economic thinking was being done for it by the agricultural exporters and by the civil service, and its political realism was fast disappearing in a welter of arrogance.

Fanning tells us that the Department of Finance had no difficulty in persuading its political masters of the totally unacceptable nature of 'deficit financing'; there was no evidence of resentment or resistance by Government ministers to Finance's strictures and Cosgrave and MacNeill, in particular, were totally pro-Finance. 'The Cosgrave administration was as loathe at the end of their decade in office as they had been at the beginning to question the policies advocated by the officials of the Department of Finance', i.e. 'to do nothing and say nothing'.[112]

Two clear examples of this are given by the Government's reaction to the Report of the state-sponsored Committee on the Relief of Unemployment, and the budget of 1931.

The Committee on the Relief of Unemployment had been set up in 1927, clearly to give the impression that the Government was prepared to do something about the problem.[113] Its recommendations included: a ten-year house-building programme; powers to local authorities to compel owners to clear derelict sites and enforce sanitary conditions and proper repairs in tenements; reconstruction or renewal of schools; expansion in afforestation; and road-building and drainage schemes.

The Report met with a stony reception from the Government. In March 1928 Finance countered that 'the Exchequer position makes it imperative that expenditure under this, as well as other heads, should be restricted within the narrowest possible limits'. Building costs, it claimed, were too high and it was not possible to proceed with the Committee's recommendations. The Government effectively buried most of the Committee's recommendations, despite protests from both the trade unions and Fianna Fáil county councils throughout late 1928 at its failure to implement the Committee's Report.

---

[111] *Irish Times*, 10 Feb. 1930.

[112] Fanning, *The Irish Department of Finance*, 107–8, 210.

[113] For comments on the Committee's work and correspondence, see NAI Finance F088/0039/28, F088/0044/28, F088/0046/28.

There was a further policy consideration behind the decision to keep expenditure on unemployment relief schemes as low as possible: the desire to keep the wages of those so employed below agricultural labourers' wages, so as not to antagonize the farmers. A Finance memorandum in February 1931, reporting on a meeting with farmers in County Limerick on just this matter, is revealing:

the money which is being spent on relief works must be provided by taxpayers generally, and taxpayers include both ordinary wage earners and farmers who complain that they are definitely suffering losses and that they are paying more than their fair share of taxation . . . it would be unfair to tax farmers for the purpose of paying a rate of wages to men of the agricultural labourers' class which would be higher than that paid by the farmers themselves, and would tend to divert labour from the farms.[114]

In reality, there was little likelihood of wages being excessively high, as they tended to be fixed by local councils, which, as a Labour Party statement in November 1927 claimed, were 'composed mainly of farmers and shop-keepers'.[115] The Government, it was claimed, was attempting to lower wages further by imposing upon contractors a maximum wage level. The Wages Advisory Commission had reported in December 1927 that, 'in view of the situation which has arisen by reason of the representations made by the Labour Party, it was generally agreed that any further reduction in wages would embarrass the Local Government Department'.[116] But Finance was considerably less sensitive to such potential embarrassment, and pressure for wage reductions continued to be applied.

The groundwork for the 1931 pre-election budget had been well prepared by Finance since the mid-1920s. Despite a 20 per cent reduction in expenditure between 1926 and 1929, Finance continued to press for all-round cuts. In September 1928 McElligott had warned Departments that his Minister was most anxious to balance the budget without raising taxes. He wrote:

The real remedy for the present financial emergency is a rigid and unswerving policy of retrenchment . . . no opportunity of effecting economies in existing services must be overlooked.

Furthermore, while existing services are subjected to a rigid and continuous scrutiny, no proposals for new expenditure should be put forward

---

[114] Ibid. F088/0010/30.   [115] Ibid. F88/5/27.   [116] Ibid.

unless for absolutely essential purposes which are not only urgent but are also balanced by compensating reductions in some other branch of the Department's activities.[117]

The 1931 budget was literally dictated by the Department. Finance advocated:

(1) No new expenditure, e.g. on pensions, housing, land purchase or division;
(2) lowering of the salaries of teachers, army, police, old age pensioners, and of health and unemployment health insurance payments. There was to be no adjustment, in the pay and pensions of civil servants;
(3) thorough revision of all other expenditure;
(4) additional taxation—but limited only.

The Government, Fanning tells us, hesitated at first, and then bowed, inevitably. A budget in compliance with the above was introduced on 30 October 1931—a matter of months before the general election—and was to prove disastrous for Cumann na nGaedheal. This is not to say that austerity programmes cannot be presented successfully to the electorate. They can, of course, as Fianna Fáil was shortly to prove. But Cumann na nGaedheal's inability adequately to represent and secure the interests of any coherent social group was ultimately to mark its decline. The party's only political tactic seems to have been the sharpening up of its 'tough-men' image. The murder of Kevin O'Higgins had made the cabinet 'more closed and stubborn',[118] and this was evident in its approach to social and economic matters also. Patrick McGilligan, for example, under question from Lemass about unemployment, told the Dáil: 'I would not be deterred from a rationalization process conducted within the country by consideration of the fact that certain men would temporarily lose employment, or even that certain men would permanently lose employment.'[119]

Cumann na nGaedheal, one commentator tells us, was overconfident of its own competence and certain that a Fianna Fáil government would collapse through ignorance and inexperience.[120] But it was Cumann na nGaedheal's political immaturity and not Fianna Fáil's alleged economic simplicity which was to prove decisive.

[117] Ibid. F039/0015/28.
[118] Manning, *Irish Political Parties*, 13.   [119] Dáil Debates, 6 Mar. 1930.
[120] T. Desmond Williams, 'De Valera in Power', in McManus (ed.), *The Years of the Great Test*, 31.

If Cumann na nGaedheal's sense of political realism was stunted by arrogance, the Labour Party's was stifled by caution, confusion, and insecurity. Labour's dilemma cannot be reduced to the simple proposition that Fianna Fáil combined social reform with republicanism while Labour represented only the former, thus appearing too extreme or irrelevant: that 'most Larkinite second preferences went to Fianna Fáil. This appealed to disgruntled workers as representing the vague Republican–social ethos as against Labour's over-extreme appearance.'[121] If this was truly the case, and Labour appeared 'over-extreme', then how does one explain the fact that these voters opted for James Larkin in the first place? In fact, the idea of Larkinite voters being alienated by the excess radicalism of Thomas Johnson and his colleagues is somewhat lacking in credibility. Nor does such an explanation account for the behaviour of the small Workers' Party of Ireland, which, in May 1927, urged support for Fianna Fáil rather than Labour.[122]

Labour fought the June 1927 general election on the basis of an eminently moderate programme. Manning does not deal sufficiently with this fact, emphasizing, instead, that Labour's campaign focused on unemployment, low wages, and Fianna Fáil's ignorance of economic affairs.[123] What is striking about Labour's June 1927 platform is how little it attempted to harness the widespread social alienation present in the community, and how much it appealed to the 'opinion formers' of the established press. Labour leaders seem to have been so shocked by the strike outbreaks of 1923–4 and by Larkinite radicalism that they concentrated upon distancing themselves from any revolutionary intent, thereby forfeiting to Fianna Fáil the opportunity to channel popular discontent.

Labour election propaganda in 1927 focused upon the 'constructive' nature of its opposition to the Government. Nothing as ambitious as Fianna Fáil's commitment to full employment was forthcoming; instead, Labour offered moderate proposals on employment and housing, couched in even more moderate language: 'it is necessary that a man must have employment and adequate wages if he is to do his duty as a father and a Christian citizen.' As already mentioned, this was coupled with a pledge to 'rigorous control of all public expenditure', and a decidedly defensive stance

---

[121] O'Connor Lysaght, *The Republic of Ireland*, 86.
[122] Reynolds, 'The Formation and Development of Fianna Fáil', 78.
[123] Manning, *Irish Political Parties*, 69.

on taxation—no mention of a wealth tax was made. No commitment to abolish land annuities was included, because Thomas Johnson considered the unilateral repudiation of the land annuities 'unthinkable'.[124] His attitude was similar to that of the editor of the *Irish Times,* who described the land annuities as a 'debt of honour'. Johnson was more concerned with attacking the doctrine of 'class warfare' and reassuring the electorate that 'I am a "community-ist", a "nation-ist", before I am a "trade union-ist".'[125]

Labour did well in June 1927, although it saw only three of its nine candidates in Dublin elected. Its respectability beyond doubt, it received support from people who had accepted the Treaty settlement but who were not enthusiastic about Cumann na nGaedheal. Labour did not yet face a serious challenge from Fianna Fáil. That party had not yet entered the Dáil and was still obsessed with questions of a constitutional and purely tactical nature; its political strategy was still in embryonic form. That it out-polled Labour even at this stage was a dangerous portent. On the basis of the evidence, it is arguable that Labour's chief weakness was not that it seemed too socialist, but that it did not seem sufficiently radical.

This fact was quickly realized and seized upon by Fianna Fáil propagandists. On 11 June 1927 the *Nation* attacked Johnson, comparing him unfavourably with James Connolly and James Larkin, and declaring that the media had 'discovered a Labour leader after their own heart . . . he will never smash any tyranny, native or foreign. He is entirely "safe" and entirely respectable.' The paper followed this up on 16 June by describing Johnson as the 'leader of the opposition which does not oppose'. Fianna Fáil propaganda in June 1927 was decidedly more radical-sounding than Labour, linking poverty and hunger to a Government in the pay of 'Imperialists'.[126]

The 12.6 per cent which Labour received in June 1927 was not to be repeated. When Fianna Fáil entered the Dáil in the summer of that year, Labour's fate was sealed. This was not simply due to Fianna Fáil's presence in the Dáil and the manner in which it elaborated its economic programme and political strategy. Labour's own reactions are important. Lyons states that Labour lacked a coherent ideology. 'It was for social reform, certainly, but not apparently for the total reconstruction of society.'[127] Here is the key to understanding

---

[124] Gaughan, *Thomas Johnson,* 238–9. [125] Ibid. 287.
[126] See e.g. UCDA MacEntee Papers P67/344.
[127] Lyons, *Ireland since the Famine,* 525.

Labour's crisis. Indeed, it did not always seem to be so certain even about social reform; social stability seemed at times to be as important. After the assassination of O'Higgins, Labour offered to join Cumann na nGaedheal in a national coalition and to forge a national agreement 'between workers, employers, and investors for increased productivity and improved wages'.[128] Such an arrangement, had it come to fruition, might well have finished Labour electorally. But Cumann na nGaedheal, always one to look a gift horse in the mouth, declined the offer; indeed, an ungrateful Ernest Blythe flung Labour's offer back in its face, declaring that Johnson's 'overtures to the Government were dictated by his insane desire to be a minister at any price'.[129] Labour similarly attempted to secure agreement with Fianna Fáil and the National League, promising that 'during the life of the coalition government no attempt would be made to pass special labour legislation'.[130] Well might Lemass tell the Dáil in November 1927 that Labour's vitality had been sapped by long association with the parliamentary establishment.[131]

Johnson and his colleagues gained a reputation as parliamentarians of great ability; and one cannot doubt their hard work within the parliamentary arena, including the tabling of numerous motions on unemployment and poverty. But their inability to influence Cumann na nGaedheal in the least, and, at the same time, their paralysis in the face of growing social and political discontent, their fear of class politics, and their anxiety to defend the parliamentary institutions with which they had come so closely to identify, left them devoid of any real appeal to the disaffected. It was precisely here that Fianna Fáil outflanked Labour; if Fianna Fáil could sharpen the edge of its perceived radicalism by raising the republican flag, so much the better; but it was not the 'green card' played by Fianna Fáil which sealed Labour's fate; it was the failure of Labour to play even a 'pink card'; it was the failure of Labour to play any card at all.

Before long, Labour was implicitly accepting a subaltern position *vis-à-vis* Fianna Fáil (as opposed to Cumann na nGaedheal). In November 1927 Johnson was quoted as saying: 'at the last election Labour was said to have suffered defeat. It is not defeat to have the cause one espouses carried far forward towards accomplishment.

[128] Gaughan, *Thomas Johnson*, 294.
[129] E. G. McKay, 'The Irish Labour Party, 1927–1933', MA thesis (Dublin, 1983), 3.
[130] NLI Johnson Papers MS 17170.   [131] Dáil Debates, 24 Nov. 1927.

Half of the Dáil is now committed to this cause.' Well might it be said that 'there is a strong identification [here] of Labour with Fianna Fáil. It was as if a Fianna Fáil victory was a Labour victory and indeed not a few would in the future make such an equation.'[132] The 1926 Labour Party conference had already called upon 'the Irish people to support the move for the development of Irish industry by purchasing on all occasions Irish made goods which are produced under fair conditions'[133]—a weakly qualified endorsement of Fianna Fáil policy.

One is left wondering to what extent even Labour's cautious advocacy of social reforms during the late 1920s was shaped and conditioned by the pace set by the elaboration of the Fianna Fáil strategy and programme for government: it would not do, after all, to be seen to be lagging behind 'the cause one espouses'. Perhaps this is unfair to the Labour leaders; it is certainly not meant to imply that they were indifferent to the plight of workers and labourers. But Labour's preoccupation with the need to establish its respectability raises the possibility that, if not forced to keep pace with Fianna Fáil on the economic and social front, it might well have been totally carried away by the anti-communist hysteria unleashed by Cumann na nGaedheal in a last-minute attempt to snatch victory from defeat in 1932. Banta has pointed out that in July 1929—even before Cumann na nGaedheal's anti-communist crusade had got fully under way—Labour was denouncing the Irish Labour Defence League as 'having all the clumsy hall-marks of communist activity inspired from abroad'.[134]

Labour's leaders had been left politically and psychologically predisposed towards anti-communism by the upheaval within both the party and the trade unions during the mid-1920s, as a result of the bitter conflict with James Larkin and the left. Larkin and his supporters had reacted to the perceived opportunism of the Labour leadership with a personalized bitterness which is certainly not exclusively Irish, but which is not exactly foreign to the national character either. Physical scuffles between rival groups; clashes between the right-wing ITGWU and the left-wing Workers' Union of Ireland (WUI), over which union had the right to organize where—the WUI spoke of the 'rank treachery and organized

---

[132] McKay, 'The Irish Labour Party', 7.   [133] Ibid. 10.
[134] M. Banta, 'The Red Scare in the Irish Free State, 1929–37', MA thesis (Dublin, 1982), 6.

scabbery of the ITGWU', which, in turn, poured contempt on 'the Larkin family organization';[135] near riots on occasion at Labour conferences; attacks upon Johnson as an 'Englishman' and an 'agent of the English government'; and libel suits: all had left their mark upon the Labour establishment's view of rank-and-file agitation. As Cumann na nGaedheal unleashed anti-communism in the run-up to the 1932 election, the Labour leaders were complaining anxiously of 'the communist-infested group led by Peadar O'Donnell, Seán MacBride, and one or two others'.[136]

I will return to this point, and other of Labour's problems, when I trace general political developments in the period, 1926–32. The point to be made here is that not only did Labour's lack of a 'coherent ideology' result in its failure to develop an economic and social programme which aimed at the 'total reconstruction of society'; but the Labour leaders' obsession with the perceived fragility of their own position and the need for social stability deprived them even of the ability adequately to respond to weaknesses in the economic strategies of their opponents. Labour, for example, looked helplessly on as its support among farm labourers was squeezed by both Fianna Fáil and Cumann na nGaedheal: those labourers who hoped for land turned to the former, while those who perceived in the Fianna Fáil programme a threat to the big farms on which they were employed turned to the latter.[137] As far as the urban working class was concerned, Labour was reduced to advocating a pale version of Fianna Fáil's policies, tentatively pointing out the dangers inherent in protection without disputing the basic strategy.

FRAMING THE QUESTION: THE IDEOLOGICAL PRESENTATION OF THE FIANNA FÁIL PROGRAMME

The Irish petty bourgeoisie is fairly mixed, including artisans, small traders, and small-scale industrial enterprises.[138] In the sense used here, the term includes small farmers. Peillon points out that, lacking a 'social project'—what might be called an aspiration to

---

[135] NLI O'Brien Papers MS 15677.

[136] Johnson to Mortished, Assistant General Secretary of the Labour Party, on 1 Nov. 1931, quoted in Gaughan, *Thomas Johnson*, 471–4.

[137] Mair, 'Labour and the Irish Party System Revisited', 66; Garvin, *The Evolution of Irish Nationalist Politics*, 167.   [138] Peillon, *Contemporary Irish Society*, 27.

economic and political hegemony—these groups tend to be float-
ing voters and hence electorally vital. 'More subject to ideological
manipulation than the more powerful social forces, they are also
more inclined to be more moderate in their political views.'[139] During
the period under examination, sections, at least, of the Irish petty
bourgeoisie did possess a 'social project': to displace the old export-
orientated bourgeoisie as the economically dominant class; but
Peillon's point remains important.

It must be further remembered that the ideological concerns of
the petty bourgeoisie—stability, frugality, security, reward, concern
with the family and with property and inheritance, religion, patriotism—enjoyed a widespread appeal. The working class was numerically weak and working-class ideology was even weaker. The
export-orientated bourgeoisie had been compromised, ideologically
as well as politically, by its association with England. There is no
doubt that the Irish nationalist movement produced strong
integrationist tendencies which facilitated the spread of petty-
bourgeois ideological concerns, not least in its emphasis upon property ownership, and in the idealization of the 'Homestead' and the
'Nation'. Moreover, the partition of the country, resulting in a near-
monolithic religious and ethnic identity, further encouraged
integrationist ideologies.

We have seen how the Fianna Fáil programme aimed at the
diffusion of property ownership; ideologically, this was portrayed
as the creation of a nation of small property owners, each family
with its stake in the country. Propaganda in favour of the small
business was forthcoming from a number of sources during the
late 1920s and early 1930s. Roosevelt, in the United States, posed
as the champion of the small farmers ruined by the Depression,
and the *Irish Press* carried numerous reports of his battles with the
banks and the large industrial concerns. Gandhi's struggle against
British colonialism was also played up by Fianna Fáil propaganda.
Roosevelt's success and UK industry's failure were used by Fianna
Fáil to reinforce the notion that 'small is beautiful'. The marked
conservatism of the small trader or producer has often been the
subject of comment. Peillon notes that the success of the small
business enterprise, depending as it does to a large extent upon
personal contact, induces a tendency to conform and to seek social

[139] Ibid. 132.

respectability and acceptability.[140] The world of the petty bourgeois is one in which the threat of economic ruin is constant, and de Valera was probably influenced by the need to reassure this longing for security and stability when he declared that 'the sinister design of aiming to bring about a sudden revolutionary upheaval, with which our opponents choose to credit us, is altogether foreign to our purpose and programme'.[141] We have, moreover, noted the emphasis which Fianna Fáil propaganda placed upon security on the eve of the 1932 election.

The insecurity experienced by the petty bourgeoisie also induces a strong hostility to competition; herein lie the roots of what was earlier described as the tendency towards 'status quo "anti-capitalism" '. Here, too, is the source of the strong emphasis upon 'reward' according to 'work', and not simply 'market value', and the hostility towards the 'idle rich', which frequently cloaks feelings of jealousy; for the aim of the petty bourgeois, in so far as he has a social project, must be precisely to join the ranks of the 'idle rich'— having got there through sheer hard work, of course. Those who succeed find that the idealization of their 'hard work' and 'simple virtues' serves to legitimize and rationalize their newly acquired privilege; those who do not, content themselves with their 'moral superiority'. Petty-bourgeois ideological traits do not necessarily decline in significance with the mutation of the petty bourgeoisie.

Daly has commented upon the 'strong anti-competition mentality' of native industrialists, and we have seen the care taken by Fianna Fáil to promise protection against alleged unfair competition.[142] This often went hand in hand with attacks upon the 'capitalists' and the idealization of petty-bourgeois strata as 'the men of no property', 'the plain people', 'the common people', 'the masses'. This, too, embraced a strong hostility to the notion of class—class was the hallmark of the Anglo-Irish ascendancy alone.

A number of examples will suffice to illustrate this point. De Valera had told his supporters that 'the Top Hats may have to be done away with' and Seán T. O'Kelly had declared that 'Fianna Fáil's policy was the policy of the plain people. It was opposed to the ascendance of capitalism.'[143] Indeed, as late as 1938, Fianna Fáil was denouncing the 'capitalist traditions left behind by Britain'.[144]

---

[140] Peillon, 26. [141] Longford and O'Neill, *Eamon de Valera*, 261.
[142] Daly, 'An "Irish Ireland" for Business?', 272. [143] *Irish Press*, 12 Jan. 1932.
[144] Ibid., 13 June 1938.

Lemass, tackled during the debate on the 1930 Finance Bill about his criticism of millionaires, had explained that he had nothing in principle against millionaires, but was concerned with the 'plain, good, honest-to-God working men whose interests were neglected when this budget was framed'. Perhaps most effective of all was a Fianna Fáil advertisement during the 1932 election campaign, entitled 'Government by the Rich and for the Rich'. It featured a two-headed Cumann na nGaedheal business man saying to a poor woman, 'I have nothing for you, my good woman, the country can't afford it', and to a well-dressed man, receiving money, 'This is to help you rear your family, my poor man'. Underneath was the punch line—'The Masses and the Classes'.

The concept of the 'pro-British classes' was a device by which petty-bourgeois resentment, ambition, and jealousy, and working-class desperation and bitterness, could be directed against the small export-orientated section of the bourgeoisie, whose destruction was perceived as a precondition for the emergence of the 'small man' as the dominant force in the nation. It was also a useful device by which Fianna Fáil's opponents, already accused of being puppets of the Unionists and the Freemasons, could be isolated from the 'mass of the people' and denounced as 'the Imperialist Party'.[145]

Fianna Fáil's appeals to the working class must be seen in this light. The notion of the working class as a social group with distinct interests was effectively denied; instead, the working class was subsumed within the concept of the 'plain people of Ireland', with interests which were essentially indistinguishable from the small farmers, traders, and domestic bourgeoisie who were in many cases their employers. The Ireland which would be reconstructed under the leadership of the national bourgeoisie would be a classless one. It is in this context that we must understand comments of Fianna Fáil speakers, such as Seamus Moore, TD, who declared that 'if there was a party which realised the rights of Labour and was determined to give Labour a fair chance it was the Fianna Fáil party';[146] or Paddy Smith, TD, who told supporters in Cavan a few months later that the policy of Fianna Fáil was designed absolutely in the people's interests: 'they did not want class warfare, but if there was a clash of interests they would be on the side of the poor

---

[145] Longford and O'Neill, *Eamon de Valera*, 251.
[146] *Irish Press*, 23 Nov. 1931.

man, realising that the small farmers and the town worker were the men who bore the brunt of the fighting and were the real producers of wealth.'[147]

The real effect of such apparently radical rhetoric was not to raise class awareness, but to channel working-class protest in the direction of a model of economic development which rested upon the strengthening of native capitalism. In a similar way, the concepts of the 'pro-British classes' and 'the plain people' were used to shape, legitimize, and limit democratic reforms such as the abolition of the Senate and of the property franchise at local-government elections.

The concern with frugality and meritocracy was a constant theme behind Fianna Fáil attacks upon the alleged extravagance and waste of Cumann na nGaedheal. Lemass declared in December 1931 that 'Fianna Fáil had gone through the various estimates for Government departments and had come to the conclusion that it was possible to maintain the Government services at the present level and even with increased efficiency at a total cost of about two millions less than the present one'.[148]

Fianna Fáil propaganda in 1932 promised to 'end the reckless extravagance of the Free State Government'. Land annuities would remain in the Irish Treasury and would go to lessen taxation: 'with that money they could almost completely derate agricultural holdings.' Farmers, it was added, were burdened with too heavy overhead charges. At the 1931 *Ard-Fheis*, de Valera had attacked the political patronage of the Government and had accused it of wasting taxpayers' money on the army.[149] An all-out attack was launched on Government pensions and gratuities to ex-Free State army men. This was coupled with a promise to review all salaries over £1,000 per annum in the public service. Such a discourse appealed to a petty-bourgeois hostility towards the public service, perceived as parasitical. This was not without its contradictions, for the public service was often the only source of employment available to the children of the Irish petty bourgeoisie.[150]

---

[147] *Irish Press*, 2 Jan. 1932.

[148] Ibid., 7 Dec. 1931.   [149] *Cork Examiner*, 29 Oct. 1931.

[150] See Andrews, *Man of No Property*, 97, 119. The author comments sarcastically on the life style of state technocrats such as those employed on the Shannon Scheme: 'smoked salmon became the symbol of the risen people'; and he adds that 'we in Fianna Fáil regarded all senior civil servants as a "crowd of Free State bastards"'.

There was another facet to this exploitation of petty-bourgeois hostility to bureaucracy and 'waste'—a demagogic attack upon the alleged Cumann na nGaedheal policy of centralization and the erosion of the powers of local authorities. Fianna Fáil accused Cumann na nGaedheal of using enormous concentration of power at the centre for 'the gift of political patronage and favouritism', and attacked as undemocratic the dismissal of local representatives. O'Kelly promised that Fianna Fáil would oppose every attempt towards 'the erection of dictatorship in local government affairs' and that Fianna Fáil policy was 'definitely hostile to the concentration of all power over local affairs in the hands of a central authority'.[151]

O'Crualaoich points out that the obsession with frugality and the elimination of material waste stands in sharp contrast to the avaricious reality of much of Irish life, as exposed by realist writers of the time, and poses the question: why, then, did this type of discourse have such appeal? His answer is enlightening: this aspect of the Fianna Fáil discourse was

peculiarly suited to a time and place where the idea prevails that a hitherto exploited and depressed peasantry is at last in the position of being able to appoint the individuals who will form its government. Surely, it is implied, self-sufficiency will be the lot of a people whose thrift and self-restraint had previously been cruelly traded on by a hated ascendancy, but who are now largely in control of their own destiny, and who live in a society where class differences are officially non-existent.[152]

Prager has produced an admirable analysis of the social and cultural basis of the party's appeal:

Fianna Fáil's vision was unequivocally Romantic. It celebrated that uniquely puritanical variant of Irish Catholicism by emphasising that Ireland could not live beyond its means. The aim, Fianna Fáil insisted, was to develop a self-sufficient Ireland neither dependent on any other nation nor expectant of a rich, luxurious life. The vision was of the rural, frugal, family-oriented Catholic society, cognizant of its limits and not envious of the wealth or economic security of other modern Nations. It was an image decisively anti-bourgeois.[153]

---

[151] Reynolds, 'The Formation and Development of Fianna Fáil', 221.
[152] G. O'Crualaoich, 'The Primacy of Form: Folk Ideology in de Valera's Politics', in J. A. Murphy and J. O'Carroll (eds.), *De Valera and his Times* (Cork, 1983), 51.
[153] Prager, *Building Democracy in Ireland*, 205–6.

Prager is, of course, here describing an image which was equally anti-organized labour.

Fianna Fáil's appeal included evocation of both religion and nationalism. The party portrayed itself as the custodian of the Irish nation, assiduously fostering the 'myth of the historic Irish nation'.[154] The very name, *Fianna Fáil*, was chosen with a view to the assimilation of party–state symbolism;[155] the letters FF still appeared on the badges of the Free State army, the name having been chosen originally by the Irish Volunteers. Indeed, the military-style discipline which characterized the party was sometimes suggested as a model for the nation to emulate: Major Vivion de Valera, in 1937, told the 'soldier-people of Kerry' that 'not professors, but soldiers, disciplined soldiers, are going to build up this nation . . . This is our job and we have no time for academic quibbles or lawyers' fine points.'[156]

The party was careful to emphasize that, in contrast to Cumann na nGaedheal, it was pledged to wipe out 'past dissensions'. 'Even those who have most vehemently opposed us are Irishmen like ourselves . . . we will need their help in building up the virile, prosperous Ireland of the future', declared a Fianna Fáil statement, penned by Boland and Lemass, in the late 1920s. De Valera, speaking in Waterford in December 1931, declared: 'The object of founding Fianna Fáil was to try to enable the forces that had been divided by the Treaty to come back and begin over again the forward march and to bring back those who believed the Treaty was a stepping stone to freedom.'[157] This shrewd tactical rejection of any easy recourse to political sectarianism was to pay dividends for the party; by 1932 its candidates included ex-members of Labour, National League, Cumann na nGaedheal, Clann Éireann, Sinn Féin, and the National Group—giving considerable credence to its claim to be a party of national unity. Two former Cumann na nGaedheal leaders—Father MacBrennan and J. J. Walsh—were campaigning for Fianna Fáil and two ex-Cumann na nGaedheal TDs were amongst its candidates.[158] Robert Barton, one of the signatories of the 1921 Treaty, campaigned for Fianna Fáil on the grounds that Collins and Griffith had been betrayed by the Cosgrave administration.[159]

[154] Bowman, *De Valera and the Ulster Question*, 126–7.
[155] Garvin, *The Evolution of Irish Nationalist Politics*, 154; Fanning, *Independent Ireland*, 97.   [156] *Irish Press*, 26 May 1937.
[157] *Munster Express*, 11 Dec. 1931.
[158] Reynolds, 'The Formation and Development of Fianna Fáil', 90.
[159] *Kerryman*, 21 Jan. 1933.

The integrationist effects of religion proved useful to the party. As Fanning states, de Valera sought support from countervailing forces within the Church and made no attempt to challenge its authority.[160] Those within Fianna Fáil who might have adopted a more critical attitude were quickly silenced and recalled to political realism. It was not long before O'Kelly called for prayers to be said in the Dáil and for the suspension of Dáil sittings on Church holidays; and attacked the Government over its failure to consult the Irish Catholic hierarchy before moves to establish relations with the Vatican. Indeed, this issue was very skilfully exploited by Fianna Fáil. Cumann na nGaedheal's hasty and mishandled efforts to have a papal nunciature established in Dublin—in order to confer legitimacy upon the Free State regime—alienated many of the Irish bishops, who resented the idea of a nunciature as an unwarranted Vatican intrusion in the internal affairs of the Irish hierarchy. As Keogh adds, 'de Valera and Fianna Fáil were quite capable of taking full advantage of the cooling of relations to demonstrate that they were a viable alternative to Cumann na nGaedheal'.[161] By 1932 Fianna Fáil was indignantly and unselfconsciously rebutting the charge of 'communism' which had been levelled against 'a party which has behind it over half a million Catholic voters, whose personnel is almost exclusively Catholic . . .'.[162]

The identification of Irishness with Roman Catholicism was soon to become a constant theme in de Valera's discourse. As Whyte puts it: 'This tendency to equate "Irish" and "Catholic" seems to have been special to Fianna Fáil and particularly to Mr de Valera himself. It is not so evident in the speeches of Mr Cosgrave and his colleagues in the preceding government.'[163] In 1931 de Valera not only supported the dismissal of a Mayo librarian on the grounds that she was a Protestant, but went on to recommend that Catholics only should be employed as dispensary doctors in mainly Catholic areas. Sectarian strictures, such as these, may not always have been enforced by Fianna Fáil in government; there is, however, evidence from within the party's own ranks of disquiet with sectarian conduct. Erskine Childers—one of the few Fianna Fáil politicians who came from a Protestant background—was years later to protest to

---

[160] Fanning, *Independent Ireland*, 129.
[161] Keogh, *The Vatican, the Bishops and Irish Politics*, 160.
[162] Editorial in the *Irish Press*, 1 Feb. 1932.
[163] J. Whyte, *Church and State in Modern Ireland, 1923–1970* (Dublin, 1974), 49.

Seán MacEntee about anti-Protestantism, listing suppression of Church of Ireland sex-education literature by the Fianna Fáil Government, alleged exclusion of Protestants from youth unemployment schemes, and 'a general feeling on the part of Protestants that in regard to Government appointments and the Local Authorities, they had better not apply'.[164] On another occasion, worried perhaps that his own political career would be blocked because of his religion, Childers wrote:

> Robert Barton (not to be quoted please to anyone) hinted to me that a Protestant was unlikely to be appointed to the Ministries of Justice, Health, External Affairs, Education, and probably Social Welfare . . . I cannot believe it but others in Fianna Fáil have hinted at this and I should be glad to know the truth.[165]

The party did not hesitate to reap whatever political capital it could by playing the Catholic card, particularly as its opponents' opposition to such a stance could be held against them as further evidence of their 'Unionist', 'Freemason' or (in the case of the left) 'communist' sympathies.

Fianna Fáil understood that an essential part of any successful ideological discourse is the shaping and conditioning of what is popularly perceived to be possible as well as desirable. This, in turn, involves rendering rival discourses either ridiculously irrelevant and illusionary, or causing such confusion as to render such discourses literally meaningless. Among the ideological terms of potential rivals which Fianna Fáil undermined was the label 'socialist'. Todd Andrews, for example, had no bother in referring to himself, and Seán Lemass, and even the women of Cumann na mBan, as 'socialists'. In 1969 Brian Lenihan, TD, described Fianna Fáil as 'the party of practical socialism'.[166] And in 1972 Fianna Fáil leader Jack Lynch declared in a radio interview that he was a convinced socialist.[167] De Valera himself, in 1975, in one of the last interviews given before his death, declared: 'in those days, I believe we could be called socialists, but not communists.'[168] Of course, such statements may reflect a genuine confusion on the part of

---

[164] Undated letter to MacEntee, probably c.1945 (UCDA MacEntee Papers P67/269).   [165] Letter dated 11 Feb. 1948 (UCDA MacEntee Papers P67/298).
[166] Quoted in Gallagher, *Political Parties in the Republic of Ireland*, 27.
[167] Quoted in T. Gallagher, 'The Dimensions of Fianna Fáil Rule in Ireland', 66.
[168] Quoted in Mair, *The Changing Irish Party System*, 17.

Fianna Fáil politicians as to what constitutes socialism. On occasion, however, the tactical use of such language has induced a sense of bewilderment, confusion, and cynicism in the general public; and seduced some of Fianna Fáil's opponents, through manipulation of their wishful thinking and capacity for self-deception, whilst forcing others more on the defensive than ever.[169]

POLITICAL DEVELOPMENTS 1926–32

The sequence of events surrounding Fianna Fáil's Dáil entrance is well known, and a brief summary will suffice. From its launch, Fianna Fáil was committed to taking its Dáil seats if the oath of allegiance was removed. In the general election of June 1927 the party scored 26.1 per cent of the vote—an encouragement, perhaps, but no improvement on the old Sinn Féin vote; the rump of Sinn Féin was decimated in the June election, polling 3.6 per cent and dropping out of electoral politics thereafter.

Concurrent with the elaboration of its programme, the search for a means of circumventing the oath began. Impatience was clearly mounting within the party. Shortly after the June election, two TDs broke ranks and took their seats as independent republicans; it has been suggested that the tendency of Fianna Fáil to rewrite the history of the Treaty debates which preceded the civil war so as to exaggerate the importance of the partition question was an attempt to use partition to 'wriggle off the hook of the "oath"'.[170] An opportunity was presented by the assassination of hardline cabinet minister Kevin O'Higgins in July 1927. Although de Valera strongly condemned the murder, Cumann na nGaedheal, apparently convinced that Fianna Fáil's parliamentary abstention contributed to an atmosphere in which such murders took place, coupled a new Public Safety Act against the IRA (including special 'death penalty courts'[171]) with an Electoral Amendment Bill aimed at Fianna Fáil. This measure entailed that deputies would forfeit seats not taken within two months. Fianna Fáil, who had earlier been refused Dáil entry because of their refusal to take the oath, and had been involved in efforts to raise a petition (in accordance with the Free

---

[169] See H. Patterson, 'Fianna Fáil and the Working Class: The Origins of the Enigmatic Relationship', *Saothar*, 13 (1988), for a succinct and important discussion of this point.　　　[170] Lee and O'Tuathaigh, *The Age of de Valera*, 96.
[171] Lyons, *Ireland since the Famine*, 498.

State Constitution) to have the oath abolished, now realized that it had to act fast. With what must have been a certain relief as well as a lot of heart-searching, the 'oath' became 'an empty formula' and de Valera led his party into the Dáil on 11 August 1927.

Fianna Fáil's presence in the Dáil certainly transformed the political situation. In the first place, Cumann na nGaedheal was deprived of the comfortable majority it had enjoyed and was forced closer than ever to the smaller bourgeois groupings: the Farmers' Party, representing the interests of the large farmers, had polled 8.9 per cent and won eleven seats in June; the National League, representing largely remnants of the old Irish parliamentary party, had polled 7.3 per cent with eight seats; and independents had polled 12.8 per cent and won fourteen seats. This last group was composed in the main of ex-Unionists and included many representatives of the financial bourgeoisie.

In the second place, Fianna Fáil's presence inside parliament undoubtedly had a polarizing effect. For the first time, a real and realistic political and economic alternative was present. Supporters of the smaller bourgeois groupings began to rally to Cumann na nGaedheal, as did some Labour Party voters; Mair suggests that it was not until 1932 that Labour voters moved to Fianna Fáil.[172] I have already noted the reasons for this: the Labour Party's obsession with stability both attracted pro-Treaty support and encouraged Labour supporters to regard defence of the political status quo as defence of a framework for progress; and Labour's support among farm labourers left it vulnerable to the clash between Fianna Fáil and Cumann na nGaedheal agricultural policies—in the beginning, at least, farm labourers were likely to have reacted cautiously to any threat to their employment. Fianna Fáil, meanwhile, could hope to win growing support from those who had regarded its position in opposition as untenable—or, to put it another way, to capture some of the 'pro-Treaty, pro-republican' vote which Cumann na nGaedheal had enjoyed; and to mobilize voters who had not bothered to vote before, including many urban workers. The smaller parties were further adversely affected by financial and organizational difficulties, although this is more likely to have affected Labour than the Farmers or independents; Labour's fund-raising

---

[172] Mair, 'Labour and the Irish Party System Revisited', 66.

campaign netted only £1,200 in 1927 and it found itself able to nominate only twenty-eight candidates in September compared to forty-five in June.[173]

In September Cosgrave's Government, its majority now reduced to a solitary vote, went to the polls again. With the turn-out increased slightly, Fianna Fáil went up from 26.1 per cent to 35.2 per cent; Labour declined from 12.6 per cent to 9.1 per cent; Cumann na nGaedheal soared from 27.4 per cent to 38.7 per cent, as the smaller bourgeois groupings—Farmers, National League, and independents—fell to 6.4 per cent, 1.6 per cent, and 8.0 per cent respectively. But the fact that both Fianna Fáil and Cumann na nGaedheal had secured substantial increases in their vote, eating into the middle ground, should not lead us to conceive wrongly that the balance of forces was potentially favourable to both; Fianna Fáil was on the offensive, conquering new ground, Cumann na nGaedheal was on the defensive, absorbing its allies.

During the period 1927–32 Labour's position worsened considerably. This was not simply to be reflected in Labour losses to Fianna Fáil in the general election of 1932; it is also reflected, indeed more forcefully so, in Labour's failure to mobilize working-class and trade-unionist voters during the late 1920s and early 1930s; it is here that Fianna Fáil proved itself successful. By 1932 the turn-out had risen to 75.4 per cent (from 66.5 per cent in June 1927). It was Fianna Fáil alone which benefited from this electoral mobilization, above all in Dublin. Instrumental in winning working-class support for the party in Dublin was Lemass, who, *inter alia*, courted the trade-union movement, combining a 'warm, cooperative approach to the trade union movement with a steely approach to the Labour Party'.[174] Lemass was insistent upon hammering home the point that Labour was incapable of offering strong opposition to Cumann na nGaedheal policies. 'I think you should make reference', he wrote to Frank Gallagher of Fianna Fáil headquarters staff on 16 August 1929,

to the fact that on practically every occasion on which the Government was in difficulties since we went into the Dáil and a tight division was imminent, members of the Labour Party left the house so as not to defeat

---

[173] Gaughan, *Thomas Johnson*, 321.
[174] C. McCarthy, *Trade Unions in Ireland, 1894–1960* (Dublin, 1977), 245.

the Government. On the occasion of many divisions I have seen members of the Labour Party sitting in the Public Gallery while the voting was going on and returning to the house after the announcement of the result was made. They have saved the Government repeatedly in this way.[175]

Whether or not Lemass's comments are accurate, his concentration upon the timidity of Labour politics is interesting. I have dealt with some of the underlying reasons for this state of affairs; however, the weaknesses in Labour's political presentation during this period require further attention.

As Hazelkorn has argued, the Labour Party opted during the 1920s to 'substitute the political project of labour for the priorities of nationalism', and was 'essentially unable to differentiate itself from other class and political interests'.[176] Labour's assimilation to nationalism may well have been facilitated by a Connollyist rhetoric which linked social and national revolution, but the party leadership was soon articulating a deeply conservative message of 'social unity' rather than radical social change, not to mention class struggle.

The argument that there was *no* potential for radical socialist politics during this period, and that Labour's acceptance of a subaltern political position was somehow inevitable or fatally conditioned by its marginalization during the period of the independence struggle, is not sustained by the evidence. The period was one of often intense industrial agitation, which extended right into the early 1930s despite the defeats suffered in 1923–4 and the fragmentation of the trade unions. There was a big lock-out of building workers in the spring of 1931, and militant miners, organized by the communist-led Irish Miners', Quarrymen's, and Allied Workers' Union, won their struggle for improved wages and working conditions at mines at Castlecomer, County Kilkenny, in the early 1930s. Moreover, even at the electoral level, there was some evidence of potential for radical socialist policies. The Irish Worker League (IWL), founded by Larkin as the Irish section of the Communist International, contested the general election of September 1927 with three candidates. Larkin was himself elected to the Dáil in north Dublin with over 8,000 votes. (He was subsequently unseated as an undischarged bankrupt following a move against him by the

---

[175] NLI Gallagher Papers MS 18339.
[176] E. Hazelkorn, 'Why is there no Socialism in Ireland?—Theoretical Problems of Irish Marxism', *Science and Society*, 53/2 (1989), 152–9.

Labour Party.) His son, James junior, polled 2,126 votes in Dublin county and, as only 10 per cent of these transferred to Labour, he cost the Labour leader, Thomas Johnson, his seat in the Dáil. The IWL candidate in Dublin south, John Lawlor, got over 2,500 votes. This was a respectable vote for the small Marxist party—1.1 per cent of the total national poll despite having just the three candidates. Equally impressive was the radical left vote in the elections to Dublin city council in 1930. The IWL ran twelve candidates—and secured a seat, with Larkin senior elected for north Dublin. The even more militant Revolutionary Workers' Groups (RWG)—formed, it seems, because they considered Larkin too reformist—ran two candidates and saw one of them elected with almost 1,000 votes. This fact must be set against the undemocratic nature of the local-government franchise; Lyons reports that, with a rates qualification to the value of £10, 20 per cent of the electorate was disenfranchised in 1929.[177] Moreover, the election of two revolutionary Marxists to Dublin city council contrasts not so unfavourably with the three seats secured by Labour and the five seats won by Fianna Fáil. This relatively promising electoral base in the capital was complemented by the existence of the WUI, founded in 1924 and affiliated to the communist Red International of Trade Unions; although it was largely confined to Dublin, it did enlist some 16,000 members in the capital.

Of course, the radical left was a small minority; but it was not very much weaker than the Labour Party itself was rapidly becoming. If Labour, as a whole, had adopted a more militant position, it might well have been better placed to exploit the weaknesses in Fianna Fáil's strategy; and it might have been able to exercise a unifying and clarifying influence upon those left-wing republicans who were struggling—ultimately unsuccessfully—to free themselves from the limitations of republicanism.

Labour, however, continued to decline, and the Marxist groups—isolated, vilified, and soon to be legally suppressed—declined along with it. Johnson's defeat in the election of September 1927, far from causing Labour to embark upon soul-searching, simply threw it into greater confusion than ever. His 'loss', reports Donal Nevin, was 'severely felt'.[178] The Labour Party had concentrated upon

[177] Lyons, *Ireland since the Famine*, 483.
[178] D. Nevin, 'Labour and the Political Revolution', in McManus (ed.), *The Years of the Great Test*, 57.

perfecting its image as a party of active, hard-working, concerned statesmen—and now it had lost the most hard-working and respected statesman it possessed. His successor, T. J. O'Connell, had little new to offer. Labour was less inclined than ever to grant a hearing to the radicalism of those who had cost Johnson his seat.

Within the trade-union movement, the weaknesses of the official Labour position were, if anything, more evident. Lyons writes that after the defeat of the Larkinites there was 'a decisive turn to the right'—with no place for a socialist programme. 'The practical consequence of the turn to the right was that the Labour movement as a whole failed to offer a credible alternative to the middle-class, conservative regime inaugurated by Mr Cosgrave and his colleagues.'[179] Split, and weakened in times of severe economic recession, the unions continued to decline; with the expulsion of the WUI from the Irish Trades Union Congress (ITUC), and the loss of members due to the recession, the total membership of the Congress fell to under 100,000 (north and south combined) in 1929—it had been twice that in 1922; union funds fell to £78,000 in 1929 from £184,000 in 1923. Meanwhile, the leadership of the ITGWU, under William O'Brien, inflicted further damage on the labour movement in 1928–9 as it attempted by the use of divisive tactics to increase its influence upon the parliamentary Labour Party at the expense of other (moderate-led) unions.[180] The Labour Party's decision in 1930 to opt for a formal break with the unions, ostensibly to jettison a narrow class base and facilitate its transformation into a mass catch-all party which could compete with Cumann na nGaedheal and Fianna Fáil, cleared the way for Fianna Fáil to penetrate the union movement. Indeed, only a minority of Irish trade unionists has ever been won to vote for Labour.

'Strictly speaking', wrote Thomas Johnson to Labour Chairman Luke Duffy in October 1928, 'there was not a Labour Party in the Saorstát [Free State] because, of the party's thirteen TDs and five Senators, no two of them would agree even on fundamentals.' Two Labour TDs, Anthony and Morrissey, were actually expelled from the party in 1931 for voting in favour of the repressive, anti-communist, and anti-IRA legislation introduced by Cumann na nGaedheal, including the establishment of military tribunals. More

---

[179] Lyons, *Ireland since the Famine*, 676.
[180] Gaughan, *Thomas Johnson*, 329.

than the two expelled were, apparently, in favour of the legislation. The party was now on the verge of internal chaos and was clutching at straws. Small wonder, then, that Labour leaders such as Johnson and William Norton, who had offered to join Cumann na nGaedheal in a 'national coalition' in 1927, were by 1932 'strong advocates of the informal coalition with Fianna Fáil'.[181] On 13 February 1932 the Labour paper, the *Watchword*, told its readers that 'we agree with the mass opinion that Fianna Fáil should get its chance now'. Labour thus ceased to be a political threat to Fianna Fáil and also lost pro-Government preferences by announcing in advance that it would put Cumann na nGaedheal out of office.[182]

Fianna Fáil, meanwhile, was warding off potential challenges on another front. Immediately after the party's formation de Valera had been careful not to alienate the republicans who had refused to join him, referring to them as 'the left-wing of the republican forces'.[183] By the early 1930s his strategy was to distance the party from the extreme republican groups in the public eye, while, at the same time, keeping sufficiently close to the IRA and other groups, at least informally, to avoid an outright break. The first aim was necessary for two reasons: IRA violence, with the possibility that it might spark off a new civil war, was clearly not a vote winner; while the radical socialist policies of some of the left-wing republicans, from about 1929 onwards, went further than Fianna Fáil was willing, or able, to contemplate and thus rendered them unwelcome bedfellows. The second aim was necessitated not least to avoid internal party turmoil; many Fianna Fáil members still felt a great deal of emotional sympathy with the IRA and the smaller republican groupings. Perhaps, moreover, Fianna Fáil hoped to absorb some of the IRA militants and to set limits to the leftwards swing of other republican organizations. Farrell suggests that Lemass's rhetoric about breaking the tradition of Irish capitalists investing abroad may have been aimed at winning support from Saor Éire.[184]

The IRA was active again from 1926, involving itself in attacks

---

[181] Ibid. 327, 339, 342. Indeed, Labour had also had talks with Fianna Fáil in 1927 about the possibility of the latter forming a government (see Hazelkorn, 'Why is there no Socialism in Ireland?', 150).

[182] Reynolds, 'The Formation and Development of Fianna Fáil', 365.

[183] Quoted in Bowman, *De Valera and the Ulster Question*, 94.

[184] Farrell, *Seán Lemass*, 30.

against the *Gardaí*. From 1929 social discontent swelled its ranks, and under the influence of leaders such as Peadar O'Donnell it began, in a confused and uncertain way, to move to the left. A measure of IRA influence at this time is that in 1929 its weekly paper, *An Phoblacht*, sold 8,000 copies while the Fianna Fáil weekly, the *Nation*, stood at 6,000.[185] In June 1931 IRA chief of staff Maurice Twomey was writing to Irish-American backer Joe McGarrity in enthusiastic terms about 'the extraordinary growth of the Volunteer Movement'.[186] (Six months later, however, he was admitting that recruitment had suffered a setback from Government repression.) In 1932 the IRA ran its own campaign during the election with the slogan 'Put Cosgrave Out'. This was clearly a tacit, if not an open, endorsement of Fianna Fáil.

The IRA was not the only extreme republican organization active at this time. In September 1931 Saor Éire was formally and publicly launched at a conference attended by over 150 delegates. Saor Éire was 'an open Republican organization with a radical social and political programme' which advocated widespread changes in the structure of Irish society, including nationalization of the banks and financial institutions. Saor Éire was not a military organization; there is no evidence that it ever engaged, as an organization, in violence. Many of its members undoubtedly supported those who did, and may have helped them; but then many members of Fianna Fáil may have felt much the same.

Fianna Fáil aimed to keep the 'left-wing of the republican forces' at arm's length: not too far to alienate them, not too close to incur any danger. The first sign of this approach came in the run-up to the June 1927 general election, when the IRA Army Council sought to get Sinn Féin and Fianna Fáil to agree on a panel of candidates; each candidate would take a pledge not to take the oath of allegiance. Fianna Fáil, not surprisingly, found this and other clauses unacceptable and the move came to nothing. In the September 1927 election Fianna Fáil put further distance between itself and the IRA, repudiating the latter's stance on partition. A Fianna Fáil election advertisement ran as follows: 'What Fianna Fáil Does Not Stand For: Attacking the North East: Fianna Fáil does not stand for attacking "Ulster". It will accept EXISTING REALITIES, but will work resolutely to bring partition to an end.'[187]

---

[185] Cronin, *The McGarrity Papers*, 150.   [186] NLI McGarrity Papers MS 17490.
[187] Quoted in Fanning, *Independent Ireland*, 137 (emphasis in original).

The IRA, and many within Fianna Fáil, were, however, given an assurance that it was a 'fact' and not a 'principle' that force would not work. It is in this context that Lemass's oft-quoted remark about Fianna Fáil being a 'slightly constitutional party' must be seen. Obviously, this is not to suggest that many people within Fianna Fáil, including many of its leaders, did not sincerely hold this position; simply that the position was dictated by the political necessities which the party faced.

At the 1929 Fianna Fáil *Ard-Fheis*, 'the Republic' was absent from the agenda for the first time, and at the 1931 *Ard-Fheis* de Valera repeated his condemnation of violence. At this *Ard-Fheis* numerous rank-and-file Fianna Fáil delegates voiced their sympathy with the IRA. One delegate declared that 'these men [the IRA] are alright; they have our sympathy'. Others insisted on the 'moral right' of the IRA.[188] De Valera, however, laid down the authoritative party line when he told the *Ard-Fheis*:

With regard to partition, I see no solution of that problem. Force is out of the question. Were it feasible, it could not be desirable. The only hope that I can see now for the re-union of our country is good government in the twenty-six counties, and such social and economic conditions here as will attract the majority in the six counties to throw in their lot with us.

'The Republic', once again, did not feature at all in the Fianna Fáil 1932 election manifesto and there was little emphasis placed on partition.

As far as the socialist inclinations of Saor Éire and the IRA left were concerned, the electorate was reassured that arms dumped after the civil war were never intended for 'class warfare or for civil war' and that 'if all came to all, I was a Catholic first'.[189] Indeed, Cumann na nGaedheal's charge that Fianna Fáil had been contaminated by 'communism' was not only easily rebutted; Fianna Fáil showed itself as concerned—and more realistically so—with the alleged danger as was Cumann na nGaedheal: the draft 'Economic Plan for the Free State' produced from within the party in 1932 justified expansion of the money supply on the grounds that 'it follows that if we can give them [the people] sufficient money to purchase such product we shall destroy for ever the desire to flirt with Communism'. De Valera could with confidence and sincerity

[188] *Irish Independent*, 28 Oct. 1931.
[189] De Valera, quoted in *Irish Press*, 29 Oct. 1931.

assure the Dáil that Fianna Fáil agreed entirely with the Government in opposing communism, and that

the right of private property is accepted as fundamental, and, as far as Catholics are concerned, there has been a definite teaching upon it ... There is nobody on these benches but is just as anxious as the people opposite that these principles will be the ruling principles as far as our own social organizations here are concerned.[190]

As Keogh adds, 'philosophically, Cosgrave and de Valera were much closer together on this issue than either of them ever fully realised'.[191]

How, then, did Fianna Fáil manage to avoid an open breach in those crucial early years, not only with the IRA, but with Saor Éire? First, the involvement of many Fianna Fáil members alongside members of Saor Éire and the IRA in campaigns such as that against the payment of land annuities encouraged the republican left to exaggerate the radical potential of Fianna Fáil and the extent of their own influence upon it. Second, Fianna Fáil's fight against all the repressive legislation introduced by Cumann na nGaedheal further helped to align the militant republicans behind it—although, as we will see later, it was to make good use of such legislation when in government. The party fought the Public Safety Act of 1927 (it was repealed at the end of 1928), the Juries Protection Act of 1929, and the Public Safety Act of 1931. The party also championed the cause of republican prisoners and their families, and promised an end to discrimination against republicans. In opposing repression, Fianna Fáil was careful to stress the part played by the economic and social situation; de Valera's skilfully worded statement that 'if men are hungry, they will not be too particular about the ultimate principles of the organization they would join, if that organization promises to give them bread' could almost be read two ways—as a partial endorsement of the left organizations, and as a shrewd warning to the bourgeoisie of the potentially disastrous long-term effects of Cumann na nGaedheal policies.

The republican left was disorientated. Although Fianna Fáil was regarded with growing suspicion, it was tacitly regarded also as part of the republican family; for years, the bulk of the republican left, as well as the IRA militarist right, searched in vain for the

---

[190] Quoted in D. Keogh, 'De Valera, the Catholic Church and the "Red Scare", 1931–32', in Murphy and O'Carroll (eds.), *De Valera and his Times*, 142.
[191] Ibid. 156.

correct way to win the stray Fianna Fáil sheep back into the fold—or to rid them of their recalcitrant shepherds. The roots of the dilemma, however, lay much deeper than de Valera's tendency to compromise on 'the Republic'. Cumann na nGaedheal's resort to repression of the political left, as well as the IRA, gave Fianna Fáil the opportunity to appear more radical than it really was and, paradoxically as it may seem, simultaneously to reassure the bourgeoisie and the middle strata of its opposition to anything amounting to social revolution.

The general election of 1932 was fought against the background of an anti-communist witch-hunt. The radical left, although not insignificant in Dublin, was a tiny minority of the national electorate; and, following political suppression, the total communist vote in 1932 was a mere 5,000. It would seem that by the early 1930s the actual or potential threat to the established order from the far left was not such as adequately to explain the extent of the reaction. Why, therefore, did Cumann na nGaedheal choose to launch an offensive of this nature?

At least three possible reasons exist. First, Cumann na nGaedheal was growing increasingly desperate in the face of mounting support for Fianna Fáil. The Government's political ineptitude had contributed substantially to its inability to maintain its dominance; the 1931 budget, for example, had not only consolidated support for Fianna Fáil among strata of society already attracted by that party's appeal, but had even alienated such pillars of the Free State establishment as the army and the police. Government minister Patrick McGilligan urged holding the 1932 general election as early as possible in order to avoid further economic decline and to enable the Government to take advantage of the 'Irregular and Bolshie situation alone'.[192] Cumann na nGaedheal had played no small part in creating, or at least greatly exaggerating the extent of, the 'Irregular and Bolshie situation'.

Second, Cumann na nGaedheal found it increasingly difficult to count upon the total support of the Catholic Church as the *rapprochement* between Fianna Fáil and the Church gained momentum. It is possible that the Government was attempting to use the 'red scare' to force the Church to take a firmer stand in its favour. Certainly, Cosgrave did ask Cardinal MacRory for a 'concise

---

[192] Quoted in Fanning, *Independent Ireland*, 104.

statement' against the IRA and the left-wing organizations, and on 18 October 1931 the hierarchy issued a pastoral letter condemning Saor Éire, the IRA, and other left-wing groups as sinful and irreligious.

Third, it is possible that Cumann na nGaedheal had lost all sense of political realism, in this as in other matters. It certainly misjudged the effect of its anti-communist crusade; driven to paranoia by increased IRA activity from 1929, worried by the apparent growth of Saor Éire, and pressurized by the reports of its own spies, Cumann na nGaedheal may well have convinced itself of the reality of a 'communist threat'. The Government was, moreover, urged on by the obsessive anti-communism of its police commissioner, Eoin O'Duffy, who demanded that IRA suspects be placed 'outside the protection of a constitution . . . and . . . in a position uninfluenced by the constitutional rights of citizenship'. O'Duffy had been furious at the repeal of the Public Safety Act in 1928. He felt that the Government was too liberal, and, complaining of the lack of support for the police by the judiciary, he was soon demanding the abolition of the jury system. 'Let us make no mistake about it,' he wrote; 'from the point of view of their outlook on so-called political crime, the Irish public is rotten. Their sense of citizenship is negligible.' By now, O'Duffy was also boasting in memoranda to the Government of 'unorthodox methods' of harassment.[193]

In October 1931 the Government introduced a ferocious Public Safety Act aimed, not only against the IRA, but against virtually all left-wing political organizations. The Act 'contained virtually everything that O'Duffy had asked for'.[194] Twelve organizations were banned, including the IWL, the RWG, Saor Éire, the Working Farmers' Conference, and, of course, the IRA (Sinn Féin escaped the ban as it had opposed the IRA's move to the left).[195] Military tribunals were set up with the power to impose the death penalty. Republican journals including *An Phoblacht* were suppressed and hundreds were arrested.

The Dáil was dissolved on 29 January 1932 and the election was

---

[193] Quotations from C. Brady, 'Police and Government in the Irish Free State, 1922–1933', MA thesis (Dublin, 1977), ch. 7, pp. 12–20.

[194] Ibid., ch. 7, p. 38.

[195] J. P. McHugh, 'Voices of the Rearguard: A Study of "An Phoblacht": Irish Republican Thought in the Post-Revolutionary Era, 1923–1937', MA thesis (Dublin, 1983), 134.

fixed for 16 February. Cumann na nGaedheal fought entirely on the basis of law and order and the 'communist threat'. The real target, however, was not communists but Fianna Fáil. De Valera was portrayed as a Kerensky-type figure—a front man for the gunmen and the communists. Cumann na nGaedheal newspaper advertisements warned the electorate that voting for Fianna Fáil meant the release from prison of communists and terrorists and posed the question: 'How will you vote tomorrow? The gunmen are voting for Fianna Fáil. The communists are voting for Fianna Fáil.' Party election posters showed the red flag superimposed upon an Irish tricolour and bore the legend, 'We want no Reds here. Keep their colour off your Flag.' Cumann na nGaedheal propaganda accused Fianna Fáil of tending 'more and more towards State Control of Industry and Agriculture' and singled out for attack that party's plans for a Wheat Control Board, a National Housing Board, and the nationalization of transport (which Fianna Fáil never promised)—in other words, practical measures which held considerable appeal for different social strata. Charges that Fianna Fáil would impose a land tax or deprive the farmer of his land were firmly answered by de Valera, as already noted.

Coupled with this were increasingly authoritarian and anti-democratic pronouncements which must have alienated at least some of the middle strata. Justice Minister Fitzgerald-Kenny warned of a greater civil war than ever if Fianna Fáil won the election. As Cumann na nGaedheal propaganda portrayed de Valera as a virtual gunman, the *Irish Press* was dragged before the military tribunals on charges of libel—it had countered with accusations of Freemason and Unionist involvement in Cumann na nGaedheal. The Cumann na nGaedheal periodical, the *Star*, hinted at the possibility of an army mutiny against a Fianna Fáil government[196] and O'Duffy openly contemplated the use of extra-constitutional means, involving dissident army and police elements.

Not only did the charges of communism against Fianna Fáil appear wide of the mark, but the hysterical reaction of Cumann na nGaedheal may have convinced some wavering voters that the real threat to the functioning of parliamentary democracy came from that party, and not Fianna Fáil. Professor Alfred O'Rahilly, who switched from Cumann na nGaedheal to Fianna Fáil in 1932

[196] O'Connor Lysaght, *The Republic of Ireland*, 81.

because 'he opposed what he believed was a vulgar attempt to harness Catholicism exclusively to Cumann na nGaedheal',[197] may not have been alone among the middle strata.

As Keogh puts it, 'armed with the national pastoral denouncing Saor Éire, Cumann na nGaedheal went to the hustings not realising that de Valera had long since come out from under the shadow of the gunman as far as many in the key sectors of Irish society were concerned'.[198] When the election results were announced, Fianna Fáil was by far the largest party, with 44.5 per cent (seventy-two Dáil seats); Cumann na nGaedheal was reduced to 35.3 per cent (fifty-six seats), despite the fact that it had by now absorbed the National League; Labour fell again to 7.7 per cent (seven seats); Farmers and independents took 2.1 per cent (five seats) and 10.5 per cent (nine seats) respectively. The way was open for Fianna Fáil to take power, with the support of Labour. As Murphy writes, of de Valera: 'Something like a millennium was promised as he came to power in 1932.'[199]

---

[197] Keogh, 'De Valera, the Catholic Church and the "Red Scare"', 135.
[198] Ibid. 155.
[199] J. A. Murphy, 'The Achievement of Eamon de Valera', in Murphy and O'Carroll (eds.), *De Valera and his Times*, 13.

4

Fianna Fáil in Power 1932–1938

Fianna Fáil took office on 9 March 1932. The cabinet was as follows: Eamon de Valera (President of the Executive Council and Minister for External Affairs), Seán T. O'Kelly (Vice-President of the Executive Council and Minister for Public Health and Local Government), Seán MacEntee (Minister for Finance), Seán Lemass (Minister for Industry and Commerce), Frank Aiken (Minister for Defence), James Geoghegan (Minister for Justice), Jim Ryan (Minister for Agriculture), P. J. Ruttledge (Minister for Lands and Fisheries), Tom Derrig (Minister for Education), Joseph Connolly (Minister for Posts and Telegraphs).

Between 1932 and 1938 Fianna Fáil sought to implement its economic, social, and political programme. The results and effects of its efforts will be the subject of this chapter. The signing of the Anglo-Irish Agreement in 1938 involved an implicit recognition of the exhaustion of the party's original project. Although the war years gave a new lease of life to the stated objective of self-sufficiency, and although it was to be another decade again before the party seriously embarked upon the formulation of a new developmental strategy, it can be argued that by 1938 Fianna Fáil had developed the Irish economy as far as was possible behind the barriers of protection. Politically, too, 1938 marks a significant turning-point: 'between 1938 and 1943 there took place a major and fundamental change in the social bases of Fianna Fáil's support.'[1]

FIANNA FÁIL AND THE STATE

Any discussion of Fianna Fáil in office must begin with a few words about its attitude to the state apparatus of which it was nominally in control in March 1932. Although there was some pressure from

---

[1] M. Gallagher, *Electoral Support for Irish Political Parties, 1927–1973* (London, 1976), 23.

within the party for changes to be made in the police and the judiciary—some *cumainn* passed resolutions to this effect—it seems clear that this was inspired by a desire to settle old scores with pro-Treaty opponents, rather than to alter the character of the state apparatus as such. Fianna Fáil was convinced that the state was essentially a neutral instrument, and such pressure for changes as existed was side-stepped in the name of fair play. No changes were made in the civil service, the *Gardaí*, and the army, or the judiciary; as Fanning puts it, de Valera 'wanted to bend the machinery of government to his own purpose, not to dismantle it'.[2] The only replacement announced was that of police Commissioner Eoin O'Duffy, whose hostility towards the new Government was so unmasked that he left de Valera with little option. Otherwise, grass-roots pressure for at least token changes seems, in part, to have been directed against the new Minister for Justice, Geoghegan, whose previous associations with Cumann na nGaedheal made him unpopular with many party members, and who was subsequently replaced. On 10 March, the day after the Government took office, de Valera summoned the heads of the various civil-service departments to assure them that there would be no dismissals.

This conception of the state apparatus as a neutral instrument is vitally important. For the state, as even a cursory examination of one of its components—the civil service—will show, was nothing of the kind. The upper echelons of the civil service were, for the most part, wedded to traditional *laissez-faire* economics, untempered by political considerations. An example of this attachment is given by Fanning, who documents the Department of Finance's devotion to the principle of the balanced budget; during the early 1930s, the Department was insisting that the reduction of salaries in the public sector 'would not only enable the budget to be balanced, but would also create the proper atmosphere to allow private employers to reduce wages and salaries'.[3]

Such sentiments were shared by property owners, and the civil service which reflected their views was destined to exercise a large influence on Government policy. Boland claims that 'policy emanated mainly from the civil service but was marginally adjusted by the cumulative effect, on individual ministers, of party opinion and

---

[2] Fanning, *Independent Ireland*, 109.
[3] Fanning, *The Irish Department of Finance*, 211–13.

of public opinion filtered by the party'.[4] It had been precisely the failure to take political considerations into account which marked the downfall of Cumann na nGaedheal. It was here that Fianna Fáil was determined to succeed and, on its way to power, had shown considerable adeptness in doing so. Yet Fianna Fáil's conception of the state meant that what it rejected as hostile in the shape of Cumann na nGaedheal, it tended to embrace as neutral, disinterested, professional, and expert in the shape of the civil service. This is not at all to say that Fianna Fáil always bowed to the advice of the civil service; rather, that its room for manœuvre was restricted, and the political opportunities which were present were not always exploited to the full, by its having ceded so much to the ideology of the civil service—an ideology which some cabinet ministers came to share in full.

MacEntee, in particular, was notoriously unwilling to challenge civil-service dictums. Other ministers, especially Lemass, were more attuned to political necessities and potentialities; others, still, such as de Valera himself, simply followed their instinct for party unity. Indeed, within the civil service, to some extent, this clash of outlooks found its reflection in interdepartmental rivalry, hostility inspired by Finance's control over other departments' purse-strings, and the loyalty of civil servants such as John Leydon, secretary of the Department of Industry and Commerce, to their ministers. This meant that Lemass, for example, could exploit contradictions within the civil service in his battle to achieve a satisfactory resolution of contradictions within the cabinet. But the influence of the dominant *laissez-faire* ideology was such that even Lemass was thwarted by his cabinet colleagues more often than he succeeded during the 1930s.

Two examples of how bourgeois ideology—reproduced as professional advice by the civil service—acted to curtail potential deviations from strictly economic rationale are given by the framework of reference of MacEntee's 1932 budget and by the Department of Finance's successful resistance to most of Lemass's proposals for economic reorganization in November 1932.

Introducing his budget, MacEntee was at pains to reassure his departmental mentors of his acceptance of the balanced budget philosophy, social-welfare improvements notwithstanding:

---

[4] Boland, *The Rise and Decline of Fianna Fáil*, 38.

No authority on public finance would attempt to justify borrowing to provide services like public works and buildings, grants to universities and
forestry . . . Public works, where these are definitely of a recurring character and are not of such a nature as will yield a certain and immediate
economic return, cannot be regarded as abnormal and should not be provided for out of borrowing.

. . . the provision of emergency relief in the case of widespread famine
or a national catastrophe could properly be classified as abnormal expenditure, whereas the expenditure necessary to relieve the continuous or
recurring distress of poverty-stricken elements of the community must be
regarded as normal and must be provided for out of normal revenue.[5]

Public-health schemes and housing schemes, for example, were
to come out of 'normal revenue'. The effect was both to limit the
range of social improvements which the Government could undertake and to slow down the rate of deflation (as a large part of the
increased 'normal revenue' came from increased indirect, regressive taxation).

In November Lemass responded to the worsening economic situation with a series of proposals, 'revolutionary in character', including the removal of the surplus population from the land and the
provision of large-scale public-works schemes to cater for around
100,000 unemployed. Again, all but those concerned with social-
welfare reform were successfully resisted by Finance on the grounds
that 'the time has not come to extend the system of public works
for the relief of unemployment but to reduce it drastically' and that
the 'principle that the State must provide work' should be fought.[6]

Fianna Fáil's unwillingness radically to challenge the state apparatus limited its ability to introduce economic and social reforms;
its potential for altering the power structures of Irish society was
already fatally affected, I have argued, by the class nature of its
economic programme. Yet, despite its all too clear limitations, the
party's electoral success is beyond dispute. The limited measures it
did introduce were sufficient to secure the allegiance of significant
numbers of the disadvantaged, given the absence of any more
attractive alternative. If the party had been able to assert a greater
degree of relative autonomy from the state apparatus and the bourgeoisie, it might have been even more successful. It has often been
claimed, though without much evidence, that social discontent and

---

[5] Copy of budget speech in UCDA McGilligan Papers P35d/56.
[6] Quoted in Fanning, *The Irish Department of Finance*, 250.

political radicalism in Ireland have been defused through the emigration of hundreds of thousands of young disaffected workers,
labourers, and disinherited; if Fianna Fáil's vision had been less
limited—if Lemass's proto-Keynesianism had won the day, and a
place, even a modest one, had been found for at least some of
these lost generations at home in Ireland—they may well have
rewarded Fianna Fáil with a even firmer hold on the Irish electorate
than it has enjoyed. However, we can only speculate on the matter.

FIANNA FÁIL AND THE ECONOMY

Industry and Agriculture

Much discussion of the economic policies of the 1930s has centred
on the course of the so-called Economic War between Ireland and
the United Kingdom which began shortly after Fianna Fáil came to
power. While there can be no doubt that the Economic War permitted the party to consolidate support for its economic strategy
under the banner of patriotic necessity, the actual conflict itself
appears almost incidental to the main thrust of party policy. Nevertheless, the effects of the Economic War on the pattern of agricultural exports, the close relationship between the prosperity of the
agricultural sector and the import of raw materials necessary to
develop industry, and the booster the conflict gave to the nationalistic presentation of the Fianna Fáil economic programme, all
mean that the Economic War forms a constant backdrop to the
progress of events in both the industrial and the agricultural sectors
throughout the 1930s.

The Economic War began in July 1932 when the Government
withheld payment of land annuities from the UK Exchequer. The
UK Government at once produced a secret agreement signed by
Cumann na nGaedheal in 1923 by which the Irish side undertook
the payment of the annuities and also certain pensions to former
members of the pre-independence police force, the Royal Irish
Constabulary. As this agreement had been kept secret from Dáil
Éireann, de Valera was able to discard it as undemocratic and to
use the issue to attack the duplicity of Cumann na nGaedheal.
When the British responded to the Irish decision to withhold the
annuities by imposing a 20 per cent *ad valorem* tax on all Irish
exports to the United Kingdom, the Irish Government answered
with the Customs Duties (Provisional Imposition) Act, imposing

tariffs on UK imports. For the British, the issue seems to have had primarily political, rather than economic, significance. Although British concern to have a ready supply of Irish food imports must have increased as the international turbulence of the decade grew, the specifically political purpose of their action is seemingly borne out by the insistence of Commonwealth Secretary, J. H. Thomas, upon linking the annuities question to the quite separate question of the oath of allegiance to the crown (his successor, Malcolm MacDonald, took a quite different attitude and quickly facilitated a change of policy), and by apparent attempts to frustrate de Valera's attempts at international mediation by an impartial third party by insisting that any such mediation be by a Commonwealth tribunal. For Ireland, the effects of the conflict were much more serious economically—96 per cent of Irish exports went to the United Kingdom—but the political aspect was also predominant; as stated, the issue allowed the Government to outflank its opponents on the ideological plane.

'The beauty of the "Economic War"', writes Fanning, 'was that "frugal fare" could be depicted as the economic price for political freedom';[7] and, indeed, the cry was taken up by various Fianna Fáil leaders, each using the issue in his own characteristic way. Thus de Valera, speaking at the 1932 party *Ard-Fheis*, declared that

the land annuities will never be paid to Great Britain; if the British succeed in beating us—then we'll have no freedom. The British policy is to make the pace so fast as to be full of hardship for us. However, we did not engage in the conflict unwittingly; we knew perfectly well that Great Britain would bully and coerce us; a leopard doesn't suddenly change its spots.[8]

Lemass used the issue to hammer home his insistence upon industrialization:

The effects of British duties upon Irish exports revealed the fundamental weakness in the national economy of the Irish Free State; and the danger of dependency on one market for the sale of a limited range of perishable products. The seriousness of the consequences strengthens our determination to remodel the economic structure of the country . . . [we are] convinced that Ireland has a considerable industrial future but this won't be brought about by 'kid glove' methods.[9]

[7] Fanning, *Independent Ireland*, 114.
[8] *Irish Press*, 9 Nov. 1932.   [9] Ibid., 26 Sept. 1932.

Not only could the pursuit of the Economic War be used to accuse Cumann na nGaedheal of national disloyalty (with some credibility, as that party's return to power was undoubtedly hoped for by the UK Government); but the presentation of Fianna Fáil economic policy in patriotic colours could be used to fend off protests from the labour movement; indeed, the Labour Party, in a vain attempt to appear more republican than Fianna Fáil, was soon demanding the acceleration of the Economic War.

Behind the screen of the Economic War, the Government implemented its economic strategy. In the agricultural sphere, the principal aim was to encourage the spread of tillage, as opposed to cattle raising, and to reorientate production towards the home market. As Meenan states, agricultural exports were 'to be the residual of production, not the prime end', and would be used to purchase raw materials necessary for the concurrent industrial drive.[10]

Irish agriculture, we have seen, was in trouble by the early 1930s. The market for all but cattle had collapsed by 1931, and the halving of cattle prices between 1930 and 1934, and the collapse of calf prices, hit large and small farmers alike. Agricultural incomes already in decline—they had fallen by 12.8 per cent between 1929 and 1931—now fell further as 'cattle exports fell in volume by 33.2 per cent between 1931 and 1934. The value of net agricultural output fell by 37.6 per cent between 1929/30 and 1934/35.'[11] The situation, which would probably have been bad regardless of the Economic War as the United Kingdom resorted to protection, worsened from 1934 with London's imposition of a quota system which limited fat cattle to 50 per cent of the 1933 figure and imposed a 100 per cent restriction on store cattle as well as prohibiting beef and veal imports. The outcome was that cattle exports to the United Kingdom fell from 775,000 (1929) to 500,000 (1934), and were in danger of falling further. Obviously, such a development had implications for employment in the agricultural sector, particularly employment of farm labourers.

So far, so good—it might be said. After all, did not Fianna Fáil policy aim precisely at such a destruction of the 'rancher classes', and would not the anticipated switch to tillage provide employment for much greater numbers? Certainly, the Government did

---

[10] Meenan, 'From Free Trade to Self-Sufficiency', 76.
[11] Orridge, 'The Blueshirts and the "Economic War"', 360.

everything it could conceive of to encourage such a switch. 'A guaranteed price was offered for Irish wheat while all millers were forced to use a stated quantity of native wheat in their flour and flour imports were strictly controlled.'[12] Import controls on bacon, sugar, and tobacco were imposed and a major effort was made to develop the sugar-beet industry. Subsidies were offered (against the advice of the Department of Finance[13]) on exports of butter, bacon, and sheep offal, and, while an orderly run-down of the cattle trade was envisaged, bounties were offered on cattle exports—presumably to offset too sudden a depression due to UK actions. Land annuities paid to the Irish Government were halved and used to reduce agricultural rates substantially: 'rate relief introduced between 1932 and 1935 gave relief to the first twenty pounds of valuation, thus freeing smaller holdings from rates completely. Further relief was given according to the amount of outside labour employed, a measure to encourage labour-intensive tillage farming.'[14]

However, the anticipated mass switch to tillage did not happen. The total number of acres under tillage increased from 21,000 (1931) to 255,000 (1936), but this has to be set against a projected target of 1,200,000 acres. Moreover, the increase in acreage under tillage was largely at the expense of other crops, and not at the expense of cattle.

Farmers did not switch from livestock to tillage. Insofar as they switched at all, it was simply from unsubsidized tillage to subsidized tillage, and tillage in any case no longer seemed to provide more employment than cattle. The province that most increased its wheat acreage during the 1930s, Leinster, also experienced the sharpest drop in the number of agricultural labourers.[15]

[12] Daly, *Social and Economic History of Ireland*, 147.

[13] Finance was horrified by the proposal. McElligott expended much effort attempting to persuade his Minister to stand firm against agricultural subsidies on grounds of budget stringency. A memorandum on 15 August 1932 put the Department's view succinctly: 'it is taken for granted by the Department of Agriculture that "the State" will bear all the additional costs, leaving it to the producers of all kinds to reap all the additional benefits. I take the view that the purpose of these schemes is to benefit the agricultural industry . . . No case whatever has been made out for obliging the State, that is to say the taxpayer who is not necessarily or indeed usually a producer, to shoulder the burden' (NAI Finance F075/0011/32, F073/0008/32).

[14] Orridge, 'The Blueshirts and the "Economic War"', 363.

[15] Lee and O'Tuathaigh, *The Age of de Valera*, 133.

By the mid-1930s an unhealthy preponderance of wheat and sugar-beet at the expense of other crops was already evident.[16] Large farmers refused to switch from cattle production, while small farmers merely jumped at the offer of subsidies. An unfavourable international climate, moreover, frustrated such governmental efforts as were made to find alternative markets for Irish agricultural produce.

The large farmers were engaged in a bitter struggle with the Government during this period and were determined to hold out in the not unrealistic hope that the Government would soon be forced to change its tune. Cattle numbers remained high and, from 1935, the old trade patterns began to reassert themselves. A bounty scheme on calf skins and free beef for the unemployed, introduced in 1934, had a short lease of life; while the move brought beef within the range of the poorer strata for the first time, and was destined to enter the Fianna Fáil pantheon of social achievements, the overall effect of developments was to increase the number of unemployed in the agricultural sector.

Lemass certainly recognized that persuasion alone would not be enough to change the production patterns of Irish farmers. In November 1932 he warned that the country was 'facing a crisis as grave as that of 1847'. The collapse of the economy was in sight, and famine was a real possibility. 'Famine can come not because our farmers cannot, but because they will not, produce food. The stoppage of exports should mean cheaper food for our own people but cheaper food means still lower prices for the farmers.' But was Government policy not aimed at providing price supports for the farmers? Lemass proposed 'drastic remedies' which 'would certainly require dictatorial powers for their execution'. These included the reduction of agricultural production to the point required to feed the country plus exports which could be profitably maintained, or exports undertaken at a loss to pay for essential imports, and removal of the surplus population from the land.

Herein lay the crux of the matter, for Irish farmers were ageing, inefficient, and unwilling to change, and successful application of the party's industrial strategy would have required the much more active involvement of the state in the restructuring of agriculture— in the forcible subordination of agriculture to the needs of industry.

---

[16] Lyons, *Ireland since the Famine*, 626.

Farrell suggests that Lemass may have been attempting to 'galvan-
ize' the Government into action.[17] Unfortunately for Lemass, his
colleagues refused to be 'galvanized'. Fianna Fáil came to accept,
under pressure, that the depopulation of the Irish countryside was
inevitable; but a combination of the party's ideological vision of a
nation of smallholders and its strong adhesion to property rights
prevented it from contemplating any moves to force the pace significantly. At the same time, the pressing need to earn revenue to
pay for the necessary raw materials for industry was leading to the
inevitable surrender to the logic of the cattle export trade. This is
the background to the Anglo-Irish Coal–Cattle Pact of January 1935,
which increased the quota of Irish cattle allowed to enter the United
Kingdom, while Ireland increased purchases of UK coal by an
equivalent value, meaning that in practice all Irish coal purchases
now came from the United Kingdom. Duties on each country's
products remained, but the Pact was a sign of a thaw and 'it arrested, as was no doubt the intention, the tendency to reduce cattle
herds and it gave hope that at some future date the restraints on
Anglo-Irish trade would be removed'.[18]

Meanwhile, the lot of the smaller farmers had not substantially
improved. They shared with the large farmers a pronounced unwillingness to change. All farmers, of course, benefited from price
supports, and small farmers in particular benefited from the halving
of land annuities, the reduction in agricultural rates, and the introduction of export subsidies and bounties. But the situation remained
bleak for the small farmer in terms of marketing, transport, and the
availability of agricultural credit. Some of the Government's measures, such as the protection of the barley industry to benefit the
maltsters, hit the small farmer who needed cheap barley to feed his
pigs and poultry, and the small farmer was further hit by an inability to take advantage of mechanization. The reinforcement of the
cattle trade saw a transfer of wealth from small to large farmers,[19]
and land clearance continued unabated from the mid-1930s.

Yet the Economic War was genuinely popular among small farmers and, although the trade agreements reached with the United
Kingdom in 1938 were to provoke the rise of Clann na Talmhan as
an autonomous expression of small-farmer discontent, Fianna Fáil

---

[17] Farrell, *Seán Lemass*, 38.   [18] Meenan, *The Irish Economy since 1922*, 101.
[19] Lyons, *Ireland since the Famine*, 627.

support amongst the small-farmer stratum has always remained strong. The reasons for this paradox are not hard to discern. Subsidies to the small farmers simply allayed the need to modernize and had the effect of drawing them into a spiral of dependence upon the party in power. Fianna Fáil was quick to discover that price supports and welfare concessions were a relatively cheap way to secure the electoral loyalty of this stratum. Moreover, for the small farmer, what was at stake was not so much an occupation as a way of life, rooted in tradition and mythology. This explains the tenacity with which small farmers clung to their land despite the increasing impossibility of achieving any level of economic viability. Emigrants' remittances, paradoxically again, helped to maintain those small farmers who remained on the land (rural emigration was overwhelmingly from the small-farmer areas, frequently the disinherited children of small farmers, although agricultural labourers also emigrated).[20]

The slowing-down of the work of the Land Commission from the mid-1930s further confirmed the small farmers in their subaltern state. The Land Act of 1933 had aimed at speeding up the work of the Land Commission and 4,000 new farms had been promised in 1934. However, Finance remained totally opposed to the policy of land division on economic grounds and, as the Government was unwilling to involve itself in the radical restructuring of agriculture, the programme of land division was abandoned after 1935. The small farmers were rapidly becoming economically and demographically doomed as a social stratum. Deprived of any real hope of improving their lot economically, they clung to Fianna Fáil, not without occasional protest, but with a desperation born of dependence. That dependence was intensified by the knowledge that their lot under any alternative government was likely to be worse, and by the feeling that Fianna Fáil offered the best possibility of employment for their offspring. Their economic situation increasingly hopeless, they could at least draw some comfort from the continuing idealization of the small-farm life style by Fianna Fáil propaganda.

On the industrial front, meanwhile, protection was not proving the panacea which had been hoped for. Industrial policy, which aimed at import substitution to diversify the structure of production

[20] Peillon, *Contemporary Irish Society*, 14–18, 185.

and promote industrialization through the development of the home market, got off to a firm start in May 1932 with the imposition of forty-three new duties. Further measures followed in July and October, and, as the hitherto existing preferential treatment given to UK goods was withdrawn, the list of protected industries grew longer and longer. Tariffs were imposed on imports of UK coke, cement, electrical goods, machinery, iron, steel, and coal. Quotas were added to the tariffs until, by 1936, duties existed on 288 articles, quotas on 1,947, and some—such as bicycles, shoes, and some clothes—were banned altogether.[21] A number of state companies were established to aid the industrialization drive and provide essential infrastructural requirements: the Irish Sugar Company was established in 1933 and was producing 80 per cent of domestic requirements by 1938; a government scheme to develop the bogs led to the Turf Development Board in 1934—however, despite an act of 1935 which conferred compulsory purchase powers upon the Board, control over turf production remained largely in private hands and production remained underdeveloped; Aer Lingus was established in 1936; and the Irish Tourist Board, Irish Life Assurance Board, and Irish Alcohol Factories Ltd. completed the picture.

This state intervention in the economy met with no significant opposition from the emerging national bourgeoisie. Opposition, in the main, came from the large farmers and the civil service. Moreover, the state's expanded economic role was undertaken with little discussion. One reason why the national bourgeoisie should feel so little concern at this increase in state activity is that the state was only prepared to get involved where its intervention was deemed necessary and functional to the requirements of the developmental strategy, and in the absence of competition from the private sector. Although no action was taken to enforce the sort of massive investment in Irish industry which would have been necessary to sustain the industrialization drive, an Industrial Credit Corporation, backed up by a Trade Loans (Guarantee) Act, came into being in 1933 to help provide financial support for budding native entrepreneurs.

Allied to this was the introduction of the Control of Manufactures Acts in 1932 and 1934 to ensure that the industries established in Ireland behind the protective shield should be Irish-controlled. The case of the Control of Manufactures Acts has been definitively

---

[21] Daly, *Social and Economic History of Ireland*, 145.

covered by Daly, upon whose account the following brief summary is based.[22] The demand for measures designed to ensure that Irish business would not be robbed of the benefits of protection by more efficient foreign-based competitors had been forcefully put by the NAIDA and (from December 1932) by the Federation of Irish Industry (FII)—'a body composed exclusively of native manufacturers and having among its aims "to secure as far as possible consistent with national requirements that industrial development shall be retained in the hands of Saorstát nationals"'.

Initially the minister concerned, Lemass, envisaged that all businesses would be licensed, 'but that those established before a certain date would be automatically entitled to a licence, while businesses established at a later date would be licensed at the minister's discretion and the licence could be subject to certain conditions'. Lemass also envisaged measures to ensure that native concerns should continue to be controlled by Irish shareholders.

The cabinet, however, had different ideas. The first cabinet committee established had been an economic committee; despite the fact that Lemass was included in its membership while the Finance Minister, MacEntee, was surprisingly excluded, Lemass's position was by no means dominant. The economic committee of the cabinet frequently frustrated Lemass's more sweeping proposals for the reorganization of the economy. The cabinet rejected any suggestion that restrictions might be placed upon domestic undertakings. Furthermore, Lemass, who perhaps had an eye to the problems which might arise as a result of greed and inefficiency, was also curtailed when the cabinet, concerned by 'possible interference with any of our nationals embarking upon business', rejected any question of the minister being empowered to restrict entry to over-crowded industries.

It was a much modified version of Lemass's proposals which was introduced. The initial act required that all companies established in the Free State after 1 June 1932 which did not have a majority of native shareholders should apply for a licence to conduct business. The decision as to whether to grant a licence rested with the minister—despite the best efforts of the manufacturers to gain an institutionalized veto. The minister could, moreover, impose conditions concerning employment of Irish nationals, use of Irish

---

[22] Daly, 'An "Irish Ireland" for Business?'.

materials, restrictions on output, and location of plant. Restrictions on output were clearly intended to ensure that native manufacturers were protected from competition and, according to Daly, this would appear to have been the major criterion governing the issue of licences. Location-of-plant restrictions were also common, and increasingly so during the late 1930s; obviously the power to direct the location of new factories conferred a considerable power of political patronage.

The restrictions imposed under the 1932 Act may not have been all that Lemass desired, but they did not satisfy the national bourgeoisie either. Increasingly, both the NAIDA and the FII applied pressure for stronger measures against foreign investors so as to eliminate the possibility of competition. A vigorous propaganda campaign was waged during the 1933 election, and Irish business succeeded in adding delegations from the ITGWU—representing workers frightened for their jobs—to the stream of visitors to the Department of Industry and Commerce, sent there to press their case. On 7 March 1933, for example, Lemass was pressed by the FII to respond to 'definite proof' that English firms, such as Alfred Bird (custard manufacturers) and Brown and Polson Ltd., were producing goods in the Free State through agents, and benefiting—despite not being themselves registered. 'Real Irish firms', the FII insisted, were outraged. The FII wanted the introduction of a new requirement as to capital registered; 51 per cent was not good enough, but 'they were not able to suggest a definite figure'. They wanted no licence granted to new entries, whether native or foreign, into an industry where 'production had reached saturation point'. According to the report of that meeting, 'the Minister promised to consider the representations made to him, but he did not hold out much hope of meeting the request of the deputation'.[23]

The 1934 Act was a further disappointment. Its chief additional measure was designed to ensure that 50 per cent of all classes of shares and at least two-thirds of shares carrying voting rights be held by 'qualified persons'. Beyond this, Lemass and the Government could not go. The need for foreign expertise and capital and the all too obvious readiness of native manufacturers to exploit protection for all it was worth meant that total capitulation would have been politically impossible. That much was obvious to an

[23] NAI Industry and Commerce TID/1207/178.

increasing number of Fianna Fáil ministers (de Valera, before long, was driven by a sense of patriotic humiliation to condemn the readiness of business men to exploit the existence of the border for further profits). Foreign expertise was increasingly welcomed during the late 1930s and a blind eye was turned to the many stratagems employed by foreign investors to evade the restrictions. The national bourgeoisie continued to bemoan the continuing penetration of Irish industry by foreign capital, but, paradoxically, the very extent of this penetration and the many guises it took meant that it became increasingly difficult to distinguish between foreign and native capital, and the Government was left with considerable leeway to beat a retreat from its more ambitious dreams.

Although some industries, such as brewing, distilling, and biscuit manufacture, which depended on the export trade, suffered after 1932, the overall effect of the new strategy was undoubtedly to raise both industrial output and employment. National industrial output during the period 1931–8 rose in value from £25.6 million to £30 million; industrial employment during the same period rose from 111,000 to 166,000. Overall employment was further boosted by a crash housing programme, designed as much to provide jobs as houses, and by the expansion of the public sector (for example, 3,000 new civil servants were taken on between 1932 and 1937):

the total numbers in employment rose, with more jobs in industry and services out-weighing the losses in agriculture. This was the first increase in numbers employed since the Famine. The increase in industrial employment of over 50,000 was the most dramatic achieved in this century.[24]

These tangible achievements were accompanied by improvements in social conditions which at least enabled those who did not emigrate to survive the ultimate failure of the industrialization strategy. What was born was not so much a 'new Ireland' in which the 'common man' had at last come into his rightful inheritance; rather, an increasingly dependent Ireland in which certain social strata were more beholden than ever to a political party whose modest achievements, combined with the lack of any brighter alternative, allowed it to continue to project itself as a modernizing force.

The strategy did yield more secure rewards for those who grew considerably richer behind the barriers of protection. Whilst no

[24] Daly, *Social and Economic History of Ireland*, 150.

effective action was taken to break the economic power of those who invested large sums of capital abroad, new money was added to old. Fortuitously for Fianna Fáil, low interest rates in the United Kingdom during the mid-1930s added a new incentive to the profit opportunities and tax concessions offered by Government policy, and the work of the Industrial Credit Corporation was complemented by at least some reinvestment of Irish capital at home. There were now 905 companies registered with capital of £7.3 million. Shares on the Dublin Stock Exchange (1933–6) were worth £6.5 million. 'Overnight a whole new business and capital world was created.'[25] Fianna Fáil had kept its promise to consolidate and expand the national bourgeoisie. But would the latter develop the Irish economy as Fianna Fáil had hoped and expected?

On the face of it, it seems an unrealistic hope: Ireland was a small, exposed, and underdeveloped economy which might, under conditions of rigorous protection, offer the prospect of short-term profits; but which called for massive investment in restructured production on a long-term basis and at a high risk if economic development was to be achieved. Such economic conditions would appear to suggest three possible ways forward: continuing economic dependence and underdevelopment, lack of production diversification, and reliance on a single dominant trading partner; full incorporation into the international economic order, involving industrial modernization carried out by foreign capital—combined with a concerted drive to find new markets—and resulting in new forms of dependence and uneven development; forced industrialization by the state, involving appropriation of the productive assets of the society, capital included. It certainly seems naïve to rely upon the patriotic altruism or redistributive zeal of a class, encouraged into existence by the promise of easy profits, to achieve the 'new republic'. This is certainly not to engage in the fruitless business of apportioning moral blame; the national bourgeoisie was incapable of solving the problems of Irish economic underdevelopment, although a more assertive role on the part of the state might have achieved greater results.

As it was, the weaknesses of the industrialization strategy were many and serious. First, insulation from effective competition led to excess profits in many cases and, sometimes, to the establishment

[25] Daly, 146.

of virtual monopolies. During 1936–7 Lemass, in particular, showed himself aware of this danger, though less sure of how to deal with it. He delivered repeated warnings to industrialists. Speaking at a Drapers' Chamber of Trade dinner in February 1936, for example, he 'warned Saorstát industrialists that if undue advantage was taken of the tariff policy to increase prices he would see that the tariff was removed or reduced in the industry affected'.[26]

The Government's policy of granting price supports to farmers similarly pushed up food prices. The inflationary effects of protection led to a serious concern with falling living standards from 1936 onwards and this was a constant theme in the propaganda of Fine Gael (in which Cumann na nGaedheal was subsumed in August 1933). Yet there was little indication that Fine Gael had any answer to the problem, having effectively ceded the case for protection by now. In 1937 Fine Gael sent a leaflet to industrialists—their names had been gleaned from Lemass's Industrial Directory—assuring 'all industrialists . . . that they need have no fears that their quotas or tariffs would be interfered with if Mr Dillon became Minister for Industry and Commerce'.[27] How, it might have been asked, did such pledges square with the urgings of the pro-Fine Gael provincial press to vote for an end to 'essential commodities at prices already prohibitive'?[28] Well might Fianna Fáil's Tom Derrig declare:

Well, they cannot have it both ways. Mr Cosgrave says the cost of living can be reduced but he does not tell us how he promises to do it. If they want to let in the foreign product . . . let them say so and the country will at least know where they stand . . . All we know is that they are as much afraid of the dairying and tillage farmers as they are afraid of the urban population to even dare to suggest that they are prepared to consider interfering with our protection policy.[29]

(Admittedly, Fine Gael leader and former Blueshirt commander, Colonel Ed Cronin, did voice some criticism of the protection policy —on the grounds that 'a crowd of aliens and Jews' were reaping the benefits. His anti-Semitic ranting was echoed by a party colleague who complained that Fianna Fáil was subsidizing 'Jewish firms' who were 'no benefit to the country'.[30])

[26] *Irish Times*, 26 Feb. 1936.   [27] *Longford Leader*, 29 May 1937.
[28] *Sligo Champion*, 26 June 1937.   [29] *Kilkenny People*, 12 June 1937.
[30] *Connacht Sentinel*, 22 June 1937.

The cost of living was further exacerbated by heavy indirect taxation. Both the provision of improved social-welfare services and the growth in state provision of infrastructural requirements called for sharp increases in revenue. Taxation was invariably defended by Fianna Fáil on the grounds that it was necessary if improvements in social welfare were to be maintained; this argument was certainly effective in neutralizing labour-movement criticism and in making Fine Gael's attacks upon taxation look like a nostalgic harkening back to the Cosgrave years.[31] Fianna Fáil, in a bid to woo capital invested abroad, was unwilling to impose direct taxation so as to take the burden off the backs of the poorest sections of the community. Despite the fact that capital was more plentiful than before, the sums invested abroad remained very large and there was a continuing shortage of capital available for industrial investment. The Government was unwilling to alter the investment patterns of the Irish banks forcibly and business men resisted appeals to their patriotic good faith: at the Drapers' Chamber of Trade dinner mentioned above, the Chamber's president, Mr Duggan, replied to Lemass that, while business men were grateful for the industrial boom, they were reproachful of the notion that 'when they had money to invest they invested it outside their own country. He did not think there was ever any real justification for that reproach . . . the only grounds that would supply a justification for the reproach were grounds that would not commend themselves to reason or commonsense.'[32]

Fianna Fáil, in its 1932 budget, had imposed a corporation surtax of up to 7.5 per cent, raised the standard rate of income tax from three shillings and six pence to five shillings, imposed new taxes on the rich by lowering the threshold for the surtax from £2,000 to £1,500, as well as increasing indirect taxation. A timid tax was also imposed on the banks: a 3 per cent stamp duty on consolidated bank notes. These measures, claims O'Connor Lysaght, had alienated many of the rich.[33] Before long, however, the measures were abandoned, as the Government sought through incentives alone to attract capital investment to Irish industry. The tax on the banks

---

[31] For example, Fine Gael Finance spokesman, Patrick McGilligan, was quoted in the Fianna Fáil press as saying that 'they [Fianna Fáil] have piled up the social services to such an extent in the country that they cannot continue without a reduction' (*Irish Press*, 24 Nov. 1936).   [32] *Irish Times*, 26 Feb. 1936.
[33] O'Connor Lysaght, *The Republic of Ireland*, 121.

was reduced to 2.5 per cent in 1937 and abolished altogether in 1942. Before that, other forms of direct taxation were reduced. The president of the Cork Chamber of Commerce, A. H. Moore, was able, in January 1935, to welcome the 'reduction in income tax of six pence in the pound' and 'look forward to the remission of corporation profits tax'.[34] The 1935 budget marked a further shift towards indirect taxation; the 1936 budget went further still in its attempts to stem the outflow of capital by reducing the average rates of income tax below the UK level. All of this inevitably meant higher levels of indirect, regressive taxation, and indeed between 1931 and 1939 the *ad valorem* tax level rose from 9 per cent to 35 per cent—among the highest in the world.

Not only was the industry fostered behind the barriers of protection costly and inflationary; it also afforded wages and working conditions which were often the source of discontent. The weaknesses of the labour movement, the anxiety of business men to make as much profit as they could while they could, and the anxiety of the Government to encourage the growth of a native capitalism at all costs, led to the exact opposite of Fianna Fáil's pre-election promise to end the 'downward pressure on wage rates'. A highly defensive labour movement issued constant pleas to the Government on low wages and poor conditions. In 1936 Labour Senator Kennedy claimed that 'the great bulk of the new industries could be rightly described as industries for child labour'; his party's national organizer was quoted as complaining that 'the Government were using every lever available to reduce the workers' wages; as an instance, men had been knocked off Unemployment Assistance, and offered certain work to which they had to travel five or six miles, at two-thirds what was paid to road-workers'.[35] Even allowing for the obvious desire of opposition politicians to make political capital, it seems indisputable that there was some truth in these assertions. Government acts, which aimed at regulating working conditions, hours, and paid holidays, were not always honoured by employers in the protected industries and many of the new industries paid low wages by UK standards. The resumption of large-scale emigration to Great Britain, as soon as that country's worst bout of economic depression had passed (in 1935–7, 75,150 persons emigrated to Great Britain, and the human flow accelerated

[34] *Evening Herald*, 30 Jan. 1935.   [35] *Irish Independent*, 24 Mar. 1936.

during the war when labour power was in demand), was proof of the attractiveness of UK wage rates. An accurate estimate of wealth distribution in Ireland in the 1930s is difficult, but Tom Johnson, utilizing the 1932/3 estate duties figures, estimated that 1 per cent of the population owned 59 per cent of taxable wealth; that 8 per cent owned 34 per cent; 10 per cent owned 7 per cent; and that 81 per cent owned nothing taxable—i.e. less than £100 in cash and goods. It is unlikely that these figures were significantly altered by Fianna Fáil's first years in power, except perhaps in a negative direction.[36]

In addition, many of the new industries were totally unsuited to competition in foreign markets. Many Irish firms were woefully inadequate in the fields of technical, managerial, and marketing expertise and many home-produced items were simply more costly and inferior replicas of well-known international brands. Entrepreneurial flair, in product innovation as in investment risk-taking, was in short supply. By 1938 the home market was saturated and no further expansion in employment or production was really possible; further profits really only lay in racketeering.

A further point worthy of consideration from the point of view of internal party conflict is that, despite the use of the power to direct the location of new industries conferred by the 1932 Control of Manufactures Act, Irish industry tended to be centred largely in the east of the country. This fact certainly aroused the anger of rural party leaders such as Joseph Connolly, Minister for Lands, who complained of the failure to locate industries in the *Gaeltacht* areas, demanded that certain industries should be reserved for the *Gaeltacht*, and warned that people in the west were poorer 'than they were before our policy was put into operation'. Lemass's attitude was typically unsentimental and unapologetic. In a memorandum outlining proposals to provide employment for people from the *Gaeltacht*, on 10 April 1935, his Department pointed out that 'in formulating these proposals the Minister has regarded the Gaeltacht problem as solely an economic one arising from the existence in these areas of considerable congestion' side by side with unfavourable economic conditions. 'He considers that the only practicable methods of dealing with that problem are such as will tend in due course to reduce the congestion of population by inducing the

[36] NLI Johnson Papers MS 17217.

younger people to migrate to other areas.'[37] While electoral worries in the late 1930s may have influenced the location of some factories in the west, it is difficult to sustain the hypothesis that Fianna Fáil industrial strategy in practice, as opposed to rhetoric, encouraged much of a bias towards the 'periphery' at the expense of the 'centre'. Connolly was nearer to the point when he complained that the west was being drawn into dependence on subsidies[38]—a realization which led to his disillusionment with de Valera and his retirement from politics.

Finally, we may comment upon the Government's failure to develop the raw materials necessary for industry. The industrialization drive remained crucially dependent upon imports. In fact, import substitution merely replaced one form of dependence upon the import–export trade with another. As Meenan points out, this failure to develop natural resources and raw materials meant that Government policy was not really one of self-sufficiency at all.[39] While exports, which were almost entirely agricultural, were halved by the Economic War between 1931 and 1934, rising only slightly in 1936, the continuing necessity to import tea, petrol, coal, iron, steel, and other essentials led to a worsening balance-of-payments situation. Imports outpaced exports rapidly. Attempts to use the state's sterling assets to offset this worsening balance of payments resulted in a reduction in sterling assets of £9 million between 1931 and 1935.[40]

Fianna Fáil had repeatedly pledged itself to the development of the country's natural resources. However, its total commitment to private enterprise, its refusal to involve the state in other than essentially non-profit-orientated ventures, and its single-minded attempts to stimulate the bourgeoisie into action all paralysed its capacity to entrust a more active role to the state. Of course, it can be argued that Ireland is not as fortunate in its deposits of natural resources as other countries, and that the necessity to import raw materials would have existed in any case; but such resources as the country does possess were left fatally underdeveloped. Lemass may well have told the FII in 1937 that the 'next stage' would be the creation of 'factories for the production of raw materials and semi-manufactured goods',[41] but nothing was done until the Second World

---

[37] NAI Taoiseach S.7441A.
[38] Ibid.   [39] Meenan, 'From Free Trade to Self-Sufficiency', 77.
[40] Lyons, *Ireland since the Famine*, 613–20.
[41] Quoted in Daly, 'An "Irish Ireland" for Business?', 270.

War literally compelled the Government to take some cautious steps. Until then, the development of the bogs was the only major scheme undertaken, and even here turf production remained ultimately in private hands. (Land and sea transport also remained in private hands and the merchant marine was allowed to decline until the war.) Nothing was done to develop the forestry industry. No co-ordinated attempt was made to develop mineral deposits: mining leases were granted to party supporters intent upon making profits through rapid exploitation. Challenged by opponents on this very point, Lemass replied that 'he thought it was a good thing for the country that there were members of the Fianna Fáil party and others who were willing to invest their money in exploring the mineral wealth of the country, and the whole purpose of the Mining and Minerals Act was to make it possible for such people to be engaged in that work'.[42] Efforts to develop Irish oil-refining capacity were even less successful. Proposals to this effect were twice turned down by the cabinet in December 1935. Lemass had proposed awarding monopoly rights to an Irish-based oil-refining company, but even the idea of sponsoring private enterprise in this field seems to have been unacceptable to the majority of his colleagues, who appear to have regarded the project as too ambitious, too risky from the point of view of state financial commitments, or simply unnecessary. By the time Lemass did succeed in finding backing for his project, in 1938, the imminence of the war forced the project to be shelved.

The failure to develop natural resources contributed to the difficulties in which the country found itself by the late 1930s. The industrialization drive had ground to a halt; its achievements had to be balanced against the growth of a bourgeoisie which, far from contributing to the further development of the means of production, was, frankly, parasitical; living standards were falling and emigration and unemployment were both beginning to rise again; a worsening balance of payments meant that the need to increase (agricultural) exports so as to pay for necessary imports was pressing. Paradoxically, the country was more dependent upon its trade with the United Kingdom than ever. Whilst the scope of the other problems mentioned was distorted, and the solution delayed, by the peculiar circumstances in which Ireland found itself during the

[42] *Irish Times*, 15 June 1935.

war years and immediately after, the solution of the import–export dilemma was perceived as crucial.

Following the signing of the Coal–Cattle Pact between Ireland and the United Kingdom in 1935, pressure for a formal end to the Economic War increased. Cattle exports were once again on the increase from 1935, and by 1938 the old trade patterns had been almost entirely resumed by Irish farmers. Following the renewal of the Coal–Cattle Pacts in 1936 and 1937, the Department of Finance was instrumental in urging its minister to push the Government towards a final resolution of the conflict.[43] Finance had always been deeply hostile towards the pursuit of the Economic War; its officials, being on first-name terms with their British colleagues, almost regarded the whole affair as a personal slight. MacEntee by now needed little persuasion. Like all Fianna Fáil ministers, he was increasingly uncertain about the conduct of economic policy; more than most, he was unwilling to contemplate increased state involvement in an attempt to sort out difficulties; his instinct was for a return to established custom. In early 1936 he was reported in the party press as saying:

There was no market which offered us an opportunity for that increase upon a scale commensurate with the requirements but the British market . . . Anything, therefore, which would tend to impede the fair course of trade between the two countries, anything which would create enmity between the two peoples, or arouse prejudice against this country, her people or her products, is a matter of the gravest concern to everyone of us but most of all to those who are the mainstay of Ireland, the farmers and tillers of the soil, upon whose well-being all of us depend.[44]

Cumann na nGaedheal had been saying much the same thing four years earlier. Later, in the same year, MacEntee's political opponents were alleging that 'MacEntee is also charged with being a menace arising out of his "Sound Finance" speech at the *Ard-Fheis*. He is charged[45] with having read a speech at the *Ard-Fheis* which he had never previously read—it being the product of an official.'[46]

[43] McElligott wrote MacEntee a stream of memoranda on this subject between 1934 and 1937 especially. Examples are to be found in UCDA MacEntee Papers P67/151, P67/152, P67/153.   [44] *Irish Press*, 22 Jan. 1936.
[45] Apparently by de Valera, Derrig, and Ruttledge.
[46] Typewritten notes on the 1936 local-government elections in UCDA Mulcahy Papers P7/C/148.

MacEntee's language may have been harsh and politically embarrassing; it may have been too obviously inspired by the 'dour and suspicious men in the Department of Finance';[47] but his cabinet colleagues were unable to come up with any alternative to the inexorable logic of Finance's urgings. Even Lemass seems, at this stage, to have been at a loss as to what to do next.[48]

On 11 November 1937, the secretary of the Department of Finance sent a memorandum to his minister advocating the immediate cessation of the Economic War:

> It is not the case that our imports are too high, but our exports are too low and will not be capable of being increased as long as we wage an economic war with our best customer. Any policy which attempts to rectify the adverse trade balance either by reducing imports or by finding markets other than the United Kingdom for our exports is doomed to failure.[49]

In line with this advice, MacEntee called for an initiative to end the Economic War. The initiative came on 24 November, with a message from de Valera to Malcolm MacDonald, the new UK Commonwealth and Dominions secretary. MacDonald was considerably more sympathetic to the Irish case than his predecessor, Thomas, had been, and considerably more aware of the political necessities facing the Fianna Fáil Government. Besides, with a major European confrontation looking increasingly likely, the United Kingdom had its own reasons for wanting to end a mutually harmful economic conflict with one of its closest trading partners. When an Irish delegation, composed of de Valera, Lemass, MacEntee, and Ryan, arrived in London for negotiations in January 1938, the spirit of agreement was already in the air.[50]

For MacEntee, in particular, achieving such an agreement was a major priority. Of the four members of the Irish delegation, he alone has left a vivid account of his reasoning at this time. While in London, he wrote a number of memoranda to de Valera, outlining his position.[51] A memorandum of 17 February 1938 is notable

[47] Williams, 'De Valera in Power', 39.

[48] Fanning (*Independent Ireland*, 147) claims that Lemass was less prominently placed in the Fianna Fáil hierarchy during the late 1930s, falling back to fourth position, just one step ahead of MacEntee.

[49] UCDA MacEntee Papers P67/153.

[50] An excellent account of the actual progress of the negotiations is given in D. McMahon, *Republicans and Imperialists: Anglo-Irish Relations in the 1930s* (New Haven, Conn., 1984), 237–93.   [51] UCDA MacEntee Papers P67/155.

for the unsentimental and utterly realistic view it contains about the Economic War, Anglo-Irish relations, and especially relations between Éire and Northern Ireland; and for its revelations also about tensions within the Government. It is worth citing at length:

I feel that the partition problem cannot be solved except with the consent of the majority of the Northern non-Catholic population. It certainly cannot be solved by their coercion. Hitherto, we as the Government here have done nothing of ourselves to secure a solution, but on the contrary have done and are doing certain things which have made a solution more difficult. The demand which we make continuously that the British should compel the Craigavonites [*sic*] to come in with us, has only had the effect of stiffening them against us.

I believe a failure to settle the Economic War will be bad for the country and disastrous for the Government and the Party . . . the country is looking for a settlement, expects to get one, and does not regard Partition as more than a theoretical obstacle to a practical agreement.

I for my part feel that the way in which we have been manœuvred into this situation by those who do not want a settlement of the Economic War upon the only basis which is practicable, and who are labouring to reverse the policy in your speech of May 1935, has destroyed the only basis upon [which] a Cabinet can last: that of agreement upon the essentials of policy and a pervading confidence that the policy having been stated, it will be accepted by all.

(MacEntee appears to have been referring to a speech which de Valera made in the Dáil on 29 May 1935, in the course of which de Valera had declared his enthusiasm for friendly relations with the United Kingdom, including his openness towards a possible future defence treaty, and had given a categorical assurance that the territory of the Free State would never be permitted to be used by any foreign power as the base for an attack on Britain.[52]) MacEntee continued:

It is clear now that your speech of May 1935 has not been accepted by the Minister for Lands nor by the Minister for Posts and Telegraphs as an authoritative statement of Government policy—though in these circumstances how the former could have remained in the Government and the latter entered it *after the speech* was made passes my comprehension. In any event it is clear that these Ministers hold themselves free to undertake a filibuster against those of their colleagues who propose to think and speak and act upon the principle laid down by you in 1935. Even upon

[52] *Ballina Herald*, 1 June 1935.

this issue alone I have no desire to remain in the Government, and therefore my resignation as Minister for Finance is at your disposal whenever you deem it advisable to accept it.

We have had differences of opinion as to wisdom or unwisdom of a line of policy and I have always been prepared in the last resort to defer to your judgement. But I cannot concede that full deference now, because in regard to Partition we have never had a considered policy. It has always been an affair of hasty improvisation, a matter of fits and starts. We are giving it first place now in the practical business of Government. When did we do that before in regard to any of those activities by which our citizens are consolidating and intensifying Partition? Why, we would not risk antagonising one Gaelic League or GAA [Gaelic Athletic Association] crank in order to undo Partition—as it could be undone in sport and amusement. And yet we are prepared to subject our farmers and our people as a whole to further and intensified hardship in order to compel Great Britain to force the Northern non-Catholics to associate with us, when with our connivance every bigot and kill-joy, ecclesiastical and lay, is doing his damnedest here to keep them out.

It was quite a statement from a man who, in February 1929, had declared at a rally that 'the people who built up Belfast were not Irish, but English and Scottish settlers, and they would not be Irish until the people of the South showed them that they were stronger than they';[53] and who was only too happy, in public, to invoke the Catholic religion, time and time again, in defence of his policies and his party and to wrong-foot his opponents. As was often the case, MacEntee's resignation threat—one of many issued in the late 1930s—was melodramatic and unnecessary; he was pushing at an open door, as far as the substance of Government policy was concerned. 'Window-dressing about Partition'[54] may have been slowing negotiations down, but window-dressing is precisely what was involved. De Valera, like Lemass and MacEntee, was intent upon reaching agreement.

Three separate agreements were eventually signed on 25 April 1938, covering finance, defence, and trade. Under the first of these, the Irish agreed to pay a lump sum of £10 million and the British agreed to drop all other claims for payment of land annuities and RIC pensions. This represented a theoretical saving for the Irish of

---

[53] Quoted in C. O'Halloran, *Partition and the Limits of Irish Nationalism: An Ideology Under Stress* (Dublin, 1987), 33.

[54] Letter to Mrs MacEntee in January/February 1938 in UCDA MacEntee Papers P67/179.

£94.05 million; its significance, though, was largely political. Despite describing the £10 million which he agreed to pay as 'ransom money', de Valera was able to claim that, as the land-annuities share of the amount claimed by the British came to only £78 million, he had not paid a penny of it—the £10 million paid was merely a portion of the £26.05 million claimed in respect of other matters. Under the defence agreement, the UK Government returned those Irish ports still under their control—Berehaven, Cobh, and Lough Swilly—without any conditions attaching. Economically, the most important agreement was that on trade. Meenan gives the following description of what exactly was entailed:

Irish goods were to be admitted free into the United Kingdom. The Irish Government affirmed its willingness to co-operate with the British Government's policy of ensuring orderly marketing of agricultural production. The British Government undertook that it would not regulate the quantity of imports from Ireland without regard to the special conditions of Irish exports and their course in the past. Irish exports to the UK would receive preferential treatment as compared with non-Commonwealth goods.

Equally, the Irish Government extended preferential treatment to British goods entering Ireland. Free entry was to be given to British coal, iron and steel and other metal manufactures, machinery, and chemicals; and a minimum duty was imposed on imports of coal from other countries. The Irish Government undertook to review its protective duties and, if necessary, to replace them with duties which would allow British producers a reasonable chance of competition while affording adequate protection to Irish industries. The review was to be undertaken by the Prices Commission, to which British firms could appeal. It will be seen that these concessions on the Irish side, which were the prelude to the re-establishment of the export trade in agricultural production, went far beyond the bounds of preferential treatment of British imports.[55]

The agreements met with some protest, as might be expected. In September 1939 the ITUC wrote to the Department of Industry and Commerce to complain about increases in food prices which the unions attributed to the Anglo-Irish Trade Agreement. The letter was acknowledged, and filed.[56] A more spirited, but ultimately no more successful, protest was lodged by the FIM, whose secretary at this stage was Erskine Childers (later, of course, a Fianna Fáil cabinet minister, and later still president of Ireland). On 25 April 1938

[55] Meenan, *The Irish Economy since 1922*, 78.
[56] NAI Industry and Commerce TID/2215/45.

Childers lodged a 'vigorous protest' against reduction in duties for UK goods, quoting manufacturers of linen, candles, soap, hosiery, paper, twine, wooden articles, shirts, cables, and ropes. The Council of the FIM, he wrote, was establishing an Industrial Bureau to 'give assistance to the Government in the matter of making statistical records from time to time of English market prices'—and sought assurances of Government co-operation. In December a senior civil servant, R. C. Ferguson, wrote to Childers that 'I am not prepared to recommend a change to the Minister until there is some evidence of the necessity for such a change . . .'.[57] In the Department's view, no such evidence existed.

In effect, the Griffithite strategy for economic development was at an end. In 1938 a Bill was introduced providing for the abolition of the Tariff Commission; in any case, nothing had been referred to it since December 1934.[58] Protective duties were retained, but as purely defensive measures and no longer as an industrial strategy.

Banking and Finance

Nothing, perhaps, better illustrates the limitations inherent in Fianna Fáil's industrial strategy than the party's failure to attempt any reform of the financial system. Lemass, as mentioned earlier, had made noises about reform. Indeed, de Valera, in an address to the League of Nations in 1932, spoke of the need to reform the system of production, distribution, and exchange and warned of the dangers of failing to do so. Fianna Fáil had, on the surface, few reasons to feel favourably disposed towards the financial institutions. Apart from the fact that banking and financial circles had been strong supporters in general of Cumann na nGaedheal, the small farmers and petty bourgeoisie were frequently under pressure from the banks to repay loans when they could ill afford to do so. Indeed, the times might appear to have been conducive to sweeping changes in the financial system, which Fianna Fáil might have presented as a necessary stage in the completion of national independence.

There was considerable debate within the party in the early days of government about financial questions. Lemass put forward proposals for a state bank and a break with sterling which were strongly resisted by the Department of Finance and, ultimately, by the cabinet. There is also evidence of some pressure from the Fianna Fáil

[57] Ibid. TID/2215/9.   [58] NAI Finance S084/0026/38.

grass roots for change. In August 1932, for example, the Mullingar Fianna Fáil *cumann* forwarded to de Valera a resolution declaring: 'That we consider that the Banks have a stranglehold of the country to a greater extent than is generally known and that the time has come to have the whole system of credit examined with a view to basing it on its real value—which is goods.'[59]

Admittedly, what this actually means is vague, to say the least. But it is evidence of unease with the operations of the existing financial system. De Valera passed the resolution to Finance 'for consideration by the Minister and for any action that might be taken'; Finance appended the cryptic note: 'I do not think we can usefully take any action on this resolution.'

Despite occasionally radical rhetoric when in opposition (he was once even regarded as a socialist), MacEntee took a characteristically conservative view. Aiken, although also conservative, possessed what can only be described as an idiosyncratic interest in questions of monetary reform. De Valera was willing to consider alterations but was cautious and distrustful of sweeping experiments.

In September 1932 de Valera invited the chairman of the Currency Commission, Joseph Brennan—former secretary of the Department of Finance—for talks. Among the subjects on the agenda were the link with sterling, the question of a more direct role for the banks in the stimulation of industry, and bank pressure on farmers to repay their loans. Brennan totally rejected all arguments for change. He denied that there was any pressure on farmers to repay loans, and dealt with the two remaining topics as follows:

So far as banking participation in industry was concerned, the continental principle was foreign to the system on which a very sound banking system had been established and maintained in Ireland. As to the link with sterling, this had so far proved a suitable arrangement from the Irish point of view and, in the Chairman's opinion, ought to be continued provided that no undesirable development threatened to arise on the side of sterling.[60]

Opposition to the break with sterling was maintained strenuously in all correspondence with MacEntee. On 23 February 1933, for example, MacEntee reported to de Valera that the Governor of the Bank of Ireland was worried about 'a more or less radical alteration' in the system of banking and currency and that

---

[59] Ibid. F009/0010/32.
[60] Moynihan, *Currency and Central Banking in Ireland*, 185.

in the course of discussions in recent months with the Governor of the Bank and with the Chairman of the Currency Commission, I have given assurances that any alteration in our existing arrangements in regard to these matters mentioned above would be made only after a searching investigation by a competent body . . . I also stated that I would undertake to discuss the terms of reference beforehand with the banks if any such investigation was contemplated.[61]

In practice, this was to amount to giving the banks an effective veto over any proposals for change.

The notion of a central bank was now a live issue. Elsewhere in the British Commonwealth the initiative was soon taken—by New Zealand in 1934 and by Canada and India in 1935. The Government announced the formation of a commission to look into this and related matters, although it took two and a half years to report. Bankers' misgivings about proposals for central banking had been deepened by the party's advent to power and both the banks and the Currency Commission went into action to resist the Government initiative.

The Cosgrave Government had fought off suggestions for reform with the explanation that it would be against the wishes of 'existing institutions'. Fianna Fáil, always more radical in appearances, went so far as to appoint a commission; but the banks had much less to fear from that commission than they anticipated. MacEntee was as good as his word, protesting to de Valera in January 1934 that the terms of reference of the Banking Commission should exclude control of internal or external credit, and insisting in March that

we are under an obligation to consult with the Irish Banks before initiating any new step in connection with national currency, banking, or credit but apart from that, as the success of the inquiry and the acceptance of its findings must depend on us securing the whole-hearted co-operation of the Banks, it is, in my opinion, vital that we should be in close touch with them in the matter from the outset.[62]

In deference to the 'existing institutions', Fianna Fáil filled the Commission with conservatives, the majority of whom had made no secret of their opposition to financial reform. The chairman of the new Banking Commission was Joseph Brennan, a man who

---

[61] UCDA MacEntee Papers P67/105.

[62] Quotations are from letters to de Valera dated 31 January 1934 and 22 March 1934 in UCDA MacEntee Papers P67/105.

spent his life saying 'no' to every suggested innovation. If Fianna Fáil was serious about change, why did it appoint such conservatives? According to de Valera, it was because it wanted to establish the objectivity of the Commission beyond doubt, and to avoid accusations of bias. This argument had been put to de Valera by Finance on 4 April 1934.[63]

In fact, Fianna Fáil simply handed the opponents of any change a platform from which they could air their views with the authority of Government sponsorship. What might have been an opportunity to suggest fundamental changes was lost through fear of alienating the financial bourgeoisie and by the failure, once again, to call the objectivity of the state apparatus into question.

In the run-up to the 1938 election, both Fine Gael and Labour cited the delay in publishing the Commission's Report as evidence of an alleged Fianna Fáil plot to suppress it. Fine Gael's James Dillon claimed that the Report would indict Fianna Fáil policy since 1932 as 'a complete failure'; and Labour's P. J. Quinn declared that 'once the Report was published they knew the people would sweep Fianna Fáil out of power'.[64] The latter claim was certainly overly optimistic, although Dillon's comments may have had a greater ring of truth. When the Banking Commission eventually published its Report (in late 1938), the full extent of the loss of opportunity became evident. As Daly says, 'the Banking Commission saw a Central Bank as a restraint on government spending' and not on the banks.[65] The Majority Report was indeed highly critical of the expansionist and interventionist policies associated with Lemass. According to the *Irish Times*, the Report was 'in many ways . . . so conservative that it might almost have been prepared in Manchester fifty years ago'. The *Financial News* found its judgement 'to be coloured by its distaste for the whole trend of economic development in Éire'. *The Economist* went further: the Report had 'very few important recommendations to make, save for the all-important recommendation to leave things as they are'. The link with sterling was upheld and the commercial banking system was 'given an equally clear bill of health'. And *The Economist* continued:

the present Currency Commission (whose functions are virtually limited to the issue of currency and the holding of sterling assets against the notes

[63] Ibid.   [64] NAI Finance F009/0011/38.
[65] Daly, *Social and Economic History of Ireland*, 155.

issued) is to be renamed and its functions are to be enlarged. But the enlarged functions are not to include those normally attaching to a Central Bank. For example, there is to be no attempt to create a money market in Dublin, the commercial banks are not to be under the obligation of keeping reserve deposits with the new institution, and it is not even to take over the Government account from the Bank of Ireland.[66]

Fianna Fáil's political instinct was sharp enough to resist any attempt to tie its hands in the field of social spending. Lemass and other ministers expressed sympathy for one of the three minority reports produced; this had been the work of Fianna Fáil TD Peter O'Loghlan, who, in the ensuing debate, made a passionate attack on unemployment and on the link with sterling 'which dominates the financial operations of the Irish Government'. De Valera, himself, made clear his sympathy with the O'Loghlan report and committed Fianna Fáil to continue with social spending, especially in the area of housing. But there was to be no break with sterling. Above all, the Minority Report associated with the ITUC, which called for the state to amalgamate existing commercial banks into a single state banking corporation, publicly owned and controlled, was rejected outright. As Moynihan puts it, de Valera 'had made manifest his distrust of monetary experiments'.[67]

In a speech in September, Erskine Childers warned that 'Fianna Fáil must strenuously resist the temptation to offer a defiant attitude to the general findings', although it 'might . . . be possible to effect a compromise by not taking at 100 per cent value some of the more conservative strictures of the Report'.[68] In other words, the party should retain a certain political leeway but without attempting any real change in the financial system. That is precisely what happened. In particular, the Government rejected any suggestion of a compulsory repatriation of investments to aid the industrialization drive. MacEntee had warned that this 'would lead to a wholesale flight of capital and of those who owned it. Even if this did not occur the net effect of the change would be simply to shift the proceeds of past savings from more productive to less productive investment.'[69] In a memo to the Government in June 1939, MacEntee

---

[66] Quotations are from Moynihan, *Currency and Central Banking in Ireland*, 223–4.   [67] Ibid. 229.
[68] *Irish Independent*, 2 Sept. 1938.
[69] In a memo to the Government dated 18 April 1936 in UCDA MacEntee Papers P67/111.

quoted bankers' leader Lord Glenavy approvingly, to the effect that the existing system was fine; defects had not been shown; the Government had no right to interfere or to make profits from banking operations, when it did not provide the resources. And he ended: 'the Minister for Finance is in entire agreement with the conclusion reached in the Majority Report and he desires to secure the concurrence of the Government therein.'[70]

The Central Bank Act of 1942 followed the findings of the Majority Report in all important respects. The Act had been submitted in advance to both the Currency Commission and the Irish Banks Standing Committee for their observations, and interviews had been granted by MacEntee to the banks' representatives to assure them of its terms.[71] It was also in 1942, as we have noted, that the stamp duty imposed on the banks was removed altogether.

Social Conditions and Social Welfare

Possibly no aspect of Fianna Fáil's programme explains the breadth and solidity of the party's popular support better than the social-welfare reforms which it introduced when first in office. Modest, but essential, social-welfare payments drew a great mass of urban and rural poor into dependence upon the party. Social-welfare reforms did not eliminate poverty, but they did make the poor conscious of their need of a 'kind' political master, a point which was rammed home by the constant attacks of the Fine Gael opposition upon social spending. In the depressed rural areas Home Assistance officers, responsible for the distribution of the benefits, were often politically appointed and suspected of bias. Acts of maladministration could include the payment of benefits being made conditional or payments being made to the unentitled.[72] The rural poor, propped up partially by the remittances of emigrant sons and daughters, did not blame de Valera for the limitations of an industrial strategy which allowed emigration to continue largely unabated; instead, they looked to Fianna Fáil with almost filial devotion and filial expectations of support—their very insecurity increasing their loyalty. It has been suggested that Fianna Fáil treated its dependent supporters as almost childlike,[73] and indeed Fianna Fáil propaganda in 1938 spoke of the party's attitude to the community as being

[70] NAI Finance F009/0023/38.   [71] UCDA MacEntee Papers P67/108.
[72] Gibbon and O'Higgins, 'Patronage, Tradition and Modernisation', 36.
[73] O'Connell, 'Class, Nation and State', 20.

'that of a reasonably decent parent in the interests of the family as a whole'.[74]

Introducing the party's first budget in May 1932, MacEntee had declared, 'one thing we shall not do: we shall not cut the social services'. That budget increased housing expenditure and unemployment benefits, introduced free milk for needy children, and raised old age pensions. Old age pensions were still means tested, but the income of other family members was no longer taken into account; still, the qualification age for the pensions remained 70 years, as late as 1973.

Perhaps the most significant of the social improvements was the crash housing and infrastructure programme the Government embarked upon. The new Minister for Public Health and Local Government, Seán T. O'Kelly, increased grants to public-utility societies, private individuals, and local authorities, and the crisis in housing conditions was at last tackled.[75] A comprehensive slum-clearance programme led to the construction or renovation of 132,000 houses between 1932 and 1942—the highest figure for a long time. These houses were picturesquely portrayed in Fianna Fáil propaganda as 'monuments to Dev'.[76]

Other adjustments seemingly validated the party's claim to be a caring, compassionate, and protective parent. The age limit for blind pensions was reduced from 50 years to 30. Workmen's compensation legislation was introduced, under the tutelage of Lemass, in 1934; widows' and orphans' pensions followed in 1935. Lemass's reputation as champion of the working man was further enhanced by the Conditions of Employment Act of 1936. This Act guaranteed shorter hours with no reduced earnings, unemployment insurance for those under the age of 18 years who lost their employment because of the operation of the Act, holidays with pay, and obligatory provisions on cleanliness, rest rooms, first aid, ventilation, employment of women, and home work. Shift work and piece work were regulated and employment of children under 14 years was prohibited.[77] At around the same time, Lemass served notice to Finance of his intention to propose a new Shops Bill to regulate the

---

[74] *Irish Press*, 4 June 1938.

[75] Needless to say, Finance was opposed to the expenditure, with McElligott arguing that local authorities were not anxious to spend money and that the Exchequer would be left to foot the bill when they did (NAI Finance F088/0005/32).

[76] *Irish Press*, 7 June 1938.   [77] NAI Taoiseach S.6462A.

hours and conditions of shop assistants. Amongst its provisions were: a weekly half-day, persons under 18 years not to be employed for more than seventy-four hours per week, seats to be made available for female assistants, and provision of meal-breaks. The Minister was to be empowered to issue an Order fixing minimum wage rates and local authorities were to be responsible for enforcement. A Wages Board, with a chairman nominated by the Minister, was to be established. Despite predictable Finance opposition, this measure was signed into law in February 1938.[78]

Although many schools remained in a state of disrepair, and little attention was paid to education in general, free schoolbooks for needy children were provided in 1937. Between 1933 and 1936 the national health insurance system was streamlined. Towards the end of 1932, Lemass had put forward two 'definite proposals' to aid the unemployed: legislation to protect lower-income 'bona fide unemployed' from eviction for rent arrears, and weekly unemployment assistance, to be paid to all unemployed persons over the age of 18 years, subject to the same means test which applied to old age pensions. After some bureaucratic foot-dragging, legislation was introduced in August 1933 which effectively incorporated the second proposal.

The 1933 Unemployment Assistance Act extended assistance to all workers, the chief beneficiaries being small farmers and rural labourers. Agricultural labourers, in particular, were subject to the usual vicissitudes of seasonal, or casual, labour. In 1935 some 110,000 persons applied for assistance, although only 18,000 were eligible for unemployment benefit. Unemployment remained high throughout the 1930s and was rising sharply from 1935. Agricultural labourers seem to have been particularly prone to economic insecurity; legislation guaranteeing them a minimum wage, introduced in 1936, may also have contributed to less of them being employed; and agricultural labourers' wages declined by an average of three shillings per week between 1931 and 1935.[79]

Fianna Fáil was quick to point out that the first ever meeting of the cabinet had decided on an old age pensions Bill, voting an additional £250,000 for the care of the old, despite opposition from Finance. During the 1933 election, party leaflets bore slogans such

---

[78] NAI Finance S084/0027/36.
[79] Note to Cosgrave in UCDA McGilligan Papers P35c/176.

as 'Fianna Fáil will Abolish Unemployment', 'Fianna Fáil is Providing Healthy and Happy Homes for All', and 'What Fianna Fáil has Done for the Old Age Pensioners'. By 1935 the party was boasting of the £7 million it had distributed 'on services which benefit directly the poorer people'.[80]

However, the dialectic of internal party struggle imposed a limit to welfarist reforms. Lemass was the most politically adventurous of the cabinet team, ever mindful that social and industrial relations reforms were a necessary part of a successful political strategy in the Ireland of the times. De Valera, whose political instinct was equally sharp but more tactical than strategic, generally supported him. This support, however, was never unconditional; it was tempered by de Valera's obvious function in unifying the cabinet team, and by his own conservative idealism in economic and social matters. Thus, Lemass's efforts to have the means test for unemployed and pensioners lowered in 1935 were rejected by the majority of the cabinet, and he found himself battling against a proposal that legislation should be introduced to 'reduce from two shillings to one shilling per week the amount of means excluded from calculation'.[81] Similarly, his efforts to ensure that men and women should receive the same unemployment benefit—'I see no reason for differentiating between single men and women,' he wrote[82]—were unsuccessful, and his proposal to deprive landlords of the right to evict unemployed tenants was rejected as 'inadvisable' by a meeting of the economic committee of the cabinet on 18 November 1932, attended by almost the entire cabinet—a familiar device used to crush the more radical of Lemass's initiatives.[83] (Lemass was probably less astute *vis-à-vis* interdepartmental and inner-party conflict at this stage than he later became, and his tactic of writing personally to de Valera with his proposals, in an effort to bypass other Departments, scarcely helped to break down resistance from cabinet colleagues.) On top of this, the blatant failure of the promise of full employment, by the late 1930s, offered a clear target for attack: in 1939 there were 98,000 registered as unemployed, with 90,000 on local-authority assistance.[84]

By the mid-1930s Finance's old battery of economic, ideological, and moral arguments against state creation of employment and

---

[80] *Irish Press*, 3 Oct. 1935.   [81] NAI Cabinet 7/219.
[82] Letter dated 29 May 1933 in NAI Finance F088/0009/33.
[83] NAI Taoiseach S.6242A.   [84] *Irish Independent*, 3 June 1938.

public spending on social welfare was confidently reasserting itself, with MacEntee emerging as Lemass's most formidable opponent within the cabinet. The years 1935–8 saw growing conservatism in economic and social matters. This was so despite MacEntee's repeated threats to resign from office on the grounds that his views were not receiving the respect and support they deserved from de Valera.[85] Despite the whining and melodramatic tone of MacEntee's resignation threats, and his constant complaint that he had been slighted, snubbed, or ignored in cabinet, the fact is that his pressure had the desired effect: de Valera tended increasingly in the late 1930s to err in the direction of caution.

MacEntee opposed the use of public works to relieve unemployment in 1936 as 'economically unsound' and as leading to 'general budgetary and economic instability'. In this, he claimed to reflect the views of the Inter-Departmental Committee on Public Works.[86] In a passage which shows just how little had changed in his Department since Fianna Fáil assumed office, he wrote:

the moral improvement is never so great when a person is provided with work automatically and without effort on his part as when he obtains it by his own efforts. The system also tends to make the unemployed look to the state for employment in the same way as the community generally now shows a decided disinclination to embark on any enterprise without promise of active state support in one form or another.[87]

The cardinal principle of all expenditure on unemployment relief should be that provision should 'not be so attractive as to induce people to abandon their normal vocation in the hope of securing the more congenial conditions'.

Fianna Fáil's opponents did little to exploit these divisions or to offer a more attractive alternative to those dependent upon meagre social reforms. The Labour Party, apart from a brief flirtation with notions of nationalization which were quickly abandoned under Church pressure, failed to evolve any alternative strategy and found itself almost embarrassed by Fianna Fáil's social reforms. The limits to Fianna Fáil's achievements for the underprivileged were becoming

[85] See UCDA MacEntee Papers P67/121, P67/125, P67/133 and P67/155 for copies of repeated resignation threats. In one of these, written in 1938, MacEntee bitterly accused de Valera of 'preparing the way for a campaign of inflationary spending' and Lemass of contemplating 'even more desperate and delusive measures'.

[86] UCDA MacEntee Papers P67/111.

[87] Memo dated 18 April 1936 in UCDA MacEntee Papers P67/111.

obvious enough—but were the measures taken not those which Labour had advocated? How could Labour, despite its support for Fianna Fáil in 1932, and again in 1937, answer Seán T. O'Kelly's boast that 'the Labour Party had no more to do with the Widows' and Orphans' Act than the King of Bulgaria'?[88] The party's evident frustration with Fianna Fáil after that party's first few years in office stemmed as much from Labour's own inability to come up with something new to say as with Fianna Fáil's growing conservatism. Fine Gael found itself increasingly irrelevant to Irish capitalism, while just as unable as ever to appeal to the underprivileged. Concern with low living standards and poverty sat uneasily alongside attacks on public spending.[89] The party might call for higher productivity as the way to create wealth; but increases in productivity had seldom meant employing more workers or raising wages for Cumann na nGaedheal–Fine Gael when in government. Its appeal to the lower social groups was as circumscribed now as it had been during the 1920s—only now it held considerably less attraction for the bourgeois strata as well.

The politics of dependency and of paternalism went largely unchallenged.[90] A good example of the paternalism which characterized Fianna Fáil's approach to its working-class support base, and which Lemass shared with MacEntee, was given in 1937 in reaction to strikes within the state-owned sugar industry. MacEntee argued that 'if the state on behalf of the people opened the sugar factories it has an equal right, and indeed a duty, the moment they cease to serve the needs of the people fairly, to close them also. Those who challenge that principle challenge all organized authority in this country.' In effect, the implicit social contract between public-sector workers and the state meant that workers forfeited the right to strike in exchange for security of employment; they owed the state a duty of obedience. Strikes in a nationalized industry were 'unpatriotic and unfair' and there was 'no just reason' why strikers should 'ever again get employment in a Government undertaking'.[91]

---

[88] *Irish Press*, 21 June 1937.   [89] UCDA McGilligan Papers P35c/259.
[90] Perhaps some idea of the level of dependency can be gauged from the fact that in October 1938 the Department of Finance estimated that 575,477 people were dependent on the Exchequer for maintenance. The figure included 431,092 adults under 70; 130,916 pensioners over 70; and 13,469 'others' (NAI Finance F200/0020/38).   [91] UCDA MacEntee Papers P67/120.

It has been noted that Fianna Fáil, from 1938 onwards, con-
quered new territory among the middle strata and the bourgeoisie,
whilst forfeiting some rural support to the newly formed Clann na
Talmhan. The party's emergence as a catch-all party in the electoral
sense should not blind us to the fact that its working-class support
base remained considerably more solid than its small-farmer base
during this period.

POLITICAL DEVELOPMENTS

The 1930s witnessed an intensification of political struggle in Ireland, with the activities of the proto-fascist Blueshirts, on the extreme right, and of the IRA (initially, at least) and of other groups,
on the left, seemingly threatening the political status quo. The process by which Fianna Fáil managed to turn these potential forces of
destabilization to good advantage, outwitting its rivals on the left
and discrediting its opponents on the far right, is worthy of some
consideration.

Within days of the 1932 election Fianna Fáil made overtures to
the IRA, seeking a fusion of the organizations; no oath of allegiance
would be required of the IRA—just recognition of the new Government, which would create a new volunteer force which the IRA
could join. The new Government came to power in circumstances
of uncertainty; in view of the campaign rhetoric of sections of
Cumann na nGaedheal, there were fears as to whether Fianna Fáil
would be permitted to take power at all, and when Fianna Fáil
entered the Dáil many of its TDs carried revolvers in their pockets.
The party sought to use the threat of a 'reactionary Government'
further to coax the IRA, and a Fianna Fáil representative told the
IRA that 'a fusion now of the national forces, that is of the labourers
and the working farmers, will ensure that the national march to
freedom and social justice and cultural and economic development
will commence with rapid movement and overwhelming strength'.[92]
Reluctant to put itself out of existence, and innately suspicious of
'politicians', the IRA resisted the call for fusion, although its approach to Fianna Fáil remained confused. De Valera rejected the
IRA offer of a 'united front' against 'British aggression', and over
the next few years the argument continued, back and forth, with

[92] Cronin, *The McGarrity Papers*, 152–3.

the IRA calling for unity between 'all national and anti-imperialist forces' and de Valera insisting that it disband.

Meanwhile the Government took a number of steps designed to win the support of IRA members, cutting the ground from beneath the feet of the organization's leadership. Although the IRA itself was in a state of ideological confusion and had by no means proven itself capable of rising above purely terrorist activity, this very confusion seemed, at least, to create the opportunity for left-wing advances within the organization. Fianna Fáil had a clear interest in arresting any such development and the new Government sought to charm, cajole, captivate, and render politically innocuous the nascent republican left. Fianna Fáil had learnt well that repression alone usually proves counter-productive. Moreover, the sympathy felt by many party members for the IRA would have made such a policy politically difficult at this stage. The 'carrot-and-stick' approach, which Fianna Fáil followed with such astuteness, was ultimately to prove much more devastating for the IRA, and the benefits were to outweigh any political liability incurred by the fact that certain social groups might feel alienated by too close an initial relationship between Fianna Fáil and the IRA.

Immediately upon taking office, the Government ordered the release of seventeen republican prisoners, suspended the military tribunals (although, significantly, the Public Safety Act was not repealed), lifted the ban on the IRA, and allowed republican journals, such as *An Phoblacht*, to reappear. The emergence in the spring of 1932 of the Blueshirts created conditions favourable to a closer relationship between the extraparliamentary republican organizations and the Government; the IRA quickly branded the Blueshirts 'fascists' and renewed its pleas for joint action. In reality, however, the Blueshirt phenomenon actually facilitated the marginalization of the IRA. Fianna Fáil warned that the Blueshirts and the IRA would jointly plunge the country into renewed civil war if left unchecked and was soon preparing the way for the suppression of the IRA, having first dealt with the Blueshirts.

The IRA looked on, largely helpless, as the Government played off one alleged threat against the other. IRA leaders have always claimed that their men were ordered not to cause trouble during the Blueshirt upheaval and that Fianna Fáil members were often responsible for violent incidents which were then blamed on the IRA. The IRA chief of staff, Maurice Twomey, in a letter to Joe

McGarrity, disclaimed all involvement in attacks upon Blueshirt meetings, adding: 'the point is that Fianna Fáil leaders are using the commotion their own followers are largely responsible for creating to attack us.'[93] Indeed, it is symptomatic of the ideological confusion within the IRA that its members were ordered not to intervene when Blueshirt mobs attacked left-wing targets because the IRA was anxious to disassociate itself from the charge of communism. An order went out that no communist could be a member of the IRA and a statement from the IRA Army Council repudiated communism.

De Valera, however, did not fail to attribute to the IRA at least partial blame for the deteriorating political situation. At the Fianna Fáil *Ard-Fheis* in November 1932, he delivered a stern warning to Blueshirts and IRA alike:

We have tried to avoid coercive measures because this has failed with our people in the past . . . but I want to give warning: it is our duty as a Government to proceed vigorously against anyone found in possession of arms. In future, anyone found in the possession of arms will be given the full vigour of the law.[94]

In January 1934, in a direct attack upon the IRA, he declared: 'If this country is not to be a Mexico or a Cuba, a basis must be found, or else the party that has got the confidence of the majority here will have to secure order by force. There is no alternative.'[95]

The way for repressive action had been cleared by a series of further measures designed to win over rank-and-file IRA members and to neutralize the Fianna Fáil ranks. A new volunteer force was created in 1934 to absorb anti-Treaty IRA veterans, and a Military Pensions Act, which enabled those who had fought against the Treaty to claim pensions for the first time, further eroded the IRA's base. Boland tells us that 'almost all Ministers recruited their official drivers from their own IRA units and, in any case where this was not done, the deficiency was supplied by men who had served with the then Minister for Defence, Mr Aiken'.[96] (It is possible that some left-wing republicans may have been further tantalized by de Valera's support for the Soviet Union's application for membership of the League of Nations.) The IRA and the republican left were

---

[93] Ibid. 157.   [94] *Irish Press,* 9 Nov. 1932.
[95] Quoted in Cronin, *The McGarrity Papers,* 158.
[96] Boland, *The Rise and Decline of Fianna Fáil,* 31.

unsure how to react to these overtures; the IRA probably maintained as much contact with Fianna Fáil as with Sinn Féin; and while the IRA leadership might warn of Fianna Fáil attempts to neuter the organization, the rank and file was probably as ambiguous in its attitude to Fianna Fáil as the Fianna Fáil rank and file was towards the IRA.

The IRA resisted pressure to disband and refused to turn in its weapons. But it resisted increasingly from a position of weakness. 'The IRA floundered in those years for lack of a policy—any policy: political, social, or military.'[97] It failed to turn the polarization of Irish politics to good effect; its attempts to do so were marred by its naïve acceptance of the logic of Fianna Fáil economic strategy which left it hanging on to the coat-tails of the Government. (In July 1932 the IRA had called for a 'conference of national forces' to fight the Economic War more vigorously—a demand which made little political sense, as Fianna Fáil had absolutely no incentive to accede to it.) In May 1933 the IRA launched its contribution to the Economic War: it appointed a Director of Boycott, announced a *Boycott British Goods* campaign, and raided licensed premises to destroy supplies of Bass beer (a British company). The only real effect of this activity—condemned by de Valera as 'damn foolacting business'—was in all likelihood to convince many within Fianna Fáil that the IRA's anarchic outbursts were threatening their Government's successful pursuit of the Economic War. Indeed, it was precisely this point which de Valera used to bring pressure on the IRA via their North American backer, McGarrity, with whom he retained good relations. On 3 October 1933 McGarrity wrote to the IRA chief of staff, informing him that he had received a letter from de Valera in which it was stated that, although de Valera had 'no desire' to 'come out in opposition' to the IRA, he would be forced to do so. McGarrity continued: 'he says if we here could use our influence with the IRA and have them throw in their weight behind the Government that tremendous progress could be made, but instead of helping to win the fight they have the Bass Raids etc.' McGarrity went on to recommend convergence with Fianna Fáil 'as whatever de Valera's party may be they have no trucking with England of a voluntary nature'. Twomey wrote back three weeks later, in highly defensive terms, complaining of Fianna Fáil's

---

[97] Cronin, *The McGarrity Papers*, 166.

'betrayal' and 'sell-out' to the 'imperialist–rancher–banker–Chamber of Commerce element', but assuring McGarrity that 'I should be sorry to do the Fianna Fáil leaders an injustice'.[98]

Towards the end of 1933 the IRA was in deep crisis. The lack of any strategy which would enable it to compete with Fianna Fáil, coupled with the hostility of most of the leadership towards communism, led to a split involving the secession of the left wing. This group, including Peadar O'Donnell, pushed for the formation of a Republican Congress which would not be a new political party but 'an organizing centre for anti-imperialist activities on the part of people irrespective of their party or organizational affiliations'. When the IRA convention of March 1934 rejected the proposal, the left walked out. The subsequent launch of the Republican Congress did little to overcome the central problem facing the radical republicans —the absence of any political strategy based on an analysis of the nature of the Fianna Fáil regime now in power. The Republican Congress made a number of crucial compromises with Fianna Fáil ideology from the outset. The organization, which exhibited a marked antipathy towards large-scale industrialization, addressed itself as much to the small farmers as to the unemployed city workers (if not more so) and would seem to have accepted the central myth of Fianna Fáil propaganda: that small is beautiful, and that only a nation of smallholders could secure the happiness and freedom of the 'people'. The corollary of this, as we have seen, is the acceptance of a small, protected home market with an inefficient and ultimately exploitative national bourgeoisie.

Indeed, the Republican Congress declared that its aim was for the 'full realization of Fianna Fáil's original policies'. How it proposed to achieve this any better than Fianna Fáil was unclear. The dilemma for the Congress lay in its belief that the Fianna Fáil programme, and the ideals which inspired it, were in some way revolutionary, in the sense of subversive of the capitalist system. This patently was not the case; but, instead of encouraging the Congress leaders to subject the republican ideology which they shared with Fianna Fáil to critical examination, the obvious conservatism of the Fianna Fáil Government merely led them to sniff the scent of 'betrayal'. O'Donnell summed up the dominant position of the Congress when he declared: 'our quarrel with de Valera

---

[98] NLI McGarrity Papers MS 17490.

was not that he was not a socialist, but that he was not a Republican.' O'Donnell envisaged that the Congress, far from becoming a socialist organization, would simply associate republicanism with small-farmer and labour struggles through uniting the IRA, the Fianna Fáil rank and file, trade unions, Sinn Féin, the Gaelic Athletic Association, the Working Farmers' Committees, etc. in an effort to seize the leadership of the 'national struggle' from de Valera and 'free the republican masses from the ball and chain formula of Fianna Fáil'. This grandiose schema (based, it might seem, upon an attempt to emulate the Popular Front strategy of the *Comintern*) depended, not upon the exposure of the class limitations of Fianna Fáil's economic strategy, but upon the subordination of class to the revolutionary potential of the national struggle. Surprisingly, the RWG, in January 1933, seemed to be possessed of a similar idea, declaring that Fianna Fáil 'will receive the support of the broad masses because of its stand (however weak) against the British'.[99] In other words, Fianna Fáil hegemony was being attacked, not at its weakest point, but at the strongest.

Far from analysing Irish society in class terms, the Republican Congress merely reproduced the old Gael-versus-Planter stereotype, so deep-rooted in Irish Catholic nationalism. Eithne Coyle, a member of the Congress, declared in June 1933 that 'we must show those tyrants in the North that the land of Ulster belongs to the real people of Ireland and not to the Planter Stock of Henry VIII'.[100] As McHugh remarks, 'thus, even at the high water-mark of radical influence in the IRA, there were still calls for revolutionary mobilization on ethnic lines, not those of social class'.

A small minority within the Congress, which refused to accept the dominant thesis and pressed for the formation of a socialist organization which would campaign unambiguously for a Workers' Republic, was defeated and forced out of the Congress in September. This further split deprived the Congress of some of its most talented leaders, such as Michael Price and Roddy Connolly, both of whom eventually joined the Labour Party. Moreover, these leaders were associated with the trade unions and the loss of trade-union support was a serious blow.[101]

The effect of these developments was to create more confusion

---

[99] Banta, 'The Red Scare in the Irish Free State', 107.
[100] Quoted in McHugh, 'Voices of the Rearguard', 453 and *passim*.
[101] Ibid. 87.

and disillusionment than ever. The IRA was in a state of clear numerical decline from 1934. Not only did the defection of the Congress members affect it directly, but the decline into sheer militarism in their absence led to further membership loss and hastened the movement's suppression. From 1935 it was involved in armed attacks upon the police; a number of IRA murders in 1935–6 shocked the country and led to calls for immediate action against it; ominously, in 1935 Fianna Fáil declared that it would no longer sell Easter lilies, the symbol of 'an organization of whose methods they disapprove'.[102] At the same time, IRA attacks upon members of the Republican Congress marching at Bodenstown in June 1935 added to the disarray and made nonsense of hopes for republican unity. On 18 June 1936 Fianna Fáil made its move. The IRA was declared illegal once more; its leaders were arrested, including chief of staff Maurice Twomey, who was sentenced to three years' hard labour.

The move had been prepared well in advance. The Fianna Fáil ranks and republican sympathizers in general were prepared by the reassurance that the Government had done everything possible to be conciliatory. Cronin estimates that IRA strength fell from 8,036 in September 1934, to 7,358 in late 1935, and to a mere 3,844 in November 1936—of whom only 2,038 could be classified as 'active'. In Dublin, the IRA had fallen dramatically from 490 men in 1934 to 93 in 1936. As Cronin puts it,

de Valera's volunteer force cut into the membership from the Right, while many followed the Republican Congress to the Left, especially in Dublin where social policies were important. De Valera's constitutional advances robbed the IRA of much of the reason for its existence in the eyes of many republicans; and it was not radical enough for those who wanted social revolution.[103]

Perhaps of even greater significance for membership levels than the 'cuts' from right and left was the simple onset of confusion, disillusionment, and disorientation.

The Government's reputation was considerably enhanced, and its stability reinforced, by the emergence in 1932 of the movement known as the Blueshirts. Ironically, the ultimate effect of the Blueshirt

---

[102] Quoted in R. Fanning, 'The "Rule of Order": Eamon de Valera and the IRA, 1923–40', in J. A. Murphy and J. O'Carroll (eds.), *De Valera and his Times* (Cork, 1983), 165.   [103] Cronin, *The McGarrity Papers*, 166.

experience was to make Fianna Fáil appear more radical than it actually was, and, simultaneously, to consolidate its appeal as a party of stability, law and order, and national cohesion.

The Blueshirt movement had its origins in the Army Comrades Association (ACA), launched on 9 February 1932, allegedly to protect Free State army officers against possible discrimination.[104] It was not long, however, until the ACA was concerning itself with broader issues, and projecting itself as the 'vanguard of the anti-communist movement'.[105] In fact, the organization took up themes prominent in Cumann na nGaedheal propaganda prior to the 1932 election—the danger of 'communism', the role of Fianna Fáil as a front for communism, and the damage which Fianna Fáil economic policy would inflict upon the class interests of the large farmers and export-orientated bourgeoisie.

Strong anti-communism, given physical expression by extreme Catholic mobs, was commonplace in Ireland during the late 1920s and 1930s. Meetings of left-wing organizations were frequently broken up by crowds organized into Catholic Action Groups—formed to press for a totally Catholic society; the Blueshirts increasingly took up this cry. By August 1932 the programme of the ACA was one of total anti-communism. By the end of 1932 its membership had reached 30,000, and the focus of its attacks was increasingly the new Government. An editorial in the publication *United Irishman* warned that de Valera was 'proceeding along the Bolshevik path almost as precisely as if he was getting daily orders from Moscow'.[106] De Valera's dismissal of police Commissioner Eoin O'Duffy in February gave the organization a new leader; in July O'Duffy officially took over the leadership of what was now renamed the National Guard. The blue shirt had been adopted as a uniform in January 1933 and membership of the National Guard was restricted to 'Christians of Irish birth'. The movement took on clearly authoritarian and fascistic traits, with O'Duffy declaring that 'communists' should not be allowed to organize—the term 'communist' covered a wide spectrum in his eyes.

---

[104] For a discussion of the nature of the Blueshirts, see, *inter alia*, M. Manning, *The Blueshirts* (Dublin, 1970; 2nd edn., 1986); J. Heatley, 'The Blueshirt Movement', M.S.Sc. thesis (Belfast, 1987); D. Keogh, *Ireland and Europe, 1919–1948* (Dublin, 1988), ch. 2; P. Bew, E. Hazelkorn, and H. Patterson, *The Dynamics of Irish Politics* (London, 1989), 48–72; and R. Finnegan, 'The Blueshirts of Ireland during the 1930s: Fascism Inverted', *Éire/Ireland*, 242 (1989), 79–99.

[105] Manning, *The Blueshirts*, 15.   [106] Ibid. 36.

There is no doubt that the Blueshirts tended to find support amongst those who had voted for Cumann na nGaedheal and its allies in the Farmers' Party (which re-emerged in September 1932 as the National Centre Party, at one with Cumann na nGaedheal in opposing the Economic War). Cosgrave, himself, later estimated that the Blueshirt movement was largely manned by large farmers and their sons,[107] and it was never to succeed in transcending its narrow social base. The Blueshirt phenomenon can be viewed, not so much as a temporary deviation from the norms of parliamentary democracy by tried and trusted statesmen who ought to have known better, but rather as the logical outcome of a political strategy which had failed totally. After Fianna Fáil's return to power with an effective overall majority in the snap general election of January 1933— the party increased its share of the vote to 49.7 per cent—Cumann na nGaedheal and its allies became more desperate than ever to prevent the new regime's consolidation. The onset of the Economic War hardened their resolve: its harmful effects were greatly feared and exaggerated in the minds of the large farmers. After the banning of the National Guard in August 1933—a Mussolini-style 'march on Dublin' had been threatened—the logical fusion of the right-wing opposition groups took place. Cumann na nGaedheal, the National Centre Party, and the blueshirted National Guard united to form a new party: Fine Gael. (Characteristically, however, they could not even agree upon a definitive name and for a time it remained unclear whether the new organization should not, in fact, be called the United Ireland Party.) O'Duffy was elected to the leadership of Fine Gael and the National Guard was re-formed as the Young Ireland Association—within Fine Gael.

The reason why Cosgrave and his colleagues should turn to a fascist-type reaction in an effort to oust Fianna Fáil is not as difficult to discern as is sometimes claimed. Emphasis upon the constitutional and statesmanlike approach of Cosgrave should not blind us to the fact that many Cumann na nGaedheal leaders had shared an IRA background with Fianna Fáil and illusions about Cumann na nGaedheal's reluctance to apply authoritarian solutions to perceived problems are dispelled by that party's last years in power. Certainly, the party handed over power to Fianna Fáil in 1932; but to attempt otherwise—as some, including O'Duffy, contemplated—

[107] Ibid. 126.

would have been to risk a renewed civil war which Cumann na nGaedheal had no guarantee of winning: the balance of forces was no longer so favourable. Probably, the party felt that the safest course was to permit Fianna Fáil to take office and then sit back and wait for the Fianna Fáil Government to collapse through sheer incompetence. When Fianna Fáil did not do so, its opponents were at their wits' end as to what move to make next. Cumann na nGaedheal found itself contesting the 1933 election with little more than a watered-down version of Fianna Fáil's policies, allowing the Government to boast that 'even Cosgrave admits that Fianna Fáil was right all along'. When defeat followed, unity with the Blueshirts seemed to offer a new policy, corporatism, and a new dynamic appeal, in the form of O'Duffy's aggressive leadership. The need for a new corporatist approach had been outlined by Eoin MacNeill in a paper in 1932. He had written:

If a party claiming to represent the national interest generally has no policy of social reform, and can promise nothing beyond 'trying to rebuild the old house on the same pattern and with the same materials', it must expect to fall down before the building itself falls down. Such a party can only put up a technical plea of Not Guilty when its opponents charge it with being capitalistic and reactionary.[108]

The intention was clear enough, but 'capitalistic and reactionary' was exactly how Fine Gael continued to appear. The new look corporatism was clumsily presented in an authoritarian and threatening manner and too much faith was placed in the power of papal encyclicals on social organization and occasional pastorals condemning the effects of the Economic War. The problem in Ireland during the 1930s was not simply one of social organization, but one of economic growth, and here Fine Gael had nothing new to offer. Promises of blissful social organization were no substitute for the jobs and houses which Irish workers eagerly awaited from Fianna Fáil, or the profits which a substantial section of the Irish bourgeoisie hoped to reap from protection. The hostility of the small farmers and farm labourers was assured by the involvement of the 'ranchers'. In fact, the 'ranchers' were the only social stratum to whose basic interests a definite appeal was made—although some support may also have been forthcoming from medium-size farmers, alienated by Fianna Fáil's attempts to regulate the wages of farm

[108] UCDA MacNeill Papers LA1/F 313.

labourers. The new look, then, was essentially window-dressing; the lessons of Cumann na nGaedheal's failure had not been learnt. By the end of the 1930s Fine Gael had reached an organizational and electoral low from which it was not to recover for over a decade. O'Duffy's supposedly charismatic leadership further contributed to the humiliation by frightening some of his own supporters, and making the Government appear distinctly moderate and respectable by comparison. Nor was the appeal to national chauvinism, or racism—characteristic of fascist movements elsewhere—open to the Blueshirt–Fine Gael movement; their identification with the British economic connection and with the Protestant minority within the state closed off that avenue effectively. O'Duffy's occasional ranting about invading Northern Ireland was an embarrassment to most of his colleagues.

Fine Gael, both during and after its flirtation with fascism, found itself shadow-boxing on the sidelines of Irish politics. This is not to deny that the Blueshirts did capture public attention for a brief period, or that the threat to democracy which they posed was real; aping of European fascist movements, complete with the Roman salute and cries of 'Hail O'Duffy!', might seem comical in retrospect, but at the time the danger seemed potent enough. But the movement found itself, time and time again, fighting on non-issues. Gross exaggerations of IRA violence, almost to the point of suggesting that the country was on the brink of total anarchy, were easily refuted by the Government, which could point out that the incidence of political violence was less than it had been when Cumann na nGaedheal was in power; and many people understandably held the Blueshirts responsible for much of the violence in the first place. Attempts to utilize the Catholic religion—as if members of Fianna Fáil were closet atheists, intent on the destruction of 'Christian civilization'—were way off the mark; de Valera was soon referring to Ireland as a 'Catholic nation', Fianna Fáil ministers were attending Church ceremonies, and bishops were being invited to open and bless new factories and housing estates.[109] Although Fianna Fáil might maintain a certain leeway—for example, it refused to join a pro-Franco Catholic crusade during the Spanish Civil War—Church–State relations were not a political issue. Fine Gael's initial opposition to the various constitutional reforms introduced by Fianna

---

[109] Whyte, *Church and State in Modern Ireland*, 47–8.

Fáil, culminating in the new Constitution of 1937, made a mockery of that party's previous commitment to use the Treaty settlement as a stepping stone to full independence, and permitted Fianna Fáil to accuse it of conspiring with the British to start a new civil war. The party's opposition to the enlargement of the local-government franchise allowed Fianna Fáil to attack the Blueshirts (since banned again, and renamed again—the League of Youth) as the 'League Against Youth',[110] as young people stood to benefit from the abolition of the property qualification; in the last local-government elections held under the old register—in 1934—Fine Gael did poorly, despite O'Duffy's proud boast that it would replace Fianna Fáil, winning control of only seven of the twenty-three councils contested. The party consistently overestimated both the plight of the large farmers and the importance of their welfare to the rest of the community. As late as 1937—after the Coal–Cattle Pact had considerably eased the pressure on cattle exporters, with MacEntee already making the turnabout in Fianna Fáil policy crystal clear, and with the Anglo-Irish Agreement now in the air—Fine Gael was contesting the general election of that year on the basis that, 'if returned to power, Fine Gael promises to put the people of this country, especially the farmers, on their feet. The only true farmers' party is the Fine Gael party.'[111] Not only was this line of argument by now in reality irrelevant, it was almost guaranteed to have a negative effect upon workers, the unemployed, and small farmers, who had suffered much more than the large farmers, whose social-welfare benefits Fine Gael was on record as attacking, and who were scarcely likely to be impressed by appeals to the selfishness of the better-off. Finally, Fine Gael's opposition to the 1938 Anglo-Irish Agreement—welcome news to the very strata which had looked to it for leadership—apparently for no better reason than the fact that Fianna Fáil had negotiated it, aptly sums up the party's continuing failure to engage with realism. The party's 1938 declaration that 'a vote for a Fianna Fáil deputy is a vote for the abolition of effective parliamentary representation. It is a vote for one-man Government' was so out of touch with reality as to serve as a fitting epitaph for the pre-war phase in the party's history.

Fine Gael's own record on 'parliamentary representation', meanwhile, had been giving cause for concern. In October 1932 Thomas

---

[110] *Irish Press*, 26 Apr. 1934.   [111] *Irish Independent*, 3 May 1937.

O'Higgins, brother of the late Kevin O'Higgins, declared that 'no country in the world needs order knocked into it as much as Ireland'. By January 1933 he was threatening to wreck Fianna Fáil meetings in retaliation for disturbances at Blueshirt rallies. Ernest Blythe, writing as '*Onlooker*' in the *United Irishman*, reported that young Blueshirts 'think that all parliaments gabble too much, and they are not at all sure that the national will can be properly ascertained by merely counting heads'.[112] O'Duffy was soon echoing these sentiments, declaring that 'there is no reason why we should make an idol of parliament' and speaking of the need to 'supplant' it. In April 1934 he was quoted as saying that 'we must make life impossible for those who will not yield to our demands', and was described as a 'would be dictator'.[113] Repeated Fianna Fáil attacks upon the undemocratic nature of the Blueshirts were given added poignancy by the violence associated with the Blueshirt campaign against payment of agricultural rates and land annuities.

This campaign yielded some positive return for the movement in the short term, but ultimately proved a disaster. The Blueshirts argued that farmers had no obligation to pay annuities, as they were penalized by the tariffs imposed upon Irish exports to the United Kingdom. In 1933 57 per cent of annuities were withheld and nearly 97 per cent in 1934 (the figures may be artificially boosted by Government reluctance to pursue collection too vigorously amongst small farmers); by 1935, however, the campaign had run out of steam and only about 30 per cent of annuities were being withheld. The attempt to withhold rates was less successful: 36 per cent of rates went unpaid in 1933/4, and 31 per cent in 1934/5. However, the naked sectional nature of the campaign limited its appeal and Fianna Fáil paraded the rates and annuities campaign as a direct attack upon the poor and the unemployed, for whom, Fianna Fáil claimed, the money was used. The campaign was accompanied by a crescendo of violence, which seemed to occur in inverse relation to the political success of the movement. In early 1934 Colonel Jerry Ryan, a member of the Fine Gael national executive, was charged with the attempted murder of a rate collector, and many other Blueshirts were charged with similar violent crimes. After Fine Gael's setback in the 1934 local elections a new wave of Blueshirt violence broke out. In late 1934 several members of the

---

[112] Quoted in Manning, *The Blueshirts*, 58.   [113] *Irish Press*, 13 Apr. 1934.

Fine Gael national executive were jailed; the Blueshirt leaders were becoming increasingly reckless. In 1934 military tribunals convicted 349 Blueshirts and 102 IRA men of violent crimes. By now, however, the movement was in a state of confusion, dissension, and decline.

The flirtation with right-wing authoritarianism had clearly not worked for Fine Gael. Conditions similar to those which facilitated the rise of Mussolini in Italy or Hitler in Germany were absent in the Ireland of the 1930s. Not only was the stability of the capitalist economic system not under threat, but Fianna Fáil's policies were rapidly expanding the ranks of the manufacturing bourgeoisie, which, in turn, was turning to Fianna Fáil for political leadership. Not only was the challenge from the left extremely weak, but the working class was increasingly being incorporated within Fianna Fáil's economic development strategy. As far as the greater part of Irish business was concerned, it wanted nothing better than the social peace and stability necessary to get on with the job of making as much profit as possible from the Government's policy of protection. Fine Gael had nothing new to offer; it had failed to learn the necessity of constructing a political bloc of diverse social forces; what was at stake was merely the immediate economic interests of a bourgeois stratum which was no longer economically dominant.

By late 1934 the failure of the attempt to impose by force what the electorate had already rejected twice was clear. Fianna Fáil's tough response to the Blueshirt threat—a new police division, equipped with armoured cars, had been established to deal with the situation; the Blueshirts, under their various titles, had been repeatedly banned; and the wearing of the Blueshirt uniform was outlawed—had the effect of bringing matters to a head. Fine Gael now faced imminent disaster, possibly even disintegration, if it continued upon a path of violent confrontation whilst lacking the social support necessary to sustain such a strategy. The immediate issue at stake was the question of O'Duffy's unstable leadership—although this might have been taken as a synonym for the whole Blueshirt strategy of tension. In September 1934 O'Duffy was removed from the leadership of Fine Gael and of the Blueshirts amid bitter recriminations; Cosgrave was restored to the party leadership and the Blueshirts were progressively marginalized. The burning of the homes of two Fianna Fáil TDs in April 1935 was condemned by the

United Irishman, the journal of Fine Gael, and in 1936 the Blueshirts were finally wound up.

The Blueshirt episode certainly strengthened the Government, not least in that it facilitated Fianna Fáil's inroads into the labour and trade-union movement, and not only in the sense of increased co-operation with the Labour Party. Labour had supported a minority Fianna Fáil Government in 1932 in return for the implementation of common aspects of the two parties' programmes and consultations on proposed welfare legislation. De Valera had been quick to cement the alliance with Labour, even to the extent of quoting James Connolly. Speaking in the Dáil in April 1932, he said: 'I never regarded freedom as an end in itself, but if I were asked what statement of Irish policy was most in accordance with my view as to what human beings should struggle for, I would stand side by side with James Connolly.' And he continued:

These two parties [Fianna Fáil and Labour] had naturally the same programme and when I differed with the Labour Party after the Treaty it was because I thought that party was making a mistake and that they did not see what James Connolly saw, and what he told me he saw, that to secure national freedom was the first step in order to get the workers of Ireland the living they were entitled to in their own country.[114]

By linking working-class living standards to 'national freedom', de Valera was able to quote Connolly against the party which Connolly helped to found in such a way as to make Fianna Fáil appear more radical, more left-wing, more 'labour-orientated' than the Labour Party. This was part of a concerted Fianna Fáil drive, not merely to confine the Labour Party to a subaltern position, but, more importantly perhaps, to enlist the support of thousands of workers and trade unionists over the heads of the Labour leaders.

By the end of 1932 many of the points common to the two parties' programmes were being implemented—and Fianna Fáil was taking the credit. The Government's willingness to consult with the Labour Party on aspects of social and economic policy neither had much effect, nor gained the Labour Party much advantage. Anxious to avoid total absorption, the Labour leaders now fought something of a rearguard action, demanding stronger efforts on the employment front. How did Labour envisage this could be achieved? The answer is illustrative of the entirely defensive and subaltern nature

[114] Dáil Debates, 29 Apr. 1932.

of the Labour position: it demanded an acceleration of the Economic War. Like the republican left, it was attacking Fianna Fáil at that party's strongest point. Indeed, Norton, who succeeded the unseated O'Connell as Labour Party leader after the 1932 election, has been described as 'more republican' than his predecessor, and he was to draw the amazing conclusion that the outcome of the 1933 election, in which his own party suffered badly, was 'an instruction to Cumann na nGaedheal and to the Farmers' League to stop fighting Thomas's [the British Dominions secretary] battle against the Irish people'.[115]

Nevertheless, by the end of 1932 the lack of an overall majority was becoming irksome to Fianna Fáil, whose exclusivist ideological outlook made it an uneasy partner in any political alliance. Accordingly, the Government, taking advantage of the disarray of its rivals on both left and right, called a fresh election in January 1933, and, using the external conflict with the United Kingdom, campaigned on the slogan: 'Today Choose your own Government. Choose a Strong Government. Choose an IRISH Government.'[116] Its economic and political strategy thus firmly presented in patriotic colours, Fianna Fáil received an increased mandate which effectively relieved it of reliance on the Labour Party and reduced Labour's share of the popular vote to an all-time low of 5.7 per cent.

At this point, it might be felt, the Labour Party was free—indeed, forced—to develop a more independent political stance, if there was any room for political manœuvre left to it. But it was precisely at this point that the upsurge in Blueshirt activity further delivered Labour into the hands of Fianna Fáil.

Labour perceived in the growing authoritarianism of the Blueshirts a serious threat to the democratic system in general, and to trade-union rights in particular. The adoption of wholesale corporatism by the Blueshirts underlined these fears. In a 1934 pamphlet in the Fine Gael Policy Series, entitled *An Outline of the Political, Social and Economic Policy of Fine Gael (United Ireland) Party*, General O'Duffy declared: 'We are out to establish the dictatorship of the people of Ireland. The people of Ireland include the capitalist as well as the worker, the farmer as well as the industrialist, the farm-labourer as well as the factory worker.' Given the nature of the Labour Party by this stage, the corporatist idea, in itself, would not necessarily have met with their certain opposition; but the use of the term 'dictatorship', the increasingly authoritarian tone of Blueshirt pronouncements, and the General's promise that in the ideal Blueshirt society there would be no such thing as strikes or lock-outs, certainly aroused their worst fears. At around this time a worried Thomas Johnson was compiling notes on the Blueshirts. Among the statements in the *Blueshirt* journal which exacerbated his fears were O'Duffy's claim that boys in their teens were joining in large numbers; the blunt statement that 'Democracy in the short space of a year has gone mad and committed suicide, and a rapid choice between Communism and some system with discipline and author-ity as its first principle is facing the young generation here'; and the warning that 'the state should fix the constitutions of the various unions and federations and take care that they are controlled by men of good character, public spirit and sound national views'.[117]

Fianna Fáil was quick to seize upon these fears, warning that O'Duffy's dictatorship 'will press most heavily upon the workers', and that 'Trade Unionism as it is known today is to disappear', to be turned into a 'branch' of employer-dominated corporations. The party further coloured the picture by claiming that the unemployed, under a Blueshirt administration, would be put into 'labour gangs' under duress. 'We know some of those he [O'Duffy] is now asso-ciated with and we know their outlook on workers' rights.'[118]

On the one hand, this increased Labour's tendency to regard Fianna Fáil as the more progressive of the two main parties, and to accept its leadership in the struggle against 'fascism' rather than attempt a third position of its own. On the other hand, Labour reacted to the Blueshirt hysteria about 'communism' with custom-ary panic. In November 1932—at a time when Blueshirt leaders were escalating their threats against the Government, and when there was now a perceptible and serious challenge from the authoritarian right—Labour leaders were pitching themselves into battle against the tiny number of communist activists who were making attempts to organize the unemployed in protest marches. The General Sec-retary of the Labour Party, D. J. O'Neill, was quoted as saying:

We have circularised all branches in the country to beware of the agents of Communism, who have been sent out to organise the unemployed. It was the policy of Communists to keep up a continual discontent amongst

---

[117] NLI Johnson Papers MS 17186.　　[118] *Irish Press*, 27 Feb. 1934.

the unemployed by the method of hunger marches on public bodies. By this means they hoped to build up an organization from which to set up a Soviet state.

He was further quoted as saying that 'large numbers of the unemployed in Dublin had joined the Communist movement' but he believed that they did not know where they were being led and he was sure 'that no matter how poverty stricken an Irishman might be, if the rules of the Soviet state were forced upon him, he would do with them [the communists] what St Patrick did with the snakes.'[119]

Given this sort of clerically inspired hysteria which greatly exaggerated the 'red scare' upon which the Blueshirts' justification rested, it is hardly surprising that the Labour Party should turn a blind eye to dangerous miscarriages of justice, such as the (technically illegal) deportation, in August 1933, of the Leitrim socialist, Jim Gralton— a deportation carried out by Fianna Fáil to appease right-wing Catholic groups led by a local Catholic priest, who had demanded action against Gralton's 'preaching' of 'subversive doctrines'. Or that the 1934 Labour conference should concentrate as much on condemning violence perpetrated by left-wing republicans against the Blueshirts as on condemning the Blueshirts themselves—going on to endorse a motion advocating a 'just social order based on Christian teaching' and rejecting all 'anti-Christian, Communist doctrines'. (In 1935 the chairman of the County Cork Organizing Committee of the Labour Party, Mr T. Quinn, was assuring the public that 'the Labour Party's programme was founded on a policy of religion and "love one another"'.[120])

Yet mention must be made of a development which in retrospect seems something of an aberration: the adoption by the 1936 Labour Party conference of the old Connollyist demand for a Workers' Republic. Labour leader William Norton told the conference: 'private enterprise has failed. The Labour Party stands for a planned economy. The political objective of the Labour Party is a Workers' Republic.' The new party programme called for nationalization of all basic industries and state control of banking and credit, as well as a rather vague demand for 'economic planning'. However, the change was more apparent than real, and was short lived. As to why Labour should have embarked upon the Workers' Republic adventure at all, there are a number of possible explanations.

[119] *Irish Independent*, 9 Nov. 1932.   [120] UCDA Mulcahy Papers P7/D/117.

First, by 1936 the Labour Party found itself with a lot more room for manœuvre. With the recession of the Blueshirt threat, with Fine Gael in obvious disarray, and with the eclipse of the various far-left groups and the suppression of the IRA, Labour was almost obliged to perform an opposition role of some description. Moreover, the persistence of economic problems, such as unemployment, low wages, and emigration, seemed to present fertile ground for a bolder political approach. Second, the need for Labour to take its distance from Fianna Fáil was finally rammed home by its inability to claim any electoral benefit or political credit from Fianna Fáil's implementation of certain of Labour's demands, and by the solid refusal of Fianna Fáil to implement the more generous social-welfare reforms which many Labour leaders (and, no doubt, Lemass) would have wished for. Labour had, moreover, apparently failed to benefit from the rise in trade unionization: in the period 1932–4 alone, trade-union membership rose once more from 117,000 to 126,000, yet Labour continued to derive negligible support from trade unionists. Finally, the adoption of the Workers' Republic programme was undoubtedly influenced also by the influx of former Republican Congress members, who joined Labour in search of a political home. One of their number, Michael Price, was actually elected to Labour's Administrative Council in February 1937.[121]

However, the new departure was much less radical than it seemed. It is doubtful if it ever received more than tactical support from the bulk of Labour's rural members, or from pragmatic trade-union officials; certainly a substantial minority never even gave it that. Alderman R. Corish, TD, undoubtedly spoke for many when he declared: 'I am neither Socialist, Syndicalist nor Communist. I am a Catholic, thank God, and I am prepared to take my teaching from the Catholic Church . . .'[122] Moreover, there were always members of the Labour Party Administrative Council, such as Mr Gilbert Lynch, ready to reassure the anxious that 'the Labour Party are not opposed to the rights of private property; but what we do say is that every citizen of this country ought to have a right to own property'.[123] The flirtation with socialism may have paid off electorally: in the 1937 general election Labour increased its vote to 10.3 per cent—its highest vote since Fianna Fáil entered the Dáil—while the

[121] NLI Johnson Papers MS 17190.   [122] *Munster Express*, 27 Nov. 1936.
[123] Ibid., 25 June 1937.

Fianna Fáil vote fell by a corresponding 4.5 per cent to 45.2 per cent. Moreover, Labour, significantly, made gains in Dublin, where it made political capital out of the rising cost of living—attributing this to the effects of the Economic War, which it had unstintingly supported before. Labour may also have been helped by industrial militancy in Dublin, where a big building strike led to large labour meetings, reportedly larger than de Valera's opening rally of the Fianna Fáil campaign.[124]

But the adoption of the Workers' Republic was merely tactical—indeed, more of a panic reflex than a serious change of heart. Behind the radical rhetoric and the sloganizing there was little evidence of strategic thinking. The programme was at most a vague social-democratic document, if even that; it certainly bore little resemblance to the revolutionary theorizing of James Connolly. Party thinking at the time was well expressed in the so-called 'Labour's Constructive Programme for an Organized Nation'.[125] The most radical proposal contained in this document was one which foreshadowed later initiatives of Lemass, seeking an Industrial Code. 'The Trade Unions would be authorised by law to assist in the enforcement of the industrial code in factories and workshops, and their co-operation would be sought to supplement the efforts of the State to improve the conditions and technique of industry generally.' This industrial code would be aimed at hours and conditions, and the 'employment of juvenile workers should be restricted to a minimum' (all pretty innocuous stuff, when one considers that Lemass sought to ban juvenile employment altogether!). Loyalty to Connolly's goal of a Workers' Republic took the form of a declaration of loyalty to the Easter Week Proclamation, 'and to the principles of Connolly enshrined in it'. Hostility was declared to the notion of a 'Dictatorship of the Proletariat'. 'Labour does not deny the rights of private property,' the Programme continued: 'Labour does not consider that in the public interest confiscation of property (e.g. ownership of ground rents), although in many cases that property may have been stolen originally or has been paid for over and over again by the community, would be desirable.' This vital compromise on the question of property rights was coupled with a plea to 'the people of this country collectively to regard

[124] *Connacht Tribune*, 26 June 1937.
[125] NLI Johnson Papers MS 17188 (n.d., after 1934).

themselves as a great Christian family'—plus a Fianna Fáil-style reference to the 'capitalist system which was imposed on us by a foreign oppressor . . .'.

It is little surprise, then, that in 1938 Labour reverted to its own peculiar brand of Catholic social teaching, deleting the references to the Workers' Republic from its programme once more. The move followed a condemnation of talk of a Workers' Republic by the Catholic hierarchy, whose intervention had actually been sought by the Irish National Teachers' Organization—one of the 'anti-communist' trade unions affiliated to the Labour Party.

In the 1938 general election Labour did quite well, holding its vote almost intact at 10 per cent; at this election Fianna Fáil, with the Anglo-Irish Agreement tucked under its arm, soared to a historic high of 51.9 per cent. Clearly, the adoption of a more independent and radical image, however short lived and however little there may have been behind the image, had given Labour a considerable morale boost. One can only speculate on how Labour might have fared in the years ahead if it had stuck to its guns in 1938 and turned its attention to the detailed elaboration of an alternative economic strategy. But with the return of Labour's habitual self-effacement the party was once more placed on the defensive and further splits and disappointments were just around the corner.

Finally, we may comment on those changes of a constitutional nature introduced by Fianna Fáil during the 1930s, in so far as they are pertinent to the party's consensus-building strategy or its ideological discourses. It is not my intention here to give a detailed historical account of the process by which Fianna Fáil came to dismantle the framework of the Anglo-Irish Treaty of 1921. But a brief summary of the constitutional reforms, culminating in the new Constitution of 1937, is necessary to a full understanding of the process by which Fianna Fáil consolidated its hold on power, not least in so far as the constitutional debate presented Fianna Fáil with further opportunities to wrong-foot its rivals.

Fianna Fáil's stated ambition to dismantle those features of the 1921 Treaty settlement which were especially repugnant to republicans was facilitated by the Statute of Westminster in 1931, which confirmed the right of British dominions to control their own affairs. Once in power, Fianna Fáil did not take long to avail to the full of the opportunities inherent in this development. First on the agenda was the abolition of the oath of allegiance to the British crown. A Bill to abolish the oath passed through the Dáil but was delayed by the Senate, eventually becoming law in the summer of 1933. The following August saw the abolition of the right of appeal to the UK Privy Council. The progressive curtailment of the powers of the Governor-General was facilitated by the appointment to that office of a man typical in many ways of a substantial section of the party's support base—Mr Donal Buckley, a small garage owner and staunch Fianna Fáil supporter, who effectively killed the office of Governor-General by refusing to appear in public or give any form of social lead, who drew only £2,000 of his salary of £10,000, and who did not take up residence in the vice-regal lodge. The whole farce was as if stage-managed to delight the party's supporters by appealing to the petty-bourgeois egalitarian myth which was to play such an important part in the ideological justification and legitimation of the new Ireland. Indeed, the handling of the Governor-General affair is reminiscent of de Valera's much-flaunted cut in the salaries of government ministers, on the grounds that government and people should 'tighten their belts' together (there, too, the image was what mattered most—for the cuts were soon restored). The Governor-Generalship was abolished altogether in 1936.

A Bill to abolish the Senate was introduced in March 1934, becoming law in May 1936. In 1935 the Irish Nationality and Citizenship Act and the Aliens Act were passed; these two pieces of legislation replaced British citizenship with Irish, and classified British subjects as 'aliens', thus pointing the way towards the full realization of de Valera's goal of 'external association' with the British Commonwealth. Finally, the UK abdication crisis of 1936 allowed the Government to rush emergency legislation through the Dáil deleting all references to the King and the Governor-General from the Constitution of the Irish Free State, and then proceeding to recognize the new king only as head of the British Commonwealth, not as king of Ireland; the aim of 'external association' had effectively been achieved.

The constitutional reforms enacted so far obviously had the advantage of appealing to patriotic sentiment. Fianna Fáil could now claim to be a 'national Government'; and those who opposed its reforms could be accused of aiding and abetting a foreign adversary with whom the country was engaged in an economic war. Moreover, these changes were essential to the Fianna Fáil leadership's legitimation of its exercise of power in the eyes of its own members, given the organization's history; and they played an obvious part in the Government's attempts to woo or coerce the IRA and the left republican groups out of existence. But there is another aspect to the constitutional changes which is too often overlooked: their democratic egalitarian aspect. Fianna Fáil's constitutional reforms could be, and frequently were, presented not only as a reassertion of the soul and spirit of the nation, but as an attack upon privilege, inequality, and undemocratic, 'imperialist' hang-overs from the past. In this way, Cumann na nGaedheal–Fine Gael, especially given its involvement with Blueshirtism, could be accused of attempting to prevent the ascent of the 'plain people of Ireland', led by Fianna Fáil. The appeal behind many of the party's constitutional reforms was not only to a sense of nationalism, but to an, albeit confused and disorientated, sense of social class consciousness. Fine Gael, obligingly, dug its heels in, and opposed every democratic reform, including the extension of the local-government franchise; it was Fianna Fáil now, not Fine Gael, which was seen to carry out Michael Collins's policy of using the Treaty merely as a 'stepping stone to freedom'.

Labour, for its part, was further thrown on the defensive by the progress of the constitutional debate. In December 1936 Labour opposed the Government's External Relations Act—which, having taken references to the king out of the Constitution, clarified the Free State's recognition of him as Commonwealth head—on the grounds that there should be no mention of the king at all! Once again, Labour exposed the weakness of its position; by its futile attempt to appear more nationalistic than Fianna Fáil, Labour simply demonstrated its incapacity to learn that Fianna Fáil could not be defeated by attacking it on its own ground. Labour continued to dance to another's tune.

By the end of 1936 Fianna Fáil was determined to press ahead with the passage of a new Constitution, the preparation of which was well under way. The existing Constitution had its roots in British law, and its symbolic repeal was essential to the credibility of Fianna Fáil's subsequent claim that full independence had been achieved in the twenty-six counties.

The new Constitution was approved by referendum on 1 July 1937, obtaining 685,105 votes (56.5 per cent) against 526,945 (43.5 per cent); it came into effect in June 1938. The Constitution was a purely republican document, although it contained no specific mention of republicanism. 'Éire' was declared to be 'a sovereign, independent, democratic state' (Article 5) with a president elected by the people (Article 12). The tricolour was established as the national flag, and the Irish language recognized as the first official language of the state. Why, then, did Fianna Fáil stop short of declaring a full republic? Fanning has suggested that the Government was anxious to avoid openly provoking the United Kingdom lest retaliatory measures such as the enforced repatriation of Irish emigrants to Great Britain (and the closing-off of the safety valve of emigration) be undertaken; and that it may have been felt that unity would be facilitated by avoiding an outright break with the Commonwealth.[126] On that point, it is true that the form of words chosen was such as to allow the UK Government to claim, rather disingenuously, that, as far as it was concerned, no change had been effected in the relationship of Éire to the Commonwealth. However, it is unlikely that de Valera paid much attention to the implications of the new Constitution for Irish unity, *vis-à-vis* its effects on Ulster unionists. As Bowman makes clear, the symbolism contained in the document was intended for southern consumption alone;[127] during the debate on the Constitution, de Valera made manifest his total rejection of a plurality of views on the question of Irish identity.

De Valera revealed the partitionist mentality in a flash when he told the Fianna Fáil *Ard-Fheis* that the constitution had been passed by 'a majority of the Irish people'. It had not been passed by 'a majority of the Irish people'. It had been passed by a narrow majority in the south, and by nobody in the north. 'The Irish people' stopped at the border.[128]

Finally, the overall attitude towards the unionist position was summed up by Articles 2 and 3, which claimed *de jure* juris-diction over Northern Ireland, thereby wishing the unionists out of existence.

A more likely explanation for the failure to declare a republic is that the Government realized that for many people the Promised Land was, as yet, far from overflowing with milk and honey; to declare 'We Have Arrived', in such circumstances, could fuel the fires of disillusionment; far better to go on holding out the promise

---

[126] Fanning, *Independent Ireland*, 118–19.
[127] Bowman, *De Valera and the Ulster Question*, 146–60.
[128] Lee and O'Tuathaigh, *The Age of de Valera*, 104.

of a better and brighter future—by keeping the myth of the 'real' Republic alive, with talk of unfinished business.

The Constitution represented a curious blend of liberal democratic and Catholic social thinking. Many of the declarations of personal rights were in line with orthodox liberal constitutional thinking; and in some respects the Constitution was even progressive: the recognition given to the Jewish community, at a time when anti-Semitism was rampant in Europe (fanned in Ireland by right-wing Catholic groups such as *An Ríoghacht*), is an obvious example. Moreover, it is clear that substantial bodies of Catholic opinion would have preferred even greater recognition given to their Church. Although Article 44 did recognize the 'special position' of the Catholic Church, and many other articles faithfully echoed Catholic teaching, extreme Catholic groups openly canvassed for a completely Catholic society, angry that recognition should be given to any religion other than their own, or that recognition should be given to registry-office marriages. Cardinal MacRory is said to have shared their integralist fervour, and to have been an advocate of the '"one, true Church" formula'.[129]

However, more than sufficient concessions to Catholic teaching were made to ensure that party and Church should not be at odds. De Valera had declared, on 17 March 1935, that 'the State would be confined to its proper function as guardian of the rights of the individual and the family, co-ordinator of the activities of its citizens'.[130] The Constitution gave full force to this pledge with a severe curtailment of the potential role of the state and with the enforcement of Catholic teaching on morality and the family. As a result, it was sufficiently satisfying to some members of the hierarchy, including Archbishop Byrne of Dublin, to enable de Valera to isolate the Cardinal's more rigid position.[131]

We have already noted that public ownership was made more difficult than it had been under the preceding Constitution. Article 43 guaranteed the primacy of the 'natural' right to private property. Article 45 declared roundly that 'the State shall favour, and where necessary, supplement private initiative in industry and commerce'. A statement on 'directive principles of social policy' paid tribute to

---

[129] Keogh, *The Vatican, the Bishops and Irish Politics*, 212.
[130] Quoted in Rumpf and Hepburn, *Nationalism and Socialism in Twentieth Century Ireland*, 98.
[131] Keogh, *The Vatican, the Bishops, and Irish Politics*, 212.

contemporary Catholic social teaching with vague references to the 'welfare of the people as a whole', the 'common interest', and recommendations that the state should guard against monopolies. But the fact that this 'directive' was not binding on parliament meant, in effect, that the lip service paid to Catholic social teaching—cum petty-bourgeois egalitarianism—should not interfere with capital accumulation.

Divorce was prohibited and the 'moral primacy' of the family guaranteed: Article 42 guaranteed the primacy of the family in educating children. Women were relegated to a distinctly subordinate position; Article 41 declared their place to be in the home—their only place in Irish society was effectively that of wives and mothers. Opposition was indeed forthcoming from feminist groups, but, as might be expected, their influence in the Ireland of the day was small, to say the least. Mrs Clarke, widow of the 1916 martyr, spoke out at the Fianna Fáil *Ard-Fheis* against the Constitution's interference with women's rights, but received a cold reception from delegates. Young women continued to emigrate from de Valera's Ireland at a higher rate than young men.

The 1937 Constitution, with its blend of cultural and moral authoritarianism and political liberalism, was a fairly accurate reflection of the dominant ideological ethos of a Catholic, nationalist, capitalist regime—an ethos which it shared in full with its principal rivals. The relatively high level of electoral opposition can probably be attributed in no small measure to the ritual opposition of Fine Gael and its allies, opposing the Constitution because they wanted full and unequivocal membership of the British Commonwealth. This apart, they shared in full the ideological concerns underlying the document. Not for the first nor the last time, Fine Gael had more in common with Fianna Fáil than it cared to admit, or perhaps even realized. Well might de Valera appeal to all who had been in the old Sinn Féin movement to support the Constitution on the grounds that it was the enactment of old Sinn Féin ideals.[132] It has been said that the Constitution achieved stability.[133] That is perhaps another way of saying that it marked the end of Fianna Fáil ambitions in the direction of social change. The 'red nightmare' of sections of the bourgeoisie was now definitively over.

[132] *Connacht Sentinel*, 12 Oct. 1937.
[133] Lyons, *Ireland since the Famine*, 548.

The debate surrounding the Constitution allowed Fianna Fáil to establish its conservative, and at the same time its popular, credentials beyond any doubt. In the Ireland of the day, the way to do both was through invocation of religion. Seán MacEntee assured voters that it required a 'moral courage almost unique in the world today to adopt as part of the Constitution the fundamental teachings of the Holy Father in regard to the Family';[134] Seán T. O'Kelly described the Constitution as 'worthy of a Catholic country'.[135] Of course, there was nothing new about this interaction between religion and politics. The Constitution merely set the seal on a process which had been under way since Fianna Fáil came to office.

It is doubtful if the overwhelming majority of Fianna Fáil members and supporters really saw much distinction between profession of Irish nationality and profession of the Catholic faith. De Valera probably spoke for a great number when he declared that it was Ireland's historic Christian mission to help 'save Western civilisation' from the scourge of materialism, just as Irish missionaries had brought the gospel to parts of the world in the past. In this speech, 'responding . . . to the accusation that modern Irish nationalism was insular and intolerant'[136]—a speech 'as dogmatic about Irish identity as it was flattering to national pride'[137]—de Valera almost seemed to portray the Irish Government as the secular arm of the Church, its relative autonomy owing as much to Thomist philosophy as to liberal-democratic political theory. Again, on 17 March 1935, he declared that 'since the coming of St Patrick fifteen hundred years ago, Ireland has been a Christian and a Catholic nation. All the ruthless attempts made through the centuries to force her from this allegiance have not shaken her faith. She remains a Catholic nation.' In the meantime, his Government had hailed the 1932 Eucharistic Congress in Dublin as 'the august resurrection of a nation', banned contraceptives, and, at the Church's behest, introduced a Public Dance Halls Act (1935) to enforce 'moral standards'. The Constitution had all the hallmarks of a final settlement between Fianna Fáil and the Catholic Church.

The Constitution achieved stability in another way. 'Full independence' having been achieved in the twenty-six counties, Fianna Fáil could claim that the last remaining justification for the IRA and

---

[134] *Irish Press*, 18 June 1937.   [135] Ibid., 24 June 1937.
[136] Brown, *Ireland: A Social and Cultural History*, 36–8.
[137] Fanning, *Independent Ireland*, 128.

its activities had been removed. The outstanding grievance of partition should be left to de Valera and his Government to solve, as that Government was now the legitimate government of the Irish people, having shaken off the shameful mantle of the Free State. Fianna Fáil could now, without hesitation and with a clear conscience, unleash the full repressive apparatus of the state—not the Free State, of course, but Éire—against the IRA.

CONCLUSION

The 1938 general election is generally held to have marked a peak in Fianna Fáil's electoral fortunes, and a turning-point in the party's social profile, heralding the onset of conventional, conservative, bourgeois politics, albeit sometimes tempered by nationalist fervour. In fact, 1938 merely marked the culmination of the party's developmental strategy, based upon the economic leadership of the national bourgeoisie. Were it not for the fortuitous intervention of the Second World War, this strategy would have been thrown into crisis sooner than was actually the case. To perceive the post-1938 period simply in terms of a 'turn to the right' is to fail to come to grips with the limited nature of the radicalism of the preceding period. Certainly a significant change in the social bases of the party's electoral support occurred during its first years in power, with the losses in support being largely concentrated in agricultural areas;[138] this shift was maintained in subsequent years. The party's failure to realize the hopes of small farmers lay behind the electoral volatility of this stratum; after 1938 Fianna Fáil faced competition from Clann na Talmhan, a party aimed specifically at small farmers. But the small farmers were a dying social stratum whose protests were soon to give way to dependency upon Government subsidy; dependency, in turn, would give way to romanticization of their life style and increased vulnerability to the party which best manipulated their ideological self-projection.

More important for the future was the process by which Fianna Fáil came to capture the support of at least a relative majority of both the working class and the industrial and commercial bourgeoisie. Although it has been claimed that only a minority of Irish capitalists supported the party in 1932, and that its first budget,

---

[138] Gallagher, *Electoral Support for Irish Political Parties*, 21.

involving increased social expenditure, alienated many,[139] the party was quick to disprove any fears that it might challenge the economic leadership of the bourgeoisie. Even in seemingly trivial matters, and where national pride might seem to have been at stake, Fianna Fáil was sensitive to business feelings: a move to change Dublin street names—many Dublin streets were (and still are) named after British overlords—was abandoned for fear of offending the business community.[140] By 1937 Tom Derrig, generally regarded as one of the more radical of the cabinet team, was declaring that 'it was only fair that those who put their money into industry should get a fair crack of the whip from Irish labour. Irish labour . . . was getting fair play from them.'[141] The Dublin and Cork Chambers of Commerce could scarcely have put it better. Moreover, the immediate issue at stake in the decision to call an election in 1938 was the refusal of the Government to relax controls on civil-service pay—the Government was defeated on this issue by Fine Gael and Labour united. Even here, however, a conservative approach to the issue of pay was sold to the working class in typically demagogic fashion. Higher civil-service salaries, claimed Fianna Fáil propaganda, would mean cuts for the poor: 'Do you want More Privileges for the Privileged at the Expense of the Plain People?'[142]

Throughout the 1930s the party's financial dependence upon business interests grew. The initial big subscriptions to party funds were soon followed up; before long a committee had been formed by business men to collect money from associates in the business world. Boland traces the origins of the fund-raising organization which became known in the 1960s as *Taca* to this period.[143]

None of this prevented Fianna Fáil from winning the support of perhaps the bulk of organized labour. This process was certainly facilitated by Fianna Fáil's skilful exploitation of splits within the trade-union movement and of the timidity of the Labour Party. For the working class especially, the limitations of Fianna Fáil policy were soon to become apparent; but so, too, was the absence of any credible alternative. Lee and O'Tuathaigh can well complain that de Valera had once pledged that 'we shall not rest until we have lifted

[139] O'Connor Lysaght, *The Republic of Ireland*, 124.
[140] Andrews, *Man of No Property*, 293.
[141] *Irish Press*, 23 June 1937.   [142] NLI Gallagher Papers MS 18376.
[143] Boland, *The Rise and Decline of Fianna Fáil*, 96–7.

the doom of exile which so long has lain upon hundreds of thousands of Irishmen in every generation', only to preside over a government which was soon 'shovelling out the Irish as quickly as Britain would take them'.[144] But what other party offered an economic programme with any credible solution to the problem?

Fianna Fáil did much to reproduce the confusion and disunity of its rivals, appropriating the 'labourist' and 'trade-unionist' mantle from the Labour Party and the 'strong government' and 'Catholic' mantles from Cumann na nGaedheal–Fine Gael. As early as January 1933 Fianna Fáil, in a classic hijack of its opponents' political clothes, was campaigning on the grounds that 'There must be Certainty' and 'Give the Nation Security—Vote Fianna Fáil'.[145] The development of a new language of politics, based on the party's ability to govern efficiently, and the branding of opponents as 'anti-Irish' and 'anti-national' which is so closely related to the virtual cult of strong government, was actually present from the start and was given a considerable boost by the Blueshirt experience. So, too, was the process by which the centralist and authoritarian nature of party organization was further developed: the emphasis on strong government, the perceived threat to the country's safety, and the pressure of some internal dissent from the shifting priorities of economic policy, all led to a further tightening of the party rules in September 1937. More power was given to the national executive which could henceforth dissolve *cumainn* 'which, in its opinion, have been guilty of a violation of the Rules', and expel anyone 'guilty of conduct unbecoming' or who had supported a non-Fianna Fáil candidate in any election. The national executive also gained the power to decide the number of candidates in each constituency and to add names to the list presented to it by *cumainn*. It could, moreover, deselect any sitting TD, and select by-election candidates.[146]

Certainly the projection of Fianna Fáil as the party which alone was capable of providing strong government in the interests of all classes played at least as significant a role as the quite separate question of irredentist anti-partitionist rhetoric. In 1938 there was something of a revivalist flavour to the party's rhetoric; realizing that the Anglo-Irish Agreement had removed the valuable ideological weapon of patriotic necessity, Fianna Fáil went forward with

---

[144] Lee and O'Tuathaigh, *The Age of de Valera*, 129.
[145] *Irish Press*, 5 Jan. 1933.   [146] UCDA MacEntee Papers P67/455.

an appeal to the electorate to 'whip John Bull'. But the party's moderation on the reunification issue had been well established, and conservative opinion had been well assured of its willingness to come to grips with the IRA. Fianna Fáil's attitude towards northern nationalists had been distinctly cool; the party had refused to share a common strategy with them, to admit them to the Dáil, or to contemplate organizing within Northern Ireland. The Government seemed to be more motivated by the fear that IRA violence or northern agitation might upset the new equilibrium which it had established south of the border. 'What seems certain is that given the nature of Fianna Fáil's political support, de Valera could scarcely have formed a more conciliatory northern policy.'[147]

In short, the politics of the new Ireland, which by 1938 had effectively reached its economic zenith, had come to be dominated by a political party which combined the economic thinking of Arthur Griffith with considerable political acumen and pragmatism, whilst displaying in ample measure the pious self-righteousness which is the most captivating and the most infuriating quality of Irish nationalism.

[147] Bowman, *De Valera and the Ulster Question*, 129–35, 139.

'Our Radicalism Implemented'
1938–1948

The outbreak of war in 1939 highlighted the need for national unity in the face of perceived external danger. Moreover, the acute shortage of imports, especially of raw materials, during the war gave an artificial boost to the concept of self-sufficiency as a viable strategy for national development, while the renewed demand for labour in Great Britain permitted the timely resumption of significant emigration.

Fianna Fáil's position in 1938 was by no means unassailable: its consensus-building political strategy was closely related to its economic strategy, and during the next decade the party would face very real threats to its social bases of support. Behind the electoral statistics one can detect mounting discontent, not merely from the small-farmer element in its support base, but significantly also from the professional strata and clerical workers whose numbers had been increased by the expansion of the public sector.

During the second half of the decade, Irish politics was in a state of considerable flux. The period witnessed the appearance of three new political forces. Two of these—Clann na Talmhan and Clann na Poblachta—respectively harnessed small-farmer and urban professional and white-collar worker discontent with Fianna Fáil; the third—the National Labour Party—was the product of splits within the labour and trade-union movement in which Fianna Fáil played no small part.

Fianna Fáil was to find itself out of office in 1948 for the first time in sixteen years—and without any clear idea of how to win back power or how to prevent the further erosion of the internal unity of the political bloc of social forces it had carefully fostered. That it managed to regain both governmental office and eventually its own composure can be attributed to the internal contradictions, weaknesses, and confusion of its opponents rather than to its own merit. There was certainly nothing inevitable about Fianna Fáil's survival of the challenge it faced in the post-war period. Indeed, until the late 1950s the resolution of the crisis opened by the weakening of Fianna Fáil's moral, intellectual, and political leadership was an open question.

These are the main contours of the period 1938–48: economic stagnation accompanied by stagnation of ideas at the level of the political leadership; and increasing discontent within the bloc of social forces which had carried Fianna Fáil to dominance, accompanied by mounting political and electoral volatility. The first point is not to deny that there was intense debate within the cabinet about economic and social policy; on the contrary, there was intense debate over many issues, which I will endeavour to trace in its essentials. What is remarkable is how little this debate produced by way of a real change of heart until the traumatic crisis of the 1950s. Nor is it to deny that the period witnessed a further expansion of state intervention in the economy; this in itself in no way contradicts the thesis of policy stagnation and loss of strategic direction. The second point is not to suggest that electoral volatility is in itself an accurate reflection of the extent of political volatility; it is surely our task to attempt to analyse the political and social trends behind the electoral statistics and the possibilities inherent in any historical situation.

I will trace the evolution of Fianna Fáil economic and social policy during the period, paying attention to the development of debate within the cabinet about its direction and the circumstances which contributed to the resolution of that debate in favour of a conservative approach in the post-war period. Next I will examine Fianna Fáil's changing relation to the balance of forces within Irish society and the underlying strengths and weaknesses in its position. Finally, I will outline the main political developments during the period, concluding with a look at the state of the party in 1948.

FIANNA FÁIL AND THE ECONOMY

Industry and Agriculture

At the end of the 1930s Lemass revived his proposal to have an oil refinery established in Dublin Bay—which, we have seen, was rejected by the cabinet in December 1935. Contacts with the London and Thames Haven Oil Wharves Ltd., while resulting in favourable terms, fell foul, in 1937, to the threats of the companies responsible for Irish oil imports—Anglo-American Oil Co., and Shell-Mex and BP Ltd.—to withdraw from Ireland if the scheme went ahead.[1] In 1939 Lemass returned to the issue, presenting a request for final authorization to proceed. He declared himself satisfied with the financial standing of Andrew Weir and Co., which had offered its backing for the scheme on the same terms originally agreed with the London and Thames.

Lemass outlined what, on the surface, seem very favourable terms. Andrew Weir and Co. had agreed to the Minister for Industry and Commerce's supervision of the company's activities and a ministerial veto over the appointment of directors; 50 per cent of shares were to be held by Éire investors; the Minister was to exercise a veto over the transfer of shares; and the Government was to have the option of acquiring the oil-refinery company after twenty-one years on payment of agreed compensation to the shareholders. Lemass had declared that what was involved was a 'large-scale oil refinery' capable not merely of producing the requirements of the domestic market but of selling in external markets: the production of 500,000 tons of petroleum products per annum was envisaged, of which 200,000 would be for export.

The Department of Finance counter-attacked, using a multitude of arguments. The Department declared itself in sympathy with the Banking Commission Report's critique of industrial strategy, and in particular the use of the Industrial Credit Corporation to provide state financial backing for industrial projects.[2] With a marked reluctance on the part of most of the cabinet to get involved in anything as ambitious as the refinery project—as witnessed by the fact that the issue was continually postponed and withdrawn from the cabinet agenda—Finance went on the offensive on 17 July, with a memorandum designed to provide cabinet opponents of the scheme with the various arguments they required—including the question of 'Irish control', which had scarcely been amongst the Department's priorities hitherto—to shelve the project once and for all. Finance argued that there was no guarantee of the financial standing of the company (Lemass, having conducted background investigations, had concluded very differently); no guarantee of the quality

[1] NAI Taoiseach S.6138.
[2] McElligott memo. to MacEntee dated 7 July 1939 in ibid.

of the products; no guarantee of 'continuity of supply of raw materials in an emergency situation'. Furthermore, there was a strong possibility that the state would end up having to subsidize 'an unprofitable export trade'. (This last point underlines the Department's consistent opposition over the years to the idea that Ireland might be an exporter of other than agricultural produce.) The memorandum concluded that Industry and Commerce should be restricted and forced to consult with Finance about the financial feasibility of the scheme.[3] The following day Lemass's cabinet colleagues decided to postpone the question once again.

On 31 July Finance returned to the attack, this time conclusively. Once again the central theme in the Department's objections to the scheme was the cost involved, the dubious financial benefit of the oil refinery, and the precarious international situation: 'the view is strongly held that the present situation is not opportune for the Government to tie itself to any scheme.'[4]

This time the scheme was shelved by the cabinet indefinitely. Whether Lemass would have made any further headway against such opposition and indifference even had the war not broken out is questionable. In any case, the oil-refinery project was never revived, and the main features of Finance's argument against state involvement in any industrial development were to recur with unfailing regularity. The incident is a good example of the extent to which the conservative economic philosophy, which had traditionally dominated the civil service from the early days of the state, was internalized by Fianna Fáil in power; and of how an alliance between the Fianna Fáil Finance Minister and his Department, combined with the innate caution and intellectual weakness of a majority of the cabinet, could serve to frustrate such interventionist and expansionist schemes as Lemass might propose.

While the war gave a renewed relevance to the strategy of self-sufficiency based upon the encouragement of a protected industrial bourgeoisie, it was a disastrous epoch for those, like Lemass, who, whilst lacking any fundamental critique as yet of the policies pursued since 1932, were becoming painfully aware of the shortcomings of the industrial bourgeoisie and the woefully inefficient state of much of Irish industry.

---

[3] Finance memo. to Cabinet dated 17 July 1939 in ibid.
[4] Finance memo. to Cabinet dated 31 July 1939 in ibid.

After the signing of the trade agreement in 1938, Lemass threatened reconsideration of tariff and quota levels for manufacturers who took advantage to make excess profits.[5] The need for an efficient industrial base was emphasized and greater competition with UK industrial products threatened. Lemass warned that 'their industries had passed beyond the infancy stage and were capable of facing comparison with industries in other countries, and they would have to be prepared to face that comparison'. The *Irish Press* further admonished business men that Irish industry should 'be reasonably expected to stand on its own feet . . . The era of spoon-feeding is over.' But by no means was a majority of Lemass's colleagues, nor de Valera himself, as concerned with rectifying the inherent negative consequences of protection, and the war effectively diverted attention from the problem. The fact that Lemass, by dint of his reputation as the most active, energetic, and imaginative member of the cabinet, acquired new and unparalleled powers during the period should not deflect us from the fact that the war years were a totally stagnant and isolationist period in Irish economic life in which the degenerative processes at work in the economy were accelerated and in which Lemass found himself continually on the defensive and frequently unsuccessful.

Preparations for an international emergency had been under way since November 1935, and an Emergency Supplies Branch of the Department of Industry and Commerce had been set up in September 1938. The outbreak of hostilities in Europe saw its transformation into a new Department of Supplies under Lemass on 9 September 1939.[6] However, little had been done to secure stockpiles of essential imports: 'the government, or more correctly the civil service, believed that Britain would continue to meet our needs in vital commodities'; almost all trading with Europe had been done through the United Kingdom, and little attention had been paid to the rest of the world.[7] Moreover, Finance had been most reluctant to release funds for the stockpiling of supplies and, despite the fact that MacEntee's move to Lemass's old Department (Industry and Commerce) eased relations with Finance, Lemass continued to meet with steady and dogged opposition from this quarter; the creation of the Department of Supplies may have

---

[5] Lee and O'Tuathaigh, *The Age of de Valera*, 140–1.
[6] NAI Industry and Commerce EHR/3/15/C2.
[7] Andrews, *Man of No Property*, 170.

weakened Finance's influence somewhat—but the battle for a more interventionist role for the state was far from won. (Interestingly, Meenan tells us that the Currency Commission held on to its sterling and bought no more gold in 1939, and suggests that 'to an outsider it does rather look as if a gentleman's agreement had been reached on the basis that if Ireland continued to hold sterling, the British government would do its best to assure some level of supplies'.[8]) In fact, Lemass's efforts to build up emergency supplies of essential imports relied to a considerable extent upon the goodwill of business men. Farrell claims that he met with a generally positive response from business men, although the oil producers were still hostile, and the FIM, pleading that its members could not afford to stockpile goods, demanded government credits.[9]

An official record of the experience of the Department of Supplies gives a picture of how ideology reduced the Government's real state of preparedness for the Emergency (as the Second World War was known in neutral Ireland):

There were a number of considerations against direct interference by the State. The acquisition of additional stocks was regarded as being primarily a matter of ordinary business prudence for the firms concerned, which would stand to benefit themselves if and when supplies ultimately became scarce.

The Government, it was believed, did not have the necessary experience and expertise of the private sector. There was a fear of encouraging dependence on Government action: '[The] State could not be expected to take the risks and, when the time came to place the reserves on sale, allow private firms to reap the profits. A large measure of direct trading by Government agencies was an alternative which did not commend itself.'[10]

The functions allocated to the Minister for Supplies were certainly sweeping; the relevant cabinet memorandum lists these as: control of exports and imports of all kinds; regulation of keeping, treatment, storage, movement, distribution, sale, purchase, use, and consumption of articles of all kinds; control of all prices.[11] However, the latter power, in particular, was certainly not availed of effectively

---

[8] J. Meenan, 'The Irish Economy during the War', in K. B. Nowlan and T. Desmond Williams (eds.), *Ireland in the War Years and After, 1939–1951* (Dublin, 1969), 30.
[9] Farrell, *Seán Lemass*, 51.   [10] NAI Industry and Commerce EHR/3/15/C2.
[11] NAI Taoiseach S.11418A.

during the war years. The Prices Commission established by Lemass in 1938 was effectively made redundant and, with the emphasis now on stockpiling rather than on efficiency, and with Irish business insulated against competition with UK industrial products, profits soared. The economic isolation imposed by war strengthened the virtual monopolistic hold which protected industries enjoyed, enabling them to thrive at the expense of the consumer. Black marketeering flourished, despite the fact that government inspectors succeeded in bringing some 5,000 prosecutions.

It was as if a tacit agreement had been reached that, in return for business co-operation with government plans to keep the country supplied with essential products, the question of price control and efficiency would be deferred until after the end of emergency conditions. Personal ties between Government ministers, especially Lemass, and Irish business circles were strengthened during the war. Andrews tells us that when the Government set up an agency—Fuel Importers (Éire) Ltd.—to stockpile coal reserves, its chairman was the 'shrewd' coal merchant, John Reihill, managing director of Connolly's Ltd. (a coal firm).

Generous subscriptions to the Fianna Fáil party funds had brought him to the notice of Seán Lemass. He formed with Lemass what amounted to a symbiotic relationship ... It would be impossible to imagine two men more dissimilar in character and motivation. Reihill lived and died in the faith of big business (Irish style) leaving behind him a thriving coal and oil empire.[12]

Dissimilar in character they may have been, but it is clear that Reihill and many other Irish business men benefited from the relationship consolidated during the period.

The failure to control profits during the war was not matched by a similar relaxed attitude to wages. In May 1940 MacEntee, at Industry and Commerce, initiated a Standstill Order on Wages, which effectively froze income levels for workers for the duration of the war. This measure was defended by Lemass, in June 1941, on the grounds that 'an expansion of wages, operating on a reduced supply of goods, would only force up prices and make more difficult the position of workers unable to gain increases and of the unemployed, who were likely to increase'. (Interestingly, Lemass seems

---

[12] Andrews, *Man of No Property*, 171.

here to be tending towards the orthodox Finance view that wage increases are the primary cause of inflation.) He further used the threat of 'complete chaos' if the Government did not take action on the wages question.[13]

The Wages Standstill Order was accompanied by the 1941 Trade Unions Act, which severely limited the right of trade unions to negotiate and to strike. Moreover, an 'Emergency budget', introduced by the new Finance Minister, Seán T. O'Kelly, in November 1939, proposed to meet the increase in expenditure necessitated by the Emergency through increased income tax and indirect taxation rather than through taxes on profits or capital export, and this was to remain the pattern in the post-war period. There can be little doubt that the period witnessed a further shift in the balance of power from the worker and consumer to the protected industrialist—a fact which may be obscured if Lemass's *dirigiste* or interventionist approach to the economy is confused with 'creeping socialism'.

That fraction of the Irish bourgeoisie which had a stake in the export market was also less than happy with the conduct of economic policy during the Emergency. The FIM wrote to the Minister for Finance on 17 June 1940, advocating an Export Department with 'authoritarian powers' designed to stimulate the export-orientated sector of the economy by purchasing necessary materials in the United States. In a significant passage, the FIM wrote:

It is the view of the Council [of the FIM] that the Government will not be able to allow industries who have a protected interest in this market to continue to ignore the necessity for export and that an element of compulsion, which is now practically universal as a result of the war, may have to be engendered in this country.[14]

Such clashes of interest between fractions of the bourgeoisie were to be skilfully exploited by Lemass and Fianna Fáil in reorientating economic policy in the late 1950s. But in the war years the Government closed ranks against any such move, albeit on significantly different grounds: Finance objected in principle to 'state regulation', Lemass took umbrage at being 'dictated to'. On 18 July 1940 Finance wrote:

external trade cannot be controlled without bringing internal trade in also and this would involve all the trappings of an authoritarian state. It is

[13] NAI Taoiseach S.11394.   [14] NAI Finance F005/0007/40.

questionable how far we could proceed along these lines without infringing the Constitution, and, indeed, such basic changes could hardly be made without the prior approval of the people by means of a referendum.[15]

Lemass repeatedly refused to meet the FIM to discuss their proposals. On 24 June 1940 his Department replied that it had informed Erskine Childers (the FIM secretary) 'that really it seemed as though the Federation were adopting an attitude of dictating to the Minister for Supplies how he should carry out the functions of his Department'. In September 1941 Lemass was still adamantly insisting upon his relative autonomy from representatives of one bourgeois fraction; a Department of Supplies memo noted that 'it is claimed that this correspondence [between the FIM and the Department] shows the very remarkable foresight displayed by that body in contrast to the grave lack of foresight in Government and public circles'; in fact, it continued, the FIM was better at giving advice to the Government than at coming up with any practical solutions or taking firm action.[16]

The supplies situation became more critical when, from December 1940, the UK Government imposed severe restrictions upon Irish trade in retaliation for Irish neutrality. Petrol was already rationed; oil shipments to Ireland were now seriously restricted, and coal imports effectively dried up from the end of 1941. British regulation of Irish commercial shipping led to shortages of tea, sugar, tobacco, bread, fruit, feeding-stuffs, and fertilizers. Needless to say, prices rose rapidly.

Only in 1941 did the Government set about the establishment of a state-owned mercantile marine—Irish Shipping Ltd.—and then only as an auxiliary to private enterprise. The Government had shown a complete indifference to maritime development up until the war: the whole navy then consisted of two boats, and was not to rise above ten; a coastal-watching service was not established until 1939; although the establishment of a state mercantile marine had been urged by Labour leader William Norton in the Dáil in September 1939, the Government acted only 'when it came to the belated conclusion that the country could no longer rely on the ships of other nations to secure its lifelines'.[17] At its peak, Irish

---

[15] NAI Finance F005/0007/40.   [16] Ibid.
[17] B. Share, *The Emergency* (Dublin, 1978), 99.

Shipping Ltd. consisted of fifteen boats—two of which were sunk by German U-boats—and private mercantile vessels were also subject to attack by both German and British planes. It became clear that in wartime conditions it would prove impossible to assemble anything like a mercantile fleet capable of keeping the country supplied, even were adequate imports available.

Likewise, 'the general principle followed in the legislation affecting the development of mines and minerals, which was in operation up to the year 1940, was based on the assumption that the development of the country's mineral resources was essentially a matter for private enterprise'.[18] It was only in 1940 that some belated action was taken to ensure supplies of essential minerals and fuels, when the Minerals Development Act empowered the Minister for Industry and Commerce to act compulsorily on behalf of mineral deposits not worked, or not worked efficiently. The Minister was given the power to grant mining leases. However, Finance blocked, on grounds of cost, a proposal from Lemass in February 1941 that a National Institute for Industrial Research be established. Lemass envisaged the functions of such an institute as being to advise the Minister for Industry and Commerce on: the utilization of natural resources; the types of research needed to ensure industrial development; scientific and technological planning; and the distribution of grants to students for training in research work.[19]

Lemass may well have avoided the odium of 'Minister for Shortages' by such populist gestures as riding to meetings on a bicycle,[20] but many people were suffering very real hardship. The shortage of bread hit the poor, who could not afford to buy meat, and the black market widened the gap between rich and poor. Despite widespread emigration to Great Britain in search of wartime employment, unemployment in 1943 stood at 70,000, and widespread malnutrition was reported by the *Church of Ireland Gazette*— scarcely a periodical which can be accused of exaggerating social distress with subversive intent. The intellectual publication, the *Bell*, alleged tuberculosis and disease due to a lack of proper food.[21] By 1943 malnutrition amongst working-class children was of such a dimension that the Irish Women Workers' Union (IWWU) and the

---

[18] NAI Industry and Commerce EHR/3/25.
[19] NAI Finance S099/0006/41.   [20] Farrell, *Seán Lemass*, 58.
[21] Share, *The Emergency*, 36.

Emergency conference of the Women's Societies—an umbrella body comprising eight societies, including the Irish Countrywomen's Association and the Irish Housewives' Committee—were petitioning the Government for rationing of fruit and jam, price control of vegetables, and steps to safeguard calcium content of bakers' loaves. 'We are alarmed by the increase in rickets, scabies, and the revelations of the incidence of tuberculosis amongst young children,' wrote the IWWU, begging the Taoiseach to meet mothers of starving children.[22] The departments of Local Government and Public Health and Supplies were asked to furnish a reply; the civil service dutifully responded with a litany of arguments against doing anything: quantities of the goods in question were too small; fruit and vegetables were perishable; price control would raise the prices of lower-grade vegetables, etc. There should be no further interference with manufacturers.

Even Lemass was at first reluctant to introduce a system of rationing. He urged the adoption of different attitudes to different commodities, arguing that some, like bread, were essential to the poor and that a system of general rationing would create great hardship: 'the correct line to take is to make available the greatest possible amount for those who cannot purchase substitute foods and to restrict proportionately the other classes of the community.' Lemass tried to convince his cabinet colleagues that rationing schemes were intrinsically unfair to the poor.[23] However, the pressure to introduce rationing and end obvious injustices was such that a system of general rationing—tea, for example, had already been rationed since January 1941—was introduced in June 1942.

In a bid to secure adequate bread supplies, the Government introduced compulsory tillage orders. By 1942 574,739 acres were producing wheat, and this figure had risen further to stabilize at around 662,000 acres by 1945.[24] There can be no doubt that the system of compulsory tillage was unpopular with the farming community; it brought forth complaints, vocally supported by Fine Gael, that farmers were being forced to produce at uneconomic prices. It has been argued that it was the small farmers, whose poultry and potatoes remained unsubsidized, who suffered most from the system.[25] Certainly this group, for whose votes Fianna Fáil was in

[22] NAI Industry and Commerce SEB/13.   [23] NAI Taoiseach S.11394.
[24] NLI Gallagher Papers MS 18376; Lyons, *Ireland since the Famine*, 623.
[25] O'Connor Lysaght, *The Republic of Ireland*, 117.

competition with Clann na Talmhan after the war, seems to have been in the minds of Fianna Fáil propagandists, who were careful to emphasize that compulsory tillage was abandoned once the Emergency had passed.[26]

On 29 January 1941 de Valera broadcast to the nation on the need to secure bread. Wheat acreage, he declared, must rise from 300,000 acres to 650,000. There was a need to avoid waste and to search for home-produced alternatives to unavailable imports.[27] On 21 March Seán Moylan, then parliamentary secretary to the Minister for Defence, wrote to de Valera on the question. Moylan, who was to play an important part in the ensuing battles over agricultural policy, urged

making of any crops produced, under any schemes adopted, a cash crop, responsibility for payment of which would rest with the Government . . . There is very little use in telling such people that if they produce the food they are sure to find a market for it. There is very little of the speculative tradition in the ordinary farmers. They are, instead, apt to be over cautious. They are not endowed with the particular type of foresight that would enable them to see that increased voluntary food production on their part is a good business proposition. And even if they had all these qualities they have not the capital resources that would enable them to produce the food . . . the only real method of securing food production to the limits of our needs is by an extension of the system of payments by which beet production was secured to the other crops needed.[28]

Moylan was shortly to replace Derrig as Minister for Lands. In this memorandum, de Valera's idealization of the small farmer is effectively jettisoned. Guaranteed prices to secure the aims of Government policy is accompanied by a cold, realistic analysis of the economic potential of the Irish agricultural producer. Moylan also urged that a public pronouncement in favour of the Government's tillage policy be sought from the Archbishop of Dublin.

The Moylan view was endorsed by the Government, which overturned an earlier recommendation from Finance that there should be no further increases in wheat prices, no further subsidy for fertilizers, and no further expenditure on the tillage campaign. Attempts by the Irish Farmers' Federation to bypass the Minister and seek a personal meeting with de Valera (who, presumably,

[26] NLI Gallagher Papers MS 18376.   [27] NAI Taoiseach S.11394.
[28] Ibid. S.11402B.

they felt would be sympathetic to the case of the farmers) met with a cold response in January 1941; the Taoiseach's Department replied that the meeting would have no purpose as the Government had 'nothing to add' to previous policy statements. The farmers' case was taken up by Fine Gael TD Patrick Belton, who pleaded that the farmers' response had been 'magnificent' and urged a new price for wheat of fifty shillings per barrel (the existing price was forty-five shillings). Whilst publicly disclaiming all criticism of its policy, this was the course of action adopted by the Government in January 1942, and a cabinet decision was taken which resulted in higher bread prices. Writing in his party's newspaper, de Valera emphasized the need to increase production of potatoes also and expressed his desire to involve the Catholic Church in impressing upon farmers their moral obligation to the whole community.[29]

This was to be a recurring theme. Repeated appeals were in fact made to clergymen from 1940 to 1944. By November 1941 the Department of Agriculture was growing increasingly concerned that 'importing wheat which we could grow at home means loss of shipping space and foreign exchange'.[30] On 22 January 1942 Agriculture wrote to the Irish Catholic bishops, seeking support for the Government's wheat-production policies: 'The Minister feels confident that the clergy will do everything possible to help in this great crisis and he appeals to you to use your influence in bringing home to our farmers a realisation of the danger that threatens the country.'[31] This naked attempt to rally the moral influence of the Catholic bishops behind what was, after all, a policy disputed by Fianna Fáil's political rivals shows to what extent the party's relations with the Church had changed since coming to power.

Tillage policy, meanwhile, necessitated a restriction of the ever-increasing emigration to Great Britain from rural areas: many farm labourers took advantage of the wartime boom in the UK economy to emigrate in search of industrial employment. Irish men and women were by now leaving the country at the rate of 25,000 per year, and net emigration from Éire in the period 1936–46 was 187,111. An order, therefore, prohibited men ordinarily resident outside towns of population of 5,000 or over from emigrating to Great Britain, and a Government spokesman specified that the

---

[29] *Irish Press*, 13 Jan. 1942.
[30] Memo. from Agriculture to the Taoiseach dated 29 Nov. 1941 in NAI Taoiseach S.11402B.   [31] Ibid.

measure was aimed at men 'with a minimum experience of agricultural or turf-cutting operations'.[32] While the emigration of women
was not restricted, the order was extended to men in jobs, men
who were sacked for misconduct or who refused the offer of work
at home, and most men under the age of 19, as well as men on a
special register of agricultural and turf workers.[33]

Emigration during the early days of the war did much to reduce
the strain of unemployment. Moreover, emigrants' remittances helped
support those who remained behind. Indeed, it was not until
1942–3, when the question of coping with the anticipated large-
scale post-war return of emigrants entered the political agenda, that
the debate over economic policy really took off within the cabinet.
However, even from 1939 to 1940 differences within the Government over the employment question can be detected.

Finance was opposed, as early as 1939–40, to any suggestion of
an increase in Unemployment Assistance expenditure, and wanted
it stopped altogether in rural areas: the departmental secretary,
McElligott, argued with characteristic social compassion that 'what
the people wanted was a good fright'.[34] This view brought Finance
into immediate conflict with Lemass. May 1940 had seen the establishment of the Cabinet Committee on Emergency Problems,
consisting of de Valera, Lemass, Aiken (now Minister for the Co-
ordination of Defensive Measures), and, from August, Seán T.
O'Kelly. This body, which functioned for a period as a sort of inner
cabinet, was one of three cabinet committees established to bolster
the policy-making apparatus during the life of the Emergency. For
a brief period, its functions were somewhat overlapped by the
economic committee of the cabinet (Lemass, MacEntee, and Ryan),
but this body fizzled out in April 1941, just two months after its
creation. Eventually, in November 1942, the functions of both
bodies were superseded by the most important of the three cabinet
committees to be established—the Cabinet Committee on Economic
Planning (de Valera, Lemass, and O'Kelly).

In July 1940 Lemass submitted a report to the Cabinet Committee
on Emergency Problems, outlining his plans to deal with unemployment in the event of total economic isolation. Envisaging acute
unemployment, as a result of a 'breakdown of means of external

---

[32] Share, *The Emergency*, 91.   [33] NAI Taoiseach S.14134c.
[34] Fanning, *The Irish Department of Finance*, 320.

communication', he stipulated a figure of 261,000 unemployed—including 180,000 newly unemployed—as external trade eventually ground to a complete halt. The note of urgency in his reports is summed up by the cryptic adjoiner that 'there has not been time to consult the Department of Finance . . .'. He argued for an increase in the Unemployment Assistance Funds, under these conditions, and a relaxation of the means test: 'It will be necessary for the Department of Finance to make arrangements in advance with the banks so that the requisite amount of currency may be available in each locality to provide for the payment of Unemployment Assistance, salaries and wages etc.' He reassured his colleagues that this, far from amounting to a social revolution, was necessary for social peace:

Social order could best be maintained if the working population knew that there was provision in a familiar form for workers losing employment . . . Money payments would permit of rent, rates, medical treatment and other family expenses as distinct from bare necessities being met in the normal way and avoid the general dislocation which would necessarily follow a departure from the normal course of money payments.[35]

It is interesting to contrast Lemass's scheme with a rival plan prepared by MacEntee in April 1941. This envisaged a figure of 400,000 unemployed, given total isolation of the country as the war situation worsened. However, the three specific proposals were modest indeed: that the Government should 'appeal' to employers to prolong employment by avoiding overtime, encouraging job-sharing, etc.; that the Minister for Industry and Commerce should consult with unions and employers as to how best this might be achieved; that proposals be formulated for the payment of partial unemployment benefit or assistance to part-time workers.[36]

Lemass's proposal was radical, and certain to bring down upon his head the ire of Finance. Fortunately for Finance, the 'breakdown of means of external communication' was not such as to disrupt the emigration routes to Britain, and the cabinet was able quietly to bury the proposals—a fate which would greet many other Lemassian schemes after the war, when, once more, the UK labour market allowed Fianna Fáil to sit back, relax, and slide into total economic stagnation. Fanning is right to add that the Government

---

[35] Memos. dated 1 and 5 July 1940 in NAI Taoiseach S.119810.
[36] NAI Finance S099/0021/41.

was watering down or amending Finance's stringent proposals for cut-backs; but Lemass's proposals for a substantial increase in employment expenditure met with an even sharper fate. For all his decisiveness and 'near dictatorial powers',[37] he found himself fighting a defensive battle. Thus, the minutes of the economic committee of the cabinet record that at a meeting attended by de Valera, Lemass, O'Kelly, MacEntee, and Ryan on 7 April 1941

the Minister for Supplies raised the question of the production policy which should be adopted in the case of industries which would be affected by a shortage of raw materials or fuel. After a discussion it was decided that as a general rule such industries should be organized on the basis of keeping the maximum number of people in employment. It was agreed however that the peculiar circumstances of some industries might render desirable the adoption of an alternative policy such as that of concentrating production in the most efficient units.[38]

In August 1941 Lemass, while retaining the Supplies portfolio, also regained his old Department, Industry and Commerce; MacEntee was shunted on to the Department of Local Government and Public Health. Even this should not lead us to conceive of a dynamic duo of de Valera and Lemass consistently forging ahead with plans for the post-war period. It is difficult to substantiate the claim that de Valera took 'the first decisive political steps towards economic planning', forming a solid partnership with Lemass against MacEntee and O'Kelly, and, with Lemass, making 'the need for rational economic and social planning visible in the bitterly hostile environment of the late 1930s and the early 1940s'. Or that the establishment of the Cabinet Committee on Economic Planning in November 1942 represented a clear victory for this partnership.[39] It is more likely that the Committee was used by de Valera to stifle Lemass in the interests of cabinet unity and caution, the economic committee of the cabinet having failed to achieve this.[40]

Thus, Lemass's proposal in June 1942 for a new Department of Labour to plan for the post-war unemployment problem met with the usual de Valera fudge. According to Fanning, Lemass had given de Valera a seven-page memorandum entitled 'Labour Policy',

---

[37] Fanning, *Independent Ireland*, 148.   [38] NAI Taoiseach S.12308.
[39] R. J. Raymond, 'De Valera, Lemass and Irish Economic Development: 1933–1948', in J. A. Murphy and J. O'Carroll (eds.), *De Valera and his Times* (Cork, 1983), 120–1.   [40] Lee and O'Tuathaigh, *The Age of de Valera*, 158.

calling for the establishment of a Labour Department to prepare post-war plans for 'construction works and other desirable development schemes to be operated when supplies become available'. De Valera shared his worries about the post-war unemployment problem which might arise because of returning emigrants, demobbed soldiers, etc., but was typically cautious. On 30 June de Valera wrote to his ministers: 'we should plan at once for such use and development of our resources and potentialities as seem reasonably practicable without a revolutionary change.' As Fanning puts it: 'this characteristic preference for the "reasonably practicable" over the allegedly "revolutionary" reveals the limitations of what the Government meant by planning.' Needless to say, it was decided that there would be no Department of Labour, and no disruption of normal bureaucratic procedures—de Valera would be personally in charge of supervising the 'plans'.[41]

Between November 1942 and May 1945 the Cabinet Committee on Economic Planning met some fifty-eight times in all, and it became the centre of an intense debate over economic policy. Unfortunately, the minutes of the committee tell us little; and, as in the reaction to the publication of the Beveridge Report in the United Kingdom, 'closer inspection quickly reveals that what was involved was not so much an overall economic plan for the post-war years as piecemeal proposals in particular areas based on the response of individual departments to the government decision of June 1942'.[42] Nevertheless, it was unique for such decisions as those on the need for economic planning which gave rise to the committee to be recorded in the cabinet minutes, and the debate within the committee, which can be traced in its essentials on the basis of important memoranda from the various departments, was one of the most intense which had ever taken place over economic policy.

It is little wonder that Finance should prove to be 'unenthusiastic' about the institution of the committee, or that the Finance Minister, O'Kelly, should warn against the 'easy line of having recourse to state aid'.[43] Initially, O'Kelly had been regarded as less of a financial conservative than MacEntee, and his elevation to the Finance portfolio at MacEntee's expense had been seen as something of a victory for Lemass. Soon, however, he was faithfully echoing his Department's ideology.

[41] Fanning, *Independent Ireland*, 149.   [42] Ibid. 150.
[43] Fanning, *The Irish Department of Finance*, 352.

The first mention of the Beveridge Report is recorded in the minutes of the Cabinet Committee on Economic Planning on 18 December 1942. The Government was under pressure in the Dáil to take similar action to that suggested in the UK plan, especially as the adoption of the Report by the Government of Northern Ireland, whose economy was booming during the war, tended to place the very legitimacy, not to mention the social stability, of Éire in question. (As O'Halloran has pointed out, since partition 'the pattern was established of presenting a contrast between a decaying unionist state in the north and a progressive nationalist state in the south'.[44]) On 3 December 1942 Hugo Flinn, parliamentary secretary to the Minister for Finance, wrote to de Valera about the Report and the promise of the 'six counties Government' to implement it, which he described as 'a "god send" for the Labour Party and, properly worked, worth quite a few seats . . . every wildest claim made by them may be made to seem possible of accomplishment . . . I anticipate that with this new ammunition a different line may have to be taken'.[45] Unfortunately, such examples of the party political considerations behind the conversion of at least part of Fianna Fáil to a form of Keynesianism in those days are seldom recorded in the cabinet and departmental files; but there can be little doubt that, if such thoughts entered the head of Hugo Flinn, they might also have occurred to Lemass, to name but one.

Certainly MacEntee feared so. When his Department of Local Government and Public Health was ordered, on 10 March 1943, to proceed with the planning of public-health works and road schemes, he sprang into action. MacEntee sought to offset any manipulation of de Valera's instinctive concern with Fianna Fáil's electoral hegemony with an appeal to the Taoiseach's Catholicism. On 16 March he wrote to de Valera, quoting an English Catholic intellectual named Dr Mess against the evils of 'Beveridgeism', and invoking Pope Pius XI and *Quadragesimo anno*. MacEntee went on to level the charge of possible enforced sterilization under a National Health Service. As regards the question of children's allowances—another Beveridge-inspired evil—he argued:

It is clear therefore, that, not only the idealogical [*sic*] basis, but the practical features of any scheme of children's allowances must be very carefully

[44] O'Halloran, *Partition and the Limits of Irish Nationalism*, 17.
[45] NAI Taoiseach S.13053a.

considered, so as to ensure that they are not patently in conflict with the fundamental principle laid down in Quadragesimo Anno.

There were, apparently, moral objections to family allowances if they were 'non-contributory, universal and not means tested'. And just in case Dr Mess was not enough to sway de Valera, MacEntee forwarded for his personal perusal a copy of an article on 'Beveridgeism' by a Catholic priest, Fr Peter McKevitt, entitled 'The Catholic Standpoint', which warned, apocalyptically, that 'we have a choice between the Papal encyclicals and the omnicompetent State'.

It was not enough to kill the question of children's allowances— de Valera possessed far too keen a political instinct for that; but it certainly recast the terms of the debate. It was the ideological cue which the conservative wing of the cabinet needed.

On 31 March Industry and Commerce was authorized to draw up plans for the development of harbour facilities with post-war economic development in mind; but this authorization came, significantly, highly qualified with the proviso that 'if necessary the plans should be prepared at state expense but, pending any further decisions, the state should not be committed to approval of the carrying out of any works in pursuance of the plans or to any expenditure in connection with such works'. In September it was decided that an organization should be set up 'to undertake detailed planning for building activities generally after the war', and that it should be a branch of an existing department acting in consultation with private building interests. On 20 October 'it was further decided, in principle, that steps should be taken with a view to the planning of a comprehensive programme of employment schemes for Dublin to give employment to say 10,000 unskilled workers for two or three years after the emergency . . .'.

Now all this was very vague; as Fanning argues, it lacked a serious scheme and issues were rarely pressed by departments.[46] The question of state intervention in the economy, and the role of the state in employment creation, had scarcely been faced squarely, let alone settled. Most of the proposals involved consultation with the private sector—supplementing and complementing the role of private enterprise, and certainly not replacing its leading function. That being so, could private enterprise not be considered

---

[46] Fanning, *Independent Ireland*, 150.

capable of doing a better job without this bureaucratic interference? This was certainly argued by MacEntee, with success in large measure.

Indeed, on 15 November, de Valera stated that he now felt that the proposed organization for the planning of building activities should be more restrictive in its functions than was previously suggested. On 22 November it was decided that the body should be under the control of the Department of Industry and Commerce— but its functions were amended so that its activities should have 'regard to financial considerations and to the relative social, economic and cultural importance of the various projects'. A week later MacEntee was questioning the feasibility of the various employment schemes just mentioned on the grounds that they would 'compete for plant, materials and skilled labour with normal schemes and with building activities', i.e. with the interests of existing private enterprise.

In January 1944 it was decided in committee to request the views of Finance and Local Government and Public Health on a Lemass proposal that

a large sum should be made available from borrowed monies, say 10,000,000 pounds, for the purpose of financing the activities of Local Authorities in improving the conditions in urban areas. This sum to be divided between these authorities on some equitable basis, related to the numbers of registered unemployed in the areas concerned, and to be made available to them by way of free grant to cover the whole cost of approved works.

MacEntee agreed to consider the plans, 'should the necessity arise'. Little more was heard from him on this subject until a memorandum from his Department, dated 20 December 1944, recorded the not surprising fact that 'generally it was his [MacEntee's] view that unless the supply situation eased no appreciable expansion of work giving constructive employment could be undertaken by local authorities'.[47]

On 4 February 1944 Lemass proposed a detailed urban renewal plan, involving the construction of swimming pools, amenities, parks, renovations to buildings, monuments, etc. Finance responded, on 8 February, in language which is breath-taking, coming as it does from an ostensibly Republican government ministry:

[47] NAI Taoiseach S.13026b.

an attempt to spend this amount would probably lead to waste and extravagance. We might find ourselves in a position not unlike that which existed in the days of the Famine when, merely for the sake of providing employment, weird and useless monuments were built, and roads made that led to nowhere in particular . . . It is, at any rate, debatable whether post-war unemployment will be bad enough to necessitate that much expenditure.[48]

In July Lemass presented the Cabinet Committee on Economic Planning with a general outline of schemes which could be undertaken in the post-war period—afforestation, drainage, fisheries, housing, hospitals, updating of public buildings, ports and harbours, health works, transport, telephones, mercantile marine, mineral development, electricity, turf-cutting, town planning, etc. It was estimated that £100 million would be spent in all: £31.6 million on housing; £20 million on rural electrification; £4.6 million on turf development; £12.7 million on drainage and roads.[49] Many of the suggested schemes were far from 'weird and useless', but were urgently required. For example, Ireland still had the lowest proportion of forestry land in Europe and a fisheries policy scarcely existed; as we have seen, Daly has estimated that the Dublin tenement problem was probably worse in 1939 than in 1914[50]—and the housing programme was actually slowed down during the Emergency; the Chairman of the National Health Insurance Council, Bishop Dignan, had described the health service as 'tainted at its roots . . . of destitution, pauperism, and degradation', and Dr Noel Browne has recorded how, even in 1948, many Irish hospitals were in an appalling state and the country lacked a disease-control programme, a BCG inoculation service, a diphtheria vaccination scheme, a mass radiography scheme, and a national blood-transfusion service.[51]

Yet no firm decision was taken on Lemass's, admittedly vague, proposals. De Valera may well have sought to give the impression in public of an energetic and thoughtful government; he told the 1943 Fianna Fáil Ard-Fheis that 'we cannot rely entirely on private enterprise' and that state action would be needed to provide for the development of natural resources, etc.;[52] and at the 1944 Ard-Fheis he was reassuring delegates that, as soon as materials again became

---

[48] NAI Taoiseach. S.13417a.   [49] Ibid. S.12882.

[50] Daly, Social and Economic History of Ireland, 191.

[51] N. Browne, Against the Tide (Dublin, 1986), 111.

[52] Raymond, 'De Valera, Lemass and Irish Economic Development', 123.

available, 'industrial development would continue full steam ahead'.[53] But in reality the Government's approach was to wait and hope for the best.

Meanwhile, the clear shift which had taken place in Fianna Fáil's electoral support since 1938, with the consolidation of business, professional, and working-class support offsetting losses amongst the small-farmer stratum to Clann na Talmhan, facilitated the emergence of debate within the Government over the future of agricultural policy. As Bew and Patterson argue, whilst landless men may have been electorally unimportant, some 240,000 small farmers on 'uneconomic holdings' were another matter.[54] In this sense, the rise of Clann na Talmhan may well have been fortuitous in that it allowed Fianna Fáil to take its distance to some extent from this stratum.

De Valera was still nostalgic for his dream of a homestead republic. In 1942 he was still urging a post-war programme of land division to ease congestion and was speaking of a figure of 50,000 acres per annum over ten years.[55] A pessimistic Land Commission complained that with staffing problems and lack of resources it would be lucky to meet half that target. The de Valera view of how Irish agriculture should be structured is faithfully reflected in an important memorandum from Kevin O'Shiel, member of the Land Commission, in 1942.[56] Agriculture should be so organized as to provide each family with no more land than it could till. The case against agricultural underproduction was based, not upon economic criteria, but upon ideological and moral principles; as Bew and Patterson put it, 'in contrast with the family farm, the sight of "vast blocks of land" not in the hands of farmers at all, but in the hands of old bachelors and spinsters was nauseating'.[57]

On 1 September 1943 Moylan, by now Minister for Lands, wrote to de Valera,[58] expressing worries which had been growing since the late 1930s that local pressures meant land was going to local landless men with no experience of farming, rather than migrants from outside the locality who had the necessary experience.[59] Moylan

[53] NLI Gallagher Papers MS 18376.
[54] Bew and Patterson, *Seán Lemass and the Making of Modern Ireland*, 21–9.
[55] NAI Taoiseach S.12890a. [56] Ibid. S.13101a.
[57] Bew and Patterson, *Seán Lemass and the Making of Modern Ireland*, 23.
[58] NAI Taoiseach S.12890a.
[59] Bew, Hazelkorn, and Patterson, *The Dynamics of Irish Politics*, 78.

began by questioning the wisdom of proceeding with land division and called for a review of the activities of the Land Commission:

If land is to be brought into fullest production it must be in the hands of trained, capable and experienced agriculturalists, and where land is to be divided these and these only should be considered as allottees . . . There has been a practice of giving plots of 3, 5 and 10 acres to cotters and agricultural labourers. This practice is economically unsound . . . The practice of such allotment should cease.

Moylan went on to accuse the Land Commission of being too generous with housing and improvement grants to landless men and 'uneconomic holders', and declared: 'a too generous allotment of public funds by way of free grant to allottees saps initiative, produces dependent traits of character in the allottee which are wholly undesirable and tends to render him unfit material for the production of a capable agriculturalist.'

De Valera was, by now, at a loss as to what to do. Challenged in the Dáil, on 16 December 1943, by Fine Gael spokesman Patrick McGilligan, who had demanded clarification of the Government's agricultural policy in the light of a seemingly ambiguous speech by MacEntee, de Valera replied that it was still Government policy to put 'social' above 'narrow economic' considerations; he was still in favour, he declared, of smaller farms, more farmers, and more farm workers. MacEntee, by contrast, took to the columns of the *Irish Times* to make it clear that he was not in favour of irrevocably multiplying the number of small farms.[60] (He had, perhaps, been preparing the way in his speech for the very opposite.)

De Valera clung, at a sentimental level, and also undoubtedly for electoral reasons, to his dream of land redistribution. But even he had recognized, as early as 1939, that the flight from the land was continuing;[61] and in any case, as MacEntee in a telling comment later revealed, de Valera's 'frugal ideal' was 'one man's dream, never party policy'.[62] His cabinet colleagues—Lemass, MacEntee, and Moylan—were beginning to lose patience. On 5 September 1944 the Cabinet Committee on Economic Planning discussed the question of post-war agricultural policy. According to the committee minutes, stress was laid on:

[60] *Irish Times*, 8 Dec. 1943.
[61] Bew and Patterson, *Seán Lemass and the Making of Modern Ireland*, 4.
[62] T. de Vere White, 'Lunch with an Enduring Veteran', *Irish Times*, 19 May 1976.

(*a*) the need to promote economic agricultural production;

(*b*) the importance of the export market from the point of view of the maintenance and improvement of the standard of living;

(*c*) the importance, from the national and social point of view, of the maintenance on the land in economic security of as many families as might be practicable.[63]

Significantly, de Valera's priority had now been relegated to third in order of importance, behind two policy goals with which it was clearly in conflict.

Meanwhile, the whole discussion on both industrial and agricultural post-war policy was being subsumed in a discussion about the relation between Irish and British economic development in the light of the publication of the UK White Paper on full employment. On 13 July 1944 the Department of Finance was asked to furnish its observations on the UK White Paper. It did so on 31 October.

Finance dismissed the view that control over fluctuations in industrial investment should be considered as a policy option, declaring somewhat sweepingly that 'the Irish problem is entirely different'. 'Irish prosperity, on which the level of employment depends, can best be increased by developing the prosperity of agriculture, by maximising its efficiency and thereby increasing its productivity.' As regards easing unemployment, 'the easiest and most obvious avenue is through an expanding agriculture'. As regards the expansion of industrial markets, manufacturers should simply be encouraged to 'reduce the costs of production'. And the memorandum continued: 'the question should be examined of whether continuance of the policy of land division is compatible with the effort to secure higher efficiency in production and increased employment on the land.' The Department's only other advice was that taxes should be reduced and 'current expenditure should be reviewed with the view to eliminating "emergency" services and the reduction of these wherever practicable. In particular, the Government should avoid commitments in regard to further "social security" measures during the difficult post-Emergency period'.[64] In short, the Government should quietly forget the existence of the UK White Paper and act according to the prescriptions which Finance had been issuing since the 1920s.

On 6 December the Cabinet Committee on Economic Planning

---

[63] NAI Taoiseach S.13026b.   [64] Ibid. S.13101a.

discussed Finance's reactions to the UK White Paper and agreed with Lemass on the need for 'an immediate employment policy, based on the placing of maximum numbers in temporary employment of a character requiring a minimum of imported materials or equipment, to be maintained until normal industrial activity revives, and our long term policy can take over'. It was an optimistic declaration: no long-term policy had ever been formulated, nor did one exist.[65]

Lemass, however, had replied to Finance with a comprehensive memorandum, dated 21 November 1944, which began his full conversion to Keynesianism (although his public stance remained very different from his private arguments within the cabinet). This memorandum, one of two key documents issued by Lemass to his colleagues, was his most comprehensive statement yet of what he saw as the way forward for Irish economic development.

Lemass insisted that investment fluctuation

must have some consequences in important fields of employment and its control can contribute to increased prosperity ... plans to secure an expansion of agricultural production will have no value in dealing with the immediate post-war unemployment situation. Plans for dealing with the post-war unemployment problem may be hampered by supply difficulties, but it is not understood how they may be hampered by financial difficulties (which are not essentially supply difficulties).

He went on to suggest that talks with the trade unions were necessary on the training of unemployed workers in skilled occupations; and he advocated compulsory training for young people on unemployment assistance.

Returning to an old bone of contention between himself and Finance, he stated:

It may be desirable to examine the adequacy of the facilities for the provision of finance capital to commercial enterprise. The functions of the Industrial Credit Corporation in the post-war situation require to be defined. It is not clear that the attitude of the Department of Finance to this Company is not based on the incorrect assumption that the recommendations of the Banking Commission concerning the restrictions of the Company's activities have been approved by the Government.

It was to be 'presumed', he continued, that Finance did not simply intend to wait for the results of the UK experience. On the

---

[65] NAI Taoiseach S.13026b.

contrary, one could not depend on a successful employment policy in the United Kingdom easing the situation in Ireland. (In the event, this is exactly what did happen.) Primary consideration should therefore be given, not to the state of the national debt, but to the state of trade.

Among the measures then proposed were:

(1) The practicability and advisability of directing exports outside the sterling area by tax remissions, transport subsidies, the creation of an exporting organization, etc. to procure foreign exchange to enable purchase to be maintained in countries which are not willing to accept payment in sterling;

(2) the regulation of capital movement so as to serve Irish economic interests;

(3) the making of claims on the UK authorities for Unemployment Insurance contributions paid in respect of Irish workers in the United Kingdom to permit payment of benefit from these contributions on the return of the workers to Ireland;

(4) the advisability of subsidizing agricultural exports (such as butter and bacon) to secure re-entry to the British market;

(5) the opening of discussions with Switzerland, Canada, etc. on arrangements to facilitate the purchase of capital goods from these countries while sterling is not freely convertible.

And Lemass concluded by attempting to head off another diversionary tactic by Finance:

It is assumed that the Government will not allow questions of land division policy, the removal of restrictions on imports, the reduction of the social services, to be considered by an inter-departmental committee. These are matters on which policy must be defined by the Government and not open to question by committees composed of civil servants.[66]

The second important memorandum issued by Lemass during this period was his celebrated memorandum on full employment, dated 17 January 1945. This detailed and lengthy document is notable, both for the lucidity with which the case for an Irish application of Keynesianism is spelt out, and for the opposition with which it met. Still, the fact that the policy recommendations contained therein were generally rejected does not diminish its historical importance as an indicator of the crisis of Fianna Fáil economic strategy in the post-war era.

[66] Ibid. S.13101a.

Lemass began by arguing that full employment must be based upon stimulation of demand and, with this in mind, went on to argue for industrial reorganization, agricultural reorganization, and the framing of a new budgetary policy.

The Finance view that an efficient agriculture could act as a motor for the economy as a whole was rejected. The necessity to eliminate underemployment in agriculture was emphasized. Three measures were suggested: '(1) The elimination of the incompetent or lazy farmers who fail to maintain a reasonable output from their farms; (2) The reduction of farmers' costs; and (3) The provision of long-term capital.' The Government should regulate wholesale, as well as guarantee prices, and limit production if necessary. 'The development of agricultural exports in the form of processed goods—meat, bacon, butter, cheese, condensed milk etc.—should be the main aim of policy.' Lemass continued:

It will be obvious that private enterprise cannot be relied on to secure the desired conditions . . . The expansion of exports, together with the maintenance of certainty of sale and stability of prices, can best be accomplished by State organizations trading in these goods, supported financially by the State when necessary, and conducting their operations in accordance with State policy.

However, while state regulation of agriculture was necessary, Lemass argued that 'conditions in other industries do not require state regulation in similar degree'. The state might have to set up some large-scale industries, where necessary: mineral development and tourism were mentioned; the nationalization of bacon, flour-milling, and superphosphate fertilizer industries was also stated as a possibility. But all this was hedged in with an important qualification: 'The transfer of these industries to state ownership is not an essential part of a full employment policy, however, assuming that efficiency of production and limitation of profits can be accomplished otherwise.'

'The State must take all necessary measures to ensure that the expansion of industrial output will not be impeded by lack of capital. The provision of adequate capital resources may necessitate the repatriation of Irish capital now invested abroad.' The state should 'take whatever steps are deemed most suitable in the circumstances', if compliance from the owners of capital was not forthcoming. The state must have the power to prevent manufacturers from raising prices instead of raising production in the face of increased demand. The state should also have the power to prevent restriction of sale of goods to small groups of traders, or to regulate profit margins. State control of monopolies in manufacturing was also advocated. 'It should be made generally understood that the State will at all times be prepared to cope with a rise in prices due to excess profits or inadequate supply, by its control of imports, or, in the last resort, by bringing the industry concerned under public ownership.'

But while the threat of state regulation was to be used to whip private enterprise towards a more efficient, dynamic capitalism, private enterprise was also to be reassured that the state, for its part, would help keep their workers in line: 'efficiency' should be rewarded and manufacturers encouraged to resist 'unreasonable demands' from their workers:

The absence of the fear of unemployment might have disruptive effects upon factory discipline, free wage bargaining in full employment might lead to constant upward pressure on money wage-rates, the obstruction by workers and Trade Unions of the introduction of new techniques might operate to defeat the expansion of output capacity and the required degree of flexibility in labour supply might conflict with many rigid Trade Union rules.

Here, Lemass—who liked to project himself as a workers' champion and a friend to the trade-union movement—is clearly recognizing that a policy of full employment might dangerously strengthen the hand of the unions and thereby disrupt the economic rationale which underlies his plan for the revitalization of the Irish economy. The solution was to be threefold: (1) the weakening of the trade-union movement through state regulation of its internal functioning; (2) the incorporation of a regulated and reorganized trade-union movement within the overall strategy for the development of a vibrant capitalist economy; and (3) the use of coercive measures, where necessary, against workers or trade unionists who resisted incorporation.

Thus, Lemass argued that unions should be encouraged to maintain factory discipline through being involved in industrial management. But first 'a reorganization of the Trade Union movement, and the elimination of duplicate unions, would appear to be necessary. It is probable, however, that such reorganization would be facilitated by a decision to recognise in legislation the rights and responsibilities of Trade Unions in this respect.' This concern with the 'reorganization' of the trade unions was not prompted by altruism towards the unions, as some of Lemass's critics within Fianna Fáil were to argue, but was a fundamental part of his strategy for the relaunch of Irish capitalism. As Hutton puts it, 'his policy became one of drawing the trade unions into a subordinate relationship with the state, one in which, in return for certain clear advantages, the central trade union body would be prepared to accept "responsibilities in relation to the maintenance of discipline"'.[67]

Lemass advocated state regulation of wages, linking wages to improvements in production:

the conclusion is inescapable that a full employment policy is incompatible with the old practice of settling wages by direct negotiation between employers and Trade Unions, or by strikes and lock-outs, and that in return for the removal of the fear of unemployment, the workers must be willing to accept the supervision of wage rates by a public authority charged with the responsibility of protecting the real value of all wages against the depreciation through the inflation of prices following higher wages in some occupations.

The state must resolve to defeat trade-union opposition to new productive equipment; the unions should have full confidence in the Government's full employment policy—it is implied that they would have no right to raise workers' complaints, given such a policy.

Lemass also advocated control of prices so as to aim at 'the elimination of industrial concerns which are unwilling or unable to operate profitably at these reasonable prices'. Measures would include compulsory reorganization of management, including the Industrial Credit Corporation taking controlling shares where necessary; encouraging competition from new firms; control of the distribution of profits pending higher productive efficiency; tax incentives for capital accumulation for new plant. 'Exceptional measures of State support' were necessary to encourage large-scale exporting industries. These would include: capital and tax incentives; free factory sites; shift-work permits; free import of materials.

[67] S. Hutton, 'Labour in the Post-Independence Irish State: An Overview', in S. Hutton and P. Stewart (eds.), *Ireland's Histories: Aspects of State, Society and Ideology* (London, 1991).

'While it is desirable that all industries should be owned and controlled by Irish nationals, there is less reason for insistence on national ownership of export industries than of industries supplying only the home market, and the employment of alien technicians will require to be facilitated . . . a foreign trading organization (to market Irish exports) should be established with ample capital resources, and authorised to pledge state credit . . .'.

Lemass suggested that increased Government expenditure would be financed by borrowing. However, the voluntary repatriation of capital funds, given the increased economic activity at home, was assumed. The policy of reducing imports of consumer goods not produced at home, so as to reduce spending, was strongly attacked. It was assumed that the banks would conform to Government policy, or that the Central Bank would be empowered to force them to do so. If the banks withheld their support, this would 'necessitate a degree of state control of Banking operations *which would ordinarily be undesirable*' (emphasis added). The budget should be used to influence the whole economic structure and not just to balance the books. In effect, Lemass advocated the adoption of the budgetary policy implicit in the Beveridge Report, arguing that, although increased state expenditure would lead to increased foreign borrowing, it would also lead to increased private expenditure due to higher incomes, and therefore to an increase in the tax yield; this, in turn, would cancel the borrowing.

What we have, here, is a quite comprehensive plan for the revitalization of Irish capitalism, under the political leadership of Fianna Fáil. It may be argued that Lemass's strategy was above class interests, interventionist, concerned simply with producing results; and that both labour and capital were to feel the thrust of his *dirigiste* mentality. This, however, ignores the fact that capitalist economic rationale is enshrined in the plan even more firmly now than it had been during the 1930s. The aim is to get private enterprise into shape so that it can perform its leadership role in developing further the Irish economy. Towards that goal, state intervention and state control are advocated 'in the last resort', 'where necessary', to a greater degree than 'would ordinarily be desirable', to clear the field of chronically inefficient industrial concerns and so enable the industrial bourgeoisie as a whole to give effect to the economic strategy. For the trade-union movement, on the other hand, the envisaged role is entirely subaltern: the most the workers have the right to ask for, essentially, is security of employment and state regulation of wages.

Lemass's plan met with overwhelming opposition—not only from the majority of his cabinet colleagues and from the civil service, but from industrialists, bankers, and farmers, more concerned with rapid profit accumulation in the short term than with long-term planning. Indeed, it was the organized working class which, in return for the promise of full employment, was to provide Lemass with most support in the post-war years. However, the period 1945–56 was a dark one for Lemass in which his skills as a politician and a tactician were strained to the utmost;[68] it was not until the crisis of 1956 that his plan began to make headway.

The Minister for Agriculture replied to Lemass's memorandum on 14 March 1945. Ryan was concerned with the electoral implications of Lemass's seemingly drastic proposal to remove 'incompetent or lazy farmers' from the land: 'Mr Lemass deals with the matter of displacement of bad farmers. This would be a most delicate and difficult matter.' Many farmers were inefficient, but had a young family growing up who would eventually inherit the farm. 'It would be unthinkable to disturb the family in such cases no matter how below the desired standard the farm might presently be.' On this specific point Ryan got his way. But Irish agricultural policy had changed considerably. While Lemass and Finance disagreed on the relative balance between industry and agriculture, and the capacity of agriculture to act as a motor for the economy as a whole, they were crucially in agreement on the inevitable fate of the small farmer.

Henceforth, the policy of land redistribution was a non-issue. There was certainly some rearguard opposition to the change from within Fianna Fáil; for example, Joe Kennedy, TD, wrote to Frank Gallagher on 18 December 1946 that 'the Land Commission has ceased to function except to collect annuities and two Ministers—Lands and Agriculture—are proclaiming in best Hogan style that there are too many people on the land'.[69] But, significantly, the protest ended with a feeble pledge of loyalty to the party, in spite of all. A more angry exchange of views took place between Fianna Fáil national executive member and rural idealist Aodh de Blacam

---

[68] Bew and Patterson, *Seán Lemass and the Making of Modern Ireland*, 12–14.
[69] NLI Gallagher Papers MS 18336.

and MacEntee in 1946 and 1947. MacEntee accused de Blacam of reading opposition propaganda; but the latter protested to de Valera and to the party executive that Fianna Fáil was under mortal threat from Clann na Poblachta and Clann na Talmhan in its rural heartland. He attacked Ryan for claiming that he did not want more people on the land and for engineering a 'deliberate starving of rural housing' and warned that 'the rural areas will revolt against us and they will suffice to throw us out'. De Blacam continued:

It is essential for us therefore to diagnose the rural malaise and to find remedies, if we are to survive another general election. If we fail, not merely will we go out of power at the coming election, with disastrous consequences; but our regime will be looked back to as that under which rural Ireland suffered its death blow.[70]

On 13 December 1947 de Blacam tendered his resignation from the Fianna Fáil national executive over the question of rural depopulation.[71]

Fianna Fáil did lose the following election. But, in the longer run, the political damage which the party might have suffered from its small-farmer support element was mitigated by a series of subsidies to all farmers, Moylan's warnings about 'dependent traits of character' notwithstanding.

Finance's reply to Lemass's 'Plan for Full Employment' was, as might be expected, overwhelmingly hostile. McElligott attacked all along the line. The plan was described as involving 'bureaucratic control of the most oppressive and objectionable kind'. 'The condition stated to be necessary for full employment would involve a control of all economic processes so complete and detailed that it could probably not be realised without the full socialisation of industry and the suppression of freedoms which no Western people would sacrifice without a bitter struggle.' Lemass was aiming at the 'socialisation of marketing of agricultural produce'. What he was really seeking was not the 'displacement' of farmers but their 'liquidation'. Moreover, employers alone were responsible for factory discipline. It was dangerous to interfere with the banks or investment. The writers whom Lemass had cited—Keynes, Kaldor, and Beveridge—all belonged to the 'Escapist school of economics'.

In fact, the cabinet took fright at the seemingly reckless nature

[70] UCDA MacEntee Papers P67/282.
[71] Ibid. P67/376.

of Lemass's proposals. His main achievements during the post-war years were to be the 1947 Industrial Prices and Efficiency Act—a very watered-down version of his earlier proposals—and his preparations for the incorporation of the trade-union movement within a future developmental strategy, culminating in the 1946 Industrial Relations Act.

In March–May 1945 it was again MacEntee who led the assault upon 'Sir William Beveridge and his school of neo-totalitarians'. Full employment, he warned, would lead to higher wages and therefore inflation. Hayek was cited in defence of the argument that state economic control would be the death knell of freedom. In a speech to the Commerce Society of University College Dublin he declared: 'We should leave men free . . . in their right, the God-given right of every son of Adam, to dispose for the benefits of themselves and their families, of what they have earned by the sweat of their brow.'[72]

By April 1945 the Cabinet Committee on Economic Planning was enlarged to include the whole cabinet—probably a tactic to swamp Lemass. On 18 May it was decided to establish an interdepartmental committee to report on future employment schemes—a diversionary tactic, against which Lemass had warned in his memorandum of November. On 15 June several other of Lemass's proposals—concerning measures to rehabilitate the long-term unemployed and 'the preparation of a unified scheme of health insurance and workmen's compensation'—were discussed without decisions being taken.

Lemass's proposals had assumed, and to a large extent their credibility therefore depended upon, an expected influx of post-war Irish emigrants in search of employment at home. However, Finance had been right in assuming that the upturn in the UK economy would continue to present a political safety valve for Irish economic stagnation. Emigration to Great Britain continued unabated after the war, with a further 119,000 people emigrating between 1946 and 1951. Politically the Government was able simply to postpone the need for innovation.

The post-war years did see a rising tide of expectations in Ireland, as the example of the welfare state now in operation in Great Britain and in Northern Ireland combined with a popular disquiet

[72] Speeches on Beveridge, 1945, in ibid. P67/570.

about the harsh downward pressure on wages since 1941: by 1944 prices were 70 per cent above the 1939 level, although wages had risen only by 13 per cent.[73] A temporary industrial boom between 1946 and 1949 led to an increase in industrial production of 50 per cent, but soaring imports by far outstripped exports, and the economy as a whole lagged far behind rising expectations. It might have been expected that Lemass would have attempted to harness this growing popular discontent in order to strengthen his hand within the cabinet. He did the opposite, and it may well have been a serious political mistake.

Lemass put the unity of his party before the necessity for radical economic change and dedicated himself in public to dampening down popular expectations and demands for innovation. He showed himself to be not an uncompromising radical, but a pragmatist given to twists and turns.[74] To the amazement of some Labour politicians, Lemass publicly attacked the social egalitarianism of Beveridge, declaring that Ireland could not afford it, and sought to 'quell a potential revolution in rising expectations'.[75] At the 1946 Fianna Fáil *Ard-Fheis* he opposed a motion from some party branches which read, 'That it is the duty of the Government to provide employment for men in town or country.' Lemass, speaking against the motion, declared his support for de Valera's statement (prepared for him by a civil servant) which rejected the motion 'as it stands' and spelt out the Government's duty as being:

(1) By its financial and economic policy to foster to the utmost of its power conditions in which (*a*) the maximum use will be made of the country's productive capacity and (*b*) the minimum number of people able and willing to work will be unable to find suitable employment.

(2) So far as the resources of the community permit to promote employment schemes to absorb, mainly, unskilled manual workers for whom employment is not otherwise available.[76]

If it is true that the Government reacted to the growing wave of strikes and industrial action after the war with increasing intransigence, it is also true that there were few more intransigent than Lemass, who reacted to the threat of a flour-milling strike in May

---

[73] Daly, *Social and Economic History of Ireland*, 156.
[74] Bew and Patterson, *Seán Lemass and the Making of Modern Ireland*, 12.
[75] Ibid. 31.   [76] NAI Taoiseach S.13101a.

1947 by getting the cabinet's agreement that he 'should take the necessary steps with a view to promoting legislation, to be introduced in Dáil Éireann in the coming week, to make strikes illegal'. This was only averted at the last moment by de Valera convincing the leaders to call off the strike.[77]

Lemass's paternalistic approach to politics, his fear and dislike of autonomous expressions of protest on the part of the disaffected, prevented him from utilizing that discontent to advance his position within the cabinet. Instead, he ended up publicly defending the political and ideological stance of the conservative wing of the cabinet, whilst fighting an ever-defensive battle internally to move the cabinet towards more innovative policies.

Lemass was now fighting within the cabinet on principally two issues: industrial efficiency, and the relationship with the trade unions. Both these questions raise considerations which we will touch upon in greater detail when we turn our attention to Fianna Fáil's relation to the balance of social forces during the period under examination.

The Industrial Efficiency and Prices Bill, introduced in 1947, was a much weaker version of the stringent controls Lemass had originally proposed. In February 1946 the Department of Industry and Commerce had proposed the establishment of an Industrial Efficiency Bureau to 'supervise and assist in obtaining efficiency in any industry', protected or not. Lemass had rejected criticism of the 'drastic nature' of the proposals.[78] The Bureau, he had insisted, would act as a 'friendly adviser', with the penal provisions kept in reserve. Finance, in a memorandum dated 4 March, had insisted that the scope of the Bill should be restricted to protected industries. 'The Minister for Finance does not see why unprotected industries built up by private enterprise and holding their own in competition with imported products should be brought within the purview of an Efficiency Bureau.'[79] On this point, Finance got its way, and unprotected industries were excluded from the purview of Lemass's inspectors. A Prices Commission was, however, to be established with wide powers of inquiry and inspection; the Minister for Industry and Commerce enjoyed the right to fix maximum

---

[77] Fanning, *Independent Ireland*, 159.   [78] NAI Taoiseach S.13814a.
[79] By now, Frank Aiken was Minister for Finance, and his tenure of office has been described as 'marked by a growing concern within the Department with the need to reduce state expenditure' (Fanning, *The Irish Department of Finance*, 393).

prices or maximum margins of profits. This measure had been necessitated by the excess profits earned during the Emergency which had led to such high costs of living; and by Lemass's mistaken belief that savings to industry resulting from the abolition of the Excess Corporation Profits Tax—for which he fought from December 1945 until January 1947, against Finance's opposition—would be used to reduce prices. In fact, the abolition of the tax was merely an encouragement to excess profits, and led to increased prices.[80]

In 1945 Lemass had established informal agreements with trade-union representatives on post-war economic policy. He now sought to pave the way for the incorporation of the trade unions within Fianna Fáil's economic strategy (as he saw it developing) by settling the thorny question of wages. His Industrial Relations Act, enacted on 26 September 1946, ended the long period of hardship, uncertainty, and rule by Emergency Powers Orders (EPOs). A Labour Court was established which, during an initial four-month transition period, had the power to 'record' wage orders and bonus orders made under the lapsed EPOs. The employer, then, was forced to pay these wage rates, but the trade union concerned lost all claim to higher rates until application had been made to, and approved by, the Labour Court. Although neither side in a dispute was legally compelled to have recourse to the Court, agreements on wages and conditions registered with the Court became legally binding on both parties. The Labour Court could set up Labour Committees to govern conditions and could register Joint Industrial Councils and publish standard wage rates (non-obligatory) for each area of industry. The Labour Court could also set up Joint Labour Committees (JLCs) 'to watch over the interests of workers in trades where the workers are not well organized, and to guard against their exploitation by the employers'. The Labour Court could, on the JLCs' recommendation, fix minimum wages and conditions. The JLCs, whose function it was to supervise industrial peace, could be registered.[81]

This Act, not surprisingly, met with strong opposition from Finance, which feared that the Labour Court would strengthen the hand of the unions and workers, and that it would award high pay settlements and thereby contribute to inflation. In April 1946

---

[80] NAI Taoiseach S.13814a, S.13776a.   [81] Ibid. S.13847A.

Finance fought unsuccessfully to have the EPO on wages retained and to have Lemass's proposals deferred; at least, argued Finance, the Labour Court should be placed under the control of the Government and not the Minister for Industry and Commerce, so that the vitally important question of appointing personnel to the Labour Court who would stand firm in the face of pressure for wage increases could be settled satisfactorily.[82] The Government should tell the Labour Court that its duty was to 'increase output and reduce the cost of living'; there could be no decrease in hours worked without an increase in output; the absolute maximum increase in wages and salaries over the 1939 level should be 40 per cent.[83] On 13 January 1947 Lemass was accused of appearing 'to favour a policy of allowing all-round wage increases to 53 per cent above 1939 on the basis that it would result in a rise in prices of only 7.2 per cent or "considerably less" to the extent that it would be met out of profits'. Finance was horrified by such suggestions.

What Lemass had actually argued, in November 1946, was that 'there is no evidence yet that wage demands sponsored by responsible Trade Unions are excessive' and that 'probably, the effect of a general all-round wage increase of 50 per cent over 1939 would have less inflationary effect than a further expansion in the total of emigrants' remittances consequent on the increase in emigration to Great Britain'. In any event, while the Government adopted a tough stance *vis-à-vis* wage demands, Lemass got his way on the issue of the Labour Court—and this was to be of crucial importance for Fianna Fáil's relationship with the trade-union movement, and, in turn, for its ability to resist pressure from sections of the bourgeoisie.

These developments apart, there was little fundamental innovation during the immediate post-war years. Certainly, the period saw nothing like an embrace of Keynesianism. Although there was a considerable increase in the size of the public sector, much of this increase was incurred after the removal of Fianna Fáil from office in 1948; thus, for example, while state expenditure on housing construction had increased substantially by the early 1950s, only 1,600 houses were built with state aid in 1947. With the decline in revenue from corporation profits tax and motor vehicle duties, customs and borrowing were the main sources of increased expenditure.

---

[82] NAI Taoiseach S.13814a, S.13776a.   [83] Ibid. S.13965a.

Borrowing increased from £2.8 million in 1945 to £49.3 million in 1951 (although it fell back considerably thereafter); a stringent budget in 1947 introduced new taxes on drink, cigarettes, and cinemas, although this was somewhat offset by food subsidies. Even with Irish involvement in the European Recovery Programme in 1948, there was no new thinking fundamentally; emphasis continued to be placed on agricultural production, and concern with the balance-of-payments difficulties took precedence over concern with employment and development.[84]

After the war, the Government faced the problem of readjusting an unfavourable balance of trade with the United Kingdom. External assets in sterling had increased greatly owing to the fact that Ireland had continued to export food to the United Kingdom while suffering from artificial import restrictions. A memorandum from Industry and Commerce, prior to the negotiations with the United Kingdom about the 1947 UK financial crisis, claimed that sterling assets had grown by £163.2 million since 1940 and now stood at £450 million.[85] However, inflation in the United Kingdom had halved the value of the holdings and the British, in an effort to solve their own financial problems, were curtailing the convertibility of all sterling earnings.

There is no firm prospect [the Department wrote] that Britain will ever be able to convert into goods even the small fraction of this sterling we are likely to want to repatriate. It would be unrealistic not to regard the future accumulation of sterling less as a loan than as an outright gift of resources to Britain.

And yet the chronic need to pay for rapidly rising imports in the post-war period obviously left Ireland with the desire to exchange sterling for dollars, so as to purchase capital goods from countries which could not accept payment in sterling.

Irish agricultural exports to the United Kingdom had actually declined during the war, and there was a need to reverse this trend. There had been a decrease of 35 per cent in agricultural exports to the United Kingdom from 1939 to 1946, which the Irish side blamed on inadequate UK prices.[86] Moreover, after the war the scope for increased agricultural exports at satisfactory prices was further adversely affected by food rationing in the United Kingdom and by

[84] O'Hagan, 'Analysis of the Size of the Government Sector', 30–3.
[85] NAI Taoiseach S.14134c.   [86] Ibid.

the fact that the UK food market was becoming saturated by cheap Commonwealth food. The Government was anxious to supply the British demand for food, even at the price of subsidizing exports, but was also adamant that imports of industrial raw materials should not be placed in jeopardy.[87]

In September 1947 top-level trade talks were held with the United Kingdom. The Government demanded equal treatment of Irish industries with their UK counterparts in allocation of fuel and materials; removal of restrictions on Irish industrial exports; availability of plant and machinery for Irish exporters; equal farm-product prices with UK prices; and equal treatment *vis-à-vis* fertilizer and farm-equipment allocation. In return, the Government pledged to step up meat exports; to give the United Kingdom a monopoly of the cattle export trade; and to curtail domestic consumption of meat and eggs.[88] De Valera was openly conciliatory, speaking of the 'dove-tailing' of the two countries' agricultural policies, while insisting on the Irish desire to import coal and plant and to export footwear and homespun products. The British gave way to some extent on the question of the Irish dollar requirement, whilst hoping to reduce the pace of Irish industrialization. The Irish effectively agreed to subsidize a cheap food policy for the United Kingdom; butter and bacon losses were now subsidized by the Irish taxpayer and Irish agriculture faced a wheat glut, a decline in poultry, pigs, and tillage, and increasing agricultural unemployment—with the live cattle trade again predominant. That, in effect, was the substance of the General Agreement on Tariffs and Trade (GATT), signed with the United Kingdom in 1947, which underlined the difficulties faced by an economic strategy which relied upon the profitability of Irish agriculture. The Irish economy, depending as it did to such an extent upon agricultural exports to the United Kingdom, found great difficulty in adjusting to the post-war situation and the balance-of-payments deficit was running at £30 million in 1947 in spite of external sterling assets.[89]

Banking and Finance

The period 1938–48 continued to be characterized by (*a*) large-scale investment of Irish capital overseas; (*b*) resistance on the part

[87] Daly, *Social and Economic History of Ireland*, 159–60; Bew and Patterson, *Seán Lemass and the Making of Modern Ireland*, 34 and *passim*.
[88] NAI Taoiseach S.14134c.   [89] Lyons, *Ireland since the Famine*, 624–8.

of the banks to any suggestion that they should alter the pattern of investment or play a constructive part in the implementation of the Government's economic development policies; and (*c*) no action, on the part of Fianna Fáil, to compel the banks to change their attitude, despite rhetoric and occasional threats from, for example, Lemass and Aiken.

In 1939 the banks gave a forewarning of the attitude which was to characterize their reactions to Government policy during the Emergency and after, refusing to afford the Government lower interest rates on Government credits to manufacturers (to encourage the latter to stockpile supplies for the Emergency), despite investing in UK loans at even lower rates! Government aid to industry, such as that provided by the Industrial Credit Corporation, simply supplemented the pattern of Irish capital being invested abroad, rather than attempting to alter it.

In May 1940, the British Fabian John Hawkins estimated that total Irish capital investments abroad amounted to 300 million pounds, that bank assets held in Ireland were less than three-fifths of the assets held outside Ireland and that Irish-held investments in foreign government stocks were eleven and a half times the value of investments in Irish government stocks.[90]

The Central Bank Act of 1942 empowered the Central Bank to control banks only through possession of their deposits; even this power was held in reserve and was to prove totally ineffectual because of the lack of any control over foreign investment powers or the power to issue British currency. Indeed, 'the Central Bank, which first opened its doors on 1 February 1943, was, essentially, the kind of central bank envisaged since the early thirties by the senior officials of the Department of Finance, and by McElligott in particular . . .'.[91]

Moynihan, upon whose account this summary is based, claims that Lemass and Aiken were pressing for extensive powers for the Central Bank at the outbreak of the war, with MacEntee and O'Kelly resisting change, and de Valera 'endeavouring to reconcile the conflicting opinions while leaning, himself, towards a progressive view'.[92] If this is true, then de Valera cannot have leaned very heavily, for nothing was done. Lemass had proposed to 'empower

[90] O'Connor Lysaght, *The Republic of Ireland*, 129–30.
[91] Fanning, *The Irish Department of Finance*, 373.
[92] Moynihan, *Currency and Central Banking in Ireland*, 289.

the board of the central bank to fix the maximum proportion of the total assets of any banker that might be held in foreign securities'. This had met with strong opposition from Joseph Brennan, Chairman of the Currency Commission, who argued that the banking system owed its stability to its investment policy and that there was no need to urge the banks to invest at home. Indeed, it was argued, this would amount to partial nationalization. Finance was no more favourably disposed to any control or influence over domestic credit.[93]

In September 1941 the Finance Minister, O'Kelly, agreed to urge his cabinet colleagues to change the offending clause by which the Government had hoped 'to provide a means of influencing the banks to increase their domestic assets and to expand domestic credit'. Under the compromise which was reached, the Central Bank Act eventually required the banker to maintain interest-free deposits with the Central Bank whenever the proportion of his internal assets to internal liabilities fell below a certain figure. This power was never invoked, and, in any case, as a further concession to the banks, there was only a fine for non-compliance—not the withdrawal of their licence. Finance continued to resist even this measure, replying to the Currency Commission that 'it is no part of the functions of a bank to establish factories and provide plant, machinery, skilled labour, etc.'.[94]

In the debate on the Central Bank Bill, the Labour Party opposed the Bill on the grounds that monetary authority was not being placed under parliament and that the Central Bank, given the restrictions placed upon it, could not promote national welfare or employment creation—which brought a stern warning from de Valera that Labour was being led in the direction of nationalization! Fine Gael supported the Government, despite complaints against the one feeble restriction upon the banks contained in the Bill—the requirement to hold interest-free deposits with the Central Bank, which Cosgrave described as 'abhorrent'.[95]

During the 1940s, Moynihan tells us, the board of the Central Bank did nothing to use its limited powers: 'in view of the membership of the Board, it was unlikely that the views of the Banking Commission would be treated otherwise than with profound respect.'

---

[93] Moynihan, *Currency and Central Banking in Ireland*, 292.
[94] Ibid. 296–9.   [95] Ibid. 301–4.

Small wonder, then, that, when Frank Aiken, Minister for Finance from June 1945, asked the banks to lower interest rates so that the Government could borrow 'cheap money', he met with overwhelming opposition from both the Central Bank and the private banks.

Aiken has been described by one commentator as 'dogged and inquisitive' and more independent-minded than his predecessors.[96] Whilst he possessed an almost eccentric interest in monetary matters, he was at heart a conservative, and his stay at the Department of Finance was characterized by a strong deflationary policy and, despite threats, no action against the banks.

In 1945 the Government pressed the banks for a 'cheap-money' policy no less favourable than that in operation in the United Kingdom. The banks, it was pointed out, had done extremely well during the war and now held double the proportion of liquid assets to deposits that they had before the war: £75.6 million in the September quarter of 1945, compared to £21.8 million for the same period in 1939. (The figures refer to balances with London agents and other banks and money at call on short notice.) Cash and balances were up from £14.2 million to £47.8 million, but deposit liabilities had increased by only 80 per cent. So ample cash was available. At a meeting with the bankers on 17 December 1945, the Government requested an advance of £1.8 million on three-months Exchequer Bills at an interest rate not exceeding that in operation in the United Kingdom—i.e. 0.5 per cent. The Banks Standing Committee refused to co-operate by reducing the interest rate from 1 per cent to 0.5 per cent and stated that they were 'strongly adverse to doing it as they regarded their deposits as the vital foundation of Irish banking'.[97]

Aiken reacted furiously with a memorandum on 21 December 1945 in which he told his colleagues that he 'went as far as any Minister for Finance could be reasonably expected to go, and further than many think he should, in order to win their voluntary co-operation'. Their refusal to offer that co-operation was 'an act of undeclared war upon our people'. The Government, he insisted, would reject the offer of an advance at 1 per cent, but there would be no effective compulsion. Instead, a decision would be taken 'to sell securities and obtain Ways and Means advances from State

[96] Fanning, *The Irish Department of Finance*, 392.
[97] NAI Taoiseach S.13749a.

funds'; it was not a good bargain, but would be accepted as necessary.[98]

On 28 December 1945 Finance, clearly on Aiken's instructions, reported that Irish banks were earning almost twice as much on money deposited with them as were UK banks, and yet refused to co-operate.

The Minister regards it as a clear and unmistakable indication that the banks are prepared to undermine the welfare of our people rather than give to them the same service as the British banks gave the British people on the basis of voluntary cooperation during the war . . . Their motive is clearly not profit; it appears rather to be power, or fear of loss of power . . . the desire to keep the public in the dark regarding their power of increasing the volume of money.

Aiken added that in other countries this sort of behaviour on the part of the banks would lead to nationalization! (But not, he failed to add, in Fianna Fáil's Ireland.)

Aiken requested the Government to approve the exercise of the Central Bank's limited powers by authorizing it to force every licensed banker to deposit (not bearing interest) with the Central Bank 10 per cent of the sum by which deposit liabilities within the state exceeded assets on 1 January 1946. The Government agreed to the proposal, but in practice nothing came of it. The Government came up against the opposition of the Central Bank itself (whose Governor, Joseph Brennan, became President of the Institute of Bankers in Ireland in 1946!), which concentrated its attention in the post-war period upon urging control of the money supply and reduction in the balance-of-payments deficit through reduction in public expenditure.[99]

On 15 February 1946 McElligott forwarded a final appeal to the chairman of the Banks Standing Committee, Lord Glenavy. The letter is enlightening, by the deference shown towards the bankers and the care taken to defend Government policy in terms which might hope to gain the bankers' approval. McElligott wrote:

In order to encourage rapid development by private individuals it may be necessary to lower the rate of taxation in certain directions and this means that the State may have to risk increasing its debt in the year or two immediately ahead. In so far as the State must invest capital in such projects

[98] NAI Taoiseach S.13749b.
[99] Moynihan, *Currency and Central Banking in Ireland*, 332–4.

as electrification, turf, housing, telephones, roads, tourist and other development, the lower the interest rate on the necessary funds the lower the taxation of profits of semi-State companies will be in the future in order to repay them. In all the circumstances, it is better for all sections of the community that the State, if compelled to increase its debt for any cause, should do so upon terms which will enable it to repay the sums it has borrowed out of a reasonable level of taxation, rather than upon terms which would compel it either to impose crushing taxation or to allow debt to rise at compound interest towards the point when the total national income would be owed to the holders of State securities . . .[100]

However, even this unassailable declaration of the Government's non-revolutionary intent was not sufficient to budge the banks. Lord Glenavy continued to resist, with the helpful suggestion that the Government should borrow 'from the public' and not from the banks. And that, basically, is what happened: in addition to increased foreign borrowing, the Government 'borrowed' from the public—through increased indirect taxation.

Social Conditions and Social Welfare

The overall period was one of negligible improvement in social conditions, with the introduction of children's allowances in 1944 being the only legislative measure of lasting importance—and that only after a long internal party struggle, as we will see. It is a sad fact that Fianna Fáil's attention to social policy during these years can be summed up in a few pages. There was little improvement in those aspects of social policy which concerned the treatment of the sick, the aged, or the unemployed: 'Indeed, by 1950, many areas of Irish social administration were probably closer to the British practice of the 1920s than corresponding policies in contemporary Britain or Northern Ireland.'[101] This was despite the increasing interest in social concerns shown by the Catholic Church; with certain members of the hierarchy apparently tiring of some of the grimmer features of de Valera's Ireland, the Archbishop of Dublin, Dr McQuaid, convened a Catholic Social Services conference in 1940, and in 1944 the Bishop of Clonfert, Dr Dignan, attacked the state's social services as reminiscent in part of the Poor Law and called for a national health insurance scheme which would involve the compulsory and comprehensive insurance of all employed

---

[100] NAI Taoiseach S.13749A.
[101] Daly, *Social and Economic History of Ireland*, 173.

persons. Bishop Dignan published a blueprint for just such a scheme which, while resonant with paternalistic Catholic social teaching—it proposed, for example, that marriage benefits should be paid to the father as head of the household, that the family and not the individual should be treated as the basic unit of society, and that single men should be forced to pay for 'assumed dependants' such as 'future wives/children, old parents etc.'[102]—represented an embarrassing challenge to the Government.

Fianna Fáil greeted such interventions with anger and resentment, and MacEntee, in particular, led the attack on the Dignan scheme, later relieving the bishop of his role as chairman of the National Health Insurance Society. The conduct of the dispute between the Government and Bishop Dignan reveals that, under the cloak of the extraordinary powers which the state had assumed in wartime, Fianna Fáil was perfectly ready to tackle the Catholic Church head-on, when the Church's social interventions were seen as potentially damaging to the party's political dominance. No doubt the conservative wing of the party had been further incensed by the fact that the Dignan scheme had drawn support from many Labour Party and trade-union branches. Although Labour leaders were critical of aspects of the scheme—voicing concern that the scheme 'accepted the permanence of poverty as a national heritage'[103]—the overall response from the labour movement was probably that expressed by the National Executive of the ITUC, which welcomed Bishop Dignan's intervention as 'an important and valuable contribution to the solution of the very grave problem . . .'.[104]

MacEntee intervened heavily with both state broadcasting and the newspapers, attempting to suppress or limit coverage of the Dignan scheme; he even enlisted the help of the Minister for Posts and Telegraphs, P. J. Little, in November 1944.[105] When this proved unsuccessful, he wrote angrily to the bishop, accusing him of 'grievous lack of responsibility' and requesting his resignation as chairman of the National Health Insurance Society so as to free him to engage in 'the controversy which you are so assiduously seeking'. The bishop, for his part, replied that the Minister's behaviour imperilled the democratic character of the state.[106]

The profoundly reactionary nature of MacEntee's position is

---

[102] UCDA MacEntee Papers P67/257.   [103] *Irish Times*, 19 Oct. 1944.
[104] Quoted in UCDA MacEntee Papers P67/257.   [105] Ibid.
[106] Ibid.

expressed eloquently in a paper which was presented to the Minister in August 1945 by a Dr T. J. O'Reilly of Bray, and at once acclaimed by MacEntee as 'admirable' and 'from an independent standpoint, a very fine statement on the whole question'. The paper argued:

A study of the plan for 'social security' put forward by the Most Rev. Dr Dignan supplies no hope that it has any other outlook [than the slave state]. Right at the beginning the assumption is made that social insecurity exists here on a large scale; that this insecurity is due to material causes; that it can be remedied by the regimentation of society on some plan—the author's plan for preference—and that security imposed on the individual by outside regimentation is good.

Health centres would at best become the resort of all and sundry and the delight of the hypochondriac, the mental defective, the lazy and the psychoneurotic—all avid consumers of medicine and such other free consumable commodities as are associated therewith.

The rearing of a family is a full-time occupation and there should be no place for the married woman in industry.

This whole plan is inspired by the city mentality of a highly organized industrial community and overshadowed by the threat of the slave state. It is not suitable to Ireland. If it worked—and there is no evidence that it would—the price in human freedom is too high.[107]

With such views being praised and congratulated by the Minister with responsibility for health and social problems, it is little wonder that progress was so limited during these years.

As regards housing, it has been estimated that in 1945 some 110,000 new houses were needed.[108] Much of the housing stock which existed was in a far from satisfactory condition.

In 1938, a survey of the tenements of Dublin found 60 per cent (6,554 out of 11,039) of tenements and cottages unfit for human habitation. In these, 64,940 were forced by economic circumstance to make their home. For those families who had been rehoused in the building programmes of the 1930s problems remained.[109]

Some of these problems were noted by a commentator in 1945:

The new settlements in Crumlin and Drimnagh are without any of the essential social amenities. There are no parks, no playing fields, no town

---

[107] UCDA MacEntee Papers P67/261.
[108] Lyons, *Ireland since the Famine*, 573.
[109] Brown, *Ireland: A Social and Cultural History*, 206–7.

halls. No schools were provided at first ... there were no factories, no technical schools, no secondary schools, no football grounds ... A fine police barracks has been provided to control the unruly crowds of workless adolescents.[110]

Conditions in what were rapidly emerging as the new working-class ghettoes of Dublin were such as to sustain those who lived there in a state of despair and dependency—not unlike the condition in which Fianna Fáil policy kept the small-farmer stratum. It is these same working-class estates of Dublin which have provided Fianna Fáil since with one of its most solid bases of political support. Despite the need for 110,000 new houses by 1945, the Government's financial backing for housing construction proceeded, as we have seen, at the rate of less than 2,000 per year in the immediate post-war period (up to 1948). Fianna Fáil did introduce some measures aimed at social amelioration during the early 1940s. Free food for the very poorest in 1941 was followed by a free fuel scheme in 1942, the latter being facilitated by the ample supplies of high-grade machine turf.[111] Help for unemployed builders was accompanied by a loosening of the wages restrictions for the worst paid in 1942. Unemployment benefits were slightly increased and shop workers' conditions of employment were regulated. These, however, were relatively minor adjustments, seemingly inspired by electoral considerations of the moment.

A more significant innovation, from the point of view of long-term change, was the introduction of children's allowances in 1944.[112] This had been a subject of intense debate within the cabinet, chiefly between Lemass and MacEntee, since 1939. In October 1939 MacEntee sent a memorandum to de Valera attacking the whole idea of family allowances on the grounds that it would 'drive the unfit into matrimony' at the expense of the taxpayer; that there was too much political egalitarianism; that the measure would weaken parental authority; and that too much state intervention would lead to the 'servile state'. Although personally in favour of the idea of family allowances, de Valera insisted upon referring the proposed

---

[110] Quoted in ibid. 207.

[111] O'Connor Lysaght, *The Republic of Ireland*, 122; Andrews, *Man of No Property*, 179.

[112] See Farrell, *Seán Lemass*, 61–2, and Farrell, 'Seán Lemass', in J. A. Murphy and J. O'Carroll (eds.), *De Valera and his Times* (Cork, 1983), 40, upon which this account is based.

scheme to a cabinet committee (from which MacEntee was excluded, but where O'Kelly argued much the same line). There then followed repeated civil-service delays—reinforced by political inertia, administrative caution, and religious conservatism—and constant pressure had to be brought to bear upon both Finance and Industry and Commerce. It was not until October 1942 that a civil-service report on the issue was circulated to cabinet members, and only in 1944 that legislation was finally introduced. Even then, the Act provided for a mere two shillings and six pence per week for the third and further children under 16 years. Nevertheless, the measure was to prove of lasting importance.

Again, in the case of the 1947 Health Act, what was left to future governments to accomplish was more than what the Act itself actually provided for. However, the Act did provide for the introduction of a Mother and Child health-care scheme—although it was the succeeding inter-party government which would introduce that ill-fated measure. The 1947 Health Act also increased county-council responsibility for health schemes in general, although it met with opposition on the grounds that it was too centralized, gave no choice of doctor to the patient, and afforded the Minister extraordinary powers of compulsion (Dr Noel Browne, Minister for Health in the succeeding government, offered to modify those provisions of the Act).

FIANNA FÁIL AND THE BALANCE OF CLASS FORCES

Fianna Fáil's success in enrolling sections of organized labour behind its political banner was facilitated by the ideological and political weakness of the labour movement. Realizing that the defence of their members' interests required economic growth, the trade unions tended to accept the leadership of political forces which could credibly assert a claim to develop the national economy. Fianna Fáil's relationship with the unions developed considerably during the period 1938–48 and was to be an important ingredient of future party strategy. The relationship, and that between the party and organized bourgeois interests, must therefore be analysed in more detail.

Despite evidence that rising prices during the war were due more to excess profits and the functioning of the black economy than to excessive wage increases, the claim that wage demands were a primary cause of economic difficulties was to be a recurrent theme of the Finance-influenced right wing of Fianna Fáil. Thus, Erskine Childers, TD, a future Fianna Fáil cabinet minister and a key link between the party and the Irish bourgeoisie,[113] launched a bitter attack upon the workers involved in the Dublin Corporation strike in February 1940, describing the strike as 'a reckless demand by highly paid, pensioned employees' which 'was a selfish outrage on the farming community'. He went on to warn that 'this strike is one more blow by a small section against orderly democratic rule and the future of Fianna Fáil depends on the Government's ability to grip this fiery nettle firmly and establish the principle that small sections of the community may not plunge the whole community into danger'.[114] MacEntee, speaking in the Dáil in May, sought to place trade-union critics of the Government's employment record on the defensive, arguing that 'instead of asking us how we are going to solve the unemployment problem, how we are going to put another 20,000 men at work' they should 'ask (themselves) how we are going to keep in employment the 19 out of every 20 at work in this country'; he went on to warn grimly that the Government should show no sympathy for those of the unemployed who were 'slackers'.[115]

But it was not merely the conservative wing of Fianna Fáil which took the offensive into the trade-union and labour camp at this stage. Lemass, speaking to the Cork Chamber of Commerce, charged the trade unions with failure to realize that higher wages for some workers 'may mean no wages for others'.[116] He warned that 'the uncontrolled actions by individual sections [of the union movement] might produce consequences seriously detrimental to the interest of the whole working class'.[117] He went on to raise the question of central control within the trade-union movement and the need 'to get general agreement among trade unionists that the reduction of unemployment is our first aim, taking priority over all others including the normal desire to improve existing working conditions'. True, he also launched an attack upon managerial 'slackness'; but the appeal to industrial employers on the overriding need

---

[113] Childers was at this time the secretary of the FIM.
[114] *Irish Press*, 1 Feb. 1940.
[115] Dáil Debates, 22 May 1940.　　　　　　　　[116] *Irish Press*, 20 Feb. 1940.
[117] Quoted in K. Allen, 'Forging the Links: Fianna Fáil, the Trade Unions and the Emergency', *Saothar*, 16 (1991), 48–56.

to cut costs left them considerable leeway as to how that worthy goal might be realized. On 1 April Derrig returned to the attack, accusing the unions of making demands for higher wages based upon higher prices without understanding that wage increases merely drove prices even higher.[118] The onus, it was clear, to break the alleged circle rested with the workers and their unions—and not with those earning increased profits.

These attempts to isolate the unions from public opinion and to make them appear sectional, out of touch with changing reality, and an obstacle to the restructuring of the economic life of the country under wartime conditions can be seen, in retrospect, to have paved the way for the introduction of the Wages Standstill Order in May 1941. Nevin writes of that measure:

It effectively prohibited any increase in wages and prevented unions from striking for higher wages by removing the legal protection of the Trades Disputes Act from such strikes . . . The effect of the Wages Standstill Order in depressing workers' living standards is clearly evident in the comparison between the increase in wages and the increase in prices over the war period. Between 1939 and 1946 the cost of living index, as it was called, rose by about two-thirds but the average weekly earnings of industrial workers rose by only one-third.[119]

Trade-union opposition to the Wages Standstill Order was united and intense, albeit unsuccessful. The ITUC condemned the measure as 'harsh and inequitable',[120] and went on the offensive with an attack upon 'open profiteering and the black market in rationed and unrationed commodities (which) had reached the dimensions of a national scandal'.[121] William O'Brien, in his presidential address to the 1941 ITUC conference, declared:

the fact is that economic conditions had very much lessened demands for wages increases because workers, while feeling the increasing pinch, were not anxious to press their claims under the increasing threat to the continuity of any employment at all. Order Nr. 83 (Wages Standstill Order) was entirely unnecessary, provocative, ill-advised, and a grave blunder on the part of the Government.[122]

---

[118] *Irish Press*, 1 Apr. 1940.
[119] D. Nevin, 'Industry and Labour', in K. B. Nowlan and T. Desmond Williams (eds.), *Ireland in the War Years and After, 1939–1951* (Dublin, 1969), 96–7.
[120] NLI O'Brien Papers MS 15684.   [121] Nevin, 'Industry and Labour', 97.
[122] NLI O'Brien Papers MS 15684.

He was somewhat underestimating the Government's political instinct, as the remainder of his address was to show. The Wages Standstill Order was accompanied by a measure which was deeply to divide the trade-union movement and render any union opposition to the Government's economic strategy ineffective: the Trade Union Act of 1941. This measure, for which MacEntee was later to claim full credit,[123] sought compulsorily to regulate the trade unions by imposing constraints upon their negotiating rights and by streamlining the polyhedral union movement. Under the first part of the Act, unions required a licence in order to negotiate about wages or other conditions of employment; such licences were to be granted only to those unions which placed a deposit with the High Court—the deposits varied from £2,000 for a union with 2,000 members to £10,000 for a union with 20,000 members or more. These were substantial sums for Irish unions at this time and the measure was clearly designed to undermine the negotiating power of the smaller unions. The second part of the Act established a Trade Union Tribunal to restrict organization in certain industries to a particular union, where that union could show that it could command the loyalty of the majority of the workers in the industry; this grant of a negotiating monopoly was only to be considered, however, in the case of Irish-based unions. The Act thus sought to exploit inter-union rivalries, both between bigger and smaller unions and between Irish-based and British-based unions. Its passage enabled Fianna Fáil to manipulate the fissile tendencies always present within both the political and industrial arms of the Irish labour movement.

The need for some internal regulation had long been recognized within the union movement itself, a factor which Fianna Fáil sought to exploit. (Lemass, for example, put pressure on the ITUC in 1937–8 to inform him of measures proposed to eliminate inter-union rivalry and offered to help if 'the Minister or his officers can be of any assistance in dealing with any particular aspects of the problems'.[124]) The ITUC established a committee in 1936 which spent the next two years examining the case for reorganization. It had been agreed that there were too many unions and too much

---

[123] UCDA MacEntee Papers P67/229.
[124] NAI Labour TIW 408. This file also contains a memo. from R. C. Ferguson to Lemass (dated 10 Mar. 1936), warning the Minister against any penalties being imposed on British-based unions, which could lead to 'far more, and far more serious, labour troubles'.

overlapping: forty-eight unions were affiliated to the Congress, eighteen of them with less than 500 members each. Many other unions were not affiliated: they were either independent or based in Northern Ireland or Great Britain. Local unions were sometimes affiliated to trades' or workers' councils and 'as Trade Union units are unknown officially to Congress'. Proposals for the co-ordination of disputes and the establishment of arbitration machinery were examined, but, as always, such initiatives ran aground amid the clashing interests of rival unions, with British-based unions fearfully resisting change and the ITGWU (led by O'Brien) greedily advocating 'rationalization' with an eye to the membership of smaller unions. The situation seemed increasingly open to Government interference and, indeed, there was a widespread fear of 'regimentation' of the union movement, as the Labour Party leader, William Norton, put it.[125]

When 'regimentation' came, it was at the worst possible moment for the movement, with union membership weakened by the war and attention concentrated upon the defensive struggle against the Wages Standstill Order. Total Congress-affiliated union membership in the state in 1941 was just 103,000, of whom 79,000 were in Irish-based and 24,000 in British-based unions. A further 47,000 trade unionists were not affiliated to the ITUC—41,000 in Irish-based and 6,000 in British-based unions.[126] A weakened union movement faced potentially disastrous clashes between unions with divergent objective interests. Nor should it be assumed that all the Irish-based unions were enthusiastic about the restrictions placed upon the Irish branches of British-based unions. The Larkinite WUI was prominent in the struggle against the Act.

Larkin's leading role in the struggle against the Trade Union Act certainly contributed to a rise in his prestige and that of his union; but the old and complex rivalry with O'Brien and the ITGWU flared into the open again. It became clear at the 1941 conference of the ITUC that O'Brien and the ITGWU had no intention of opposing those sections of the Act which aimed at the elimination of their rivals in the smaller and British-based unions. O'Brien, in his presidential address, warned the unions that it was their own fault if the Government had found intervention in their affairs necessary. He continued:

---

[125] NLI O'Brien Papers MS 13971.   [126] Ibid. MS 13974.

We all, of course, can understand that no matter what the proposals in the measure were, there would be an outcry from the superfluous unions which we all want to see eliminated—or, to use an expression in fashion in some quarters, 'liquidated'. These were sure to protest no matter what form 'the surgeon's knife' took. But apart altogether from these 'fifth wheels to the coach' and the grounds of their opposition, there is a strong feeling in the unions against Government regulation of Trade Unions.[127]

This was scarcely a declaration of war upon the Act and, indeed, opposition from the ITGWU was to be negligible. Instead, that union echoed Fianna Fáil propaganda calling for the elimination of 'foreign' unions on 'patriotic' grounds and hurling the charge of 'communism' against both the Labour Party and rival trade unions. As Allen has argued convincingly, 'the emerging twenty-six county nationalism brought the ITGWU leadership ever closer to the political terrain of F[ianna] F[áil]. The key concern of both the union and F[ianna] F[áil] was the protection of the state.'[128]

The first ominous signs of the pending split came when the ITGWU refused to join a campaign mounted by the Dublin Trades Union Council (DTUC) against the Act; the ITGWU had earlier resigned from the DTUC because that body had accepted the WUI into membership. At the 1941 ITUC conference—the first which Larkin had addressed since 1914—Larkin clashed bitterly with O'Brien. The ITGWU delegation remained silent during the debate on the Trade Union Act and Larkin was not contradicted when he alleged that MacEntee had stated that 'the Bill had not come of his initiative and that what he was doing was with the knowledge and approval of some trade union officials whom he declined to name'.[129]

The Larkin/O'Brien split soon involved the Labour Party. Larkin rejoined Labour in 1941 and was elected a TD in 1943 when the Labour Party did particularly well electorally, especially in Dublin. Labour was soon afterwards to claim that he was followed into the party in 1941 by thousands of new members.[130] Certainly the split which was soon to tear asunder both the party and the trade-union movement cannot simply be reduced to a personality conflict between the two powerful union leaders; nor, even, to a revolutionary–reformist ideological dichotomy, despite the ritualistic propaganda by the ITGWU lobby about an alleged communist take-over of the

[127] NLI O'Brien Papers MS 15684.   [128] Allen, 'Forging the Links', 52.
[129] Nevin, 'Industry and Labour', 99.   [130] NLI Johnson Papers MS 17197.

Labour Party. After all, many Labour leaders who had previously shared O'Brien's personal and political dislike of Larkin—Johnson and Norton included—now ended up on the same side as the 'fiery trouble-maker'. The truth is that the 1941 Trade Union Act aroused widespread opposition throughout the union movement, as witnessed by the fact that, when the split came, the majority of unionists remained loyal to the ITUC. Apart from the obvious objection in principle to Governmental regulation of trade-union affairs, few unions stood to benefit from all the terms of the Act taken together—apart from the ITGWU. Moreover, the attempt to eliminate non-Irish-based unions could be seen as nakedly sectarian and partitionist: the ITUC had always covered the entire island of Ireland and in Northern Ireland the great majority of Protestant workers belonged to British-based unions. However, the demands of the ITGWU leaders for 'patriotic' unions based almost entirely within the southern Irish state certainly appealed to nationalist sentiment and, of course, met with the whole-hearted endorsement of the Government. MacEntee, in 1943, sought to invoke the name of James Connolly in the midst of an anti-communist outpouring, declaring himself to be as proud of the Trade Union Act as he was of 'the moment when James Connolly gave him a special message in 1916 . . .'. Once again, nationalist rhetoric was used by Fianna Fáil to demobilize its opponents and, in this case, facilitate penetration of the trade-union movement and the incorporation of an important part of that movement—the ITGWU—within the party's political strategy.

The formal split in the union movement was preceded by a split in the Labour Party (see below). The ITGWU disaffiliated from Labour in December 1943, following the election of Larkin as a Labour TD, and five Labour deputies who were members of that union promptly resigned to form the National Labour Party (NLP). Three other deputies belonging to the ITGWU chose to remain in Labour. In January 1944 O'Brien wrote to each branch secretary of the ITGWU announcing disaffiliation from the Labour Party and attacking Larkin.[131] The ITGWU executive then launched a pamphlet charging Labour with being communist-dominated. (This was followed by the decision of the NLP to republish, as a party pamphlet, a tract written by Alfred O'Rahilly, the President of University

---

[131] Copy of letter in UCDA MacEntee Papers P67/535.

College Cork, entitled 'The Communist Front and the Attack on Irish Labour'.) Labour replied that the ITGWU was waging a struggle for factional control of the trade-union and labour movement; that some of the union's officers had 'appeared to welcome the Bill' which Labour believed 'infringed the Constitutional right of freedom of association'; that ITGWU leaders supported MacEntee's denunciation of Labour TDs who attacked the Bill; and that the NLP was 'a bogus rump, financed, directed, controlled and coerced by a handful of semi-literate trade union officials thirsting for power and influence' and 'the chosen instrument of the Fianna Fáil Government'.[132]

The split within the union movement which followed was much more serious than that within the Labour Party itself and its roots 'lay deeper and were more complex'.[133] On 21 March 1945 a conference of fifteen Irish-based unions led by the ITGWU withdrew from the ITUC, alleging that it was 'controlled by British Trade Unions' and on 25 April the rival Congress of Irish Unions (CIU) was formally established. A manifesto, ringing with declarations of Irish nationalism, was issued. Two rival congresses of trade unions were now in existence:

The Irish TUC, with both Irish-based and British-based unions in affiliation, represented the great majority of trade unionists in the country as a whole. It included 15 Irish-based unions, among them the Workers' Union of Ireland, which now after years in the wilderness was accepted into the Congress, and almost all the British-based unions. The Congress of Irish Unions on the other hand consisted of 16 Irish-based unions, including the ITGWU, and its membership was almost wholly confined to the Twenty-Six counties.[134]

The ITUC, after the admission of the WUI, had some 145,000 members in 1945; the CIU had around 77,500.[135] Despite O'Brien's retirement in 1946 and the death of Larkin a year later, and despite many eloquent appeals for trade-union unity, the split persisted for some time, and the trade-union movement entered the crucial post-war period weakened, divided, and stultified.

The Government, whose legislation and nationalistic crusade against 'foreign unions' had played such a role in splitting the union movement, now sought to project itself as the 'honest broker'. Fianna

---

[132] NLI Johnson Papers MS 17197.   [133] Nevin, 'Industry and Labour', 102.
[134] Ibid. 105.   [135] Lyons, *Ireland since the Famine*, 680.

Fáil, and Lemass in particular, played a double game—taking full advantage of the split in the labour movement at both the political and industrial levels whilst, at the same time, urging the reconstruction of a central, unified trade-union body (on terms acceptable to, if not actually dictated by, the Government). Thus, it may be said that Lemass kept the split between the Irish- and British-based unions on the boil; but, when the Congress formally divided, he expressed the Government's preference for one central union body with which to negotiate.[136]

He also did his level best to strengthen the hand of the CIU against the ITUC. During the debate over trade-union representation on semi-state bodies or consultation by the Government, his Department intervened in a nakedly partisan way. On 13 July 1945 Seán Leydon was told by R. C. Ferguson that Lemass had decided to exclude civil servants, postal workers, and teachers from the figures for trade-union membership, thereby arriving at the figure of 47,000 for the ITUC and 58,000 for the CIU! The conclusion which followed from this exercise in imaginative accounting was clear:

My Minister has instructed that—(*a*) for all purposes, the new organization is to be regarded as having at least equal status with the Irish Trades Union Congress; (*b*) when an informal opinion on Trade Union matters is desired, the query should be addressed to the new Congress of Irish Unions unless otherwise directed; and (*c*) the new Congress is to be invited to make nominations when representative personnel is required for Committees, discussions etc.[137]

By June 1945 the CIU was also co-operating with Lemass in agreeing the terms of an Appeal Board to hear the appeals of persons refused membership of a union affiliated to the CIU.

On 8 November 1945 Lemass wrote to the secretary of the ITUC, pushing for a reunited Congress which would 'supervise and facilitate the process of withdrawal by British unions . . .'. And, indeed, a joint committee was established by the ITUC and the CIU, with his blessing, in September 1946 to act as a medium with a view to 'eventual reunion'.[138]

Lemass, meanwhile, acted upon the spirit of Ferguson's memorandum of 13 July. Although he maintained relations with both the

[136] O'Connell, 'Class, Nation and State', 7.   [137] NAI Labour W63.
[138] NLI O'Brien Papers MS 13974.

CIU and the ITUC, only the former was invited to nominate to the Road Transport Advisory Board and to attend the International Labour Conference.[139] Following the decision of the Supreme Court in 1946 which found the principal provision of the 1941 Trade Union Act—which aimed at the elimination of British-based unions—unconstitutional, Lemass sought to involve the CIU in consultations concerning the revision of the Act. On 8 April 1947 the decision was recorded that

the Sub-Committee [of the CIU] . . . recommend that the Central Council should not agree to further legislation to control Trade Unions unless such legislation is aimed at the restriction or abolition of the operations of Foreign Unions, and that the Central Council should meet the Minister for discussion before making suggestions to bring about the above object.

Lemass met with the CIU on 21 April, and in a written communication he invited the organization to 'frame a new Act, to define, as it were, what in your opinion should be defined as a Trade Union, what rules should govern such a body having regard to the objects to be achieved'.[140]

In the event, the Trade Union Act of 1947 was a fairly innocuous affair; the main provision was that the ministerial power to reduce the deposits paid by unions, on grounds of hardship due to prevailing 'abnormal' conditions, was extended.[141] However, as has been pointed out, the efforts of the Government to repress British-based unions because of the 'impropriety of non-national popular organizations continuing to exist here' were 'initially successful'. And the Supreme Court decision can hardly have brought much comfort to the unions: 'it was not for the purpose of protecting trade unions but because of certain principles of individualism of which the British-based unions themselves would not have approved.'[142]

It was not until 1959 that the union movement was reunited. In the meantime, the political significance of the trials it had endured should not be underestimated. The notion of the trade-union movement as 'transcending national boundaries' and 'deriving strength

---

[139] Farrell, *Seán Lemass*, 76.

[140] The CIU Sub-Committee minutes also record, however, that 'he would not undertake to say that the Government would implement all such proposals, more especially if they were in conflict with the general good'.

[141] NAI Taoiseach S.12910a.

[142] C. McCarthy, 'The Development of Irish Trade Unions', in D. Nevin (ed.), *Trade Unions and Change in Irish Society* (Dublin, 1980), 30.

in its leadership from a common socialist tradition' had been damaged. Fianna Fáil influence within the union movement, and within the ITGWU in particular, had been strengthened. Finally, a substantial section of the trade-union leadership had come to accept the Government's regulation of trade-union affairs and, through meetings and correspondence with Lemass, to conceive almost of a partnership with the Government in pursuit of common objectives in union organization. It was a logical step to conceive of a partnership with the Government in pursuit of its (or, at this stage, Lemass's) strategy for economic development.

It is scarcely surprising, then, that Lemass's 1946 Industrial Relations Act which established the Labour Court should receive a general welcome from a divided union movement, clutching at straws in pursuit of its members' interests and its own place in Irish society. The Council of the CIU, which had been involved in framing the terms of the Bill, warmly welcomed the measure. Its secretary, Cathal O'Shannon, wrote to Lemass on 17 June 1946: 'Sincere personal congratulations . . . your establishment of the Labour Court will certainly be a great landmark in our industrial history and in worker–employer relations.' Lemass replied on 19 June:

I should like to take this opportunity of expressing my personal thanks for all the help given to me in the preparation of this measure by you and the Council of the CIU. The constructive approach of you and your colleagues to every problem made it a pleasure at all times to meet with you to discuss them.[143]

The ITUC merely tempered its welcome for the new law with a call for a National Development Council to plan nation-wide production—a call which may have sounded vaguely socialistic, but was not at all out of line with Lemass's neo-corporatist thinking.[144] Well-meaning sympathizers with the trade-union movement may have portrayed the establishment of the Labour Court as a symbol of the 'victory of trade unionism in its fight for a respected and influential place in the social and economic life of modern Ireland';[145] but, as Pratschke adds, a docile and subaltern trade-union movement, plagued by internal divisions and a bad economic

[143] NAI Labour IR/19.   [144] NAI Taoiseach S.13814a.
[145] James Plunket, quoted in J. L. Pratschke 'Business and Labour in Irish Society, 1945–70', in J. J. Lee (ed.), *Ireland, 1945–1970* (Dublin, 1979).

climate, putting forward largely moderate wage demands, and facing a lack of success in the growing clerical and service sectors of the economy, also faced new and daunting responsibilities.[146]

Of course, the establishment of the Labour Court *did* secure for the union movement a new status and a more secure corporate identity; but it also involved incorporation within the framework of an economic development strategy articulated by a political party which, 'assuming in its entirety the project of the bourgeoisie, proclaims itself as the party of free enterprise and does not hesitate to preach the philosophy of capitalism'.[147]

Thomas Johnson, cerebral as ever in his old age, summed up the essence of the Act which established the Labour Court in a pamphlet entitled *The Industrial Relations Act, 1946.* The Act, he wrote,

has no revolutionary purpose; it will not effect any change in the social order. It has been devised in order to enable the existing capitalist system to work more smoothly . . . But, by removing friction, the machinery of wealth production and distribution may work more efficiently, the gross output may be increased. Out of that increase, provided the trade unions act up to their opportunities and responsibilities, the wage-earning class in particular may derive some benefit. This is a modest hope, perhaps, nevertheless it is worth an effort to attain.[148]

MacEntee lamented to the Dáil in January 1940 that, while the workers were well organized in the ITUC for the purpose of consultation on general policy, 'there was no such corresponding body among employers' and 'this was a serious handicap'. He warned that 'there is a natural tendency for the State to "nazify" industry, and wise businessmen would refrain from encouraging that tendency'.[149] In other words, business men should organize better the representation of their own corporate interests.

In fact, while Government legislation and regulation meant that the union movement emerged from the war years weak, divided, and defensive, business men, who experienced a veritable boom during the war, vastly improved their organizational capabilities by 1945. The Federated Union of Employers (FUE) registered in 1941 under the Trade Union Act and rapidly expanded its organization among employers.[150]

[146] James Plunket, quoted in J. L. Pratschke 'Business and Labour in Irish Society, 1945–70', in J. J. Lee (ed.), *Ireland, 1945–1970* (Dublin, 1979).
[147] Peillon, *Contemporary Irish Society*, 72, 111.
[148] NLI Johnson Papers MS 17226.   [149] Dáil Debates, 17 Jan. 1940.
[150] Nevin, 'Industry and Labour', 107.

The FIM also prospered during the war, and its main concern then, and immediately after, was to ensure that the policy of protection remained unchanged, and that the interests of the industrial bourgeoisie should not be sacrificed to those of the agricultural sector. To this end, it sought ever closer consultations with the Government and with Lemass, the relevant minister, and ever stronger representation within the decision-making structures of the state. The dilemma which faced Lemass was precisely to ensure that the Government retained sufficient autonomy from the corporate bodies of the bourgeoisie to pursue measures—such as price control, greater productive efficiency, and the corporatist involvement of the trade unions—the desirability of which was far from understood by the various business organizations.

It has been written that 'the bourgeoisie has no need of a special organization to back up a project which is to a large extent underwritten by the State'.[151] That statement is altogether too simplistic. It ignores internal contradictions between the interests of the industrial and financial bourgeoisie, for example. It also ignores a clash of interests between the industrial and agricultural sectors. Finally, it ignores the fact that the state in a democracy is 'inhabited' by political parties which, even if they share a commitment to capitalism, must outbid each other with competing strategies to secure the political allegiance of non-bourgeois social groups such as the working class and, indeed, the unemployed and dependent. This requires a successful political party to avoid underwriting completely the economic project of any single social stratum or class.

Certainly, the industrial bourgeoisie during the war period, and especially the immediate post-war period, felt the need for a 'special organization' to guard against any change in direction by Lemass. We saw earlier that Lemass, in 1938, had begun warning of the need to eliminate inefficiencies and was hinting that the policy of protection would have to be reviewed where necessary as a means to achieve this: he had become increasingly disenchanted with the often shoddy quality of goods produced behind the protective barriers. The war had given a new lease of life to protectionism, and business men were determined to keep the chill wind of competition at bay for as long as possible. They were still smarting from their self-perceived humiliation during the 1938 Anglo-Irish Trade negotiations, when, they felt, their lack of corporate organization

---

[151] Peillon, *Contemporary Irish Society*, 55.

had deprived them of their rightful influence in the corridors of power and had seen their interests sacrificed to those of the agricultural sector.

The minutes of the FIM record, from the earliest days of the war, an anxiety to win ministerial recognition, whilst at the same time to avoid becoming an appendage of the Lemass administrative machine. In short, the FIM sought direct political decision-making powers on matters affecting their interests and, in a vague and never openly articulated manner, pursued the sort of neo-corporate society envisaged in the Report of the Commission on Vocational Organization of 1943. Fianna Fáil, however, was united in rejecting any such notion. De Valera was singularly unwilling to devolve power to bodies outside the control of the party and Lemass, who played a leading role in the campaign against the Report—describing it as 'a slovenly document' with 'a querulous, nagging, propagandist tone'[152]—had no intention of handing the control of economic policy over to bodies like the FIM. His corporatist vision entailed a role for the state far greater than that of a mere umpire.

In October 1939 the Minister for Industry and Commerce appointed a civil servant, Mr St John Connolly, as Liaison Officer to the Federation; but, at the same time, kept FIM offers of 'assistance' at arm's length: Seán Leydon, secretary of the Department of Supplies, informed the Federation that 'his Department was in the process of organization and that at the moment he could not envisage the Federation taking part as a regular machine. The Federation, however, could be valuable in grouping manufacturers for conference purposes and in a consultative capacity.'

This was not enough for the FIM, which proposed that

each importing interest for a particular production should appoint an executive committee of three, one of whom should be a Chairman and should actively advise the (governmental) official in charge of the industry concerned, and accompany him on journeys to London for the purpose of consulting with the British and other interests.[153]

Lemass would have none of this.

From about 1942–3 relations became more strained. Lemass was by now speaking about the need for greater efficiency in order to maintain employment in the post-war period—although there was, as yet, no talk of abandoning protection. It was in June 1942, as we

---

[152] Farrell, *Seán Lemass*, 72.   [153] FIM minutes, 6 Oct. 1939.

have seen, that Lemass produced his memorandum on 'Labour Policy' and in November that the Cabinet Committee on Economic Planning was established. It was also in late 1942–early 1943 that the impact of the Beveridge Report was first felt. In short, it was at about this time that Lemass began seriously to turn his attention to the necessity for economic planning in order to meet the economic strains of the post-war period, particularly the strains of mass un-employment. It was also becoming evident to Lemass that the Government would have to take measures to ensure greater effi-ciency, and that such measures might involve the removal of cer-tain protective duties—although it was his strategy to distinguish, at least initially, the question of efficiency from that of protection, thus offsetting a united opposition from the bourgeoisie. All of this, in Lemass's view, required the Government to maintain a consider-able degree of autonomy from business organizations. Seán Leydon summed up Lemass's attitude when he

doubted the capacity of groups of traders—and by implication of most vocational groups—to reach decisions in the public interest. 'I think we could not trust them to do the job' of distributing supplies to retailers. Price fixing 'would be the last thing I would entrust to them'. Government de-partments did consider the public interest, businessmen did not.[154]

Of course, Government ministers were also, sometimes, attuned to electoral necessities; business men somewhat less so.

The FIM grew increasingly concerned at what it regarded as its lack of influence with the Government. In March 1942 the FIM Council expressed grave concern at the Government's failure to utilize the services of its Liaison Officer to open a two-way channel between the Government and the Federation. Whilst appreciating the personal qualities of the civil servant involved, the Council recorded its concern that 'whereas members of the Council collec-tively and individually use the services of the Liaison Officer in giving information to the Government, the reverse procedure rarely, if ever, took place'.[155]

Discontent with Lemass's refusal to act as the agent of the FIM grew with the increasing coherence, from 1945, of his quite radical proposals for the restructuring of Irish industry. As Bew and Patterson

---

[154] J. J. Lee, 'Aspects of Corporatist Thought in Ireland: The Commission on Vocational Organisation, 1939–43', in A. Cosgrave and D. McCartney (eds.), *Studies in Irish History* (Dublin, 1979), 338.   [155] FIM minutes, 27 Mar. 1942.

state, he 'faced opposition from real material forces' and had to be a considerable politician. The banks disliked his criticism of their failure to play a larger role in the Irish domestic economy and native industrialists feared abandonment of protection.[156] In February 1946 FIM president, P. L. McEvoy, warned: 'In theory, private enterprise is accepted as the base of our economy. Both the Taoiseach and the Minister for Industry and Commerce have repeatedly professed that it is so, but the actions of the Government belie their words.'[157]

Hostility was also forthcoming from industrialists on the conduct of the 1947 trade negotiations with the United Kingdom. The FIM feared 'that the attitude of the Government in relation to Trade Agreements appeared to be the procurement of an advantage for agriculture at any cost and generally at the cost of industrial welfare'.[158] These comments were recorded at a time when Fianna Fáil had been succeeded in office by the Inter-Party Government; but they faithfully reflect the constant fear of the industrial bourgeoisie throughout the trade talks. Indeed, Lemass was more skilful than those who succeeded him in office; FIM criticism of the Inter-Party Government's alleged devotion to agriculture at the expense of industry was to be recurrent. Lemass, on the other hand, reassured the Federation that he

was conscious of criticism levelled at him by the Federation in 1938 on the absence of any information even after the negotiations that took place then, and, as far as it was possible for him, he wished the members of the Federation to have information of a more detailed character than would have been possible to convey to them through the public process.[159]

He sought, however, to deflect FIM demands for a direct input into the trade negotiations: 'he could not agree that consultation should be entered into in matters affecting the national welfare, as such were essentially a Government matter.'[160]

Despite often having to compromise and water down his original ideas, Lemass's measures for the restructuring of Irish industry were of considerable political importance and can be seen as having laid the basis for the later relaunch of the Irish economy under Fianna

[156] Bew and Patterson, *Seán Lemass and the Making of Modern Ireland*, 12.
[157] Quoted in L. Skinner, *Politicians by Accident* (Dublin, 1946), 71.
[158] FIM minutes, 11 May 1948.   [159] Ibid., 10 Dec. 1947.
[160] Ibid., 2 Apr. 1947.

Fáil's political leadership. The Industrial Relations Act paved the
way for the incorporation of the trade unions within the economic
strategy and the more 'consensual' resolution of industrial conflict.
The Industrial Prices and Efficiency Act of 1947, which bestowed
upon the Minister widespread powers of intervention, was a significant step away from the disastrous effects of protection and towards a more corporatist approach to industrial organization. Lemass,
in his discussions with the industrialists, had denied that the Government was in the process of abandoning protection altogether.
He had warned that 'most of our pre-war tariffs had been too high
and that quantitative restrictions were of a variable quality' but had
immediately agreed that 'he would willingly accept any case put up
to him by the groups interested'.[161] Despite this 'cat-and-mouse'
game, the Industrial Prices and Efficiency Bill ran into strong opposition. 'It was inevitable that the legislation which seemed to both
increase State and trade union power at the expense of the businessmen should have provoked a major furore.'[162] The Bill was
attacked by the Minister for Finance, by the media, and by the FIM,
which warned against 'communistic' ideals. Fury was directed, especially, against the Developmental Councils, in which trade unions would participate.[163]

Why, then, did Fianna Fáil succeed in deflecting such open criticism from the very business classes which it had helped to bring
into existence? Lemass's strategy had gained the party a considerable
political leeway. Well might Lemass declare in 1944 that he was
confident that Fianna Fáil's aim of developing the Irish economy 'on
a sound financial footing' and 'mainly through private enterprise'
commanded 'the support of the whole business community'.[164] In
fact, to the industrial bourgeoisie there seemed little alternative to
Fianna Fáil at this stage, and defections were few in number. We can
distinguish at least four reasons why this should have been the case.

First, the industrial bourgeoisie was overwhelmingly in whole-
hearted agreement with Fianna Fáil economic strategy to date—it
just wanted to ensure that it continued to enjoy its benefits and to
minimize the costs of increased efficiency which Lemass deemed
politically and economically necessary. Despite rhetoric about
'communistic' ideals, the FIM never shared the Department of

---

[161] Ibid.
[162] Bew and Patterson, *Seán Lemass and the Making of Modern Ireland*, 45–6.
[163] Ibid. 46.   [164] Quoted in O'Connell, 'Class, Nation and State', 6.

Finance critique of Lemass's strategy and cannot have been insensitive to the argument that the continuing political dominance of Fianna Fáil was in its own interests. There was, perhaps, a realization in such quarters that, if increased efficiency was the price that had to be paid for political stability and industrial growth, then the cost of refusing to pay that price might well be too high. Fianna Fáil propaganda in 1948 seized upon this theme, linking the goal of a more dynamic capitalism to a greater competitive capability, and underlining the party's commitment to the private sector.[165]

Second, the manufacturers could hope for nothing better from any of Fianna Fáil's rivals. Fine Gael, with its traditional hostility to industrial development and its continuing emphasis upon the welfare of the large farmers, scarcely appealed much to an industrial bourgeoisie which already felt that its interests were too often sacrificed to the demands of the agricultural sector. The prospect of a government which might include the 'radicals' of Clann na Poblachta or Clann na Talmhan, or a minority government dependent upon their support, filled most business men with deep foreboding. Fianna Fáil alone could best guarantee both their long-term interests and the political stability they desired. It was not so surprising, then, that, in spite of all the business criticism of Fianna Fáil, and Lemass in particular, some sixteen leading business men, including D. Guiney, Chairman of Clery's Ltd. (whose financial support for Fianna Fáil was important), signed a public declaration supporting Fianna Fáil during the 1948 election and warning against an unstable coalition which might include either of the two Clanns.

Third, Lemass's tactical manipulations—separating the issue of protection from that of efficiency and reassuring business men that no general abandonment of protection was on the cards, and pledging that ministerial powers of intervention would be kept in reserve and agreement sought at all stages—drove something of a wedge between the more efficient and the most inefficient sectors of Irish industry and induced confusion in business circles as to what exactly their reaction to the Government's policy should be.

Finally, Lemass's relationship with the trade-union movement allowed him, and Fianna Fáil, to withstand criticism from sections of the bourgeoisie.[166] Despite business opposition to specific proposals

---

[165] See e.g. NLI Gallagher Papers MS 18376.
[166] Bew and Patterson, *Seán Lemass and the Making of Modern Ireland*, 14.

to give unions representation on developmental councils within industry, the incorporation of the unions within a new institutionalized arrangement was a guarantee of greater industrial peace. It meant greater cohesion within a restructured trade-union movement, with fewer small 'irresponsible' unions and less likelihood of unofficial strike action; and it reduced the chances of industrial action spilling over into the political arena, as had happened in 1941 when union opposition to the Wages Standstill Order had contributed to a new wave of militancy which had benefited the Labour Party electorally, especially in Dublin, in 1942–3. The dispersion of potential organized working-class opposition to the Government, combined with the enlistment of a substantial section of the union movement behind the Government, enabled Fianna Fáil to withstand electoral pressure from the working class, particularly in the difficult post-war period. This, in turn, proved a valuable asset to the party in asserting a certain relative autonomy from business pressure.

After 1938 Fianna Fáil began to experience electoral losses in the west of the country, and its vote in Dublin exceeded the national average for the first time in 1943. In Dublin, the 1940s saw a decline of general labourers and the growth of white-collar and skilled workers. Employment opportunities were increasingly in business, in administration, and in personal services—all of which had increased since Fianna Fáil came to office. Thus, in Dublin in 1946, 21.1 per cent were employed in commerce and finance; 12.0 per cent in administration and defence; 8.9 per cent in the professions; 13.7 per cent in personal services; and 32.3 per cent in non-agricultural production. Fianna Fáil would have to cope with increasing discontent from professional and white-collar workers employed in the growing state and semi-state sector, in particular. However, its support amongst the urban petty bourgeoisie was not necessarily as volatile as that of its small-farmer base during this period.

Given the lack of real economic initiatives during the 1940s and the considerable political volatility of the period, it is remarkable how Fianna Fáil managed to maintain its political centrality, even if its position during the late 1940s and early 1950s cannot be described as hegemonic. I argued earlier that this owed as much to the confusion and uncertainties of the party's rivals as to any intrinsic merit of the party itself. However, the party possessed a number of underlying strengths, and to grasp these we must bear in mind Fianna Fáil's handling of the changing balance of class forces.

The party's agricultural policy now clearly favoured the interests of the large, export-orientated farmers, whilst, at the same time, the interests of the agricultural sector were not allowed to eclipse the leading role of the industrial bourgeoisie. The financial oligarchy could rest assured that, rhetoric and threats apart, the party would do nothing to alter the pattern of Irish capital investment overseas. The party maintained sufficient distance from the industrial bourgeoisie to begin the delicate, but politically essential, task of correcting the obvious inadequacies of the business class which it had helped to create. The trade-union movement was divided and incorporated, workers being assured by Lemass that, in return for their support and their co-operation, the Government would guarantee employment creation. The emergent white-collar strata, especially in Dublin, frequently had a stake in the protection and expansion of the state sector (although, as we will see, the challenge of Clann na Poblachta would make its presence felt here).

The party's position was far from secure, as will become evident when we turn our attention to political and electoral developments during the war years and immediately after. But Fianna Fáil enjoyed considerable political leeway, as well as embodying potential contradictions—both more readily understood when viewed within the context of its changing relations with the various social forces. As Peillon puts it:

the problem is not so much to discover which particular social classes determine Fianna Fáil policies, since such an approach assumes that political parties simply mirror the interests of one class or coalition of classes. Parties actively mobilise their social support and are by no means passive instruments. They create a particular support by deciding on certain policies, and they manipulate it for their own benefit.[167]

This was certainly true of Fianna Fáil, and in particular of the career of Seán Lemass, who became its deputy leader and Tánaiste (deputy Prime Minister) in June 1945.

POLITICAL DEVELOPMENTS

During the 1938 election campaign, Fianna Fáil raised the flag of Irish nationalism; with the Anglo-Irish agreements on trade and

[167] Peillon, *Contemporary Irish Society*, 113.

defence under its arm, the party portrayed itself as a 'national Government',[168] defending the interests of the country as a whole against the threat of external domination. The advent of war in 1939 greatly strengthened the potential for this type of propaganda and presented the Government with new and powerful opportunities to exploit patriotic loyalties and to place its rivals on the defensive. However, the war years also saw an increase in political volatility due to rising socio-economic expectations and mounting dissatisfaction with the Government's economic performance. Several new challenges to Fianna Fáil's political dominance emerged, and it is with the fate of those challenges that this section will be largely concerned.

From the outset, the Government decided that Ireland would remain neutral in the conflict now engulfing Europe. De Valera's reasons for neutrality were threefold: his conviction that, after the collapse of the League of Nations, small states should not allow themselves to be used as the tools of any great power; his belief, obviously related, that Irish neutrality would be the acid test of national sovereignty; and the still unresolved question of partition. The policy was an immensely popular one which commanded the support of the entire Dáil (with the exception of James Dillon, who was expelled from Fine Gael for opposing neutrality), and robbed Fine Gael, in particular, of its most distinctive policy—its somewhat confused commitment to 'good neighbourliness' with the United Kingdom.[169]

The question of just how genuine Irish neutrality was need not detain us long. It is certainly the case that the sympathies of both Government and people (apart from a small minority) lay with the allies; over 50,000 Éire citizens joined the British army during the war, for example. Fanning has produced an impressive list of secret military and intelligence assistance which the Irish authorities afforded to the allies—so much so that the Pentagon innocently suggested awarding the American Legion of Merit to three of Ireland's highest ranking army officers for their co-operation during 1943–5, until informed that the award might be rather embarrassing to the Irish Government in view of its declared neutrality.[170] What is undeniable, however, is that the policy of neutrality was genuinely popular, and de Valera would have been politically unable to abandon it even had he wanted to.[171]

[168] *Irish Press*, 11 June 1938.   [169] O'Leary, *Irish Elections, 1918–1977*, 35.
[170] Fanning, *Independent Ireland*, 123–4.
[171] Bowman, *De Valera and the Ulster Question*, 254.

The overwhelming popular enthusiasm for neutrality and the sense of the urgent need to guarantee the security of the state enabled the Government to dispose, for another decade and a half, of the IRA threat. The IRA took advantage of the outbreak of war to commence a bombing campaign in England and to carry out a spectacular arms raid in Dublin. The Government reacted furiously, claiming with credibility that IRA sabotage in England would place in jeopardy the neutrality and sovereignty of Éire. The IRA (which had been legalized with the passage of the 1937 Constitution) was again banned under the new legislation which greeted the Emergency, and Special Criminal Courts sentenced IRA men to death. Nor did the Government's resolve weaken under the impact of IRA hunger strikes, the public protests of Patrick Pearse's mother (a Fianna Fáil senator) notwithstanding; de Valera flatly declared that 'the lesser evil is to see men die rather than that the safety of the whole community should be endangered'.[172] That is precisely what happened, and the new Minister of Justice, Gerry Boland, did not hesitate to use internment without trial against the IRA.

The IRA, in any case, was deeply divided and without any coherent policy. The complete triumph of the militarism of its right-wing chief, Seán Russell, in 1938–9 had led to the defection of 'antifascist' elements, including Tomás MacCurtain and Tom Barry (who accused the Germans of being behind Russell's bombing campaign in England) and the movement's clumsy involvement with Nazi intelligence throughout the war was greatly to discredit it.[173] Despite the emotional impact of deaths from hunger strikes, IRA supporters continued to do badly in by-elections even in the home constituency of one of the hunger strikers. Not surprisingly, the IRA showed no interest in social protest and 'did not associate with the unions in fights against the wage orders or the 1941 Trade Union Act' and could subsequently be characterized as 'a movement more to the "Right" of Fianna Fáil than of the "Left" '.[174]

Fianna Fáil faced little danger of being outflanked by extreme republicans on the 'national issue', and had scarcely even to try to place its Fine Gael opponents in an embarrassing position. Fine Gael's reluctance to support Government plans to resist a possible British invasion of the country, its advocacy of a defence pact with

---

[172] Quoted in Fanning, 'The "Rule of Order" ', 167.

[173] Cronin, *The McGarrity Papers*, 159–81.

[174] M. McInerney, writing in *Irish Times*, 15 Oct. 1968.

the United Kingdom, and, on occasion, its quixotic plan for a joint Irish/French/British force under a French general to defend the whole island of Ireland, simply left its commitment to defend national independence against all potential aggressors in doubt. Both Fine Gael and Labour could call in vain for a national coalition, but in practice were helpless to do anything other than participate in the powerless and cosmetic consultative defence conference summoned by de Valera. Simultaneously, the old debate between pro- and anti-Treaty factions was being rendered obsolete. The question now concerned which party was best placed to defend against the danger of the state becoming involved in the war, or, which seemed to amount to the same thing, against the danger of Northern Ireland becoming so integrated in the British war effort as practically to extend the war front to the very boundaries of the state. Here, Fianna Fáil clearly had the advantage. De Valera's success in deterring the UK Government from introducing conscription in Northern Ireland and his image of 'a lonely stand in defence of neutrality against the combined might of the United Kingdom and the United States'[175] greatly helped his standing as a national leader. So, too, did the customary ineptitude which Great Britain displayed in its confrontation with Irish public opinion. The United Kingdom never gave any assurance of its acceptance of Irish neutrality and Churchill even went so far as to declare that 'I do not personally regard Irish neutrality as a legal act.'[176] Faced with a British threat to seize Irish ports in November–December 1940, de Valera, in a broadcast to the United States, replied with that emotive language which brought a lump to the throats of Irish nationalists and did much to mobilize Irish-American opinion against an allied attack on Éire. Declaring that any attack on the ports would be resisted by force, he added: 'and we can only pray that God will give might to our arms as he gave to David's, and that we shall successfully defend our liberty with the same determination and endurance with which it was regained'.[177]

The swelling of the ranks of the defence forces to some 250,000 symbolized a sense of national unity, unparalleled since 1918; at the head of the nation, so it must have seemed to many even amongst its opponents, stood Fianna Fáil. The party enjoyed the political

[175] Fanning, *Independent Ireland*, 125.
[176] Quoted in Share, *The Emergency*, 5.   [177] NAI Taoiseach S.11394.

advantages which real external threat to the existence of an independent state bestows upon any government in power. Yet its handling of the economy, in particular, was to lead to the emergence of challenges which Fianna Fáil would have to fight hard to offset.

The first, and perhaps least worrying, electoral threat to Fianna Fáil dates back to the launch of Clann na Talmhan in 1938. Clann na Talmhan originated in the coming-together of local small-farmer groups in Galway, Mayo, and north Roscommon. Inspired by a feeling that small farmers should have got more from the Economic War than had been the case and that they had been betrayed by 'the politicians', the movement's anger focused above all on the officials of the Land Commission—who seemed to embody the negligence and foot-dragging of the Government.[178] Amongst the grievances felt by small farmers was the persistence of land-flooding due to inadequate drainage, and the demand for a national drainage system was quickly formulated. At first, the Clann seemed more of an agricultural pressure group—with perhaps something of a romantic throwback to the old days of the Land League—than a new political party; indeed, Fianna Fáil leader Gerry Boland announced that the party did not object to its members becoming involved so long as the Clann remained outside political competition and did not contest elections.[179] However, in August 1939 the decision was taken to enter the electoral arena.

The Clann's first electoral test came when its leader, Michael Donnellan, a former Fianna Fáil councillor, contested a by-election in the constituency of Galway West. The contest saw the defection of Fianna Fáil supporters to the Clann cause; Fine Gael, hoping to damage Fianna Fáil by proxy, tended to take 'a more lenient attitude' towards the Clann and even stood aside, on occasion, to let the Clann have a straight fight with Fianna Fáil. But, as Fine Gael supporters defected to Fianna Fáil in the ensuing polarization, and as the former party saw its very existence increasingly in question in the rural areas, its vote in the west virtually collapsed.[180] Helped by Fine Gael timidity, Clann na Talmhan did well in the 1942 local-government elections, and in the general election of 1943 it secured 8.6 per cent of the vote nationally (19.8 per cent in the regions it contested, and 33.3 per cent in its three central regions—Galway,

---

[178] L. Fallon, 'Clann na Talmhan—Popular Movement or Political Party?', MA thesis (Dublin, 1983).

[179] Ibid. 24.   [180] Garvin, *The Evolution of Irish Nationalist Politics*, 173.

Roscommon, and Mayo). Fianna Fáil, in that election, secured 41.9 per cent—10 per cent down on the 1938 result—and was three seats short of a parliamentary majority; Fine Gael was sliced to just 23.1 per cent; while Labour increased its vote to 15.7 per cent—its best performance ever.

Yet the Clann suffered from a number of fatal weaknesses. First, it was clearly a voice of rural petty-bourgeois protest. It represented the sense of alienation felt by a stratum which saw itself 'ignored and misunderstood by a remote government bureaucracy and exploited by big business and rapacious unions'.[181] This sense of frustration and insecurity was expressed in the Clann's hostility to politicians in general—seen, invariably, as corrupt, self-seeking, and concerned only with the interests of the new business classes and the civil-service bureaucracy (Fianna Fáil), or the large farmers and town bourgeoisie (Fine Gael). The Clann's political programme embodied these concerns, with derating of small farms, fixity of tenure for the tenant farmer, tillage subsidies, and pensions at 65 instead of 70 (which would certainly benefit the ageing small-farmer sector), intermingled with attacks on corruption in high circles and proposals for the abolition of ministerial pensions. In other words, not only was the Clann's social base largely composed of an agricultural stratum which was 'declining and ageing',[182] but its programme offered no challenge to the spiral of subsidies and dependency into which this stratum was plunging.

Second, the Clann, despite its attempts to recapture the radical flavour of the early Land League, was essentially a conservative party. (Some might argue likewise of the Land League, but that is another story.) Its electoral transfers may have helped elect two Labour deputies in 1943, and it may have seemed superficially close to Labour; but behind the rhetoric of 'Farmers and Workers Unite' was the reality that the party's fundamental purpose was the defence of the land-ownership rights of the smaller agricultural producers. Its real message was summed up in a statement of 'Policy and Aims', published in 1944, which declared: 'The farmer has a God-given right to complete ownership in the land he inherited from his forefathers.'[183] This, plus the aforementioned hostility to

---

[181] M. Manning, 'The Farmers', in J. A. Murphy and J. O'Carroll (eds.), *De Valera and his Times* (Cork, 1983).
[182] Garvin, *The Evolution of Irish Nationalist Politics*, 173.
[183] Quoted in Fallon, 'Clann na Talmhan', 33.

trade unions, must cast doubt on the likelihood of any Clann na Talmhan–Labour–Clann na Poblachta centre–left fusion ever having been a possibility. In the event, Clann na Talmhan would prove to have more in common with Fine Gael than with Labour, and it was with Fine Gael that many of its supporters and leaders eventually aligned themselves.

Third, the Clann's limitations as a potential challenger to the mould of Irish politics were heightened by internal contradictions which became most acute after the decision, in 1943, to merge with the Farmers' Federation of Leinster. This decision was apparently taken in an attempt to widen the Clann's social base and give it the appearance of a more or less national party, in terms of geographical spread. However, the interests of the large and profitable capitalist farmers of the east were totally at odds with those of the small western farmers; the former were suspicious of any radical rhetoric, and more interested in the revival of the old Farmers' Party of the 1920s as an answer to the increasing ineffectiveness of Fine Gael. The decision to unite the two groups 'proved to be a strain, and although the party remained primarily one of small farmers of the west this unification was a retrograde step, taking away from its homogeneous nature and forcing it to compromise on essential principles'.[184] The party's decision to abstain on the nomination of de Valera for Taoiseach after the 1943 election aroused the opposition of the large-farmer elements who suspected that Donnellan had capitulated to his old party leader. (This was despite the fact that Donnellan had been the target of a quite vicious campaign of personal abuse led by MacEntee, who had referred to Donnellan as 'the boss of the Galway totalitarians' and 'the Galway dictator . . . Herr von Donnellan'.[185]) The concentration on small-farmer grievances further alienated large farmers and, although the party held its vote in the snap election of 1944, Fianna Fáil's success, at the expense of Labour, ended whatever influence it might have had in the Dáil.

When Donnellan, whose radicalism offended the more prosperous elements, was succeeded by Joseph Blowick as party leader, enthusiasm began to wane. The organization went into decline, its TDs becoming more or less independents (as the old Farmers' Party

---

[184] Quoted in Fallon, 'Clann na Talmhan', 30.
[185] UCDA MacEntee Papers P67/364.

had frequently been). Large-farmer defections in 1945 were followed in 1946 by renewed defections due to conflict between farmers and the landless. By the time the 1948 election gave Clann na Talmhan a chance to taste power, it had really ceased to have any coherent purpose or corporate identity. Inevitably, the agricultural reforms which its members in government claimed as their achievement tended rather to benefit the larger and more coherent farmers' party—Fine Gael—which before long absorbed the Clann completely.

A far greater threat to Fianna Fáil was posed by the revival of labour militancy in response to the Wages Standstill Order and the Trade Union Act of 1941. The imposition of the two measures sharpened urban working-class discontent and trade-union militancy; despite the attitude of the ITGWU, the leadership of the Labour Party rallied in opposition to the Trade Union Act thereby winning strong support from unions opposed to the measure, and the morale of the party was raised by focusing attention upon the struggle. However, it is also worth noting that this new mood of militancy was not matched by any fundamental radicalization of the party programme. Labour, in 1941, was calling for nationalization of credit and transport but had little to say about the management of industry; and, in terms of its ideological appeal, was still challenging Fianna Fáil on grounds of that party's choosing.[186] Yet it seems evident that the new militant mood of Labourism, which seemed to save the party from the complete loss of any distinct identity, must have been responsible for the impressive results obtained, especially in Dublin, in 1942 and 1943.

In the local-government elections of August 1942, Labour emerged for the first time as the biggest party in Dublin and was able to capture the position of Lord Mayor. A year later, despite attempts by Fianna Fáil to utilize 'red-scare' tactics,[187] Labour polled 200,000 votes—15.7 per cent—and won seventeen Dáil seats. It was the best Labour performance ever, and the new parliamentary party

---

[186] O'Connor Lysaght, *The Republic of Ireland*, 122.

[187] MacEntee led a campaign of unprecedented ferocity against Labour, accusing that party of being run by 'communists'. Lemass wrote to him on 10 June 1943, urging him to modify his attacks on Labour; Lemass reported that a number of candidates had telephoned to complain that the red scare was backfiring and that Labour was gaining by the attacks. Jim Ryan and Oscar Traynor, he claimed, shared his view. MacEntee refused to compromise, insisting that Labour was more anti-Fianna Fáil than anti-Fine Gael. See UCDA MacEntee Papers P67/362, P67/363.

included both James Larkin and his son. The result, together with the success of Clann na Talmhan, meant that Fianna Fáil now faced electoral pressure on two fronts—in the rural west and in working-class Dublin. This, moreover, despite the fact that the lack of news-print and censorship, plus the rationing of petrol (which hampered public meetings), must have especially hit the opposition parties; and despite Fianna Fáil invoking to the full the need for national unity in wartime conditions, and contrasting 'strong government' with the danger of 'factional coalition'.[188]

Fianna Fáil was well aware of the potential threat which Labour posed. MacEntee had led the attack on 'that group of politicians which calls itself the Labour Party' during the 1943 election cam-paign, accusing Labour of taking its orders from Moscow, and of being a threat to the independence and security of the country. At the same time he had not hesitated to quote James Larkin's earlier attacks on Labour as a party with 'no policy, no programme and no faith in the working-class'. The 'red-scare' tactics had also been extended to embrace Clann na Talmhan, and to associate that party with Labour's alleged communism. MacEntee was quoted as saying:

Mr Norton was preparing the way for the Red Shirts, but his Moscow friends had imitators, if not allies, elsewhere in this country. Down in Galway a movement had been started to establish in this country a one-party State.

We do not know the terms of the pact which exists between the captives of Dublin communism and the boss of the Galway totalitarians. But it is certain that this alliance is an unholy alliance and bodes no good for honest, Christian men.

Recent recruits to the Labour Party were singled out for special treatment. They were members of a 'middle class intelligentsia who thought that the workers of this country might be talked—or should he say tricked—into selling their birthright for a mess of pottage'.[189]

In fact, MacEntee was making full use of intelligence reports—many of which were no doubt wildly exaggerated, if not wholly fabricated—which had been submitted by spies inside the labour movement and passed on to MacEntee by the Department of Jus-tice for use against the Labour Party.[190] Amongst these reports was a 'Record of Communist Activities from January 1942 to December

---

[188] *Irish Press*, 15 June 1943.   [189] UCDA MacEntee Papers P67/364.
[190] See ibid. P67/522 and P67/528, which contain copies of such reports.

1943' which named John de Courcey Ireland and John Nolan as leading communists plotting through the Connolly Clubs to take over the Labour Party.[191] The Government's spies apparently kept a watch on the comings and goings at New Books—a left-wing bookshop—on Pearse Street. The desperate deeds perpetrated by these 'subversives' included a meeting held on 7 November 1943, under the auspices of the 'Central Communist Committee for Ireland' (sic) at which 'books on Russia were on sale at two tables in the room'; even more horrifying, 'tickets were on sale at the door for a concert organized by the Cabra Branch of the Labour Party'! One can only sympathize with the poor informant who was so reduced to justifying his existence and keeping his masters happy.

These attacks were to herald a co-ordinated campaign by Fianna Fáil to split both the Labour Party and the trade-union movement, and to brand its potential rivals as communists. In this, Fianna Fáil was to receive enthusiastic support from right-wing elements within the labour movement, and be granted ample room for manœuvre by a Labour leadership which allowed itself to be panicked into joining, and thereby justifying, the anti-communist hysteria.

It was at just this juncture that the split within the trade-union movement burst into the open, to be followed by a split within the Labour Party itself. On 7 January 1944 five TDs—Everett, O'Leary, Spring, Pattison, and Looney—left Labour to form the NLP. They gave as their reason that the Labour Party was now under 'communist influence', and the old antagonism against James Larkin and the brand of trade-union militancy associated with his name soon came into the open when the ITGWU charged Labour's Dublin executive with being 'the hub of Communist organization inside the Party'.[192] This, presumably, was a reference to the role played by the Dublin Labour Party in the campaign against the Government's Trade Union Act.

Labour hit back, alleging that the NLP was the artificial creation of both Fianna Fáil and the ITGWU, the sole purpose of which was to help Fianna Fáil damage the Labour Party.[193] Certainly, Fianna Fáil did not hesitate to play one party against the other, indicating its preference for the 'patriotic' NLP—just as Lemass had indicated

---

[191] These attacks certainly had an effect; in 1944 the Labour Party expelled John de Courcey Ireland and others from membership in an effort to protect itself from such allegations. See ibid. P67/548.   [192] NLI Johnson Papers MS 17197.
[193] Ibid.

his trust in the Congress of Irish Unions. The difference, of course, was that, while Lemass was playing a double game, the conclusion of which would be the reunification of the trade-union movement on terms and in circumstances more favourable to the Government, Fianna Fáil never had any desire to see the reunification of the Labour Party.

From its foundation, the National Labour Party sought to portray itself as a nationalist Labour Party, dedicated to the Catholic religion and stripped of any contamination with socialism. It did not hesitate to seek 'character references' from figures hitherto associated with Fianna Fáil. Thus, the Cork NLP wrote to seek support from Professor Alfred O'Rahilly, President of University College Cork, who had supported Fianna Fáil in 1932, assuring him that the NLP was 'in the best interests of our people, clear and definite on fundamentals, intertwined with Faith and Nationality'.[194]

The same Professor O'Rahilly was praised in a letter from the Cork secretary of the NLP shortly afterwards. Writing to William O'Brien, he stated that O'Rahilly 'has at all times been a very great friend of ours here . . . He is a good Nationalist in the widest sense, and a good lay Catholic . . .' And the NLP secretary continued 'there is a golden opportunity for a party veering closer to National Issues with men who have FAVOURABLE NATIONAL RECORDS' (emphasis in original). With sentiments like these, it is difficult, perhaps, not to think of the NLP as Fianna Fáil's Labour Party. Certainly Lemass seemed to think so, for he confessed in 1948 that the formation of the Inter-Party Government came as a complete shock to him; he had expected the NLP to facilitate the formation of a minority Fianna Fáil Government.

The NLP also sought, and received, support from the Catholic clergy in its bid to stigmatize the Labour Party and trade unions belonging to the ITUC as 'communist'. An unsigned letter to William O'Brien from a Cork NLP official (dated 16 February 1944) boasted that 'Dean Sexton preached twice last Sunday in strong terms about the Labour Party and praising the action of those who broke. Several other Parish Priests . . . in outlying parts also beginning to speak.'[195]

Fianna Fáil, short of an overall majority after the election of June 1943, moved to take full advantage of labour-movement divisions.

[194] NLI O'Brien Papers MS 13960.   [195] Ibid.

An acrimonious debate within the Dáil on a transport bill ended in defeat for the Government on 9 May 1944, with allegations of Fianna Fáil corruption in stock-exchange dealings related to the transport bill. The Government resigned the next day and, to the dismay and protest of opposition parties, another election was held.

De Valera was able to exploit to the full the electoral advantage of the so-called 'American note' affair. Prompted by the increasingly anti-de Valera vehemence of the US Minister in Dublin, David Gray, the US Government had delivered what amounted to an ultimatum in February, calling for the closure of the Axis missions in Dublin. Needless to say, this apparent threat to Irish neutrality and sovereignty rallied public opinion behind the Government. If Gray expected de Valera to capitulate under such pressure, then he seriously misunderstood the psychology of the man—not to mention his political acumen. In a dramatic response, bridges to Northern Ireland were mined, the army was mobilized, and de Valera went before the electorate in May as 'the leader of a united people'. In the subsequent election the Government made much of the themes of unity and strength, arguing that 'these are not the times for a weak government or a rickety government'.[196]

Fianna Fáil exploited the division and demoralization of its rivals. MacEntee argued that unlike the 'Internationale' Labour Party, the National Labour Party was in 'the Pearse–Connolly tradition'.[197] In the subsequent election, Labour division and internecine warfare had its effect. Fianna Fáil jumped to 48.9 per cent and regained an absolute parliamentary majority; Fine Gael fell again to 20.5 per cent; Clann na Talmhan, as yet, managed to hold steady at 10.8 per cent. The real losers were Labour, which won just 8.8 per cent (eight seats), and the NLP which took 2.7 per cent (four seats). Labour's revival was, it seemed, over.

It might have been expected that Labour, comparing the disastrous results obtained in division with those achieved during the 1942–3 period of struggle, would have sought to repair internal unity and turn outwards again, towards opposition to Government economic policy and away from internal polemics. The exact opposite happened. The NLP, tied to the ITGWU, fired by personal animosities, and encouraged by the support it received from the clergy, became more strident in its anti-communist rhetoric.

[196] *Irish Press*, 26 May 1944.   [197] Ibid., 23 May 1944.

Perhaps the leaders of the NLP cherished the hope that they might one day share power with Fianna Fáil, with whom they seemed to share an ideological affinity and, through the ITGWU and the CIU, a working relationship in trade-union and industrial matters. It is more likely that questions of long-term political strategy scarcely entered their minds; their *raison d'être* had now become the destruction of the Labour Party. That party, for its part, reacted to the intensification of the anti-communist campaign and the disastrous defeat of 1944 by turning to the right, expelling former communists who had joined with Larkin in 1941, and utilizing anti-communist rhetoric against the ITGWU! Thus Labour assured the public that 'nobody will be allowed to masquerade as a member of the Labour Party with the object of promoting Communist objectives'; and raged indignantly that the ITGWU, prior to 1944, 'was usually considered to be the haven of Communists, as it still is'.[198]

The turn to the right was further evidenced by a retreat from resistance to the Government's trade-union policy or, indeed, economic policy in general; ironically, one of the most politically damaging industrial challenges which Fianna Fáil faced in the postwar period—the teachers' strike of 1946—was mounted by a union which had disaffiliated from Labour in sympathy with the NLP in 1945!

During the 1948 election campaign, Labour and the NLP turned their wrath upon each other. The NLP returned to the 'communist' theme, despite the fact that James Larkin was now dead and safely buried, and that the most 'communist' threat on offer from the Labour Party was that posed by the legendary *bon vivant*, Mr William Norton. John O'Leary, TD, spoke of the Labour Party as being 'now known generally as the "Red Labour Party" and under the domination and control of the Communists'.[199] While his fellow NLP deputy, Pattison, told the people of Kilkenny that 'they [the NLP] made many attempts to rid the Labour Party of its Communist members before they left but they failed in their object. What they [the Labour Party] demanded was their surrender to the Communists in their ranks.' The Labour Party retaliated, as it had in 1944, with allegations of a Fianna Fáil plot and attacks on the personal integrity of the NLP leaders. The Chairman of the NLP, Thomas Foran, had been a Fianna Fáil nominee to the Senate, Labour propaganda

[198] Labour propaganda in NLI Johnson Papers MS 17197.
[199] *Enniscorthy Guardian*, 17 Jan. 1948.

pointed out, and William O'Brien had himself accepted appointment by Fianna Fáil to membership of the Central Bank (the uncharitable might have interjected that Thomas Johnson had been a Fianna Fáil appointee to the Housing Board in 1932). This was surely evidence that Fianna Fáil was using the NLP to split the Labour vote, it was claimed. Moreover, such was the personal integrity of the NLP men that even Fianna Fáil was 'not anxious that National Labour Party candidates will get into a key position. Nobody trusts them. Lemass knows they would sell out on him in the morning if it suited the interests of those in charge of the ITGWU that they should do so.'[200]

The Labour leadership allowed itself to be forced once more on to the defensive. William Norton told the *Irish Independent* on 23 January 1948 that 'The Labour Party will use all its strength to ensure that Communism will not stain the political and religious life of the Irish people.' Communism was, moreover, 'a pernicious foreign creed'.[201] The truth is, of course, that there can be few European countries in which communism was less of a 'threat' in the post-war period than Ireland. Labour was legitimizing the ludicrous notion that Ireland was a nation under mortal siege by Moscow's agents— and thereby undermining its own ability to offer a real critique of Fianna Fáil.

Given the prevalence of such fratricide, and an almost complete policy vacuum on the part of both Labour and the NLP, the outcome of the 1948 election was somewhat predictable—even if the subsequent congelation of political forces was considerably less so. Labour and the NLP polled 8.7 per cent and 2.5 per cent respectively, although, benefiting from a strong pattern of anti-Fianna Fáil transfers—and the appalling electoral tactics of Clann na Poblachta —they did rather better in terms of seats, with fourteen and five respectively.

Before we move on to an examination of the post-war rise of Clann na Poblachta, a few words on the state of health of Fine Gael during the war years are called for; Fine Gael, however, cannot by any stretch of the imagination be labelled a challenge to Fianna Fáil during this period; the era was one of unrelieved stagnation and decay for a party which had once considered itself the natural party of government.[202]

[200] NLI Johnson Papers MS 17197.   [201] UCDA MacEntee Papers P67/376.
[202] For a discussion of Fine Gael's fortunes during the period, see G. M. McCormick, 'The Electoral Appeal of Fine Gael, 1938–1943', MA thesis (Dublin, 1990).

By 1943 Fine Gael 'seemed to be drifting into oblivion'.[203] General Richard Mulcahy, who succeeded Cosgrave as leader after the 1943 election, had actually lost his Dáil seat. Under Mulcahy—a civil-war strong man whom republicans held responsible for the execution of republican prisoners in 1922–3—the party continued to decline. By 1944 its share of the popular vote had sunk to 20.5 per cent, and in by-elections in 1944–5 Fine Gael either failed to nominate a candidate or was beaten into third place by Clann na Talmhan.[204] The party's imminent demise was now forecast. During the presidential elections of 1945, Fine Gael benefited from the polarization of the contest, and a popular candidate in the person of Seán MacEoin, to poll an encouraging 30.9 per cent; but it soon became clear that the vote was simply an exception to the general tendency; the decline continued.

Fine Gael was now lacking in any real appeal to any social class; its message to the urban working class was as unappetizing as ever; its decision to encourage Clann na Talmhan in the hope of damaging Fianna Fáil simply permitted Fianna Fáil to press ahead with those agricultural changes which accommodated the party more clearly to the interests of the larger capitalist farmers (although the collapse of Clann na Talmhan would eventually redound to Fine Gael's favour); and it even seems that Fine Gael's opposition to the 1941 Trade Union Act—ostensibly because it anticipated the Report of the Commission on Vocational Organization, but really because it was drafted by Fianna Fáil—may have alienated some business supporters. There seemed to be little rationale left for a party which, by the early 1940s, had become 'a Dublin and Cork middle-class minor party with a few rural allies'[205]—apart, perhaps, from nostalgia, personal and familial loyalty, and 'snob value'.

The total policy vacuum is well expressed in some of the statements of the time. Thus, the most inspiring which Mulcahy could manage in his address to the 1946 Fine Gael *Ard-Fheis* was the claim that:

We are fundamentally different from Fianna Fáil . . . We have a completely different conception of how Irish life should be developed and strengthened. We believe that the source of the nation's strength lies in the personal liberties of the citizens . . . Fianna Fáil always had the dictatorial mind and trend.

[203] Lee, *Ireland, 1912–1985*, 241.
[204] O'Leary, *Irish Elections, 1918–1977*, 37.
[205] Garvin, *The Evolution of Irish Nationalist Politics*, 169.

He continued, berating the 'poverty-producing, liberty-destroying, bureaucratically-controlled state'.[206] Thus, Fine Gael's answer to rising post-war economic and social expectations was, in essence, Cumann na nGaedheal economic policy of the 1920s. The same theme was echoed in July 1947, in a pamphlet entitled *Political Searchlight on Some Aspects of Fianna Fáil Humbug and on Some Points of Fine Gael Policy*:

The tendency of the present Government is towards extending the power of the state over agriculture and industry and shopkeepers and individuals, so that personal liberty is much less than it was. A further result of this is that in a great many places Government patronage and influence are important and the individual has not a fair chance of getting on by his own efforts. This is one of the causes of emigration.[207]

If the message was aimed at those most likely to be in line for the emigrants' boat, it offered little in the way of hope for the future or an alternative vision of how society might be organized. If it was aimed at the business classes whose support Fine Gael had ceded to Fianna Fáil, then it is most likely to have been seen as inspired by fine sentiments, but vacuous and, by now, irrelevant.

During the 1948 election campaign, Fine Gael propaganda assumed an almost surrealist aspect, despite its impressive doctrinal faith. In the face of widespread dissatisfaction with economic stagnation, mounting social discontent, and pressure for change, Fine Gael assured the electorate that it would be even tougher and more conservative than Fianna Fáil. Party candidate Colonel Austin Brennan complained, in characteristic vein, that 'the mania for state control has spread to all walks of life—agriculture, transport, business, and education—killing initiative and hindering progressive development in any sphere'.[208] The party spelt out its recipe for full employment—tax cuts—adding that 'some of the expensive factories were a burden instead of a benefit because they had to be subsidised from the taxation paid by the farmers'.[209] Fine Gael coupled this with a pledge of 'fresh acceptance' of membership of the British Commonwealth and, on the subject of social welfare, a call for the abolition of the free-footwear scheme (introduced by Fianna Fáil for the very needy) on the touching grounds that it was 'degrading' to the poor. In an effort to keep pace with Clann na Poblachta, the party leadership added a commitment to abolish

---

[206] UCDA Mulcahy Papers P7/D/144.   [207] Ibid.
[208] *Clare Champion*, 10 Jan. 1948.   [209] *Anglo-Celt*, 24 Jan. 1948.

means tests for widows and the blind, and some rather vague proposals for food subsidies and child-benefit increases; the amounts
were not specified. These latter details were the only 'progressive'
policies the party offered.

In the 1948 election Fine Gael sank to a historic low: just 19.8
per cent of the poll. Yet, as we will see, on the very brink of what
seemed like collapse, it was saved—by a miracle. Or rather, it was
saved by Clann na Poblachta. And it is to Clann na Poblachta, the
most serious challenge to Fianna Fáil to emerge during the 1940s,
that we must now turn.

The first rumblings of what was to emerge as Clann na Poblachta
were sounded during the presidential elections of 1945 when, against
the candidates of the two largest parties, Labour, Clann na Talmhan,
and others united in support of the independent campaign of Patrick
MacCartan. Aided by a variety of factors—social and economic
discontent, industrial unrest, and nationalist unease with Fianna
Fáil's as yet unfulfilled promise to 'do something about partition'—
the independent candidate scored an impressive 19.5 per cent of
the vote. As Garvin has written, 'in the east, the correlations suggest
that the third-party vote was a combination of mainly urban liber-
als, socialists and radicals, whereas in the west, it benefited from
agrarian, Gaelic-speaking areas with traditions of rural radicalism'.[210]

This uneasy marriage between urban 'liberalism' and small-farmer
unrest, between 'socialists' and republicans, was to characterize the
new party, Clann na Poblachta, launched in 1946; the failure of a
party leadership 'as variegated as its vote'[211] to achieve a synthesis
between the various strands was to prove the organization's fatal
weakness. The leadership included such disparate figures as Seán
MacBride, a former chief of staff of the IRA, and many ex-IRA men
who looked to him for leadership; Noel Hartnett, a former member
of the Fianna Fáil national executive, who seems fairly typical of
the disillusioned Fianna Fáil nationalists who joined; and Noel
Browne, a young radical-minded intellectual with a passion for
improvements in the health and social services. As Browne put it
many years later, 'each of us saw Clann na Poblachta as answering
our own special needs. The ex-IRA men simply wanted an end
to partition and a united Ireland. I wanted our health services

---

[210] Garvin, 'The Destiny of the Soldiers', 340.
[211] Garvin, *The Evolution of Irish Nationalist Politics*, 174.

restructured. Jack McQuillan, another radical, hoped for a serious land and agricultural policy.'[212] The presence within the Clann of so many heterogeneous elements was initially welcomed by the party leader, Seán MacBride, who sought to keep the organization as broad as possible.

The lack of political coherence was compounded by the failure 'to establish a properly structured organization, with clearly defined radical, social and economic policies';[213] and Browne has alleged that real power within the Clann was exercised by the ex-IRA group around MacBride, viewing members who lacked their republican pedigree with suspicion. Given what is known about the nature of Irish republican political culture since the civil war, this claim is not implausible.

Clann na Poblachta was formally launched in 1945 at a time when socio-economic stagnation and political crisis were assailing Fianna Fáil. The post-war era was a time of continuing shortage of goods and some foodstuffs; the country suffered from a severe shortage of raw materials and capital equipment, and critically low levels of fuel, with gas and electricity consumption cut and coal supplies very scarce. Severe weather conditions in 1945 adversely affected the harvest, necessitating continuing bread rationing. Clothes remained rationed. Inflation was rising and low wages combined with high prices. Against this background, the Government faced a rash of strikes for higher wages, beginning with the normally pro-Fianna Fáil Irish National Teachers' Organization (INTO). The teachers, who held out for several months in 1946, were helped by the sympathetic intervention of the Catholic Archbishop of Dublin, McQuaid, who, to the Government's fury, added respectability to the teachers' cause and, by implication, flatly rebutted the accusations of the Education Minister, Derrig, who had accused the teachers of holding the community to ransom and challenging the authority of the state. The teachers were soon followed by bank clerks, journalists, and others, emphasizing an interesting aspect of the post-war industrial unrest: that it was largely the white-collar or professional workers who were involved in challenging the economic record of the Government. Lemass's trade-union reforms had perhaps served to contain the unrest from spreading to the more 'traditional' sectors of the working class.

[212] Browne, *Against the Tide*, 97–8.   [213] Ibid. 98.

The situation was further complicated for Fianna Fáil by a series of political scandals which cast doubt on the party's proud boast to be above the corruption of party politics—to be a national movement, uninfluenced by venial considerations. Three scandals hit the party in a row. In 1944 it was alleged that Lemass had been involved in dubious transactions concerning the sale of railway shares, on the eve of the Government's Transport Bill; then, in 1946, Conn Ward, parliamentary secretary to the Minister for Public Health and Local Government, was found guilty of tax fraud concerning his bacon factory business in County Monaghan; and Lemass, again, was in the firing line over the alleged improper authorization of the sale of Locke's distillery in Kilbeggan to foreign financiers. Although the minister was cleared of any criminal suspicion, the effect of three investigatory tribunals in a row certainly reflected badly upon the reputation of the Government.

Clann na Poblachta won two by-elections in the autumn of 1947—a clear sign that it was beginning to harness discontent with Fianna Fáil. To prevent the new organization from consolidating its position or building an effective electoral machine, de Valera dissolved the Dáil and called a general election for 4 February 1948. He may also have been motivated by the danger of internal disintegration within Fianna Fáil. In a letter to MacEntee in 1947, Erskine Childers reported on growing hostility in Fianna Fáil ranks which he had encountered at a meeting with local party organizations in North Longford. Childers summarized the demands emanating from the grass roots as: (1) for new blood in both the Government and the party leadership; (2) that old age pensions be increased considerably; (3) that there should be subsidies on children's clothing; (4) that there should be an 'austerity cut in "luxury services"'. Childers, sounding a clear note of panic, makes the startling revelation that discussions had been under way amongst some leading party figures on the possibility of founding a new party. He wrote: 'We may be too late. It is possible that we should have founded a new Party at the end of the Emergency embracing National Labour, Fine Gael and ourselves. Unless we take risks and appoint new, young or immensely popular candidates, we shall founder.'[214]

In the campaign which followed, the weaknesses of the challenge to Fianna Fáil, despite the potential which may have existed

---

[214] Letter has no precise date—1947—in UCDA MacEntee Papers P67/293.

for a real alternative, became all too clear. Clann na Poblachta was merely attacking the failure of Fianna Fáil to live up to the hopes vested in it—not the assumptions upon which such hopes and expectations had been based. The Clann was not advocating anything like a socialist critique of Fianna Fáil; but a radical social programme based upon Catholic social teaching (in line with the new vogue for Christian Democracy in Europe), wedded to militant nationalism and, to a lesser extent, rural nostalgia. 'The banner it raised was similar to that which had once been zestfully borne by Fianna Fáil.'[215] Even the Clann's attacks upon corruption—whilst particularly wounding to Fianna Fáil—were an echo of earlier Fianna Fáil propaganda against its Cumann na nGaedheal opponents in 1927–32; indeed, it was precisely for that reason that such attacks were so wounding.

The Clann's dilemma was a serious one. Having more or less adopted the programme of the early Fianna Fáil as its own, the most the Clann could logically and coherently aspire to—if it was to have any hope of translating its aspirations into reality—was to act as a thorn in Fianna Fáil's side, forcing that party to adopt more 'radical' republican policies; the Clann's subsequent alliance with Fine Gael made no political sense to many of its supporters. The Clann faced an even more serious problem: the composition of Irish society had changed since 1932; what may have seemed radical, dynamic, and necessary to large strata of society in 1932 had little more than nostalgia value, or protest value, in the very different circumstances of 1948. The Clann offered no alternative vision of the strategic development of Irish economy and society to either the business classes or the working class, to name two social forces increasingly enrolled, as we have seen, behind the Fianna Fáil banner.

Clann na Poblachta fought the election on the basis of social-welfare proposals—and, in particular, appeals to the economically dependent and the rural poor—militant nationalism, and many familiar petty-bourgeois themes, including attacks on taxation, corruption, and the civil service, and calls for an end to increases in TDs' and ministers' salaries. The party called for the abolition of means testing for pensions and for pensions to be fixed at the level

---

[215] J. A. Murphy, ' "Put Them Out"—Parties and Elections, 1948–1970', in J. J. Lee (ed.), *Ireland, 1945–1970* (Dublin, 1979).

pertaining in Northern Ireland; for a basic minimum wage of £6 per week—sometimes it was £5; and for food subsidies of 50 per cent on essential commodities. It promised free secondary and university education for all; compulsory education until the age of 16; and, in an obvious attempt to benefit from the momentum set by the teachers' strike, equal pay for male and female teachers. The conversion of public buildings and barracks into flats for the poor was demanded. It was made clear that the party certainly did not consider any radical break with private enterprise necessary to give effect to these welfare improvements. On the contrary, Clann na Poblachta called for free credits for private employers to encourage them to invest more; the role of the state was simply to run industries 'in which private enterprise fails'.[216] Moreover, the party sought to square its advocacy of welfare expenditure with business interests by including a sharp attack on the 'burden of taxation'; additional taxation was ruled out as a policy option, and it was assumed that the necessary revenue could be found through foreign loans, 'alterations' in the money supply—essentially the printing of money —and the repatriation of capital assets overseas. The last option appealed to MacBride, more, one suspects, because of its patriotic flavour than because of the economic arguments behind it. This was borne out by the republican tone of the leader's rhetoric; MacBride was quoted in January as saying: 'Our financial system, our purse, is in the hands of England who uses it to her own advantage.'[217]

The appeal to small farmers was emphasized with an attack on rural depopulation: 'year by year we are producing less food because the people are leaving the land,' MacBride claimed;[218] and the attack on emigration was linked to the Government's alleged betrayal of its previous policies of land reform.[219] Both Clann na Poblachta and Fine Gael pledged that no foreign nationals would get land in future.

To this welfarist programme, the party added a militantly republican stance, attempting here too to outflank Fianna Fáil. MacBride called for the appointment of 'six-counties' representatives to the Senate, and for the declaration of a republic. The Clann promised the use of Irish embassies abroad in a propaganda war against partition.

---

[216] NLI Gallagher Papers MS 18376.   [217] *Leinster Leader*, 3 Jan. 1948.
[218] Ibid.   [219] NLI Gallagher Papers MS 21260.

Finally, the Clann called for the establishment of military tribunals to try corrupt government ministers, and launched an attack upon civil-service perfidy and extravagance; MacBride, in particular, harboured a lifelong hostility against elements of the civil service, which was undoubtedly shared by many of his ex-IRA colleagues.

Fianna Fáil responded to the threat posed by Clann na Poblachta with another 'red scare'. As might be expected, the leading role in this campaign fell to MacEntee, although Lemass did not hesitate to throw in his tuppenceworth. For many people, the parallel with 1932 must have seemed clear; but the similarity was merely superficial. Fianna Fáil was certainly not prepared to compete with the social-welfare proposals of the opposition (although Lemass, had he been stronger, would undoubtedly have taken a different line), and correctly sensed that the divided opposition possessed no strategic alternative to the party in power. Fianna Fáil, then, sought merely to limit the damage to itself, trusting in the impossibility of any alternative government arrangement to do the rest. De Valera's complacency, shared by many of his colleagues, was evident in a speech he made in Ennis in 1948 in which he declared 'there is probably not in the whole world at the present a country in which there is such a decent standard of living as there is in this part of Ireland'. Well might it be remarked that he 'actually seemed satisfied with the social progress already made'.[220]

Fianna Fáil warned against the advent to power of a weak government including Clann na Poblachta or Labour; such a government would betray the independence of the country. MacEntee alleged that one of the Clann's leaders, Peadar Cowan, was involved in a conspiracy 'to establish a Socialist (i.e. Communist) Republic in this country, and to make it a member of a European Federation of Socialist (Communist) Republics'.[221] Again, MacEntee warned voters to look at what had happened in France and Italy, both good Catholic countries which were falling prey to the 'red menace': 'wherever the Russian system had succeeded in seizing power, the Church had been persecuted, property confiscated, and the liberties of the great mass of the people completely suppressed.'[222] In January 1948 MacEntee alleged that he had seen a

[220] Ryle Dwyer, *Eamon de Valera*, 131.
[221] From a speech dated 20 Oct. 1947 in UCDA MacEntee Papers P67/372.
[222] Ibid. P67/373.

letter written by a priest which stated that the Clann was financed by the 'international communist movement' from its 'Belfast office'. This drew a sharp rebuke from Clann na Poblachta director of elections, Noel Hartnett, who offered to co-operate in establishing a committee of auditors, chaired by a priest of MacEntee's choosing, to examine the finances of both the Clann and Fianna Fáil over the previous twelve-month period. Hartnett also demanded publication of the letter to which MacEntee had referred. Needless to say, both the demand and the offer were turned down![223]

Lemass joined this campaign, warning that Ireland was 'on the hit list for attack in the campaign now being waged to destroy Christian Democracy in Europe'; only by keeping a sense of nationality and of national unity alive—i.e. by voting for Fianna Fáil—could this international red offensive be stemmed. Partition, in this respect, was important: 'we cannot take the risk of its being overshadowed in the minds of our people by economic and social matters.'[224] Major Vivion de Valera declared that the traditional nationalist ideals incarnated in Fianna Fáil 'were the common bond that could link the various sections of the community . . . Without that common bond, selfish interests might prevail.'[225]

The Cold War atmosphere against which these events were played out must certainly have lent some credence to Fianna Fáil propaganda, ludicrous though that propaganda must seem in retrospect;[226] Fianna Fáil quoted both Attlee and Truman as warning of a new world war against the USSR, and hammered home the message: Cold War = need for a strong, anti-communist government = Fianna Fáil. The conduct of the campaign clearly forced Clann na Poblachta —like Labour before it—on to the defensive, pleading that it was not 'communist'.[227]

Fianna Fáil was also lent some credence by the campaign of the opposition parties. Apart from the Clann's amateur electoral tactics—it naïvely spoke of a 1918-style landslide, for which there was no objective evidence whatsoever, and fielded a wide variety of candidates sometimes at odds with each other—the various

[223] From a speech dated 20 Oct. 1947 in UCDA MacEntee Papers P67/376.
[224] Quoted in O'Connell, 'Class, Nation and State', 24.
[225] *Irish Press*, 30 Jan. 1948.
[226] MacEntee, for example, raised the rather unedifying spectacle of atom bombs falling on Ballina, Co. Mayo, if Fianna Fáil lost the election and 'they had Communists at the head of the Government' (*Ballina Herald*, 17 Jan. 1948).
[227] UCDA MacEntee Papers P67/378.

opposition parties seemed to be more at war with each other than with Fianna Fáil. Labour and the NLP concentrated their fire on each other, NLP propaganda in particular lending credence to Fianna Fáil's 'red scare'; Fine Gael and Clann na Poblachta exchanged mutual insults; and all the opposition parties attacked the idea of coalition with each other—Clann na Poblachta, Clann na Talmhan, and the NLP specifically seeking votes on the basis that they would not enter coalition.

When the votes were cast, Fianna Fáil had 41.9 per cent (sixty-seven seats); Fine Gael 19.8 per cent (thirty-one); Clann na Poblachta 13.2 per cent (ten); Labour 8.7 per cent (fourteen); NLP 2.6 per cent (five); Clann na Talmhan 5.3 per cent (seven); independents 8.5 per cent (twelve). The result was particularly disappointing for Clann na Poblachta, which did badly on transfers. The percentage of electors voting for neither of the two civil-war parties had grown from 14.8 per cent in 1938 to 38.3 per cent in 1948.[228] This, however, was due more to the collapse of Fine Gael between these dates than to any parallel collapse of Fianna Fáil. (It also oversimplifies the concept of 'civil-war parties'—the Clann na Poblachta vote could reasonably be considered to be as 'anti-Treaty' as the Fianna Fáil vote; and such a juxtaposition would tell us little about the underlying reasons for the political volatility noticeable throughout the period.) The Fianna Fáil vote of 41.9 per cent, considering the climate of economic stagnation, social unrest, allegations of corruption, political challenges from several new parties, trouble with the Church and the Supreme Court, was far from disastrous.

CONCLUSION

It is a commonplace of political commentary that war frequently brings in its trail great social and political change. That was true of Ireland, also, during the decade 1938–48, even though Ireland did not participate directly in the Second World War. Fianna Fáil survived this process of upheaval remarkably intact; a balance sheet, however perfunctory, of the party's strengths and weaknesses during these years may help us understand the position it had reached by 1948.

---

[228] Rumpf and Hepburn, *Nationalism and Socialism in Twentieth Century Ireland*, 143.

The 41.9 per cent of the poll which it obtained in 1948 was a full ten percentage points below its 1938 vote, and reflected growing social unrest and discontent in the country as a whole, a growing sense of weariness with the party and its leaders,[229] and the evident volatility of sections of the electorate. In no sense can the party's position in 1948 be described as hegemonic. The war years had seen increasing economic stagnation; in a sense, this had been understandable, as a small exposed country struggled to secure the minimum requirements necessary to guarantee its political and economic survival. But the gratuitous reinforcement of an increasingly parasitical model of economic production meant that the Government was ill-equipped to meet dilemmas posed by rising post-war expectations plus severe structural economic problems. A national bourgeoisie, emerging from the war with increased prosperity and with its corporate representation strengthened, was unwilling to contemplate measures designed to increase industrial efficiency at the expense of profit, or to interfere with the policy of protection. In this, it had the tacit support of the majority of the cabinet, which, as soon as the political danger posed by returning emigrants seemed to have passed, was content to slump into lethargy.

Lemass, in a not always consistent way, foresaw many of the problems and the measures which might have served to reinvigorate the economy; but against the opposition of the bulk of the cabinet, his ideas and schemes during the 1940s are memorable chiefly for their defeat. The party, by 1948, could make no claim to be voicing a dynamic economic development strategy and it is no accident that it should have endeavoured to turn attention elsewhere—to partition, to national unity, to the need for 'stability'. Its 1948 election manifesto had concerned itself with listing past achievements. As to the future: 'there is but one major problem left for Irishmen to solve—that of the re-union of free Ireland and the lost province.' The complacency inherent in this was striking: 'some day—perhaps next month or next year—a combination of circumstances internal and external, will erect the right moment [*sic*] to strike to end Partition.' Until then, patience was all that was required, and 'a leader with the wisdom to read the signs aright'.[230]

---

[229] This was acknowledged by Erskine Childers in a letter to party general secretary Tommy Mullins on 10 Feb. 1948 (UCDA MacEntee Papers P67/299).
[230] Ibid. P67/382.

In actuality, Fianna Fáil no longer offered moral or intellectual leadership; the ideological basis of its claim to 'lead' the Irish nation had been further eroded by a succession of scandals, which may also have somewhat undermined the propagandistic effect of its 'strong-government' message.

The party's position was no longer hegemonic but it was still dominant, and this dominance was underscored by a number of strengths, some positive, some negative. First, the party's claim to leadership of the country was fortified by its presence at the helm of government throughout the war years, its successful pursuance of a policy of neutrality, and its defence of, and appeal to, a sense of national pride and dignity (as in de Valera's famous reply to Churchill's attack on Irish neutrality immediately after the war). Second, the party, largely through the efforts of Lemass, had succeeded in laying the groundwork for a new, closer relationship with the trade unions—through the incorporation of the unions within certain of the economic apparatuses of the state and the subsequent widening of the gap between the industrial and political wings of the labour movement. The full fruits of this initiative were perhaps only realized after the launch of the new economic policy in the late 1950s, when Lemass's dream of a neo-corporatist state came significantly close to realization. But even in the immediate post-war period, the trade-union reform programme may have helped to reduce industrial unrest and alleviate a potential threat to the party's working-class support base. Third, the party's closer relationship, during the war years, with both bourgeois and working-class organized interests permitted it to extricate itself from too strong an electoral dependence upon the small-farmer stratum, thereby facilitating changes in agricultural policy to bring it into line with the requirements of post-war industrial policy. The party was thus relieved at a time of political and social change of a relationship with a non-productive, ageing, and declining stratum which might otherwise have proven suffocating.

Did this add up to a sudden, qualitative change in the nature of the social interests advocated and defended by Fianna Fáil, to a rupture with its past and an accommodation to big business? This thesis has certainly been favoured by the party's republican critics, and by traditionalists within the party from Joe Connolly to Kevin Boland. Superficially it is an attractive explanation for the changes in the social bases of Fianna Fáil support which took place, and it contains a grain of truth. But on a deeper level the argument is fatally flawed. The party's championship of the small farmers had always taken second place to—had been part of—its advocacy of industrial production to secure the interests of the small manufacturer and commodity producer. It was industrial policy which took pride of place, and that policy aimed at the development of the Irish economy through the enrichment of a class of native manufacturers. It was not a 'small man's' policy; it was a policy which aimed at enabling the 'small man' to become a 'big man'—i.e. a successful capitalist. That was the very essence of the policy. Now it is in the nature of capitalist economics—in the nature of competition—that not every 'small man' can successfully make the transition from low-capital, family labour or self-employed, commercial or retail outlet to viable capitalist manufacturing concern; for every one who succeeded, many would fail and be cast into economic dependence, proletarianized, or, more likely, forced to emigrate. Naturally, it was not in those who failed that Fianna Fáil placed its hopes of economic development, but in the successful. The point is that Fianna Fáil did not begin life as a petty-bourgeois party only to capitulate later to the big interests it had despised in the 1920s; it grew, organically, with the class of native manufacturers which it had helped to create: the business circles with which the party enjoyed such a close relationship by 1948 were representatives of the class of 'small men' to whom the party had promised the New Jerusalem in 1928—those who had succeeded.

The economic health of the bourgeoisie continued to be the party's close concern. Lemass's demands for efficiency, and the measures he introduced in pursuit of that goal, were aimed at making the bourgeoisie more vigorous, more competitive—at strengthening its capability for economic leadership, not challenging or supplanting it. In the context of the late 1920s it had been an alliance of small farmers and petty bourgeois which had helped Fianna Fáil to power. By the 1940s the dreams of the small farmers had been jettisoned and the leadership of the industrial bourgeoisie demanded a rationalization of agriculture (and, Lemass realized, ultimately of industry). Finally, it was, perhaps, logical that the loss of small-farmer support should coincide with the consolidation of support amongst the working class—the economic coadjutors of the industrial bourgeoisie, whose incorporation within Fianna Fáil economic development strategy was, Lemass realized, politically desirable.

And what of the negative strengths underpinning Fianna Fáil political centrality even during the party's loss of hegemony? First, the party's introduction of legislation which split the trade-union movement allowed it effectively to manipulate latent divisions, and to contribute to a disastrous split within the Labour Party itself. The Labour threat of 1942–3 was thus neutralized and the subsequent civil war in the Labour camp politically decapitated the labour movement at the very moment when Fianna Fáil was seeking to depoliticize the unions.

Second, parties such as Clann na Talmhan tended to be based upon social strata which were essentially in decline; the same is true, to a lesser extent, of Clann na Poblachta. Fine Gael had totally failed to grasp the changes which had taken place in Irish society since Fianna Fáil's assumption of office. Moreover, the most worrying threat to Fianna Fáil in 1948, Clann na Poblachta, was bitterly divided internally between social reformers and republicans, urban professional ambition and agrarian discontent, and proved incapable of transcending this dilemma. The party 'twin-peaked' between its urban radical and rural republican wings in 1948 and thereafter the 'Republican and liberal wings of the "Clann" did not get on well, and the party soon started to disintegrate'.[231] In other words, Fianna Fáil could legitimately point to the absence of any credible alternative to its own continuation in office.

Yet the incredible happened: Fianna Fáil found itself out of office for the first time in sixteen years. The desire of both Labour parties for power proved greater than their mutual antipathy (in any case, both Larkin and O'Brien had left the scene); Clann na Poblachta felt that by putting Fianna Fáil into opposition it would stand to gain further from the credibility bestowed by office; Fine Gael was delighted by the prospect of escaping from the seemingly interminable spiral of decline; Clann na Talmhan was anxious to put Fianna Fáil out of office at all costs. A five-party inter-party government—Labour, NLP, Fine Gael, Clann na Poblachta, and Clann na Talmhan—took office under the leadership of Fine Gael's John Costello, the party having shed Mulcahy in its eagerness for agreement. No one was more surprised than Fianna Fáil, which had confidently expected the NLP to facilitate a minority Fianna Fáil Government.

[231] Garvin, *The Evolution of Irish Nationalist Politics*, 175.

Fianna Fáil reacted to defeat, once it had recovered from the initial shock, in characteristic style, emphasizing the party's ability to contain dissent and avoid ever admitting to mistakes. The 1948 party conference solemnly declared that 'Fianna Fáil is not prepared to put its policy into abeyance and could not, therefore, have any part in a coalition'. The loss was blamed entirely on organizational weaknesses, not on policy.[232]

The lack of sociological or socio-political analysis in the conference's post-mortem is striking. It was to be another decade before the depth of the economic crisis facing Ireland was so undeniable as to force a radical change in policy and economic strategy. Until then, Fianna Fáil stumbled on in the belief that tighter organization and greater commitment from party workers would suffice to rekindle the flame.[233]

This is not the place to trace the subsequent history of the interparty government, except to point out that differences within the cabinet over economic policy (similar to those already encountered in our discussion of Fianna Fáil) were now accentuated by interparty rivalries. The new administration, in its three years of existence, would have certain achievements to its credit, including the fact that it first publicly promulgated Keynesian economic principles and launched (in 1949) the Industrial Development Authority—opposed by Lemass for opportunist reasons. But divisions of policy, of temperament, and of purpose within the cabinet were to prove fatal, and disastrous especially for the smaller parties.

When the Government collapsed in 1951, over the Mother and Child affair,[234] it was Clann na Poblachta, now irrevocably split, which suffered the brunt of the defeat, sinking to just 4.1 per cent. Clann na Talmhan, too, proved unable to take advantage of the land-reclamation schemes introduced with Marshall Aid—the credit going, such is the logic of coalition politics sometimes, to Fine Gael. Labour and the NLP, reunited following their pursuit of similar policies in government, polled roughly the same vote as their combined total in 1948.

The 1951 election is important, not so much because it marked the return of Fianna Fáil to office; rather, because it marked the end

---

[232] See analyses in UCDA MacEntee Papers P67/466. [233] Ibid.
[234] For a discussion of this matter, see E. McKee, 'Church–State Relations and the Development of Irish Health Policy: The Mother and Child Scheme, 1944–53', *Irish Historical Studies*, 25/98 (1986), 159–94.

of the real or potential Labour, Clann na Poblachta, and small-farmer challenges to Fianna Fáil which characterized Irish politics during the 1940s. In a sense, the political volatility which marked the late 1940s was already giving way to a new stability by 1951; discontent with the existing pattern of politics was still widespread and it was not until after 1958 that Fianna Fáil hegemony was re-established; but the possibility of a real strategic alternative to Fianna Fáil leadership of Irish society was considerably diminished by the collapse of Clann na Poblachta and the resurrection of Fine Gael.

Was there another possible course of action in 1948? In retrospect, it is easy to say that Clann na Poblachta made a serious and fatal political mistake. But, even at the time, the decision of the Clann leaders to enter government with their old enemies in Fine Gael, with whom they had absolutely nothing in common apart from a shared rivalry with Fianna Fáil, must have been disconcerting to their supporters. If Clann na Poblachta's leaders had devoted more attention to political strategy and less to the pursuit of short-term advantage, they might have chosen to remain aloof from the formation of a new government. Such a decision might have forced a minority Fianna Fáil administration to take power with the support of the NLP. Given such an outcome, the continuing decline of Fine Gael seems likely. Clann na Poblachta and Labour might then have been in a position to mount a real challenge to Fianna Fáil, if the Clann's increasing maturity in these circumstances had enabled it to confront its internal contradictions.

All of this, of course, is speculation. What is not speculation is that the decisions of Fianna Fáil's opponents enabled a party which emerged from the election of 1948 dominant but no longer hegemonic, and with a question mark clearly hanging over its future, to stumble through another full decade of economic crises and policy stagnation before moving to re-establish its political hegemony from 1958 onwards.

Conclusion

This book has focused on the emergence and persistence of Fianna Fáil as the dominant party in Irish politics, and on the political strategy which underpinned that dominance even through periods when the party's hegemony was under threat. I have emphasized the role of Fianna Fáil and its rivals in opposition and in government; the effects of party policy upon different social strata, the changes Fianna Fáil helped to bring about in society and in the distribution of economic and political power, and the effects of changes in the social structure upon the party; and the function of ideology. I have attempted to analyse the party's reproduction of its own centrality against the background of a matrix formed by an ever-changing balance of political and social forces. In other words, by focusing on the party's interaction with a changing society, I have tried to reconsider changes in the party itself and in its support base in a dialectical way. Peillon puts it thus:

relations between social classes and political parties are not just a matter of one mirroring the other. Political agents can never be considered as mere appendices, as representing social forces in another guise. The two types of agents confront as well as complement each other, manipulate as well as co-operate with each other. Within this dialectic we are obliged to grant that political parties have both an identity and their own presence and this dialectic simultaneously complicates and illuminates their interrelations.[1]

This emphasis upon the changes wrought by Fianna Fáil on the balance of social forces, and vice versa, obviously assumes that the vitality of the party as a political force proceeds from a continuous process of social and political change—the result of social and political tension—the corollary of the absence of change being decay.

Attempts to explain the long-term stability of the Irish party system

---

[1] Peillon, *Contemporary Irish Society*, 120.

(and the continuing predominance of Fianna Fáil—so obviously a related question) in the face of deep-rooted social change, and to place the Irish party system in a comparative perspective, have been influenced by the theoretical models developed by Lipset and Rokkan and by Sartori. The former have pointed to the determinant influence of fundamental social cleavages (mainly class, religion, and region) upon party systems and political oppositions, whilst arguing for the concept of the autonomy of political divisions, so produced, to account for the apparent persistence of 'out-dated' political alignments in the face of destabilizing social change. Obviously, then, attention should be focused on those decisive periods of political mobilization and institutional development when fundamental social cleavages became operational at the political level.

So far, so good. But the theory of the autonomy of the political does not resolve the inherent weakness of such a model—the inability of social determinism to account for the apparent disjunction which arises between the social and the political. In the Irish context, this is interpreted as the continuing predominance of Fianna Fáil and the competition between Fianna Fáil and Fine Gael in the first instance, long after the political issues which divided the two parties had lost urgency and the social bases of Fianna Fáil support had changed. The point is that the assumption of political stability upon which this apparent disjunction of the social and the political rests is unwarranted.

This is so for two reasons: first, because the mere persistence of a party in no way means that what such a party represents to various strata in society remains stable over time; and, second, because social changes do not determine political changes in the first place. The relationship is much more complex. What requires explanation, in other words, is not the illusion of political stability, but the political changes—the strategic and tactical choices, conscious or otherwise—which were effected in order to reproduce that 'stability'. The object of investigation should be precisely the interactions between social and political agents.

It is not altogether surprising that the notion of the autonomy of political divisions from the fundamental social cleavages which gave rise to them, inherent in the Lipset and Rokkan model, should lead some scholars who have attempted to utilize the model closer to Sartori's emphasis upon élite management of social and political divisions. As Sinnott points out,[2] Mair attempts to employ the Lipset and Rokkan theme of the autonomy of the political to substantiate his claim that Fianna Fáil introduced a new language of politics between 1937 and 1943 which emphasized the ability of a party to govern, rather than the previous supposed emphasis on the national question. Mair clearly sees the emergence of this new dialogue as the essential ideological accompaniment of the changes which took place in Fianna Fáil's support base during those years— changes which saw Fianna Fáil become less dependent upon a small-farmer base and more of a catch-all party. Sinnott's remark that 'an alternative reading of Lipset and Rokkan's applicability to Ireland would accept the point about the autonomy of the political but would tend to interpret that autonomy as maintaining the original alignment rather than contriving a new one'[3] raises the question as to what extent Mair has moved towards the more obviously voluntaristic emphasis of Sartori.

In any case, the attempt to explain the maintenance of the significant changes in the social bases of Fianna Fáil support in terms of the introduction by that party of a new language of politics between 1937 and 1943 leads Mair to emphasize the active role of political élites in breaking free from social cleavages:

The emergence of strictly political, as opposed to socio-political, cleavages in Ireland from the early 1940s onward reinforces the argument that political divisions should not be seen as emanating purely from social oppositions within the polity, but should be recognised as being capable of achieving a certain autonomy of their own.[4]

The question is, however, whether any relationship whatsoever, other than purely coincidental, now remains between 'political divisions' and 'social oppositions within the polity'.

Thus, Mair paints a picture of the party in search of a 'new source of voter appeal' to combat the effects of the 'declining demographic importance of its original support base'. It is said to have hit the nail on the head with the emergence of a new language of politics which emphasized the ability to govern issue, enabling Fianna Fáil to 'extend its appeal eastward' and don the clothes of a catch-all party. In this way the pattern of Irish political alignments 'floats free' of the fundamental social cleavages which had originally structured it.[5]

---

[2] Sinnott, 'Interpretations of the Irish Party System', 295.   [3] Ibid.
[4] Mair, 'The Autonomy of the Political', 458.   [5] Ibid. 452–3.

Sinnott has cogently argued that Mair, in fact, has got his time-scale wrong; that the decisive breakthrough for Fianna Fáil in transcending the limitations of its original support base came much earlier—as early as 1933, when Fianna Fáil secured 43 per cent of the vote in Dublin and Dun Laoghaire—and that, in consequence, the increasing resort to the ability to govern issue was more to 'bolster a predominance already established and to consolidate an eastern break-through already achieved' than the basis on which the original social cleavages were transcended.[6]

My argument is not so much with the time-scale—though Sinnott's case is convincing—as with the methodology involved. In actuality, Fianna Fáil was evolving *with* Irish society—as much the subject of the demographic and social class changes to which it is said to have 'adapted' as the object. Fianna Fáil did not suddenly find its social base in a state of decline, but hit upon an ideological discourse which enabled the party to transcend that support base. If such were so, then the question as to how a party dependent upon declining social strata could suddenly succeed in convincing the 'healthy' social strata of its superior ability to govern would obviously require urgent answers. Rather, Fianna Fáil economic policy during the 1930s helped to shape the face of Irish society: the protected national bourgeoisie grew in numbers and in economic and political weight, and Fianna Fáil's organic links with that class—in terms of party finance, policy consultation, direct and indirect political influence, and ideological integration—grew also. The working class grew in numbers and in trade-union organization, and Fianna Fáil's articulation of working-class concerns and its links with the trade-union movement also increased. The small-farmer stratum declined in numbers with the abandonment of any effective attempt at land redistribution from the mid-1930s, and was reduced drastically in political weight, and Fianna Fáil's growing interrelations with the more economically dynamic social classes (industrial bourgeoisie and working class) enabled it to escape dependence upon that stratum. In fact, the interactions between the party and social classes at both the economic and political levels can be said to have led to the gradual supersession of the original social cleavages underpinning political alignments by a new fundamental social cleavage—that between socio-economic forces

[6] Sinnott, 'Interpretations of the Irish Party System', 294–5.

which possessed the potential for economic growth and those which did not.

This concern for economic growth came to dominate a society characterized by chronic economic underdevelopment and persistent levels of poverty and emigration. The poverty was felt all the more acutely as a result of the close cultural proximity of Great Britain and Northern Ireland; emigration further strengthened the economic dependence of the state upon its British neighbour. Fianna Fáil's emergence as a catch-all party was due to its successful self-promotion as the political agent of economic growth and prosperity—the protector of dynamic economic forces. The role entailed obvious contradictions, for the interests of the dynamic economic forces were not always seemingly identical and conflict was endemic. But the promotion of growth entailed clear advantages: properly articulated at the ideological level it could force those strata which no longer had an independent social project to advance into political, as well as economic, dependence, and it could force political rivals on the defensive, faced with the necessity of formulating an alternative scheme of their own for the dynamic development of the Irish economy.

The thesis about the new language of politics which centred on the ability to govern question is evidently related to precisely this aspect of the situation; Fianna Fáil's governmental credibility (and the lack of its opponents') rested on a claim to provide best for the prosperity and well-being of the Irish nation. An overemphasis upon the behaviour of political élites, without due regard to the social matrix which alone helps to explain the significance of their actions, can lead one to underestimate the relationship between governmental competence and the promotion of economic growth.

This postulation of the emergence of a new social cleavage between those social strata and classes which possessed the potential for economic dynamism and those which did not should not lead us back into a new deterministic trap.

First, the claim that Fianna Fáil's move to a position of centrality within the Irish political system was rooted in its promotion of economic growth does not mean that the project of economic growth was without internal contradictions. Clearly, the party's simultaneous capture of both bourgeois and working-class support presented it with the difficult task of reconciling the often conflicting demands of both groups. In theory, this task would appear more difficult, and the party most vulnerable, in periods when the party's claim to promote growth came under most strain. Indeed, this is what happened during the 1940s, when Fianna Fáil's hegemony faced potential challenges from a number of sources. In other words, the party's successful reproduction of its new social bases of support cannot be taken for granted. Rather, the internal debate within Fianna Fáil over political and economic strategy requires careful attention precisely because it reveals the influence of the matrix formed by the conflicting demands of those socio-economic groups upon whose support the party's political dominance now rested.

Second, it is clearly not the case that this new social cleavage arose 'autonomously' to 'determine' political alignments from the late 1930s and early 1940s onwards. The changes which took place in the social composition of the body politic were shaped and influenced by the actions of Fianna Fáil in government; consequently, attention needs to be paid to the *political* matrix within which Fianna Fáil played out its part—a political matrix formed by the interactions between Fianna Fáil and its political opponents. It is this attention to the social matrix formed by the conflict of class interests and group interests, the political matrix formed by party and ideological competition, and the interactions between them, that distinguishes an attempt to explain dialectically the rise of Fianna Fáil to predominance and the maintenance of that centrality in the face of social change from a deterministic or voluntaristic approach.

Other attempts to explain Fianna Fáil's predominance concentrate less upon the thesis of the autonomy of the political, and more upon the alleged applicability of Lipset's and Rokkan's three main social cleavages—region, religion, and class—to the continuing divisions between Fianna Fáil and other Irish political parties. I have already dealt with my objections to Garvin's thesis of the 'periphery-dominated centre'—the most thoroughly argued and sustained of this type of approach—and there is no need to cover the ground again. I have also covered the evidence produced by commentators including Mair and Garvin to support the view that political parties other than Fianna Fáil—Fine Gael and Labour, for example—do exhibit a 'class bias' in the social bases of their contemporary electoral support; and that Fianna Fáil, in seemingly drawing significant electoral support from every social class, is more of an exception to the rule than conclusive proof of the totally unstructured nature of Irish political alignments. McAllister and

O'Connell have further argued, on the basis of survey data, that there is a clear discrepancy in the class images of party supporters, with Fine Gael supporters showing a greater propensity to see themselves as middle class and Labour supporters less likely to see themselves as such. They conclude that class image 'is unimportant in predicting Fianna Fáil support but that it is a significant influence for the other two parties'.[7]

I have indicated my sympathy for the efforts made to counter the thesis that Irish political alignments are unrelated to social cleavages through a more detailed analysis of regional and class voting trends. But there is no doubt that a counter to that thesis which rests on purely psephological analysis will not suffice, for Irish voting patterns do indeed appear to bear a much weaker correlation to class membership, religion, and region than do the voting patterns of many other European countries. The thesis that Irish politics and Irish political parties are therefore *sui generis* cannot be successfully refuted whilst remaining on psephological ground alone.

What is required is a concept of power, and an analysis of political alignments and political competition in terms of power and the changing balance of power in Irish society. For example, whether it is sustained, with Garvin, that a significant regional discrepancy in party support existed at least until 1943, or, with McAllister and O'Connell, that 'political influence of region is moderated once other things are controlled for',[8] a conception of the varying economic and political weight of different regional groups is missing.

The present argument rests upon two assumptions: first, that social groups which possess a potential for satisfying needs perceived as vital by society as a whole—for example, economic growth—are thereby better placed to exercise ideological leadership; and, second, that the promotion of the economic and social project of such groups thereby confers a decisive political advantage, also in terms of winning or retaining the electoral support of decaying or stagnant social groups, upon a political party. If these assumptions are valid, then it can be argued that an apparently even spread of support for a party such as Fianna Fáil throughout society tells us less that political alignments have drifted free of their social bases

---

[7] I. McAllister and D. O'Connell, 'The Political Sociology of Party Support in Ireland: A Reassessment', *Comparative Politics*, 16/2 (1984), 197–8.

[8] Ibid. 200.

than that Fianna Fáil has succeeded in articulating the social project of the dominant groups—a project which, meeting the perceived needs of the whole society, is shared far beyond the confines of the dominant social groups alone.

Likewise, the not altogether convincing attempt made by McAllister and O'Connell[9] to attribute a religious dimension to Irish party alignments raises other fundamental questions. Their argument that church-going Catholics are more likely to vote for Fianna Fáil really adds little to our knowledge. After all, the overwhelming majority of the population of the Irish Republic are church-going Catholics. A more interesting and fruitful exercise would be to trace the ideological usage which Fianna Fáil made of the Catholic religion, and of related themes of morality, respect for property, and national identity, in undermining the efforts of its rivals to formulate independent political strategies and in consolidating the social project it had embraced.

What lessons may the period in Fianna Fáil history which we have examined hold for those seeking to understand the prospects for future changes in the centrality of Fianna Fáil in Irish politics, and in the Irish party system? Irish politics is currently in a state of unprecedented flux, central to which is the almost existential crisis which Fianna Fáil has faced for over a decade. Writing from the perspective of the mid-1990s, five unique factors appear to distinguish the current phase in the country's political life.

First of all there has been the emergence, since the mid-1980s, of a clear challenge to Fianna Fáil in the name of bourgeois orthodoxy from within its own ranks—the Progressive Democrats. In the election of November 1992 this party seemed to consolidate its presence on the political scene polling just under 5 per cent and winning ten Dáil seats.

The second factor has been the simultaneous emergence of a challenge from the left—as yet relatively weak and contained, but concentrated, significantly, in working-class Dublin, one of the foundation pillars of the Fianna Fáil edifice. During the 1980s, the left in Dublin was galvanized by the electoral advances of the Workers' Party, which all but collapsed amid an acrimonious split in 1992. In the general election of November 1992 a revitalized Labour Party

---

[9] I. McAllister and D. O'Connell, 'The Political Sociology of Party Support in Ireland: A Reassessment', *Comparative Politics*, 16/2 (1984), 196.

successfully harnessed a growing constituency for a liberal social agenda combined with a moderate social democratic programme and polled its highest ever vote—19.3 per cent, winning thirty-three Dáil seats. Simultaneously, the Republic's newest political party— the Democratic Left—which was created by the reform-centred majority of the Workers' Party in spring 1992, retained a electoral and Dáil presence to the left of Labour.

A third development has been the election of a left-of-centre candidate, Mary Robinson, as President of Ireland in October 1990— the first successful non-Fianna Fáil candidate since 1945. President Robinson's victory was soon seen as heralding the emergence of new political subjects—above all, women—and of a new political agenda, centring on the liberalization (if not yet secularization) of Irish society.

The disintegration of Fianna Fáil's internal unity, after a decade of in-fighting around the controversial figure of Charles Haughey, must be set against this background. Haughey was forced to resign the party leadership and the office of Taoiseach amid allegations of corruption and inappropriate behaviour in February 1992.

Finally, the growing realization by commentators, politicians, and the electorate alike that the era of single-party government may well be over, for the immediate future, and that coalition politics may not only become the 'norm', but, in the process, involve more intricate strategic and tactical play on the part of the parties. December 1992 saw the formation of a Fianna Fáil–Labour coalition; that had followed three years of an equally unprecedented Fianna Fáil–Progressive Democrats coalition. Moreover, both Fine Gael and the Democratic Left joined Labour in a new coalition in December 1994. Indeed, the whole-hearted endorsement of the fundamental thrust of Fianna Fáil budgetary policy, in the late 1980s, by Fine Gael suggested to some that a coalition between the 'big two' sometime in the future is no longer unthinkable. As ideological distinctions between the parties become ever more difficult to grasp, and all five major parties—and possibly even the tiny Green Party— become potential future partners in shifting coalition alignments, so party strategy assumes ever greater importance.

It is clear by now that I regard Fianna Fáil's political strategy— which aimed at the construction at the political, institutional, and electoral levels of a bloc comprising potentially fissile social classes and groups—as the key to its past success. Fianna Fáil, far from being wholly autonomous from the social classes and groups which have formed its electoral bloc, has always reflected the leadership of the dominant forces mediated by the political necessity to maintain the cohesion of the bloc as a whole. Such cohesion ultimately depends upon the successful execution by the party of its role as 'intellectual-organizer'—i.e. upon its success in convincing the social groups which comprise its support base of its optimal advocacy of the shared objective of economic growth.

Clearly, then, the party's political dominance is placed under greatest threat when its identification with the healthy development of the economy is called into question. This is because the fissile tendencies inherent in an electoral bloc comprising social groups with mutually antagonistic demands then become potentially operational; and because marginal and economically unproductive social strata which lack an independent social project tend under these conditions to undergo greater political volatility. Two possible resolutions of the political crisis facing Fianna Fáil under these circumstances are possible, but neither can guarantee the survival of the party's hegemony, and much would depend upon the behaviour of other political agents.

First, under conditions of economic recession and a chronic burden of apparently 'unproductive' public spending, the party might attempt to harness the ideological appeal of economic growth to an effort to effect the 'modernization' and 'rationalization' of the Irish economy in accordance with orthodox capitalist economic rationale. But if electoral volatility and political instability are to be minimized, this would require favourable ideological and political conditions. These would include a careful and sustained ideological offensive to convince those social groups likely to be most harshly affected— the working-class and dependent strata—of the unavoidability of such changes if *future* economic growth is to be sustained, backed up by *either* a political solidarity on the right (between Fianna Fáil and Fine Gael and/or the Progressive Democrats) *or* the successful conversion of the Labour Party to the 'unavoidability' of privatization and rationalization. But even under such favourable conditions there is no guarantee that Fianna Fáil could wholly contain the potential damage to its links with the organized working-class movement—the trade unions—or its working-class support base, especially in Dublin. Some attempt to harness the trade-union movement to such an economic programme might be necessitated, and the success of this initiative, in turn, would depend to a great extent on the trade-union movement's assessment of the balance of political forces. The situation is moreover further complicated by the fact that Irish society is currently undergoing a quite profound process of social, cultural, and moral questioning and transformation, during which individual and collective identities are being reforged to some extent, and existing certainties called into question.

Alternatively, the party could attempt to spend its way out of the economic recession through a policy of borrowing. This might well postpone a clash with its working-class support base, but a policy of unproductive public spending financed through borrowing would clearly run counter to the demands of the bourgeoisie, and ultimately to Fianna Fáil's acceptance of the economic leadership of the private sector; in other words, as the terms of the party's advocacy of economic growth are defined by its acceptance of bourgeois economic leadership, such a policy would ultimately prove much more damaging, ideologically, to the party's identification with the health of the economy than the former strategy. It would, moreover, come up against the restraints imposed by Ireland's membership of the European Union and anxiety to participate in European monetary convergence.

In retrospect, it is evident that the latter course was effected by Fianna Fáil in government during the late 1970s and early 1980s; and that it contributed to a severe crisis of identity for the party and to the emergence from within Fianna Fáil of the Progressive Democrats, and the strengthening of Fine Gael. On the other hand, the former course was the chosen strategy of Fianna Fáil between its return to office in February 1987 and the end of 1992. There is as yet no reason to believe that the formation of a coalition with Labour in December 1992 marked a rupture with this strategy. Much will continue to depend on Labour's ability to articulate and adhere consistently to an alternative strategic vision.

The reproduction of Fianna Fáil centrality in conditions unconducive to the party's credible promotion of economic growth—the essential common denominator which binds together otherwise fissile social groups—requires the decisive 'neutralization' (condemning to a subaltern political position) of one of the two fundamental social groups which still form a large part of the party's support base—the working class and the bourgeoisie. It seems that the party has now chosen, in accordance with its acceptance of the economic leadership of the private sector, to effect the further neutralization of its working-class support base, and it is probable that it will assess the performance of its coalition with the Labour Party in this light. Fianna Fáil and Labour are involved in a deadly contest—in which each must try to suffocate the other. The stakes are high. For Labour, the challenge is to exploit the contradictions inherent in Fianna Fáil's support base by setting an agenda of economic, social, and political reforms which Fianna Fáil can respond to only at its peril; and thus to supplant Fianna Fáil, above all in the urban areas. For Fianna Fáil, the priority is to reverse Labour's gains in working-class Dublin, exploit Labour's vulnerability to Fine Gael and Progressive Democrat challenges amongst the liberal middle class, detach Labour from the left, and condemn that party to a subaltern position. Offers of an electoral pact (for the exchange of second preferences) in by-elections and European Parliament elections which Fianna Fáil made to Labour[10] in early 1993 must be seen in this light: as an attempt to accustom Labour voters to transferring to Fianna Fáil, to prevent any voter solidarity on the left (for example, as witnessed by transfers between Labour and Democratic Left), and to co-opt Labour to a 'junior' position within Fianna Fáil's electoral politics while the latter party searches for a convincing strategic response to the new political situation. In the light of the collapse of its coalition with Labour, Fianna Fáil faces a difficult future, and no amount of organizational 're-vamping'[11] will suffice. The party has never seemed so unsure of itself.

It is clear that a temptation exists to attempt to retreat into an increasing reliance on the integrating ideologies of Catholicism and cultural traditionalism. Such 'ideologies of consolidation' may well, as Bew, Hazelkorn, and Patterson argue,[12] be articulated with an eye to the working class, seeking to rally working-class sympathy with an offensive against the 'liberal, cosmopolitan élite'. Powerful right-wing Catholic pressure groups exist within Fianna Fáil which favour such a course; however, the party leadership must balance the perceived benefits of such actions against the damage which would be inflicted upon Fianna Fáil's standing with middle strata,

---

[10] *Irish Times*, 12 Feb. 1993, 15 April 1993.
[11] See remarks by Seamus Brennan, the Fianna Fáil national director, in *Irish Times*, 12 Feb. 1993.
[12] Bew, Hazelkorn, and Patterson, *The Dynamics of Irish Politics*, 217.

above all in Dublin and the east coast. Moreover, the political climate effectively blocks such an option for the foreseeable future. Fianna Fáil's acceptance of Labour demands for legislation on gay rights, for example, combined with the obvious change in the mood of the country since President Robinson's election, make a retreat into Catholic or nationalist fundamentalism a very risky option.

Fianna Fáil may yet emerge with its centrality reinforced but with the social compromise formulated since 1959, which has underpinned its political dominance ever since, greatly altered. It may lose part of its working-class support base to a new, Labour-led, alignment on the left, but gain through the redimensioning of Fine Gael and/or the Progressive Democrats. Or it may prove unable to transcend its internal contradictions and itself be redimensioned, perhaps paving the way for a new and stronger formation of the right. Much will critically depend upon the behaviour of Fianna Fáil's political rivals and of the social agents with which it must interact.

SELECT BIBLIOGRAPHY

PRIMARY SOURCES

Private Papers

University College Dublin Archives

Ernest Blythe Papers
P. J. Brennan Papers
Seán MacEntee Papers
Eoin MacNeill Papers
Patrick McGilligan Papers
Richard Mulcahy Papers
Jim Ryan Papers

National Library of Ireland

Frank Gallagher Papers
Thomas Johnson Papers
J. J. McGarrity Papers
William O'Brien Papers

Government Records

National Archives of Ireland

Cabinet minutes
Cabinet Secretariat files
Department of the Taoiseach archives
Department of Finance archives
Department of Industry and Commerce archives
Department of Labour archives
Department of Agriculture archives

Other Unpublished Records

Public Debates Dáil Éireann
Federation of Irish Manufacturers archives

Newspapers and Periodicals

An Phoblacht
Blueshirt

Cork Examiner
Irish Independent
Irish Press
Irish Times
Sunday Independent

Anglo-Celt
Ballina Herald
Connacht Sentinel
Connacht Tribune
Evening Herald
Kerryman
Kilkenny People
Leinster Leader
Longford Leader
Mayo News
Meath Chronicle
Munster Express
Offaly Independent
Sligo Champion

SECONDARY SOURCES

ALLEN, K., 'Forging the Links: Fianna Fáil, the Trade Unions and the Emergency', *Saothar*, 16 (1991).

ANDREWS, C. S., *Man of No Property* (Dublin, 1982).

BANTA, M., 'The Red Scare in the Irish Free State, 1929–37', MA thesis (Dublin, 1982).

BAX, M., 'Patronage Irish Style: Irish Politicians as Brokers', *Sociologische Gids*, 18/3 (1970).

BEW, P., and GIBBON, P., 'Some Aspects of Nationalism and Socialism in Ireland', in A. Morgan and B. Purdie (eds.), *Ireland: Divided Nation, Divided Class* (London, 1980).

—— and PATTERSON, H., *Seán Lemass and the Making of Modern Ireland, 1945–66* (Dublin, 1982).

—— HAZELKORN, E., and PATTERSON, H., *The Dynamics of Irish Politics* (London, 1989).

BOLAND, K., *The Rise and Decline of Fianna Fáil* (Dublin, 1982).

BOWMAN, J., *De Valera and the Ulster Question* (Oxford, 1982).

BRADY, C., 'Police and Government in the Irish Free State, 1922–1933', MA thesis (Dublin, 1977).

BREEN, R., HANNAN, D. F., ROTTMAN, D. B., and WHELAN, C. T., *Understanding Contemporary Ireland: State, Class and Development in the Republic of Ireland* (London, 1990).

Briscoe, R., *For the Life of Me* (Boston, 1958).

Brown, T., *Ireland: A Social and Cultural History* (London, 1981).

Browne, N., *Against the Tide* (Dublin, 1986).

Bruton, S., 'Peadar O'Donnell: Republican Socialist Visionary', MA thesis (Dublin, 1989).

Carroll, J. T., *Ireland in the War Years 1939–1945* (New York, 1975).

Carty, R. K., *Party and Parish Pump: Electoral Politics in Ireland* (Kerry, 1983).

Chubb, B., 'Going about Persecuting Civil Servants: The Role of the Irish Parliamentary Representatives', *Political Studies*, 11/3 (1963).

—— *The Government and Politics of Ireland* (Oxford, 1974).

—— *The Politics of the Irish Constitution* (Dublin, 1991).

Coakley, J., 'Minor Parties in Irish Political Life, 1922–1989', *Economic and Social Review*, 21/3 (1990).

—— 'Political Science in Ireland: Development and Diffusion in a European Periphery', *European Journal of Political Research*, 20/3–4 (1991).

Cosgrave, A., and McCartney, D. (eds.), *Studies in Irish History* (Dublin, 1979).

Cronin, S., *The McGarrity Papers* (Dublin, 1972).

—— *Washington's Irish Policy, 1916–1986* (Dublin, 1987).

Daly, M., *Social and Economic History of Ireland* (Dublin, 1981).

—— 'An "Irish Ireland" for Business? The Control of Manufactures Acts, 1932 and 1934', *Irish Historical Studies*, 24/94 (1984).

—— *Industrial Development and Irish National Identity, 1922–1939* (Dublin, 1992).

Daniel, K., 'Griffith on his Noble Head: The Determinants of Cumann na nGaedheal Economic Policy, 1922–1932', *Irish Economic and Social History*, 3 (1976).

de Vere White, T., 'Social Life in Ireland, 1927–37', in F. McManus (ed.), *The Years of the Great Test, 1926–39* (Cork, 1967).

—— 'Lunch with an Enduring Veteran', *Irish Times*, 19 May 1976.

—— *De Valera: The Man and the Myths* (Swords, Co. Dublin, 1991).

Elliott, M., *Wolfe Tone: Prophet of Irish Independence* (New Haven, Conn., and London, 1989).

English, R., 'Socialism and Republican Schism in Ireland: The Emergence of the Republican Congress in 1934', *Irish Historical Studies*, 27/105 (1990).

Fallon, L., 'Clann na Talmhan—Popular Movement or Political Party?', MA thesis (Dublin, 1983).

Fanning, R., 'De Valera Plays the Green Card', *Irish Times Supplement*, 19 May 1976.

—— *The Irish Department of Finance, 1922–1958* (Dublin, 1978).

—— *Independent Ireland* (Dublin, 1983).

—— 'The "Rule of Order": Eamon de Valera and the IRA, 1923–40', in J. A. Murphy and J. O'Carroll (eds.), *De Valera and his Times* (Cork, 1983).

FARRELL, B., *Seán Lemass* (Dublin, 1983).

—— 'Seán Lemass', in J. A. Murphy and J. O'Carroll (eds.), *De Valera and his Times* (Cork, 1983).

—— (ed.), *De Valera's Constitution and Ours* (Dublin, 1988).

FAUGHNAN, S., 'The Jesuits and the Drafting of the Irish Constitution of 1937', *Irish Historical Studies*, 26/101 (1988).

—— 'De Valera's Constitution: The Drafting of the Irish Constitution of 1937', MA thesis (Dublin, 1989).

FIANNA FÁIL, *The Fianna Fáil Story* (Dublin, 1951).

FINLAY, T. (ed.), *The Constitution: 50 Years On* (Dublin, 1988).

FINNEGAN, R., 'The Blueshirts of Ireland during the 1930s: Fascism Inverted', *Éire/Ireland*, 24/2 (1989).

FULTON, J., *The Tragedy of Belief: Division, Politics and Religion in Ireland* (Oxford, 1991).

GALLAGHER, M., *Electoral Support for Irish Political Parties, 1927–1973* (London, 1976).

—— 'Societal Change and Party Adaptation in the Republic of Ireland, 1960–81', *European Journal of Political Research*, 9 (1981).

—— 'The Pact General Election of 1922', *Irish Historical Studies*, 21/84 (1981).

—— *Political Parties in the Republic of Ireland* (Manchester, 1985).

GALLAGHER, T., 'The Dimensions of Fianna Fáil Rule in Ireland', *West European Politics*, 4/1 (1981).

GARVIN, T., 'Political Cleavages, Party Politics and Urbanisation in Ireland —the Case of the Periphery-Dominated Centre', *European Journal of Political Research*, 11/4 (1974).

—— 'Political Action and Ideology in Dublin', *Social Studies*, 6/1 (1977).

—— 'Nationalist Élites, Irish Voters and Irish Political Development: A Comparative Perspective', *Economic and Social Review*, 8/3 (1977).

—— 'The Destiny of the Soldiers: Tradition and Modernity in the Politics of de Valera's Ireland', *Political Studies*, 26/3 (1978).

—— *The Evolution of Irish Nationalist Politics* (Dublin, 1981).

—— 'Theory, Culture and Fianna Fáil: A Review', in M. Kelly, L. O'Dowd, and J. Wickham (eds.), *Power, Conflict and Inequality* (Dublin, 1982).

—— *Nationalist Revolutionaries in Ireland, 1858–1928* (Oxford, 1987).

—— 'The Return of History: Collective Myths and Modern Nationalisms', *Irish Review*, 9 (1990).

GAUGHAN, J. A., *Thomas Johnson* (Dublin, 1980).

GEARY, R., 'Irish Economic Development since the Treaty', *Studies*, 11 (1951).

GIBBON, P., and HIGGINS, M. D., 'Patronage, Tradition and Modernisation: The Case of the Irish Gombeenman', *Economic and Social Review*, 6/1 (1974).

GILMORE, G., *The Irish Republican Congress* (Cork, 1974).

GIRVIN, B., *Between Two Worlds: Politics and Economy in Independent Ireland* (Dublin, 1989).

GOLDRING, M., *Faith of our Fathers: The Formation of Irish Nationalist Ideology* (Dublin, 1982).

GRAMSCI, A., *Selections from Prison Notebooks* (London, 1982).

HAZELKORN, E., 'Why is there no Socialism in Ireland?—Theoretical Problems of Irish Marxism', *Science and Society*, 53/2 (1989).

HEATLEY, J., 'The Blueshirt Movement', M.S.Sc. thesis (Belfast, 1987).

HEDERMAN, M. (ed.), *The Clash of Ideas: Essays in Honour of Patrick Lynch* (Dublin, 1988).

HESSION, M., 'Women and the 1937 Constitution', M.S.Sc. thesis (Belfast, 1988).

HOGAN, G. W., 'Law and Religion: Church–State Relations in Ireland from Independence to the Present Day', *American Journal of Comparative Law*, 35/1 (1987).

HOPKINSON, M., *Green against Green: The Irish Civil War* (Dublin, 1988).

HUTTON, S., 'Labour in the Post-Independence Irish State: An Overview', in S. Hutton and P. Stewart (eds.), *Ireland's Histories: Aspects of State, Society and Ideology* (London, 1991).

—— and STEWART, P. (eds.), *Ireland's Histories: Aspects of State, Society and Ideology* (London, 1991).

INGLIS, T., *Moral Monopoly: The Catholic Church in Modern Irish Society* (Dublin, 1987).

JOHNSON, D., 'The Economic History of Ireland between the Wars', *Irish Economic and Social History*, 1 (1974).

JOHNSON, J., 'The Outlook for Irish Agriculture', *Studies* (1939).

KELLY, M., O'DOWD, L., and WICKHAM, J. (eds.), *Power, Conflict and Inequality* (Dublin, 1982).

KENNEDY, L., *The Modern Industrialisation of Ireland, 1940–88* (Dundalk, 1990).

KEOGH, D., 'De Valera, the Catholic Church and the "Red Scare", 1931–1932', in J. A. Murphy and J. O'Carroll (eds.), *De Valera and his Times* (Cork, 1983).

—— *The Vatican, the Bishops and Irish Politics, 1919–1939* (Cork, 1986).

—— *Ireland and Europe, 1919–1948* (Dublin, 1988).

KOMITO, L., 'Irish Clientelism: A Reappraisal', *Economic and Social Review*, 15 (1984).

LAVER, M., 'Are Irish Parties Peculiar?', *Proceedings of the British Academy*, 79 (1992).

LEE, J. J., 'Seán Lemass and his Two Partnerships', *Irish Times Supplement*, 19 May 1976.

—— 'Continuity and Change in Ireland, 1945–1970', in J. J. Lee (ed.), *Ireland: 1945–1970* (Dublin, 1979).

—— (ed.), *Ireland, 1945–1970* (Dublin, 1979).

—— 'Aspects of Corporatist Thought in Ireland: The Commission on Vocational Organisation, 1939–43', in A. Cosgrave and D. McCartney (eds.), *Studies in Irish History* (Dublin, 1979).

LEE, J. J., 'Ireland and the Marshall Plan', unpub. lecture delivered at the European University Institute, Florence (Feb. 1985).

—— *Ireland, 1912–1985: Politics and Society* (Cambridge, 1989).

—— 'The Irish Constitution of 1937', in S. Hutton and P. Stewart (eds.), *Ireland's Histories: Aspects of State, Society and Ideology* (London, 1991).

—— and O'TUATHAIGH, G., *The Age of de Valera* (Dublin, 1983).

LITTON, F. (ed.), *The Constitution of Ireland, 1937–1987* (Dublin, 1988).

LONGFORD, LORD, and O'NEILL, T. P., *Eamon de Valera* (London, 1970).

LYONS, F. S. L., *Ireland since the Famine* (London, 1973).

—— 'De Valera Revisited', *Magill* (Mar. 1981).

—— *Culture and Anarchy in Ireland* (Oxford, 1982).

LYONS, R., 'Stagnation, Rise and Subsequent Fall: Labour and the 1920 Local Elections', MA thesis (Dublin, 1989).

MCALLISTER, I., and O'CONNELL, D., 'The Political Sociology of Party Support in Ireland: A Reassessment', *Comparative Politics*, 16/2 (1984).

MCCARTHY, C., *Trade Unions in Ireland, 1894–1960* (Dublin, 1977).

—— 'The Development of Irish Trade Unions', in D. Nevin (ed.), *Trade Unions and Change in Irish Society* (Dublin, 1980).

MCCORMICK, G. M., 'The Electoral Appeal of Fine Gael, 1938–1943', MA thesis (Dublin, 1990).

MCHUGH, J. P., 'Voices of the Rearguard: A Study of "An Phoblacht": Irish Republican Thought in the Post-Revolutionary Era, 1923–1937', MA thesis (Dublin, 1983).

MCINERNEY, M., *Eamon de Valera, 1882–1975: The Controversial Giant of Modern Ireland* (Dublin, 1976).

MCKAY, E. G., 'The Irish Labour Party, 1927–1933', MA thesis (Dublin, 1983).

MCKEE, E., 'Church–State Relations and the Development of Irish Health Policy: The Mother and Child Scheme, 1944–53', *Irish Historical Studies*, 25/98 (1986).

MCMAHON, D., *Republicans and Imperialists: Anglo-Irish Relations in the 1930s* (New Haven, Conn., 1984).

MCMANUS, F. (ed.), *The Years of the Great Test, 1926–39* (Cork, 1967).

MAGUIRE, G. E., 'The Political and Military Causes of the Division in the Irish Nationalist Movement, January 1921–August 1923', D.Phil. thesis (Oxford, 1986).

MAGUIRE, M., 'The Dublin Protestant Working Class, 1870–1932: Economy, Society and Politics', MA thesis (Dublin, 1990).

MAIR, P., 'Labour and the Irish Party System Revisited: Party Competition in the 1920s', *Economic and Social Review*, 9/1 (1978).

—— 'The Autonomy of the Political', *Comparative Politics*, 11 (1979).

—— 'Ireland, 1948–81', in I. Budge, D. Robertson, and D. Hearl (eds.), *Ideology, Strategy and Party Change* (Cambridge, 1987).

—— *The Changing Irish Party System: Organisation, Ideology and Electoral Competition* (London, 1987).

—— 'Explaining the Absence of Class Politics in Ireland', *Proceedings of the British Academy*, 79 (1992).

MANNING, M., *The Blueshirts* (Dublin, 1970; 2nd edn., 1986).

—— *Irish Political Parties* (Dublin, 1971).

—— 'The Farmers', in J. A. Murphy and J. O'Carroll (eds.), *De Valera and his Times* (Cork, 1983).

MANSERGH, N., *The Unresolved Question: The Anglo-Irish Settlement and its Undoing, 1912–72* (New Haven, Conn., 1991).

MARKIEVICZ, C., *What Irish Republicans Stand For* (Glasgow, 1923).

MEENAN, J., 'Irish Industrial Policy, 1921–43', *Studies* (1943).

—— 'Irish Industry and Post-War Problems', *Studies* (1943).

—— 'From Free Trade to Self-Sufficiency', in F. McManus (ed.), *The Years of the Great Test, 1926–39* (Cork, 1967).

—— 'The Irish Economy during the War', in K. B. Nowlan and T. Desmond Williams (eds.), *Ireland in the War Years and After, 1939–1951* (Dublin, 1969).

—— *The Irish Economy since 1922* (Liverpool, 1970).

MILOTTE, M., *Communism in Modern Ireland* (London, 1990).

MITCHELL, A., *Labour in Irish Politics, 1890–1930* (Dublin, 1974).

MORGAN, A., and PURDIE, B. (eds.), *Ireland: Divided Nation, Divided Class* (London, 1980).

MOSS, W., *Political Parties in the Irish Free State* (Columbia, NY, 1933).

MOYNIHAN, M., *Currency and Central Banking in Ireland, 1922–60* (Dublin, 1975).

—— *Speeches and Statements by Eamon de Valera, 1917–73* (Dublin, 1980).

MURPHY, J. A., *Ireland in the Twentieth Century* (Dublin, 1975).

—— '"Put Them Out"—Parties and Elections, 1948–1970', in J. J. Lee (ed.), *Ireland, 1945–1970* (Dublin, 1979).

—— 'The Achievement of Eamon de Valera', in J. A. Murphy and J. O'Carroll (eds.), *De Valera and his Times* (Cork, 1983).

—— and O'CARROLL, J. P. (eds.), *De Valera and his Times* (Cork, 1983).

NEARY, P., and O'GRADA, C., 'Protection, Economic War and Structural Change: The 1930s in Ireland', *Irish Historical Studies*, 28/107 (1991).

NEVIN, D., 'Labour and the Political Revolution', in F. McManus (ed.), *The Years of the Great Test, 1929–39* (Cork, 1967).

—— 'Industry and Labour', in K. B. Nowlan and T. Desmond Williams (eds.), *Ireland in the War Years and After, 1939–1951* (Dublin, 1969).

—— (ed.), *Trade Unions and Change in Irish Society* (Dublin, 1980).

NOWLAN, K. B., and DESMOND WILLIAMS, T. (eds.), *Ireland in the War Years and After, 1939–1951* (Dublin, 1969).

O'CARROLL, J. P., 'Eamon de Valera, Charisma and Political Development', in J. A. Murphy and J. P. O'Carroll (eds.), *De Valera and his Times* (Cork, 1983).

O'Carroll, J. P., 'Ireland: Political Dominance of Business', in M. C. P. M. van Schendelen and R. Jackson (eds.), *The Politicisation of Business in Western Europe* (London, 1987).

—— 'Strokes, Cute Hoors and Sneaking Regarders: The Influence of Local Culture on Irish Political Style', *Irish Political Studies*, 2 (1987).

O'Connell, D., 'Political Sociology in Ireland', MA thesis (Dublin, 1980).

—— 'Sociological Theory and Irish Political Research', in M. Kelly, L. O'Dowd, and J. Wickham (eds.), *Power, Conflict and Inequality* (Dublin, 1982).

—— 'Class, Nation and State: The Real Fianna Fáil Story, 1927–1952', unpub. paper (Dublin, 1982).

O'Connor, E., 'Agrarian Unrest and the Labour Movement in County Waterford, 1917–1923', *Saothar*, 6 (1980).

O'Connor Lysaght, D. R., *The Republic of Ireland* (Dublin, 1970).

—— 'A Saorstát is Born: How the Irish Free State came into being', in S. Hutton and P. Stewart (eds.), *Ireland's Histories: Aspects of State, Society and Ideology* (London, 1991).

O'Crualaoich, G., 'The Primacy of Form: A Folk Ideology in de Valera's Politics', in J. A. Murphy and J. O'Carroll (eds.), *De Valera and his Times* (Cork, 1983).

O'Dowd, L., 'Neglecting the Material Dimension: Irish Intellectuals and the Problem of Identity', *Irish Review*, 3 (1987).

O'Faolain, S., *The Irish* (London, 1980).

O'Hagan, J., 'Analysis of the Size of the Government Sector, 1926–1952', *Economic and Social Review*, 12 (1980).

O'Halloran, C., *Partition and the Limits of Irish Nationalism: An Ideology under Stress* (Dublin, 1987).

O'Leary, C., *Irish Elections, 1918–1977* (Dublin, 1979).

O'Neill, T., 'In Search of a Political Path: Irish Republicanism, 1922–1927', *Historical Studies*, 10 (1976).

O'Rourke, K., 'Burn Everything British but their Coal: The Anglo-Irish Economic War of the 1930s', *Journal of Economic History*, 51/2 (1991).

Orridge, A., 'The Blueshirts and the "Economic War": A Study of Ireland in the Context of Dependency Theory', *Political Studies*, 31 (1983).

Patterson, H., 'Fianna Fáil and the Working-Class: The Origins of the Enigmatic Relationship', *Saothar*, 13 (1988).

—— *The Politics of Illusion: Republicanism and Socialism in Modern Ireland* (London, 1989).

Patterson, M., 'Fianna Fáil and the National Question', M.S.Sc. thesis (Belfast, 1987).

Peillon, M., *Contemporary Irish Society: An Introduction* (Dublin, 1982).

Philpin, C. H. E. (ed.), *Nationalism and Popular Protest in Ireland* (Cambridge, 1987).

Poulantzas, N., *Classes in Contemporary Capitalism* (London, 1975).

Prager, J., *Building Democracy in Ireland: Political Order and Cultural Integration in a Newly Independent Nation* (Cambridge, 1986).

Pratschke, J. L., 'Business and Labour in Irish Society, 1945–70', in J. J. Lee (ed.), *Ireland, 1945–1970* (Dublin, 1979).

Probert, B., *Beyond Orange and Green* (London, 1978).

Pyne, P., 'The Third Sinn Féin Party, 1923–26', *Economic and Social Review*, 1 (1969–1970).

Raymond, R. J., 'De Valera, Lemass and Irish Economic Development: 1933–1948', in J. A. Murphy and J. O'Carroll (eds.), *De Valera and his Times* (Cork, 1983).

Reynolds, B., 'The Formation and Development of Fianna Fáil, 1926–1932', Ph.D. thesis (Dublin, 1976).

Rumpf, E., and Hepburn, A. C., *Nationalism and Socialism in Twentieth Century Ireland* (Liverpool, 1977).

Ryle Dwyer, T., *Eamon de Valera* (Dublin, 1980).

Sacks, P., *The Donegal Mafia: An Irish Political Machine* (New Haven, Conn., 1966).

—— 'Bailiwicks, Locality and Religion: Three Elements in an Irish Dáil Constituency Election', *Economic and Social Review*, 1/4 (1970).

Share, B., *The Emergency* (Dublin, 1978).

Sinnott, R., 'Interpretations of the Irish Party System', *European Journal of Political Research*, 12/4 (1984).

Skinner, L., *Politicians by Accident* (Dublin, 1946).

Smullen, E., 'Fianna Fáil and the Small Man Economy', *Teoiric* (summer 1976).

Smyth, J., 'The Changing Nature of Imperialism in Ireland', *Bulletin of the Conference of Socialist Economists*, 3 (1974).

Therborn, G., *What does the Ruling-class do when it Rules?* (London, 1980).

Thornley, D., 'The Blueshirts', in F. McManus (ed.), *The Years of the Great Test, 1926–39* (Cork, 1967).

Twomey Ryan, P., 'The Church, Education and Control of the State in Ireland', *Éire-Ireland*, 22/3 (1987).

Walker, G., 'Propaganda and Conservative Nationalism during the Irish Civil War, 1922–1923', *Éire-Ireland*, 22/4 (1987).

Walsh, D., 'Fifty Years of Fianna Fáil', *Irish Times Supplement*, 9 May 1976.

—— *The Party: Inside Fianna Fáil* (Dublin, 1986).

Whelan, B., 'The European Recovery Programme (the Marshall Plan) and Ireland: Summary and Assessment', *Éire-Ireland*, 24/3 (1989).

Whyte, J., 'Ireland, Politics without Social Bases', in R. Rose (ed.), *Political Behaviour: A Comparative Handbook* (London, 1974).

—— *Church and State in Modern Ireland, 1923–1970* (Dublin, 1974).

WICKHAM, J., 'The Politics of Dependent Capitalism: International Capital and the Nation State', in A. Morgan and B. Purdie (eds.), *Ireland: Divided Nation, Divided Class* (London, 1980).

WILLIAMS, T. D., 'De Valera in Power', in F. McManus (ed.), *The Years of the Great Test, 1926–39* (Cork, 1967).

INDEX